"Jack Caputo is clearly on of the great 1
century. This archive will allow scholars
important body of work." —Drucilla Corne.., ..._,. .. ...._ ....

"Caputo is one of our greatest philosophers of religion, and this monumental project makes the bulk of his work available to scholars, readers, and other interested souls who want to think about what matters most in the world." — Clayton Crockett, Professor of Religion, University of Central Arkansas

"John D. Caputo is one of the leading religious thinkers of the last 50 years, and these archives will be immensely valuable for scholars tracing the development of his thought and for those seeking to read him for the first time." —Neal DeRoo, Canada Research Chair in Phenomenology and Philosophy of Religion at The King's University

"The John D. Caputo Archives comprise an essential resource for all scholars working in contemporary European philosophy, especially Continental Philosophy of Religion." —Kevin Hart, Edwin B Kyle Professor of Christian Studies at the University of Virginia

"The Caputo archive is an indispensable treasure trove of ideas for anyone interested in contemporary debates on the hermeneutics of religion and justice." —Richard Kearney, Charles B. Seelig Chair of Philosophy, Boston College

"John D. Caputo has been for the last forty years (and continues to be) one of the most important philosophers writing in the phenomenological tradition. His original works on religion have changed the way we conceive the relationship between philosophy and religion. Therefore, the formation of the 'John D. Caputo: Collected Philosophical and Theological Papers' archive is an essential undertaking, which I completely support." —Leonard Lawlor, Sparks Professor of Philosophy, Pennsylvania State University

"Professor John D. Caputo's monumental work in philosophy and theology is crucial to the mediation of contemporary European thought to a much wider readership." —Patrick Masterson, President Emeritus, Professor of Philosophy Emeritus, University College Dublin

"The 'John D. Caputo Archives' gathers together many of the works of one of the most original, influential, and uniquely American voices in continental philosophy and theology of the past fifty years. It is an invaluable resource for anyone wanting to know more about everything from phenomenology, hermeneutics, deconstruction, and negative theology to questions regarding the very future of philosophy and possibility of religion in our time." —Michael Naas, Professor of Philosophy, DePaul University

"The Collected Papers of John D Caputo is a valued resource. He is a wonderfully accomplished and creative philosopher/theologian in the Continental tradition, especially noted for his pioneering and influential work in the postmodern 'rethinking' of religion." —James Olthuis, Professor Emeritus of Philosophical Theology, Institute for Christian Studies (Toronto)

"The singular achievement of John D. Caputo's work has been to demonstrate that radical philosophy is so far from being a threat to Christian theology as to have been the means by which theology is directed to its own radical and therefore defining commitment to attend to the creative-recreative force of the insistent call that all things are possible. His is an exuberant path of thinking that dares to sit lightly to the conventional boundaries of the academy and is therefore able to confront us with what is most worth thinking about. The publication of his collected works will be a resource for both philosophy and theology for a long time to come." —George Pattison, Formerly Lady Margaret Professor of Divinity, University of Oxford; 1640 Professor of Divinity (retired), University of Glasgow

"John D. Caputo's extraordinary work from his earliest work on Eckhart, Heidegger and others to his later work on Derrida, and his contemporary philosophical theology have been a singular resource for all serious contemporary scholars. I heartily endorse this project." —David Tracy, Andrew Thomas Greeley and Grace McNichols Greeley Distinguished Service Professor Emeritus of Catholic Studies at the University of Chicago Divinity School

"Philosophers should not be allowed to have as much fun as Jack and I have had over the years debating what would make a truly radical hermeneutics. These writings are an important chapter in the development of 'continental' philosophy of religion as it has developed from Kierkegaard, Nietzsche, Heidegger, Derrida, and on into the present century." —Merold Westphal, Distinguished Professor of Philosophy Emeritus, Fordham University

John D. Caputo

The Collected Philosophical and Theological Papers

Volume 2: 1986–1996
Hermeneutics and Deconstruction

Eric Weislogel, Editor

The John D. Caputo Archives

TABLE OF CONTENTS

THE DECONSTRUCTION OF ETHICS

DECONSTRUCTION AND RELIGION

CONVERSATIONS AND CONTROVERSIES

BOOK REVIEWS

AUTOBIOGRAPHICAL

JOHN D. CAPUTO ARCHIVES

Eric Weislogel, General Editor

The mission of John D. Caputo Archives is to publish a series of volumes consisting of all of Professor Caputo's journal articles, book chapters, book reviews, interviews, and unpublished papers from 1969 to the present. Our aim is to make this body of work available in one place, handily and inexpensively. To that end, instead of working more traditionally with an academic press, we have chosen to publish the volumes that will comprise this series directly, both as e-books and in a print-on-demand format.

Under the general title, *John D. Caputo: Collected Philosophical and Theological Papers*, the plan is to publish at least seven volumes of papers over the next few years. In addition to these volumes, we intend to publish several of Professor Caputo's lecture courses as well as both his master's thesis and doctoral dissertation.

We have chosen to arrange the papers in chronological order rather than grouping them topically, reflecting the course of development of the main themes of Professor Caputo's work:

Volume 1. 1969–1985: *Aquinas, Eckhart, and Heidegger: Metaphysics, Mysticism, and Thought*
Volume 2. 1986–1996: *Hermeneutics and Deconstruction*
Volume 3. 1997–2000: *The Return of Religion*
Volume 4. 2001–2004: *Continental Philosophy of Religion*
Volume 5. 2005–2007: TBA
Volume 6. 2008–2012: TBA
Volume 7. 2012–2018: TBA

Readers interested in any specific topic or particular thinker with whom Professor Caputo has engaged can easily conduct a search in the e-book versions of the volumes. Each volume will contain a short introduction by Professor Caputo to provide some personal and historical context to the included papers. To facilitate the scholarly use of these volumes, full bibliographical information of the original publication is supplied at the beginning of each entry, and the page numbers of the original publication are inserted in square brackets in the body of the text.

Many of the essays in the *Collected Papers* originally appeared in edited books containing articles by various other authors. The reader is reminded when encountering references in our volumes to "essays appearing elsewhere in this book" and the like that this refers to the original publications and not to the present volume.

Note that certain previously published essays by Professor Caputo were incorporated into his books. When these essays were more or less substantially unchanged when included in published books – like the essays found in his *More Radical Hermeneutics, Demythologizing Heidegger* or, more recently, *In Search of Radical Theology* – we have chosen not to include them in this collection. But if the previously published essays were revised to any great extent for incorporation into books, then we believe there is something to be learned from consulting the original publication and the original context, and those essays are included in this series.

John D. Caputo Archives Board

Hermeneutics and Deconstruction

Radical Hermeneutics

The essays collected here emerge from the standpoint established in *Radical Hermeneutics* (1987), in which, as Kierkegaard would put it, I found "my point of view as an author." In this view, hermeneutics is only possible as deconstruction and deconstruction is only possible as hermeneutics. Hermeneutics can be true to itself only if it is fully exposed to deconstruction, and when deconstruction is true to itself, it discovers it is a kind of hermeneutics. I deliberately make hermeneutics the noun and radical the adjective because the radical is always the radicalization *of something*, of the pregiven, of what is always already there (*immer schon*), presupposed, over which we have had no say. That is the "hermeneutic situation," the one in which we find ourselves (*sich befinden*), which is inescapable, the presupposition within which any positioning or de-positioning takes place. The radicalization is parasitical upon the situation which it de-situates or disturbs or destabilizes. I could not call it radical deconstruction because deconstruction is the radicalizing agent and as such always occurs in the adjectival or adverbial, as a *how* not a *what*. To embrace the strategies and the resources of deconstruction is a way to come to grips with the hermeneutic situation. It is decidedly not a way to escape it. I have never entertained any such desire, never thought it even possible. Why on earth would one ever want to do that? The whole idea of radical hermeneutics is to show that if you start with the deconstruction of hermeneutics, you will end up with the hermeneutics of deconstruction. That is the central argument (Chapter 1).

Radical hermeneutics issues from the tension between the deconstructive left, which is the destabilizing agent, and the hermeneutic right (chapter 2), which provides the measure of stability in what is being destabilized. This is not entirely unlike the tension between Dionysus and Apollo. Radical hermeneutics is concerned with what James Joyce called the "chaosmos," the disorder in the order which keeps the future open. It sustain a perilous position of optimal disequilibrium, a state of built-in unrest, flux, instability, just enough to keep things sufficiently off-balance without tipping over. This is a peripatetic operation which, like walking, is a kind of falling forward without landing on your face. Radical hermeneutics is "cold" hermeneutics, meaning a hermeneutics which views with suspicion the heart-warming assumption that the reason traditions endure is their deep truth, not their violence. Radical does not mean radically grounded but radically exposed, willing to take the truth straight up, unattenuated, unsweetened, ameliorated. Both hermeneutics and deconstruction are theories of reading, not in the empirical sense, which is confined to reading books or other written materials, but in the widest, transcendental, or rather quasi-transcendental sense of interpreting, construing. Hermeneutics takes up what is readable in deconstruction while deconstruction points out what is unreadable in hermeneutics, where the readable and the unreadable are joined at the hips and mutually condition each other.

When I speak of hermeneutics I have in mind not Protestant seminaries, Schleiermacher, or Dilthey, but Heidegger's "hermeneutics of facticity," which describes the inescapable, inextricable, unsurpassable situatedness of our condition. As soon as I come to be, I find that I am already there, Heidegger claimed – in the middle of a time and place, of a language and a culture, of a body and a geography, of a time of life and an historical age, and so on, all making up the prevailing background understanding. That is the hermeneutic situation, where we find ourselves, like it or not, whatever our other aspirations, however angelic or spiritualistic, transcendent or transcendental. Philosophizing is not a matter of escaping this inescapable pre-givenness but of penetrating it all the more thoroughly, searchingly, as far as that is possible, since it is, in fact, impossible to ever do a complete search, which does not discourage us but makes it all the more compelling. It was Schelling who first made this point in the famous Berlin lectures – which were pitched against Hegel and attended by Kierkegaard – under the name of *das Unvordenkliche*, literally, the un-pre-thinkable, meaning that being is always and already (*immer schon*) up and running by the time thinking arrives on the scene. Contrary to the most profound assumption of Kant and the Enlightenment, it is not thinking that sets forth the conditions under which things may be but being which sets the conditions with which thinking must come to grips. Being deals the cards thinking is given to play. The ultimately unconditional condition is being, whatever else thinking may have had in mind. Being is the unconditional, the wall against which thinking bounces. That spelled the end of German Idealism and the beginning of radical hermeneutics.

The line I began promoting in the mid-1980s was that this was a new way to think not only about hermeneutics but also about deconstruction. While we may not often think about it this way, deconstruction in fact shares this view with hermeneutics. But does not Derrida keep his distance from hermeneutics? True, but he is thinking of the hermeneutics of Paul Ricoeur, not Heidegger's hermeneutics of facticity, with which, in my view, what he calls deconstruction is of a piece. The inescapable hermeneutic situation continually shows up in deconstruction. It is found when Derrida says we always begin where we are, *in medias res*, in the middle of a language which is already up and running; and when

2

he says there is nothing outside this (pre-given hermeneutic) context, which is what he means by a *texte* in the famous, even notorious declaration that there is no (*il n'y a pas*) getting outside one (*hors-texte*). The misunderstanding here is to take *texte* in the empirical sense of a bit of paper, papyrus or pixels, instead of the transcendental sense of a formal set of differential relationships, such that significance is achieved only by situating oneself within a differential system and learning to work its levers (like learning how to speak) in order to produce differential effects. The differential system is the pre-given situatedness, and it is not only linguistic; it is also social, cultural, historical, gendered, found in any kind of "coded" system at all, up to and including biological (DNA) codes and global-environmental systems. Derrida is saying we never get to say or do something *outside* of a preestablished differential system or quasi-system, which does the work of setting up our (hermeneutic) presuppositions. In *Of Grammatology* the concern was not to find a way to escape them but to keep them open-ended, so that everything is not pre-programmed. When he described that deconstruction as an "exorbitant" method, that presupposes the orbit; deconstruction is the productive reading which presupposes a meticulously *re*productive reading. When Derrida argues in "Violence and Metaphysics," his monumental article on Levinas, that a *tout autre* cannot be absolutely *tout autre*, that such a thing makes no sense, that the *tout autre* is always *tout autre* relative to a differential system, *that* is to acknowledge the inescapable hermeneutic situation (see chapter 20). He once used the word "hermeneutics" to say that deconstruction occupies the distance between the impious hermeneutics of the poet and the pious hermeneutics of the rabbi, between the prankster Hermes and the messenger boy, between the two interpretations of interpretation, between what we command when we speak or act and what we cannot command.

In *Radical Hermeneutics*, deconstruction is pushing the hermeneutics of facticity to the limits, explaining how even our most precious and profound inherited notions, like being and truth, God and self, are so many constituted factical effects. This does not mean embracing anomie or anarchy, skepticism or despair; it just means facing the facts, the facticity of the things we inherit (the tradition). This is an act of confession, of the circum-fession of our factical condition, of describing the conditions in which we find ourselves, always and already, described most memorably by Augustine's *quaestio mihi magna factus sum*. This represents a radical questioning of any possible autonomous or interior "self," and that self-questioning is who the self *is*. I, the "I," is the one who is a question to itself, the I who cannot say I, the we who cannot say we. Hermeneutics has to do with understanding, and in particular with reaching a self-understanding, and in radical hermeneutics the understanding is the impossibility of ever reaching a satisfactory understanding – and understanding that this does contradict the possibility of a self-understanding; it *constitutes* it. This inability to understand the being which we ourselves are *is* who we are. This is not the abjuration of hermeneutics but the radicalization of it. You get the best results by facing up to the worst, to the "difficulty of life," as Kierkegaard's Johannes Climacus says. That is radical hermeneutics.

All of this came together for me in *Radical Hermeneutics*, in the mid-1980s, not in a flash, but after a long and patient study over a couple of decades – of Aquinas and Eckhart, Kant and German Idealism, Kierkegaard and Nietzsche, Husserl, Heidegger and Gadamer, and finally of Derrida, who was the *agent provocateur*. The book was written in 1983-84. I was on a research leave that year, supported by a grant from the American Council of Learned Societies, which I had been awarded – my current readers will find this amusing – based on a proposal to defend hermeneutics from deconstruction! I began that year with a careful study of Derrida's interpretation of Husserl, with whose work I had become intimately familiar from over a decade of teaching graduate seminars on Husserl (chapters 5-7). That was my road to Damascus, the year I stopped persecuting Derrida. When I realized how meticulous Derrida's reading of Husserl was, which exposed the deep tensions between the theory of constitution and the valorizing of pure presence, when I realized that it was the very opposite of arbitrary or careless, as his critics charged, when I realized that this was not a "critique" of Husserl but the reinvention of a more radical Husserl, when I saw what a deconstructive reading *does*, I realized what deconstruction *is*.

I had reached these conclusions only after conducting a considerable debate with myself, at a point when orthodox doctrinal Catholicism had lost its grip on me. Although I happily continued to live in a Catholic world, the culture, the universities, in which I spent most of my life, Catholic orthodoxy had become a thing of the past for me, or more precisely, not simply past, over, *vorbei*, but an ingredient in my having been, *gewesen*, where *Wesen* is always already *gewesen*. The Thomistic metaphysics of my youth had yielded to the project of "overcoming metaphysics," first in the form of existentialism and phenomenology, Heidegger and hermeneutics, which were in turn exposed to the further disruption of deconstruction. By this point, I took myself to be a philosopher, pure and simple, and I put my theological beginnings behind me, an illusion of which deconstruction itself would soon enough disabuse me, there being nothing pure and simple in deconstruction. But as I mentioned in the Introduction to Volume 1 of these collected papers, *Radical Hermeneutics* was not solely the product of a research grant; it was also the fruit of an undergraduate course I taught for many years at Villanova entitled "German Existentialism and Phenomenology," in which I covered Kierkegaard and Nietzsche, followed by Husserl and Heidegger. Teaching that course, I used to think, is cheating; it was so much fun that I should not have been paid to do it. If I cannot make this material interesting to the students, I thought, I need to look for another way to make a living!

The Essays

Looking back over this collection of articles, I am struck by how many of these papers reflect the disputes of the day. This was a time of considerable controversy in continental philosophy, when the traditional verities of existentialism, phenomenology and hermeneutics were coming under increasing fire from critical theory, race and gender theory, the post-structuralist theories of Foucault and Deleuze, and, in my case, of Lyotard, Derrida and the ever unclassifiable Levinas. To take one but quite instructive example, the growing restlessness of women in continental philosophy would bring about a major restructuring of the Society of Phenomenology and Existential Philosophy. Indeed, the very name was obsolete, so we also argued about that! I remember an annual business meeting when Hugh Silverman, then a SPEP executive co-director, weathered a fierce storm of criticism by the women members of the Society. There but for the grace of God go I, a lot of us guys were thinking, shrinking down in our seats.

Coming around to seeing what Derrida was up to is not easy because Derrida is an avant-garde writer who demands patience and close-reading and a familiarity with the texts he is reading. So I found myself defending him against criticisms that I myself initially shared. A number of these papers are responses to readers who were not as patient with Derrida as Derrida demands. My most extended exchanges took place with Gadamerian critics of deconstruction (Chapters 1–3, 22, 24–25, 27), where there are Heideggerian impulses on both sides of the debate. We spent a lot of time trying to out-other each other, arguing about whether the *tout autre* and "openness to the other" was more the characteristic mark of hermeneutics or of deconstruction, which I think now is a somewhat idle debate. The genuine distinction between the two is well summarized by Derrida when he differentiates polysemy, Ricoeur's term for a multiplicity of different meanings gathered together in an analogical unity under the same name, from dissemination, which is not a semantic category at all but a formal, syntactical, diacritical and syncategorematic property. Dissemination includes chance equivocations, puns, even multi-lingual ones, misspellings, textual corruptions, and the like, and it cannot be domesticated into some ultimate unity of meaning by showing how all these errant marks ultimately make a logical or logocentric point. Deconstruction means that polysemy cannot be protected from dissemination. That is what I was getting at in "Finitude and *Différance*" (chapter 3), a previously unpublished paper that I gave at Warwick in 1988, when David Wood was still teaching there. It was also at that conference that I first met Richard Kearney.

There was a lively debate between post-structuralists and the Habermasians about reason and rationality (chapter 30), a point I had addressed in the penultimate chapter of *Radical Hermeneutics* and in a debate with James Marsh, which was moderated by Merold Westphal, both of Fordham University. Westphal quipped that he won that debate because he occupied the postmodern slash between us. In a book we co-authored under the title *Modernity and Its Discontents*, I argued for the primacy of having "good reasons" over establishing the transcendental conditions of rationality. This was an all-Fordham event. I had, for family reasons, declined an appointment at Fordham and instead become a "distinguished visiting professor" in the doctoral program (1985–88).

I also spent time trying to convince some old friends in the American Catholic Philosophical Association that Derrida was not the devil himself. I had been elected President in 1987–88. I argued in my presidential lecture (chapter 4) that the Catholic idea of tradition can be revitalized by contemporary hermeneutics, a point I also made to the Catholic faculty at Utrecht (chapter 21) and more recently at Loyola University in 2016. During my tenure as President I managed to accomplish several things. I invited David Tracy to be a plenary speaker at the annual meeting. I had attended a meeting of the Catholic Theological Society of America and noticed that the Catholic theologians had a great interest in hermeneutics, in particular in Ricoeur, and were far ahead of the Catholic philosophers, who remained immured in Thomism.

I nominated Wilfrid Desan, who taught at Georgetown University, for the Aquinas Award lecture for that year. Wilfrid, a native Belgian and arguably the leading Sartre scholar in the Anglo-phone world at the time, was one of several distinguished Catholic scholars who had come to the United States and helped establish a footing for continental philosophy in America. We also succeeded in retiring the name of the Association's journal, *The New Scholasticism*, and replacing it with its current name, *American Catholic Philosophical Quarterly*, on the grounds that no scholasticism, however new, would do. We appointed Robert Wood, a Catholic philosopher in good standing at the conservative University of Dallas, with a serious interest in the history of philosophy and in continental philosophy, as the new editor-in-chief. This was all in an attempt to broaden the horizons of the Association. We did a lot that year but it would not be enough to forestall the growing movement of "analytic Thomism" in Catholic doctoral programs, which were increasingly scared off by post-structuralism.

The publication of "Telling Left from Right" in the very analytic *Journal of Philosophy* (Chapter 2) reflects another battle being waged at the time, this one within the American Philosophical Association. The APA was uniquely un-true to its name. It systematically excluded and repressed any kind of philosophy that was *not analytic,* including classical *American* philosophy – which was risible – but especially continental philosophy. So it was hostile to *philosophy* in general. Finally, it mightily resisted being an *association,* since it strenuously dissociated itself from non-analytic philosophy by relegating it to the "satellite" groups. The only thing members of the APA had in common was that we all stayed in the same hotel at the annual meeting of the Eastern Division. This we did because of its timing, not its philosophical merits; it was the main opportunity to conduct job interviews. Non-analytic philosophers should have gotten a bigger discount on our hotel rooms! The situation was so bad that it provoked a counter-movement, the formation of the "Pluralists Society," meaning the American Association of Everything that was not Analytic Philosophy. We were led by Bruce Wilshire, a tall and impressive figure with a stentorian voice who bellowed out baritone barbs against our oppressors at the annual business meetings. We were never able to make a dent in the real corridors of analytic power, the hirings in the elite universities, but we were able to get the occasional non-analytic voice on the main program, instead of being marginalized to the "satellite" groups. This paper is an example of that.

It was also a time of strife among the Heideggerians, which can be seen in my exchange with my good friend Fr. William (Bill) Richardson, SJ, (Chapter 14), a man whom I deeply admired both as a Catholic priest and a philosopher; he was the model, the very soul of both. The "Heidegger Affair," a controversy which continues to this day as the *Black Notebooks* appear in the *Gesamtausgabe,* had been ignited by Victor Farias's *Heidegger and Nazism* (1987). This was an important if sensationalized and polemical revelation of Heidegger's involvement with the Nazis *after* he had stepped down, or been induced to step down, from the rectorship in 1934. Historian Hugo Ott's *Martin Heidegger: A Political Life* (1993), by contrast, was a coolly documented book which laid out the case against Heidegger in a decisive and less polemical way. I would later on contribute to a Festschrift for Professor Ott (Chapter 13).

7

This controversy sent me back to the drawing board (Chapters 10–11). I had up to then swallowed the official line that Heidegger's involvement was a temporary aberration which he soon regretted. So, I was forced to ask myself, just what was of lasting philosophical value in Heidegger and what was contaminated by his odious political views? That question has been brought home to me again today, as the nationalistic poison of Donald Trump courses its way through American democracy. In the case of Heidegger, it turns out, the problem lay in what I had objected to on strictly philosophical terms in an essay entitled "Demythologizing Heidegger." I was referring to the *mythos* of Being in Heidegger, his penchant for grand narratives which always turn on the logic, the mytho-logic, of the greatness of the beginning where what follows is a history of decline. When still a Christian, the young Heidegger had identified a primordial Christianity found in Paul's letters to the Thessalonians, taken to be the oldest documents in the New Testament, just as later on he singled out the fragments of Anaximander, the oldest of the presocratic fragments.

This narratival logic, the logic of a myth, fits hand in glove with his nationalism in which he fantasized that there was an inner spiritual connection between (his version of) "early Greek thinking" (never the "*pre*-Socratics, which he though demeaned them) and "Germania." This Latinism, referring historically to the barbarian land that was not Latinized, not conquered by Rome, was a mythopoetic amalgamation of everything primordially German, where the German language and the poetry of Hölderlin enjoy pride of place, a privilege which entitled the German *Volk* to rule the world and lead it out of world-historical spiritual decline. As Paul Tillich had pointed out in *The Socialist Decision* (1933), a book that cost him his job at Frankfurt, such nostalgic memorializing of a Great Beginning, now lost, is the structure of fascist time, the reactionary time of National Socialism, just as today it is the time of Donald Trump, the time of making Germany or America great *again*, the time of repeating the imaginary lost but Great Beginning whose restoration justifies the most extreme authoritarian violence. I collected the essays in which I detailed and documented my brief against Heidegger in *Demythologizing Heidegger* (1993), which, please note, also argued for a demythologiz*ed* Heidegger turning on the *es gibt* and returning to the early hermeneutics of facticity.

Demythologizing Heidegger was originally intended to be the first half of a larger book, which, for reasons of both economics and logic, I decided to publish separately. What was to be the second half of the book was published the same year under the cheeky title *Against Ethics*. This was intended to be the "ethics," or anti-ethics or hyper-ethics, which would mime and mimic Heidegger's monumental, monomaniacal – everything is either Greek or a decline from the

Greek – mythologizing of Great Beginning, a kind of Greek Big Bang. For Heidegger, the glory that is Greece utterly erases the Jew, both literally (Spinoza does not belong to Heidegger's history of Being) and as a figure of the outcast, the excluded, the marginalized. Taking my stand *against this* would be my ethics, or ethics beyond ethics, ironically entitled *Against Ethics*, which I decided to write in the spirit of Kierkegaard (whence the pseudonyms), Derrida (whence the playfulness), and Lyotard and Levinas (whence the emphasis on obligation). Against ethics, if ethics means (as it does for Kierkegaard) universal rules, but for obligation, which means the claim made upon by us by the singularity of the other (Kierkegaard's "religious" but Levinas's "ethics"), not the claim of a mythological Great Beginning but the claim of the last and least among us. That is what Lyotard called the *différend, les juifs*, what Derrida and Levinas called *tout autre*, and what St. Paul called *ta me onta* in one of the most explosive texts in the New Testament (1 Cor 1) in which Paul explores the logos of the cross, of a humiliating execution, not the all gathering gleaming logos of Heraclitus. Paul had captured something basic to the later synoptic gospels, the figure of "Yeshua," who healed the man with a withered hand (obligation) even though it was the Sabbath (ethics). The Sabbath was made for us; we were not made for the Sabbath. This provides an interesting commentary on the hypocrisy of the evangelical right today who would rather gather unvaccinated on the sabbath than protect the health of their neighbors, whom they say they love. In short, this would represent everything that Heidegger had come to disdain – instead of a glittering white sun-drenched Greek temple, a bloody torn Jewish body hanging lifeless against a darkened sky. The later Heidegger had embraced a *theologia gloriae*, of the glory that was Greece, in oblivion (*Vergessenheit*) of his own point of departure, of the roots of his hermeneutics of facticity in the *theologia crucis* of Luther. The threads of this argument can be found in "The Poetics of Suffering and the Deconstruction of Ethics" (Chapter 17). *Against Ethics* is my most Lyotardian and Levinasian book; their presence in this book is stronger than Derrida's.

It turns out that I was, in these years, also being drawn back into the question of religion, which I thought I had put behind me. One can see *The Prayers and Tears of Jacques Derrida* (1997) beginning to take shape in these essays. The figure of "Yeshua" was coming into focus, not the God-Man conjured up in High Hellenic Christology, the Lord of my youth, nothing about a divine infusion of supernatural grace, not the *theologia gloriae*, but the Galilean healer, exorcist and prophet announcing the coming the kingdom of God, of the rule of the God of Israel, who was crucified for his trouble. Accordingly, my attitude towards the mystical, with which I tended to identify religion up to that point, was beginning to shift, not because I was about to drop it, which I never did (chapter 31), but because I wanted to make room for the *prophetic*, for justice for the least among us. That shift can be detected in the critical discussions of Marion (chapter 20), in which it became crystal clear to me that the classical notion of the mystical as unmediated unity, pure givenness, being "saturated" in light, is up to its ears in Neoplatonic metaphysics. As Derrida says, when someone speaks of the unmediated, be prepared to be inundated in a tidal wave of mediations – which is why the unconditional givenness of Marion's saturated phenomenon is accompanied by the unconditional authority of Roman church, of Marion's "bishop" (chapter 21). That is what led me recently (*Specters of God*, 2022) to distinguish the edifying apophaticism of classical Neoplatonic mysticism from the more radical apophaticism of being left genuinely in the dark.

The "religion," if that is what it is, to which I was being drawn back would show up in a religion without religion – more prophetic than mystical, more Jewish than Christological, more theopoetic than theological – the subtitle of *The Prayers and Tears of Jacques Derrida*. This book was, in part, meant to be an updating and revising of Mark Taylor's thesis that deconstruction is the hermeneutics of the death of God, which was at that time, more or less, the received view of deconstruction and religion. That is what I contested (Chapters 28-29). I was arguing that Derrida's religion, if that is what it is, his religion without religion, is the circum-fession of his prayers and tears, his affirmation of the event that is harbored in the name of God, which he signaled in the expression "the possibility of the impossible." That is not well described as the death of God. In deconstruction, if you say something is dead, it will come back to haunt you (*revenant*).

Finally, I wish to point out that several of these articles have been previously unpublished (Chapter 3), unavailable (Chapter 9), published only in German (chapter 13), or available only in rather hard to find sources (chapters 8, 17, 21, 31).

John D. Caputo
Wayne, Pennsylvania
August 2022

RADICAL HERMENEUTICS

1

FROM THE DECONSTRUCTION OF HERMENEUTICS TO THE HERMENEUTICS OF DECONSTRUCTION

[In *The Horizons of Continental Philosophy: Essays on Husserl, Heidegger, and Merleau-Ponty*, ed. Hugh Silverman (The Hague: Martinus Nijhoff, 1988), 190–202]

[190] My thesis is that even as there is a deconstructive element in hermeneutics, so there also is a hermeneutic element in deconstruction. Hermeneutics cannot go about its work, which I see to be essentially one of retrieval, without an accompanying violence which enables it to recover what is hidden. But neither can deconstruction escape the hermeneutic circle; it cannot carry out its work without also cooperating in the work of recovery.

The first thesis is uncontroversial and belongs to Heideggerian orthodoxy. The second thesis is controversial and indeed contradicts the letter of Derrida's text.

I want to offer passing support for the first thesis, just in case there are any remaining infidels about, and then get right to the second thesis.

The First Thesis. Heidegger has been attacked from the right as a nihilist, and from the left as a victim of nostalgia and hope. (That probably means he is on to something!) The charge of nihilism is directed against the deconstructive element in Heidegger, while the charge of nostalgia is directed against the hermeneutic element. In *Being and Time* the hermeneutic element means, first, the recovery of the pre-understanding in which Dasein always and already stands and to which we gain access only by wresting it loose via a certain hermeneutic violence. Heidegger says [191] that hermeneutic interpretation must follow the opposite course (*im Gegenzug*) to the direction in which we are always and already falling.[1] By this violence we have not violated Dasein, but on the contrary, we have dis-closed (retrieved, recovered) what tends of itself to remain closed.

The hermeneutic element in the existential analytic only prepared the way for the hermeneutico-deconstructive reading of the history of ontology which wants to shake loose from the paradigmatic figures in the history of ontology the implicit interpretation of Being as time. And while this destruction does a superficial violence to the "authors" whom it treats, it does not violate Being, but on the contrary retrieves its originary meaning.

In the later works the project of "overcoming metaphysics" performs a deconstructive service in the name of the *Sache*. There can be no straightforward and unmediated thought of Being. Rather, the matter (*Sache*) for thought is always delivered to us in the history of its concealments. Whence the task of thought is always to dismantle the apparatus of metaphysics in order to enter all the more primordially into the movement of the *Sache*. The deconstruction of the metaphysics of modernity, for example, of the distinction between subject and object, is undertaken in the name of recovering the more primordial belonging together of Being and Dasein. The deconstruction of "logic" is made in the name of recovering the originary *logos*. The deconstruction of the will-to-power is undertaken in order to recover the non-willing of *Gelassenheit*. And so forth. Deconstruction always assists as a preparatory work for hermeneutic recovery.

The Second Thesis. But if it is relatively uncontroversial to hold that there must needs be a deconstructive element in hermeneutics, the reverse is not true. For deconstruction wants to deconstruct hermeneutics itself, to number hermeneutics among its victims. In commenting upon [192] Heidegger's critique of humanism, e.g., Derrida says there is at best here a kind of "archeological radicalness" which ends up with a deeper "revalorization" of the essence of man, a deeper repetition – or recovery – of his essence.[2] Derrida objects precisely to the moment of hermeneutic recovery or retrieval as an *Aufhebung*, a *relève*, which puts man, or *logos*, or whatever, in higher – or deeper – relief. If there is a violence in hermeneutics, it is not disruptive enough, but remains in complicity with what it puts under duress.

And we know too that in *Dissemination* Derrida is sharply critical of hermeneutics as a philosophy of "meaning." Meaning for him is always an effect, a product of the differential matrix, of the code of repeatability, and hence does not enjoy any privileges. Meanings are constituted by their place in the system of differences, but that place is held precariously and is subject to infinitesimal, differential shadings off. *Dissemination* shows the drift, the slippage, the instability of the "semantic," and hence of any "thematic" reading of literature or philosophy. Derrida wants to subvert the primacy of meaning by systematically exploring all the surfaces of language, all the possible graphic, phonic, etymological, rhythmic and psychoanalytic linkages among words. He

14

wants to exploit every connection, follow up every possible link that connects one word to another, in defiance, in reduction, of meaning. And if it is true that he is thinking more of Ricoeur in this text, it is clear that the same criticism is made of "onto-hermeneutics" in *Spurs*, because of Heidegger's interest in the "meaning of Being."[3]

And so our work is cut out for us. The second thesis is contestable, and indeed it is contested by the letter of Derrida's own text.

I would like to support this thesis, first, by asking what Derrida is up to – not an uncommon question!—and, [193] secondly, by showing that, if I am right, what he is up to has hermeneutic import.

I begin with an example. We all know that Derrida criticizes Heidegger's view of authenticity, and I would say rightly, insofar as the word "*Eigentlichkeit*" moves within the metaphoric of proximity, self-nearness, and hence self-consciousness.[4] Derrida is interested in making metaphysics tremble (*ébranler*), which is what he means by "solicitation." Thus he is on the alert for every attempt by metaphysics to give itself comfort, to relieve its anxiety with a measure of presence and identity, to arrest the flux. Hence he is sensitive to the lingering metaphysical and ethical overtones of the word "authenticity" and he succeeds in issuing a warning against thinking that one has found a sure footing and a safe refuge with this word. And he is right – for it is surely the point of this notion to undermine such assurances. He makes Heidegger clean up the existential analytic on this point.

Now my question is this. Granting this criticism, is there any *difference* between the comfort-seeking philosophy of presence and the critical vigilance (which Heidegger initiates and which Derrida wants to be more ruthless about) which exposes its ruses? And if there is, what do we say about it? In other words, how is one to characterize the difference in Derrida himself between the *repressive* movement – which is bent upon arresting the play of signifiers, which is nostalgic and in search of security, which fears the dangerous play, which enforces normal discourse – and the *Dionysiac* who embraces everything dangerous and elusive, everything playful and void of foundation? Now the right answer to this question is to say, *that* difference too is undecidable; it is part of the flux that that difference too wavers in insecurity. Then we ask, how is one to characterize the difference between facing up to such undecidability and repressing it, between keeping [194] open the wound of undecidability and trying to close it up with a cure?

I think that Derrida would be in principle unwilling to answer that question, for once it is answered a decidable distinction is enforced and the flux of signifiers is brought to a halt. It is part of Derrida's strategy to remain a moving target, never to take a position, always to be on the run, never to rest long enough to let the vitiating movement of the paradoxes of self-reference overtake him. And that is a good *strategy*, one which keeps us honest about our beliefs, which keeps us from worshipping idols, i.e., philosophical constructions of our own devising. I applaud the liberating effects of this strategy.

My question is whether it does not arise from a certain understanding of ourselves, a certain pre-understanding of the kind of being which we ourselves are. Can the *praxis* of Derrida, his deconstructive strategy, escape the dynamics of the hermeneutic circle? Does it arise from nowhere? Does it, as he likes to ask with Husserl, drop from the sky, or does it proceed from a certain preunderstanding? In my view, it draws upon a certain hermeneutic impulse, viz., one which wants to resist the attempt which metaphysics makes to insulate man against his finitude and the *difference* by which he is inhabited. Deconstruction is not innocent. Derrida's choice of texts and heroes – Nietzsche and Freud, Artaud and Bataille – is not made without a guiding assumption. Together his authors suggest a being of desire which tries systematically to mask its desire from itself. And Derrida's strategy, like the masters of suspicion whom he admires, is to unmask such a ruse, to bring us face to face with *difference* and to cut off the escape routes metaphysics devises for itself. The result is an increase in "self-understanding." Now this very metaphysical expression does not mean that we achieve some luminous self-transparency, but rather that we expose ourselves to an uncanny sense of the darkness, the *difference*, by which we are invaded. If Ricoeur would call [195] this a hermeneutics of suspicion, I would add that it is also a delimitation of hermeneutics which sees to it that hermeneutics is prepared to live without consolation.

But Derrida would never agree to say this much. Derrida himself thinks that any attempt to state or explicate such a preunderstanding will inevitably be in complicity with metaphysics, that it will drift into metaphysical discourse – just as we, for example, find it necessary to use a metaphysical expression like "self-understanding" – become a new orthodoxy, want to defend its distinctions, and so on. As long as it remains a strategy without a "position" it retains its methodological invulnerability. And there is something to that. The great advantage of deconstruction is that it is primarily a strategy. But is it a strategy which represses its own preunderstanding? Let us look more closely at just what kind of strategy it is.

In *Positions* Derrida refers to his work as "a unique and differentiated textual 'operation,'" which he also describes as an "unfinished movement."[5] Deconstruction is thus an ongoing work, not a position but a *praxis*, not a

16

theoretical outlook or standpoint, but an activity which is always *in actu exercitu* and resists being formulated *in actu significato*. It is an exercise in disruption, a disruptive work which displaces whatever is inclined to settle in place. Now it is true that deconstruction gives every appearance of being an aestheticism. It is bent on perpetual transformation and alteration, on a repetition which seems to be guided only by its desire for innovation, whose only "rule" appears to be always to avoid boredom and to seek what is interesting, which is how Kierkegaard describes the "rotation method" in *Either/Or*. One sometimes gets the sense that all that matters for Derrida is enjoying the play.

Now Derrida may indeed have such moments, but it is not my impression that that is what he is up to. In my view, it is not the Kierkegaardian aesthete whom he has adopted as a [196] paradigm, but rather Nietzsche's tragic hero, which is more like the "religious stage" in Kierkegaard, as Louis Mackey, Mark Taylor and Sylviane Agacinski have recently been saying. (Indeed Derrida is contributing to a book of essays on *Fear and Trembling* to be edited by Taylor.) The play of which he speaks is not meant as an aesthetic divertissement but rather as a deeply unsettling and disruptive movement. I come back to solicitation, the *ébranler*. Derrida wants to disturb the placidity of everydayness, to put the self-evidence of normalcy into question. That above all is what he shares with Heidegger and which separates him by an abyss from the self-indulgence of aesthetic repetition, even as the normalcy of everydayness is separated from anxiety in *Being and Time*. The metaphysics of presence is for him a philosophy of comfort, which seeks to reassure, to arrest the play. And Derrida will have none of that. He wants instead to expose everything to the risk, to the abyss, to the play.

Deconstructive work is first of all a practice (*"une opération"*), not a theory, and, secondly, a practice of disruption aimed at keeping the play in play, refusing it rest or arrest, not for the sake of aesthetic pleasure, but in order to heighten our sensitivity to the contingency and, as Husserl would have put it, the "destructibility of the world" (*Ideas I*, §44), to heighten our "readiness for anxiety." To what "end"? Can we ask about the "ends" of Derrida? Then, let us ask instead, what is the thrust of this dagger tip, this style, this stiletto? Once again, if I have felt the effect of this textual operation, this is all carried out in the name of what philosophy would call *liberation*. It is perhaps not so much a "philosophy" of liberation, in the sense of working out a liberationist standpoint, as it is a strategy or praxis of liberation. It is a textual operation performed in the name of, with the intended effect of, liberation; it is not an attempt to work out the theoretical contours of liberation.

17

[197] Derrida is extremely good at exposing the contingency of human arrangements, the vulnerability of everything "normal," the oppressiveness of everything which (poses as) present, established, unchangeable. What after all are the concrete social and political issues which concern Derrida? In 1968, on the occasion of delivering "The Ends of Man" in New York City, he expresses his grave concern at speaking in a country which was then waging the Vietnam War.[6] The essays on Lacan and *Spurs* are highly critical of phallo-centrism (actually, phal-logo-centrism). One of Levy-Strauss's greatest accomplishments for Derrida is the delimitation of ethno-centrism and the exposure of Western Europe to its "other." In "White Mythology" he says that metaphysics and logo-centrism are white not only because of their cold conceptuality but because they are European-white.[7] In *Limited Inc a b c*, part of the satire of Searle is the call for the police to enforce normal discourse.[8] He has become more and more involved in the reform of educational institutions, delimiting the artificial divisions of the disciplines, the systematic exclusions, the "discipline" which thereby gets enforced in the schools, to the point that he has recently organized his own academic institution. The goal of the *"College Internationale de Philosophie"* is to scrutinize totalitarianism, physical and psychical torture, organ transplants and genetic engineering, human rights, the relationships between politics and religion and other issues which "solicit" philosophy today and make it "tremble" (*ébranlements*). Militarism, sexism, torture, totalitarianism, ethno-centrism, racism, the academic establishment: these are the concrete targets of deconstructive critique, the sociological embodiments of the "metaphysics of presence."

Derrida is a great and gifted critic of established authority, of the "powers that be," as we say in English. And that is a revealing expression, suggesting as it does the powers that proceed (or which pretend to proceed) from Being-as-presence. Derrida is exceptionally good at showing these are only powers that pretend to be, appear to be, and [198] that they are, from the ground (which they lack) up, subject to *kinesis*. They are the powers that *become*, that have *come* to be and that will sooner or later come to grief, to kingdom come. Derrida wants systematically to show that every such established authority is an effect, a product; that it has not fallen from the sky. One cannot fail to see in this portrait of Derrida the figure of Socrates, the practitioner of disruptive strategies whose point – whose style, stylus, stiletto – is to unmask pretension, to foil the claim to knowledge. And as Socrates did not avoid the semblance of sophism, neither does Derrida avoid the semblance of aestheticism. Like Socrates, Derrida does not intend to offer guidelines for construction. We do not need encouragement to construct schemes, to lay things out in a political program, in a metaphysical panorama or a Weberian bureaucratic flow-chart. It is always in the name of these totalizing views that the police do their work. Blood is usually shed in the name of Being, God, or truth, even and especially when it is shed in the name of "country." *Pro deo et patria.* (It makes no sense to enforce skepticism, even though it can happen.) The constructions of metaphysics, like the poor, we have always with us. But it is the Socratic role to keep us honest about these schemes, to remind us of their contingency and alterability, to make the police think twice, or perhaps think in the first place.

Now let us return to the question of a hermeneutic impulse in Derrida. I do not see what other effect his work can have than to expose us to ourselves, to make it plain to ourselves, that we bear the responsibility for our own fictions. He does not attempt to put an end to fiction – for he does not think that there is anything other than fictions, contingencies, alterable configurations of the code of repeatability – but only to dispel the ring of illusion which we weave around them. If, as Nietzsche said, truth is a fiction which have *forgotten* is a fiction, then the work of Derrida is to make us *remember.* But is that not an exercise in self-knowledge, in recollection, an attempt to find a [199] moment of self-understanding, where we do not conceal from ourselves the flux, the draft, the slippage, the alterability of every human arrangement? Is this not an attempt to force into view everything which we try to repress, to bring us face to face with ourselves, not in a moment of limpid Cartesian self-consciousness, but in a moment of vigilance, of alertness to the dark powers which are at work on us, and the dark play in which we are caught up?

Should we not be led by Derrida, should not Derrida himself be led, to a moment of self-understanding, to a point of self-confrontation, like the moment of which the Judge speaks in *Either/Or* when he warns the aesthete that there is a midnight moment when all masks must be removed? Is not this critique of repression a call *back* to what has been repressed, a *recollective* moment in which we become aware of the ruses which are at work – at play – within us? The real dominion of darkness, of the kingdom of *Irrtum,* is not found in the darkness and errancy itself, but in our own ignorance of its work. And does not Derrida's suspicious eye raise our level of alertness, and by increasing our distrust, thereby increase our self-knowledge?

But Derrida's distrust is so great that he distrusts even this hermeneutic moment. He will say nothing of the kind. His distrust extends to a distrust of all talk of recollection, retrieval, recuperation, self-return, self-understanding, as modes of self-presence. If he practices a hermeneutics of suspicion this includes a suspicion of all hermeneutics. And perhaps, as a deconstructive *strategy,* we should expect nothing else. He fears making his work *safe,* domesticating it, taking away the sting of the Socratic sting-ray. He fears that if he takes this hermeneutic turn, if he says all of this, deconstruction will pose itself as the latest metaphysics of presence. It will then have something to defend, become part of the powers that be, want to insulate itself against critique, repress dissent, and assert its own authority.

[200] At this point, I think, we need a kind of meta-hermeneutics, a non-metaphysical hermeneutics which goes beyond a naive belief in meaning, a hermeneutics which takes into account the dark play in which all things are caught. One needs a hermeneutic which will be, let us say, a hermeneutics of trembling, of the *ébranler*, a hermeneutics without comfort.

In fine, we need a kind of thinking which is at once hermeneutic and deconstructive, both unsettling and recuperative, which exposes us to the abyss but which understands that in that exposure one has reached a deeper understanding of the beings which we are. "*Da-sein heisst: Hineingehaltenheit in das Nichts.*"[9]

But is that not itself one more comforting reconciliation of opposites, one more *Aufhebung*, in the manner of Ricoeur's hermeneutics of reconciliation? I think not. For hermeneutics and deconstruction do not cooperate in preparation for some coming *parousia*. On the contrary, whenever hermeneutics finds itself lured by that temptation, the Socratic sting-ray drifts its way.[10]

Notes

[1] Heidegger, *Sein und Zeit*, 10. Aufl. (Tübingen: Niemeyer, 1963), 311; Eng. trans. *Being and Time*, trans. J. Robinson and E. Macquarrie (New York: Harper & Row, 1962), 359.

[2] Jacques Derrida, *Marges de la philosophie* (Paris: Editions de Minuit, 1972), 153; Eng. trans. *Margins of Philosophy*, trans. Alan Bass (Chicago: University Press, 1982), 128.

[3] Jacques Derrida, *Spurs: Nietzsche's Styles/Éperons: Les Styles de Nietzsche*, Bilingual edition, trans. B. Harlow (Chicago: University Press, 1978), 106–107, 110–15.

[4] *Marges*, 74n26; *Margins*, 64n9.

[5] Derrida, *Positions* (Paris: Editions de Minuit, 1972), 11; Eng. trans. *Positions*, trans. Alan Bass(Chicago: University Press, 1981), 3.

[6] *Marges*, 131–35; *Margins*, 111–14.

[7] *Marges*, 254; *Margins*, 213.

[8] Derrida, "Limited Inc a b c...," *Glyph 2* (Supplement) (Baltimore: Johns Hopkins Press, 1977), 250–51.

[9] Heidegger, *Was ist Metaphysik?*, 9. Aufl. (Frankfurt: Klostermann, 1965), 35; Eng. trans. *What is Metaphysics?*, trans. W. Hull and A. Crick in *Existence and Being*, ed. W. Brock (Chicago: Regnery, 1949), 339.

[10] Portions of this paper were subsequently incorporated into my *Radical Hermeneutics: Repetition, Deconstruction and the Hermeneutic Project* (Bloomington: Indiana University Press, 1987). Acknowledgment is gratefully made to Indiana University Press for permission to use this material.

2

TELLING LEFT FROM RIGHT: HERMENEUTICS, DECONSTRUCTION, AND THE WORK OF ART

[In *The Journal of Philosophy,* Vol. 83, No. 11, Eighty-Third Annual Meeting American Philosophical Association, Eastern Division (Nov. 1986), 678-685]

* APA symposium on Hermeneutics and Deconstruction, December 30, 1986. Alexander Nehamas, co-symposiast; Hugh J. Silverman, commentator.

[678] The topic of the symposium is "hermeneutics and deconstruction." That is neat enough: hermeneutics on the one side, deconstruction on the other. Presumably: hermeneutics on the right, deconstruction on the left. A hermeneutic right wing and a deconstructive left wing. Retrieval and memorial thinking here, disruption and active forgetting there. The safely delivered messages of Hermes on the one hand (the right hand, no doubt), the dead letter box on the other. Heidegger on the right, Derrida on the left. Each side neatly framed and assigned its proper table with Pythagorean precision.

But the topic is "hermeneutics *and* deconstruction." The "and" complicates everything and forces us to face the question of how these two are connected, interlaced. How should we approach this question, hermeneutically or deconstructively? Should we set out in search of a fusion of horizons which sees in deconstruction a "hermeneutics of suspicion," a negative moment on the way toward a higher reconciliation? Or is that just a way to make deconstruction safe, a way that philosophy has of assimilating its "other" (M x-xvi)?[1] Then should we treat this "and" deconstructively and show that deconstruction is irreducibly, irreconcilably to the left of hermeneutics? Should we let deconstruction loose on hermeneutics, let it disturb hermeneutic memory, disseminate hermeneutic truth, let it subject Heidegger to Derridean critique? This troublesome "and" forces our hand. But which hand, left or right?

Perhaps the best way to get at the issue between hermeneutics and deconstruction is to let them decide it for themselves, to put a [679] common question to both and let them play themselves out. To that end I propose to take up the question of the work of art and to track the movements, first of a hermeneutic (Heideggerian) and then of a deconstructive analysis. Then, at the end, I will face up to the question of the "and" and ask whether and how the lines between the two can be drawn, whether and how we can tell left from right.

I

According to Heidegger the work of art is an event of truth which discloses the world and opens up the space within which a historical people dwells. But in modern aesthetics the artwork is not left to "rest in itself" (Or 50), but is instead reduced to an aesthetic "value," *objet d'art,* an object for the esteeming subject (Or 68). In modernity artworks hang helplessly enframed on museum walls, are taught in "literature" classes. They ornament the lives of those who seek "culture," are consumed by aficionados and experts in aesthetic value judgments. Having become the "raw material" of the art "industry" they are safely assimilated by the age of "enframing" (*Gestell*) which thereby insulates itself from the disruptive claim that the work of art makes (QCT 23-35). The museum and the literature class are safe places to confine the artwork while the fury of the *Gestell* goes unchecked. Like Foucault's lepers and madmen, the artwork is institutionalized and hence effectively excluded from "truth" and "objectivity."

The boundaries that enframe "aesthetic objects" are clearly drawn by Kant's three *Critiques.* The first *Critique* marks off the realm of strict and objective science, of categories that determine the objects of outer (empirical) intuition. The second *Critique* stakes out the inner realm of moral duty which transcends and supersedes empirical fact. Finally, Kant attempts to create a middle kingdom with boundaries of its own, but with the function of maintaining lines of communication both with moral ideas and with the sphere of sensuous intuition, within which he situates aesthetics. The whole critical operation is one of setting off limits, laying down markers. Kant means strictly to separate the *ergon* from the *par-ergon,* to keep the realm of the aesthetic pure and uncontaminated – from all truth and moral force on the one hand, from all ornamentation and merely private pleasure on the other (VP 44 ff). Kant wants the lines drawn around the artwork to be sharp, its margins clean, the right hand of science clearly set off from the left hand of values. The three *Critiques* enframe the work of art and hold it in place on the museum wall.

24

Against Kant's act of confinement, Heidegger situates the work of art in the realm of the open expanse (*das Freie*). Against Kant's [680] enframing of the artwork, which forcibly excludes it from truth, Heidegger assigns it the radical function of opening up ("dis-closing") the world (Or 57-78). Heidegger does not argue that the artwork *also* has "truth value" – which is to play according to the rules of value thinking – but that the artwork enters into the very coming to pass (*Wesen*) of truth. The artwork is not just one more truth alongside science, but rather belongs originarily to the happening of truth, opening up the realm of truth *within* which science itself is contained. As a form of propositional or calculative thinking, science is itself always already dependent upon the prior disclosure of the world by the artwork. Heidegger turns metaphysical aesthetics on its head. For the artwork provides the clear expanse (*Lichtung*) within which the scientific and ethical practices of a particular world or epoch of Being take place. The artwork is ontologically "older" than or prior to science.

Heidegger can make such an extraordinary claim in virtue of his radical idea of truth as *a-letheia*. In the originary Greek experience, "*axios*" – as opposed to value – means the commanding look of things which elicits our respect, the dignity that issues from the shining forth of the things themselves and thereby subdues the subjectivity of the subject (SG 34-35). The shining forth of *axios* is *phainesthai, phainomenon,* the self-showing appearance which means all at once self-emergent Being (*physis*), un-concealment (*aletheia*), and shining beauty (*Scheinen, Schönheit*). The modern "axiom" as a fundamental proposition artfully constructed by a mathematical intelligence and modern "axiology" as the "science of values" are metaphysical and subjectivistic renderings of originary *axios, axioma.*

Understood not as value but as *axios*, not as what is posited by an esteeming subject, but as an event that overtakes us, the work of art is a commanding, subduing event in which an entire world is opened up. The work of art is not a particular object *within* the world – let alone an art object contained within an aesthetic frame – but a matrix which institutes (*stiftet*) and forms its world. The Greek temple sits in a rock-cleft valley, or on a hilltop overlooking the Mediterranean, its white marble flesh gleaming in the sun, full of *phainesthai* and shining truth. The temple is not merely a building where rites are performed, which houses the gods or representations of the gods, but rather the place that makes the gods present, that lets them come to presence. For the Greeks, art belongs not in museums, a phenomenon of the world-as-picture, but in public view, in the *polis* and *agora*. The artwork is not so much "in" this world as it is constitutive or disclosive of it (Or 41-42).

25

[681] Emancipated, let out of its frame, the work of art then returns the favor and, in a magnanimous gesture, sets us free, admitting us into the open expanse that it itself provides.

II

For Derrida, Heidegger takes the first, necessary step in the overcoming of aesthetics and the liberation of the work of art from the rule of metaphysics. As Derrida says, any work of deconstruction must first "catch up" with Heidegger, must begin by placing itself within the opening of his questions (M 128). But it does not suffice merely to stand metaphysics on its head; for every such "reversal" remains itself under the spell of metaphysics and requires a more radical movement of "displacement" (M 329).

Heidegger's critique of aesthetic values is carried out in the name of truth. Heidegger takes the step back into the more primordial expanse of *aletheia* within which the critical philosophy has neatly carved out the domains of science, ethics, and aesthetics. But for Derrida such a transgression of metaphysics is carried out by means of the most familiar, because Platonic, gesture of metaphysics: the distinction between the originary and the derivative (M 63-64). By opposing originary truth to derivative propositional discourse Heidegger invokes the fundamental binary scheme that is "meta-physics." Derrida thus undertakes a transgression of Heidegger's transgression, a marginal note on Heidegger which pits *Nietzsche aujourd'hui* against Heidegger's last metaphysician of values.

For if Heidegger has liberated the artwork from aesthetic values, he has in the same gesture delivered it over to the rule of truth. If he has defied Kant's attempt to police the borders between the cognitive and noncognitive, he has done so by setting the truth into the artwork. But for Derrida that setting (*setzen*) remains a higher mode of framing, a metaphysical operation of positing and centering. Heidegger centers the truth of Being in the work (*Werk*) and he centers the work on the experience of truth. Derrida on the other hand wants to un-settle the truth and to question the distinction between *ergon* and *parergon*, to decenter, disseminate. For Derrida the artwork does not have clear borders, but rather spills over its frame, producing uncontrollable, multiple effects. Heidegger takes an onto-hermeneutic step back into the primordial truth of the work of art, letting it "rest in itself." Derrida lets the artwork tremble in instability and undecidability, without defining or enframing its function, letting it be by letting it waver with many worlds, many truths, too many truths, producing many other effects than truth.

Consider the case of Heidegger's discussion of Van Gogh's painting of the shoes (Or 32-36). Derrida "defends" Heidegger against Meyer Schapiro by arguing not that Heidegger is innocent, but that [682] there is nothing innocent about Schapiro (VP 291 ff). If Heidegger's interpretation is a projection of his own rural ideology, Schapiro's claim that these are the shoes of Van Gogh himself, "by that time a man of the town and the city," is the projection of the urbane art critic, the expert and aficionado who is an authority on Van Gogh (Heidegger is trespassing on Schapiro's field). Carrying around a correspondence theory of truth (VP 362-3), Schapiro tries like a good detective to track down whose shoes are being depicted and to return them to their proper owner, which, all the hermeneutic clues confirm, is "clearly" the owner/author of the painting who has signed his proper name, "Vincent." Schapiro's *Kunstwissenschaft,* his scientific, mimetic hermeneutics, is even more steeped in metaphysical dogma than Heidegger's onto-hermeneutics. If Heidegger accomplishes no more than a reversal of metaphysics, Schapiro offers metaphysics no resistance at all (VP 425).

But Derrida finds in both Schapiro and Heidegger the same hermeneutic gestures and assumptions: the same assumption that the shoes are a matched pair, left and right, which must belong on someone's feet, not just an abandoned odd pair; the same gesture of identification, attribution, restitution, appropriation (VP 417). In both cases the same attempt is made to tie the shoes down to one truth and one sex, to restore them to their rightful owner, to Van Gogh himself, now a townsman, or to the peasant woman whose world they disclose (VP 410-18). But for Derrida the shoes cannot be returned; they are like the letters in *La Carte postale* which cannot be delivered (CP 71-75). For Derrida, the unlaced shoes cannot be definitively laced up one way or the other. No one has the authority to tie up their meaning, to pronounce a master name on their behalf, to resolve their undecidability. He writes, "No one is accused or condemned or even suspected. (Not Heidegger or Schapiro.) *There is (il y a)* painting, writing, restitutions; that is all" (VP 425). The shoes in the painting are there *"for the painting,"* not in order to be reattached to Van Gogh's feet or to the feet of the peasant woman, but there for the painting, for repeated lacing and relacing, for multiple repetitions which alter and produce new effects.

This is not to say that we have come full circle, back to the separation of art from truth, which is the essential gesture of the metaphysics of aesthetic values. The deconstruction of Heidegger's onto-hermeneutics has nothing to do with the re-subjectification of the artwork. For Derrida has undertaken a critique of a more radical sort which puts the very idea of truth in question. There is no privileged domain that claims cognitive rights over and against the sphere of subjective values. The very notion of "value" belongs to a binary [683] system requiring a notion of "objective truth" which Derrida *also* deconstructs. There can be no fact/value distinction here because there are, for Derrida, in rigorously Nietzschean fashion, no facts, only interpretations, writings, paintings.

Heidegger's critique of aesthetics remains an aletheo-onto-hermeneutics, keyed to the truth of Being, tuned to the soundings of Greek master names (*physis, ousia, logos*). Such words give voice to Being's own name; they say what Being would say, were it able to speak. Indeed, they do enable Being to speak, to utter its own proper name. Heidegger's deconstruction of aesthetics is made in the name of the master name. It makes a reduction from value to primordial *axios,* from correspondence to *aletheia.* It remains an operation of hermeneutic retrieval, not deconstruction, of memorial thinking, not active forgetting. It is bent not on exposing the flux by which things are inhabited, not on disseminating the temporary stability of the master names and metaphysical *archai,* but on locating their deeper truth. It reverses metaphysics by arguing that the artwork not only has truth but *is* truth; but it shrinks back from letting truth itself tremble in instability.

III

Now it is time to face up to the question of the "and." It appears that we were right to begin with, that there is a sharp distinction between hermeneutics and deconstruction, between memorial retrieval and disruptive dissemination – in short, between right and left. We have returned hermeneutics to Heidegger, and deconstruction to Derrida, their rightful owners. And yet... (*Und dennoch, Et pourtant*) (Or 33; VP 394).

We cannot help but notice that Derrida's disseminative gesture, which disseminates even the truth of Being, is made in the language of Heidegger: *il y a; ça donne; es gibt;* there is, it gives (VP 313, 320–391, 425; CP 74). Now that is a sign of trouble. Everything has been going too smoothly. This "there is/it gives" crosses freely back and forth between hermeneutics and deconstruction, weaving its way between them, lacing and interlacing them. It will not stay put on one side, but wanders brazenly across their boundaries, defying our border patrols, resisting identification, attribution, arrest, refusing to confine itself solely to the left or the right.

This wandering produces an odd, mutant effect, a more deconstructive, leftish Heidegger, and a Derrida with a different twist. It produces an altered reading of Heidegger which shows that the dissemination and delimitation of the truth of Being has already taken place in Heidegger's text. (This is not so surprising; the business of deconstruction is not to destroy texts, but to open them up in a different way.) On this reading, Heidegger may be understood to [684] end up where he started out. He began by asking with Brentano about the manifold sense (*mannigfache Bedeutung*) of Being and he ended by thinking this manifold *as* a manifold, as a multiple unfolding of the many senses ("truths") of Being. The meaning of Being ends up as the multiplicity of meanings – in the plural – which unfold in the history of the West. The manifold meaning is the meaning of the manifold, of the unfolding of irreducibly plural senses of Being. He started out by attempting a reduction *of* this plurality and ended up by making a reduction *to* it. In short, the search for the unitary meaning of Being culminates in the discovery of the *dissemination* of meanings, the irrevocable pluralizing of its senses, of its truths.

Thus understood, Heidegger's path of thought wends its way beyond onto-hermeneutics, beyond the truth of Being, climaxing in the *Ereignis,* which is not the "meaning" or "truth" of Being ("Being as *Ereignis*") but that which gives Being, gives the manifold meanings or truths of Being, thus making of truth an "effect" in Derrida's sense (TB 21–24). The truth of Being is that there are many truths of Being, too many truths, playing themselves out in the history of the epochs. *A-letheia* does not mean the truth of Being granted to some historical people, but the very process, the a-lethic process, by which whatever is granted arises from the withdrawal of what is granting. We must learn to think *a-letheia,* "over and beyond the Greeks," as the epochal dispensation of the multiple and manifold truths of Being (TB 71). *A-letheia* does not mean, cannot be translated as, truth (TB 69). It is not a historical name; its nominal unity has been disrupted by the hyphen. *A-letheia* is not a Greek word. It points to that process by which Being and truth are granted without privilege, to us as well as to the Greeks, to the Greeks as well as to everybody else. No more privileging of the Greeks, no more Greek privileging. It points to that which produces Being and truth as historical, epochal effects.

Ereignis; Es gibt; a-letheia: markings which are neither words nor concepts, in which the meaning and truth of Being, the Being and meaning of truth, are subjected to radical dissemination and pluralizing. It gives because it gives (TB 24). It plays because it plays – and always "without why" (SG 188).

Es gibt: that is neither Heidegger's own, nor Derrida's own; we do not know where to return it. Hermeneutics *and* deconstruction: all the force of the "and" is contained in the *Es gibt* which crosses back and forth between the two, crisscrossing them, interlacing them, blurring the lines between them, disrupting our attempt to tabularize them. The *Es gibt* issues in a hermeneutics that concedes the dissemination of truth, on the [685] one hand, *and* a deconstruction interlaced with an idea of *a-letheia,* on the other.

The good intentions of our symposium to clear these matters up have been confounded. We cannot even tell left from right.

Notes

1 I employ the following abbreviations:

CP: Jacques Derrida, *La Carle Postale* (Paris: Flammarion, 1980).

M: Derrida, *Margins of Philosophy,* Alan Bass, trans. (Chicago: University Press, 1982).

Or: Martin Heidegger, "The Origin of the Work of Art" in *Poetry, Language, Thought,* Albert Hofstadter, trans. (New York: Harper & Row, 1971).

QCT: Heidegger, *The Question concerning Technology and Other Essays,* W. Lovitt, trans. (New York: Harper & Row, 1977).

TB: Heidegger, *On Time and Being,* Joan Stambaugh, trans. (New York: Harper & Row, 1972).

SG: Heidegger, *Der Satz vom Grund* (Pfullingen: Neske, 1957).

VP: Derrida, *Verité en Peinture* (Paris: Flammarion, 1978)

3

FINITUDE AND DIFFÉRANCE: GADAMER AND DERRIDA

[Previously unpublished, this paper was originally given at a conference entitled "Beyond Translation," sponsored by the University of Warwick (England) in July 1988 and directed by David Wood.]

For Gadamer translation is a paradigm of hermeneutic understanding. A translation is a fusion of horizons, a way of putting one's own meaning at risk in order to make one's own what is said in a text (WM 366/350).[1] A good translation does not reduce what is foreign to its own proportions, stripping it of its otherness, but rather it lets something other be said, lets something different be heard. Thus in the translation our own understanding is opened up to something foreign even as the foreign is brought within the horizon of our own understanding.

Now it is an interesting question to ask whether everything that is disruptive and scandalous, whether all the otherness of deconstruction, can be "translated" the terms of hermeneutics. Is it possible to assimilate what deconstruction does into the terms of hermeneutics, to open up the horizons of hermeneutics to deconstruction? This would amount to a translation in two of the three senses that Roman Jakobson itemizes.[2] It would be primarily an intra-linguistic translation, in which one would try to put deconstruction in other words, in the words of hermeneutics; but it would also involve translation "proper," for it would involve a translation from French to German (not to mention English). The question is whether such an undertaking inevitably results in a certain domestication of deconstruction which robs it of its disruptive, disseminative energy. Does such a translation transform the parasite into a host, turning the glitches and the glue of *glas* into the smooth glide of the Hegelian eagle?[3] Indeed does hermeneutics set out with a notion of translation in mind which deconstruction means to disrupt?

I want to explore this question by using Gadamer's notion of the "finitude" of hermeneutic understanding as a test case, for on the face of it finitude is a point at which hermeneutics and deconstruction seem to touch. It is his notion of finitude that sets Gadamer off from Hegel, and which situates his philosophical hermeneutics within the line of criticism which Kierkegaard made of Hegel and which Heidegger made of Husserl. One might well argue that by accenting the finitude of human understanding, Gadamerian hermeneutics contains in principle all the resources required for accommodating what deconstruction does. *Écriture* and *différance*, supplement and trace, would all be elements in an analytic of finitude. Situated within the horizon of philosophical hermeneutics, deconstruction looks like a patient, scrupulous, pitiless unfolding of the limitations and constraints under which human understanding labors, exposing in a bold and novel way the multiple illusions and traps to which we are subject in virtue of our finitude. Being bound up in the double bind would be part and parcel of the boundaries of a finite being. Deconstruction seems to explore in ruthless detail the domain of finitude, but that domain has been marked out in advance by hermeneutics. Deconstruction would be a special case of hermeneutics, a moment in the larger act of hermeneutic understanding. Deconstruction pushes hermeneutics further than it is inclined *of* itself to go, but always in a direction that hermeneutics itself recognizes, that of finitude. Hermeneutics thus would not be annulled by deconstruction; on the contrary, deconstruction would be a more radical element within hermeneutics.

So the question is, how good a translation of deconstruction does the finitude of understanding provide? My view is that finitude will not do, that finitude functions in Gadamer in a profoundly Hegelian and metaphysical manner, and that it is of a piece with a metaphysics of infinity of a most classical sort. Hence all this owning up to finitude on the part of Gadamerian hermeneutics is a cover for a closet theory of essence, ideality, and infinity. In short, finitude is not difference; it is a bad translation and we had better check the "original."

But of course if that is right, then there is trouble of another sort around the corner. For that appears to treat deconstruction as an original, an untouchable, a pure language whose unique modality cannot be translated, a core which is itself inexhaustible by any translator, in accord with the metaphysical distinction between original and copy which informs the classical concept of translation which Derrida analyzes in *Des Tours de Babel*. That may just be a problem with deconstruction, that it is so idiosyncratic, so properly itself, that it resists translation, which means that all we can do is imitate it, mime it, copy it, talk and sound like Derridean clones. It may be that every time anyone lays a hand on deconstruction, sets it to work, that Derrideans will protest, "that is a bad translation, that is not what deconstruction is at all." That would make deconstruction an inimitable original. That is why, at the end of these remarks, I will ask whether we need to surrender this whole project of translating deconstruction into hermeneutics, of giving it a ride on a ferry (*fero, ferre, latus sum*) across (*trans*) the Rhine and then across the Atlantic; whether there is a way of radicalizing hermeneutics which does not sell deconstruction down the river.

I will suggest that while the Gadamerian version of hermeneutics can never translate deconstruction, it is possible to radicalize hermeneutics by opening it up to deconstruction in a more pitiless way, a way which repeats deconstruction even as it alters it, which repeats hermeneutics even as it alters it, which is I suggest about as much as we can hope for from any translation.

Gadamer's Analytic of Finitude

I begin with Gadamer's critique of Dilthey which is, in my view, what Gadamer has gotten right about the notion of finitude. Dilthey's search for historical objectivity is essentially an effort at infinite understanding (WM 218/205). Dilthey's infinitism takes the form of an objectivist historical consciousness which thinks it can cure itself of its finitude by means of methodological controls. The mind is finite but the historian can correct for that by exerting a rigorous, purifying reflection which strikes out the distorting contingencies of one's particular historical circumstances. As a being endowed with the capacity for reflection the historian can raise himself above the fortuitous and ultimately prejudicial circumstances within which he is himself situated, thus effectively neutralizing the effects of finitude.

Gadamer rightly rejects this notion as a kind of Cartesian dream, an illusion of self-transparency which arises from an exaggerated notion of the power of reflection. Gadamer adroitly criticizes Dilthey by showing that Dilthey's historical objectivism is at odds with his own *Lebensphilosophie*. For the upshot of Dilthey's notion of life is so to bind the thinking subject to the conditions of life as precisely to disallow the kind of distantiation which his concept of historical consciousness demands, something which, as Gadamer shows, comes out in the famous correspondence between Dilthey and Count von Yorck (WM 229 ff./214 ff.) Dilthey's notion of historical objectivity requires an abstract, disengaged, epistemological subject while his *Lebensphilosophie* commits him to a concrete, living, historical subject whose relationship to the past is not an objectifying one, but a living one, one which takes up, assimilates, and is nourished by the past.

Gadamer here is being quite Heideggerian, insisting as he does on the finitude of factical understanding, and hence on the impossibility of clearing away the encumbrances of historical situatedness. Finitude cannot be

33

neutralized; prejudices cannot be annulled. Finitude is an ontological structure of Dasein and it can be laid aside only at the cost of the very structure of understanding itself. Dasein does history (*Historie*) because it is in its very being historical (*geschichtlich*), and the past is the stuff of which Dasein's existential projects are made. Understanding is a mode of self-understanding, a way that Dasein has of projecting its own possibilities (WM 246–47/231). In short, the very fact of Dasein's factical finitude, its being bound and limited to its own existential projects, makes historical understanding possible. Finitude does not merely limit, but also enables historical understanding. That is the basis of Gadamer's rehabilitation of prejudice in the next section of *Truth and Method*, the net effect of which, he says, is to open the way towards "the appreciation of our finitude" (WM 230/244).

There is, Gadamer confesses, a paradox attached to affirming the finitude of the understanding (WM 324–29/305–10). For such an affirmation amounts to a self-limiting reflection, an understanding which declares itself to be limited, which knows that it knows only so much and knows that it knows no more. If consciousness can mark off its own limits so, if it can draw a boundary line around itself, then it must at the same time know what lies on both sides of the limit. If that is so, then consciousness is not limited after all, for it has mediated its own limitation, moved beyond it, and taken another step forward in its own progressive self-possession. In short, reflection is able to transform the effective reality of history (*Wirkung*) into scientific knowledge (*Wissen*). That of course is Hegel's critique of Kant, and it applies in advance to all of Hegel's later critics who want to hold speculative idealism to the fire of existential, historical, linguistic, or – in this case – hermeneutic finitude.

In response to this Gadamer points out that such a merely formal consideration cannot settle the matter, which is why Plato used a myth to brush off the sophistic argument about the impossibility of learning anything. The issue is a substantive (*sachlich*) one and cannot be settled on merely formal grounds. To address the question substantively Gadamer takes up an analysis of our hermeneutical "experience" – our experience of the work of art, of the effective power of history, of the universal mediation of language – and he offers us an interesting, enlightening phenomenology of experience which shows the inherent limitation or negativity which is built into experience.[4]

Gadamer explicates the negativity of experience by shifting the concept of experience from the horizon of science – where experience carries the rather upbeat, positivistic sense of progressive accumulation, of the positive confirmation of a law – to the horizon of life in the *Lebenswelt*. In concrete, factical life, experience acquires a ring of negativity, a dialectical sense of "learning by" experience. In the realm of science, everything disconfirming and negative is to be gradually erased until a fully positive universal emerges. But in living experience things are different. Experience is acquired in the school of hard knocks, where to have acquired experience_means to have learned one's lesson and to be wary of what is coming next. Thus in the life-world, the point is not to annul the negative but to be ready for it, to be ready for the unforeseeable, for what goes against our expectations (maybe even ready for anxiety, *Angstbereit*). Experience was described best of all by Aeschylus: *pathei mathos* – we learn by suffering, by running up against our limits, by the thunderstorm which is visited upon our plans and expectations (WM 339/320).[5]

Now the interesting thing is that this both is and is not a Hegelian idea of experience. It is certainly a dialectical idea of experience, inasmuch as experience is sharpened and strengthened by exposure to the negative, where the security of the positive must be tested, proved, and fired by the negative. But Gadamer rejects the Hegelian conception inasmuch as it is not Gadamer's intention to supersede negativity once and for all by reaching a standpoint where the disruptiveness of the negative is simply transcended, put in its place, assigned a place by a reflection which has managed to slip past it. On the contrary, experience for Gadamer means to be a continual openness to negativity, or readiness for it, *ad infinitum*. Experience means finitude *ad infinitum*. But a finitude which keeps revisiting itself upon us infinitely, which keeps deferring its completion, is a bad infinity, albeit a good finitude, indeed the very best.[6]

So it looks like it is possible for hermeneutics to accommodate deconstruction, to locate deconstruction on the hermeneutic horizon, to find in the texts of Gadamer the resources to undertake a fair translation of deconstruction. "Deconstruction": that means – here comes the translation – hermeneutic experience pushed to its limits, radicalized, pursued ruthlessly, without pity, without appeal, without nostalgia, without a desire for presence.

But I have my doubts. For it is my view that in the Gadamerian analytic of finitude the ground has shifted from Heidegger to Hegel, that a more radical Heideggerian facticity has been subverted from within by a creeping Hegelianism, that something has been lost in the translation. That is what I want to show now.

Gadamer and the Metaphysics of Finitude

Gadamer is arguing for the limits of reflection, that is, for the irreducibility of being to thought, of the *Sache* to knowledge, of *Wirkung* to *Wissen*. In particular, he is arguing three more specific theses about our experience of the work of art, our historical experience, and our experience with language. First, he claims that the artwork never yields itself up to conceptual thinking, that it is jealous of the meaning which it harbors, indeed selfish about it, and keeps it to itself – which is what Heidegger meant by its standing in itself.[7] Secondly, in historical experience we run up against the strangeness and alienness of the past which functions like the mysterious recess of another "thou," an inaccessible source of initiatives that we can neither predict nor control. Finally, we live and think and have our being in the fluid medium of language which is irreducible to the univocity of a pure grammar and fixed significations. Language is a play in which mobile and shifting assertions do their best to stay in play with the play of the *Sache selbst*. Yet it is precisely here that I press my point that Gadamer's infinity becomes a good one, that his finitude is *aufgehoben* in a metaphysics of infinity.

Consider Gadamer's argument against assigning canonical validity to the intention of the author. He delimits the authority of the author in a two-fold gesture which reflects the way the Heideggerian side of his hermeneutics is redirected by the Hegelian side. Gadamer wants to show 1) that the act of understanding, including the author's understanding, is always finite (the Heideggerian side); 2) that what is understood – the artwork, the historical event, the work of language – has a certain infinity (the Hegelian side). The author no less than later interpreters must reckon with "the non-definitiveness (*Unabschliessbarkeit*) of the horizon of meaning within which his understanding moves" (WM 355/336). There is thus a certain "noetic" finitude, a finitude which besets human understanding, which is unable to encompass or circumscribe its object because of its own factical, historical limitations. But corresponding to this, let us say on the "noematic" side, there lies a veritable infinity of both historical event and written text which likewise accounts for the impossibility of canonical interpretation. This correlativity of noetic finitude and noematic infinity is particularly clear in the following passage:

> Historical tradition can be understood only by being considered in its further determinations resulting from the progress of events. Similarly the literary critic who is dealing with literary or philosophical texts knows that they are inexhaustible (*Unauschopfbarkeit*). In both cases it is the progress of events that brings out new aspect of meaning in historical material. Through the new actualization (*Aktualisierung*) in understanding, the texts are drawn into a genuine happening (*Geschehen*) in exactly the same way as are the events (*Ereignisse*) themselves through their continuance. This is what we described as the effective-historical

element within the hermeneutical experience. Every actualization in understanding can be regarded as an historical potentiality (*Möglichkeit*) of what is understood. It is part of the historical finiteness of our being that we are aware that after us others will understand in a different way. And yet it is a fact equally well established that it remains the same work, the fullness of whose meaning (*Sinnfülle*) is proved in the changing process of understanding, just as it is the same history whose meaning is constantly being further determined. (WM 355/336; translation modified)

To the noetic finitude of understanding (factical Dasein) there corresponds the noematic infinity of what is understood, a kind of infinite spirit. To the limited horizons within which the act of understanding must function there corresponds the inexhaustible depth of the historical material. There is a richness of meaning in historical events which just keeps unfolding, which is certainly not grasped by the original protagonists, which gradually unfolds over the course of time, and which is in principle never fully unfolded. By the same token literary and philosophical texts are inhabited by the same sort of inexhaustibility or infinity which can be mastered neither by the original authors nor by the succession of subsequent interpreters. The event or text is not an isolable (finite) historical entity but a whole history – which is also a history of wholeness – a continuity of movement made up of both the original and the history of its effects which follow after it like a comet's tail. The fullness of meaning is never fully unfolded. It is an excess which keeps spilling over like a neoplatonic emanation. It cannot be contained by either author or interpreter who are too meager of understanding, too finite to contain the fullness which sweeps over them and holds them under its claim.

The subversiveness of Heideggerian facticity has been reinscribed within the reassuring framework of a classical, Aristotelico-Hegelian metaphysics of infinity. The text is a potentiality, a potential infinity, a potentially good infinity, an infinite potential, and every new understanding is a new actualization, a new way in which what is understandable in potency becomes understood in act. But this Aristotelian process of actualization is carried out in a Hegelian process of historical unfolding. The essence (fullness, meaning) does not yield itself up at once, but rather its being is its becoming, its essence is to unfold its essence through an historical process. That is because of its inner infinity or intelligibility on the one hand and the finitude of the understanding on the other. I would go so far as to say that the model for Gadamer's position on this point is a classically theological one, that it reminds us of nothing so much as the excess or the infinity of the divine being vis-à-vis the finitude of the human intellect.[8] The latter can do no more to compensate for its limitations than to multiply the names of God and to proclaim its own inability to exhaust the infinite riches of the godhead.

My point is supported in an interesting way by Gadamer's occasional essays on modern art, many of which have been recently translated under the title of *The Relevance of the Beautiful and Other Essays*.[9] Here Gadamer is addressing art works such as the "pure poetry" of Mallarmé, "absolute" music, and contemporary non-representational painting (RB 75). These art forms would seem on the face of it to resist traditional aesthetic categories like mimesis. They seem to represent a case not of the inexhaustibility of meaning but of a radical break with meaning and so to represent a rupture with the past history of art. But Gadamer's aim is to close this gap, to fuse these horizons, and to reconcile these differences. One might ask whether this is not a domesticating gesture, whether it is really ready to hear something new in modern art, something troubling and indigestible.

Gadamer insists that the modern artwork does not lack meaning or unity; rather it has decided to draw us more fully into its play by making us, the observers, work harder in order to find meaning and unity. It leaves a certain leeway or space which needs to be filled in by an active construction or synthesis on the part of the observer. Thus Cubism does not represent the loss of the object but the necessity for the observer to superimpose for oneself the different aspects in order to attain the unity of a perceptual object (RB 27). It is as if Picasso and Braque were Husserlians with a theory of intentional adumbration (*Abschattungen*) up their sleeve, as if Duchamp's nude descending a staircase is an illustration of transcendental phenomenology. To perceive is to perceive an object – perception according to the reassuring German word is *wahrnehmen*, taking as true, taking in the solidity of a substantial unity – and what Picasso does is make this a bit harder to do. Again, the painting is a potentiality for meaning, and the observation or "reading" of the painting is its actualization.

It appears thus to be a fundamental metaphysical assumption on Gadamer's part that the modern artwork cannot be aimed at the disruption of perception itself, that it cannot mean to effect a deeper disturbance than merely to make perception more difficult. But what if the real difficulty posed by cubism or by the more extreme forms of non-representational art were the way they set about disturbing the very idea of a deeper substantial unity? What if they were trying to insist on the unmotivated, conventional character of experience, on the instability of our ideas of truth and reality? What if, in short, these were indeed

Husserlians but Husserlians who were more interested in the famous thesis of the annihilability of the world? That appears to be a horizon that Gadamer has no intention of fusing. Gadamer's theological model is not troubled in the least by modern art. He simply shifts into the mode of negative theology where the mystery of the divine being is not laid out cataphatically, in a succession of divine names, but evoked apophatically, by daring mystical paradoxes and bold negations which draws the faithful more deeply into the divine mystery. The only difference which shows up in modern art on Gadamer's accounting is that the modern artwork puts up a tougher fight – its deep potential is a lot more resistant to actualization than traditional art – but it remains within the horizon of the actualization of its inexhaustible potentiality.

I hasten to add that I do not regard Gadamer as an outright, but as a modified, Hegelian. Man for Gadamer is a finite being and he seeks fulfillment in the wholeness of the artwork. But this fulfilling meaning cannot be simply disengaged from the artwork like a message from its medium (RB 36–37). It is important to see that Gadamer does not reject the idea that the artwork bears a message (RB 142) – and to that extent he understands art very much in terms of a postal metaphysics[10] – but he does reject the idea that the message can be abstracted or distilled from the artwork in which it is embedded. He rejects the idea that art can be transcended by philosophy, that artworks can be thematically condensed into a conceptualizable *meaning*. Rather they represent a unique intensification or magnification of meaning – the mimesis does not diminish, it increases the being – which is uniquely embodied in this artwork, in this *hoc aliquid*. The horizon within which the artwork is considered is meaning but meaning is realized with such sensuous immediacy as to be rendered non-transcendable by a desensualizing *nous*.

The result of this is not to destroy the infinity and inexhaustibility of meaning but to let it sink even deeper into the artwork and to make the observer work even harder to actualize it. Gadamer speaks in terms almost of the stinginess of modern art in its refusal to give up its meaning, to let itself he appropriated, to surrender a fixed sense (RB 37). Its *Bedeutung* has become more and more *zweideutig*, its meaning more a riddle, its depths harder and harder to plumb.

All of this comes to a head when Gadamer speaks of the special "temporality" of the artwork, which is the temporality of making present again, of a sacramental repetition which Gadamer explicitly compares to the theology of the real (as opposed to the merely symbolic) presence of Christ in the Eucharist in Catholic theology. Indeed Gadamer's is a deeply "eucharistic hermeneutics,"[11] a good gift really present and made present again and again over the ages, in works of art, historical events, and literary and philosophical texts. In the temporality of the artwork we become contemporaneous with a meaning and truth which transcends time, which is omni-temporal. Of this Gadamer writes – and here the Gadamerian cat leaps out of the bag:

> When we dwell upon the work, there is no tedium involved, for the longer we allow ourselves, the more it displays its manifold riches to us. The essence of our temporal experience of art is in learning how to tarry in this way. And perhaps it is the only way that is granted to us finite beings to relate to what we call eternity. (RB 45)

Différance is not Finitude

Now that, I suggest, is simply to abdicate the finitude of Heideggerian facticity in favor of a finitude enlisted in the service of a neo-Hegelian metaphysics of infinity. And that is why Derrida writes that "the return to finitude" would not represent "a single step out of metaphysics." He continues:

> It is that conceptuality and that problematic that must be deconstructed. They belong to the onto-theology they fight against. Difference is also something other than finitude.[12]

Finitude in Gadamer is not a scandal or rupture but part of an argument for infinity, a transcendental finitude, a kind of *felix culpa* which receives its reassuring complement from the infinity of what is understood. Human finitude is a broken *symbolon* which is made whole by the ideality and infinity of the artwork. The artwork is our other and better half with which we can be fitted together to form a whole. In virtue of its symbolic make-up, the artwork is according to Gadamer:

> ...that other fragment that has always been sought in order to complete and make whole our own fragmentary life...the experience of the beautiful in art is the invocation of a potentially whole and holy order of things, wherever it may be found. (RB 32)

Consider the shock of juxtaposing the Gadamerian thematic of the fragment with the Derridean "remain(s)":

> what, after all, of the remain(s), today, for us, here, now, of a Hegel? (*Glas* 1a)
>
> "what remained of a Rembrandt torn into small, very regular squares and rammed down the shithole" is divided into two. (*Glas* 1b)

The Gadamerian fragment is a *symbolon* which is to be fitted together with its missing half, which is a perfect match for it, a token by which we can recognize infinity, the whole, the holy. The remain(s) in deconstruction are the remnants and fragments which clog the Hegelian system, the loose ends in the texture of its garment which keep coming undone, the jammed gears which grind the Hegelian machine to a halt, the cut up pieces which can be glued together this way or that, the scrambled messages that get all gummed up in the postal works, the *symbolon* which was shattered too badly ever to be fitted together, indeed which never was a whole.[13]

That is why hermeneutic finitude is ill equipped to serve as a translation for *différance*. If hermeneutics is a philosophy of transcendental finitude – a finitude which tends beyond itself and is stretched out into infinite fullness – then deconstruction is taken up entirely with infinity, with that bad infinity which just goes on and on, spread out of control in every direction. Deconstruction is the denial of finitude – of a certain Gadamerian, theological finitude – in the name of the uncontrollable transfers, transmissions, translations, and exchanges which just go on and on *ad infinitum* in the postal play. Deconstructionist infinity is the mirror play *en abîme*, the endless transformation of phonic and graphic chains.[14] It is not the infinite and eternal depths of the excess of meaning but the endless play of grammatological superficiality.[15]

The reason for this is not hard to find. Gadamerian hermeneutics functions within the classical metaphysical distinction between essence (or ideality) and its concrete actualizations. Gadamer endorses Husserl's claim that the artwork performs a spontaneous eidetic reduction, and he uses it to back up the Aristotelian claim that art is more philosophical than history. The artwork is not a less than real copy of an original but an intensification of reality which exceeds reality as the universal exceeds the particular, as the essential exceeds the contingent, as the ideal exceeds the empirical. The historian merely records individual events, but the poet brackets empirical contingencies and grasps the essence (RB 133–34, 120, 129).

Consider in particular the difference between Gadamer and Derrida on writing (WM 367 ff./351 ff.) For Gadamer, writing (*Schriftlichkeit*, being written, writtenness, in proper written form) is the defining characteristic of the linguisticality (*Sprachlichkeit*) of the hermeneutic object (*Gegenstand*). It is distinguished by him from the hermeneutic "act" (*Vollzug*) which is executed or carried out on the object, that is, the act of understanding (*Verstehen*). Thus the distinction between what is understood and the act of understanding, between object and act, comes down to a distinction between object and actualization, between potentiality and actualization. The hermeneutic object (writing) is a

41

possibility for actualization. As such, it is an ideality, an ideal carrier of meaning which can be transformed into actuality by anyone with linguistic competence. Once again, we will see the correlativity of noetic finitude and noematic infinity played out again.

The key to Gadamer's notion of writing is that in writing language is detached (*abgelöst*, WM 367/351)) from its actualization. That is both its advantage and its weakness. In writing, language is reduced to a *diminished but ideal* condition, to a linguistic concentrate, put in a sort of deep freeze which needs the thaw of speech or reading, the living *Vollzug*, to bring it back to life. Yet that is precisely what enables writing to survive, to live on, to acquire a deeper permanence than is granted to the finite, mortal readers and speakers before whose gaze it passes. Many living eyes have passed over these pages only then to pass away themselves. But this writing, not just this book which can deteriorate, but this ideality, this permanent possibility of meaning, endures. It is precisely because writing has lowered the body temperature of language to near death, slowed down its living functions to a point of almost perfect immobility, that language can acquire the permanence which makes a tradition possible. It is just in virtue of this linguistic freeze that the ideality of meaning can go into dormancy, a deep linguistic sleep, from which it can be awakened again and again by the living breath of the *Vollzug*. You see then the set of equivalences we are working with: writing: potentiality: ideality: meaning – and finally, and this is not to be forgotten, alienation. For language is not at home, is still a stranger, is half dead, a ghostly shade, in writing, and it can be relieved of its exile in this land of shades only by the warmth of the living subject. A strange thing on earth is writing.

It is just this ideality, this ghostly *Geistigkeit*, which gives the tradition its real power to hand itself down, to endure, to make memory last (WM 369/353), to become present (contemporaneous) again and again, in short to assume a certain infinity. The ghost returns. "I will speak of the *revenant*."[16] Oddly enough, Gadamer here is never so close and never so far from Derrida – maybe here we are touching on a possible translation – especially when a few lines later he remarks that this ideality is not restricted to writing:

> But that language is capable of being written is by no means incidental to its nature. Rather this capacity of being written down is based on the fact that speech itself shares in the pure ideality of the meaning that communicates itself in it…. Writing is the abstract ideality of language. (WM 370/354)

If writing is the abstract ideality of language, then speech is its concrete or living ideality. Gadamer thus, if only momentarily, erases the distinction between writing and speech and identifies in both a common structure. But he characterizes this common structure as ideality or repeatability. He thus links ideality and repeatability in the classical metaphysical manner, for he makes repeatability a function of ideality, representation a function of presence. The defining characteristic of writing, and its great advantage, is that it provides a long term medium for passing on meaning; its disadvantage is, as Plato says in the *Philebus*, that it cannot fend for itself. The defining characteristic of speech, and its great advantage, is that it can pass on meaning in a fluid and self-correcting, self-interpreting way which minimizes misunderstanding; but its disadvantage is its transiency, for it literally disappears into thin air. But in both cases we have to do with media which bear meaning, which have ideal content, which are carriers of ideality.

What Gadamer resists, what he never allows, is precisely the deconstructionist reversal which makes ideality a function of repeatability, presence an effect of representation, meaning the result of the trace.[17] It is certainly true that he has bound meaning to language much more closely than the metaphysical tradition before him. He does not think that language is the expression of a preconstituted meaning, but that language is the very emergence, constitution, or coming into being of meaning (and indeed being itself). But it is the coming to be of meaning. Language is related to meaning as the explicit to the implicit, the emergent to the latent, the actual to the possible. Towards the end of the book he identifies the neoplatonic theory of emanation as a good model for articulating the relationship between being (or meaning) and language: language is the way that being which is understood emanates forth, comes into presence (WM 453/440; 134/124–5). All of the suppleness, play, and fluidity upon which he insists, which gives speech its advantage over writing, arises from the necessity which language is under to serve the needs of this emanation process, to be responsive to meaning, to let being and meaning emerge, to let it be.

What Gadamer never permits thus is precisely what Derrida calls the thought of the trace, not the trace which follows after and copies an original, but the trace which produces, which effects, which predelineates, precedes, and makes possible the multiple unities – of "meaning", "being" and even of "language" itself – within which Gadamerian hermeneutics functions. That is why there is such a vast difference between Gadamer's treatment of Mallarmé, which seems intent as it were on containing the damage, on striking a balance between meaning and mark, sense and sound, and Derrida's, which finds in it all the energy of dissemination.[18] Gadamer does not want to enter that abyss which opens up with artists like Mallarmé or Joyce, where what hermeneutics regards as the very surface of language comes into play. Gadamer's play must always stay in bounds, within the bounds of sense. So too with modern, non-representational painting: Gadamer is reluctant to enter that abyss where the pure play of lines and color comes into play. Even though the modern painting has lost the frame which once contained it and centered it upon itself, it has not lost its unity (RB, 88–89). He will never say, as Derrida says, that there is painting, that's all; and the shoes are there for the painting, not to tell us about the dark mystery of the peasant woman's world, but for the painting, for multiple lacings and unlacings, to be tied and untied, cut up and glued together in multiple, uncontrollable ways.[19]

It is precisely the point of the Derridean stylus to stick us with the sharp cutting edges of the trace, to draw us into the land of the shades, of dormancy and the deep freeze, of the marks which can be made with pens and pencils, with a pulmonary organ forcing air out in measured and modulated ways, with paint, brushes, with hands and feet, with arched eyebrows, with green phosphorous screens, with paws and tails, with who knows what. Derrida sticks our head back into the text whenever hermeneutics comes up for the air of living speech, its eyes bulging and a look of panic on its face. Derrida cuts and glues, pasting things together in the strangest ways, making things look and sound so very odd, whenever hermeneutics tries to fit together the two exquisitely matched pieces of the *symbolon*. Derrida irreverently celebrates the fag First Communion whenever Gadamer bows his hermeneutic head at the Catholic theology of the Eucharist. Derrida hears the hissing of the disseminative "s," like air leaking from a tire, whenever Gadamer tries to strike a balance between sound and sense. Derrida shows the impossibility of the frame to maintain the distinction between inside and outside whenever Gadamer looks for the deeper unity which the frame once helped protect.

But, the Gadamerians will say – hermeneutics never gives up trying to fuse horizons – *that is the finitude*: all those scandalous things that renegade Derrida does, they are all testimony to the finitude of human understanding and the difficulty which besets the search for meaning. That is how to translate deconstruction into hermeneutics!

Now for all the reasons that I have been developing in these pages I must insist that this is no translation, or a bad translation, a trick, an evasion, a way of copping out, a way that hermeneutics has found of not listening to something different, of reducing what is other to its own terms, of making its *other* into *its* other. You cannot translate *différance* with finitude if for no other reason than that *différance* is a lot more like a wild and formless infinity than a well-formed finitude. "*Différance* is also something other than finitude." Gadamerian finitude

44

is transcendental finitude; it is practically a Cartesian proof for the existence of God, a way of bearing testimony to the infinite, an edifying discourse which is meant to tell us that we float on a sea of infinite being, meaning, and truth, whose depths we can never fathom, whose bounty we can never consume.

So if this is finitude it has no teeth in it; it is a toothless facticity with all the bite gone. Nobody ever gets cut, castrated, guillotined, stuck in the behind (*Glas*). It is a pointer in the direction of infinity. It is a good finitude, an edifying one, which points us in the direction of an equally good infinity. Gadamer is pulling one over us when he tells us he is arguing for a bad infinity. Gadamerian infinity is a classical infinity which has cleaned up its act, which does not think that we ever get the infinite in canonical form, which has the good sense to recognize that the infinite keeps taking new forms.

Whenever Gadamer bows his finite head deconstruction does a shocking, lewd dance of in-finity which scandalizes the faithful and sends them heading for the doors. Deconstruction is bad and it makes no bones about it. It dines with sinners and thieves and it hangs around with drag queens. It prefers the wild(er)ness of the *apeiron*, of infinity, to Greco-Germanic form and finitude.

Radical Hermeneutics

I mentioned at the start of this paper that insisting upon the irreducibility, the untranslatability of deconstruction into hermeneutics can lead to trouble for deconstruction. double trouble, a double bind. For pushing the radicality of deconstruction can make it look like an untouchable original, a pure language. I am myself interested in a translation of deconstruction, and even a hermeneutic translation.[20] Up to now I have been arguing not against hermeneutics, but against Gadamerian hermeneutics. Let me now risk a translation.

Suppose for a moment that one were actually convinced by what was said above, and that one were actually to "hear" what deconstruction "says," and hence motivated to "appropriate" it for oneself, to "apply" it to one's own "hermeneutic situation"? That is a bad translation; let me try again. Suppose we were actually to get stuck by a deconstructionist stylus/stiletto, and suppose it drew some blood? Would that not be a lot like getting stung by a stingray?

Again: suppose there would be a moment of "self-recognition," suppose that in all the havoc deconstruction produces, I were to recognize "that is you," just like when I hear a good sermon on Sunday which tells me I am sinner? That's a bad translation; I must give it another go. Suppose that there would be a moment when we realized we were bleeding, that we were "hit," that one of those arrows must have found its mark? Suppose we realized that the bad news is there is no "you", that that is a fiction, an effect, something constituted not constituting? There is no you – that is you!

That is the point at which I speak of the cold shiver (*phoebe*), the *ébranler*, of the *kinesis*. That is what I have called cold or radical hermeneutics. That is my translation. The idea is not to dodge the arrows of the trace, the displacement of the subject, the dissemination of meaning, the real difficulty in life. Now let us recall that back in 1921, after citing the *Nicomachean Ethics* to the effect that life is hard, which was itself a novel translation, Heidegger went on to say that pursuing that thought is what he means by the "hermeneutics of facticity."[21] The idea is not to edify ourselves with the thought of transcendental finitude, which is what Gadamer does with Heideggerian facticity, but to face up to the infinite slippage, the grammatological infinity, which makes a mess of everything determinate and definite and decidable. That is a big part of what it means to raise the question of Being as presence, to make it questionable, and to hold it there, in question, hanging in suspense.

But why call this "hermeneutics"? Why this nostalgia for this old word. Because hermeneutics means beginning where we are (Derrida),[22] in the hermeneutic situation, *in-der-Welt-sein* (Heidegger), where we are under the "metontological" necessity to think and act and hope, to press ahead, even as we understand the trouble we are in, to make the swing back into the existentiell-ontic order. Because in this hermeneutics more radically conceived, the assumption is that no matter how bad things get, we always have our being to be, whoever or whatever "we", "being", and "be" may be. That is my translation.

Notes

[1] WM: Hans-Georg Gadamer, *Wahrheit und Methode: Grundzüge einer philosophischen Hermeneutik*, 4th ed. (Tübingen: Mohr, 1975). This will be followed by a cross reference to the English translation, which should be used with caution: *Truth and Method*, ed. C. Barden and J. Cumming (New York: Seabury, 1975). [Note: a second revised edition of *Truth and Method* was published in 1989. –Ed.]

[2] See Derrida's discussion of Roman Jakobson's essay "On Translation" in Derrida's "Des Tours des Babel," in *Difference in Translation*, ed. Joseph Graham (Ithaca: Cornell University Press, 1985), 173–74.

[3] Jacques Derrida, *Glas*, trans. John P. Leavey and Richard Rand (Lincoln: University of Nebraska Press, 1986). *Glas* I think is the most utterly inassimilable of Derrida's works from the standpoint of hermeneutics.

[4] Gadamer is not claiming that we are free to hold to assertions which are formally contradictory. On the contrary, from a strictly logical standpoint, he seems to be invoking the old logical maxim *ab esse ad posse valet*: if something is actual, then it must be possible. If experience actually is limited, then there must be some accounting for that fact which does not fall victim to a self-referential paradox.

[5] See the excellent account of the tragic quality of Gadamerian experience in Gerald Bruns, *Inventions* (New Haven: Yale University Press, 1982).

[6] Hans-Georg Gadamer, *Reason in the Age of Science*, trans. Frederick Lawrence (Cambridge: MIT Press, 1981), 40, 59.

[7] Martin Heidegger, "The Origin of the Work of Art," in *Poetry Language Thought*, trans. Albert Hofstadter (New York: Harper & Row, 1971), 15–87.

[8] Theology has never been at a loss to reappropriate Heidegger's notion of finitude. It has no trouble reinserting it within a theology of infinity, within a project of transcendence towards infinite Being. That is what Rahner did with Heidegger in *Geist im Welt*. It is also not insignificant to me that the Gadamer translator Frederick Lawrence is also quite interested in the Jesuit theologian Bernard Lonergan. Rahner and Lonergan are the preeminent representatives of "transcendental Thomism ," which sees inscribed in the finitude of human *intellectus* an intrinsic "dynamism" towards the infinite Being of God.

[9] RB: Hans-Georg Gadamer, *The Relevance of the Beautiful and Other Essays*, ed. Robert Bernasconi (Cambridge: Cambridge University Press, 1986).

[10] In *The Post Card: From Socrates to Freud and Beyond*, trans. Alan Bass (Chicago: University of Chicago Press, 1987), Derrida criticizes classical theories of meaning, in which meaning can be disengaged from its medium, as theories of "message-bearing," and he uses the postal metaphor to do this. This is a problem for hermeneutics which takes its start from Hermes, the first postman. On my accounting Gadamer holds a modified postal theory. See RB 142.

[11] I borrow this expression from Jean-Luc Marion, *Dieu sans l'être* (Paris: Fayard, 1982), 210ff., who uses it in an even stronger and straightforwardly theological sense that the only interpretation of the Scripture which allows it to yield its gift must be guided by participation in the Eucharist.

[12] Jacques Derrida, *Of Grammatology*, trans. Gayatri Spivak (Baltimore: Johns Hopkins University Press, 1974), 68.

[13] *Glas* relentlessly disrupts the attempt to give Genet's work a comfortable readability or to let Hegel's work settle into systematic unity. "Why make a knife pass between two texts? Why, at least write two texts at once?...There is a wish to make writing ungraspable, of course." *Glas*, 64b.

[14] "If polysemy is infinite, if it cannot be mastered as such, this is thus not because a finite reading or a finite writing remains incapable of exhausting a superabundance of meaning. Not, that is, unless one displaces the philosophical concept of finitude and reconstitutes it according to the law and structure of the text...Finitude then becomes infinitude, according to a non-Hegelian identity." Jacques Derrida, *Dissemination*, trans. Barbara Johnson (Chicago: University of Chicago Press, 1981), 253.

[15] "'There is no name for it [*différance*],' a proposition to be read in its *platitude*." Jacques Derrida, *Margins of Philosophy*, trans. Alan Bass (Chicago: University of Chicago Press, 1982), 26.

[16] I cite here the opening lines of Jacques Derrida, *De l'Esprit* (Paris: Galilée, 1987), 11. Derrida is interested in the recurrence of the *Geist* in Heidegger's writings, how it keeps coming back like a ghost. In Gadamer, we are suggesting, it is in virtue of the *Geistigkeit* of writing that meaning can keep coming back.

[17] This is precisely Derrida's argument against Husserl in *Speech and Phenomena*, trans. David Allison (Evanston: Northwestern University Press, 1972), and it applies, *mutatis mutandis*, to Gadamer.

[18] Contrast the balance between sense and sound which Gadamer seeks in Mallarmé (RB 134–35.) with Derrida's critique of Richard's hermeneutic interpretation of Mallarmé in *Dissemination*, 246 ff.

[19] Jacques Derrida, *Truth in Painting*, trans. Geoffrey Bennington and Ian MacLeod (Chicago: University of Chicago Press, 1967), 371–72.

[20] That is indeed the whole point of my *Radical Hermeneutics: Repetition, Deconstruction, and the Hermeneutic Project* (Bloomington: Indiana University Press, 1987).

[21] See Heidegger's early Freiburg lectures in *Gesamtausgabe*, vol. 61, *Phänomenologische Interpretationen zu Aristoteles* (Frankfurt: Klostermann, 1935), 108–10; vol. 63, *Ontologie: Hermeneutik der Faktizität* (Frankfurt: Klostermann, 1988), passim.

[22] Derrida, *Of Grammatology*, 162.

4

RADICAL HERMENEUTICS AND THE HUMAN CONDITION

[In *Proceedings of the American Catholic Philosophical Association*, 61 (1988), 2–14]

[2] I propose to address the question of hermeneutics and the tradition not by speaking *about* the tradition but by undertaking a hermeneutic inquiry which philosophizes *with* the tradition. My aim is to situate myself within the tradition, within its deepest and most radical concerns – with being, God, and human existence – and to bring to bear upon these issues the discipline of a hermeneutic more radically conceived. My aim is to show that this radical hermeneutic, far from abandoning us to the wolves of irrationalism and nihilism, marks out for us in an incisive way the contours of our human condition.

Intelligere Sequitur Esse:
Hermeneutics and the Factical Being of Dasein

When Heidegger said in *Being and Time* (§13) that knowing (*Erkennen*) is a founded mode of being-in he was in no small part resurrecting a classical thesis: that epistemology takes its lead from ontology, that knowing is a function of being: *intelligere sequitur esse*. Heidegger was insisting that the conditions under which knowledge is possible are set by being, that the *modus intelligendi* is a function of the *modus essendi*. Heidegger's argument was directed against the Neo-Kantianism of the day, indeed the whole of Cartesian modernity, which privileges purely cognitive and epistemic life. Heidegger wanted to show that long before cognitive Dasein begins puzzling over this proposition or that, Dasein is always and already in the world, that all of its powers have long since been fully engaged, caught up in the sweep of worldly life. Dasein's implication in existence antedates and founds the purely epistemic relations which philosophy has for so long privileged. Merely knowing (*Erkennen*) is not the primary matter for thought, *prima philosophia,* as the modern philosophical tradition from Descartes to Husserl contends. On the contrary, knowing depends upon being, which has been from of old the matter for first philosophy.

In the memorable analysis which Heidegger gave of the being of Dasein, Heidegger identified not a stable substance looking on (*anschauen*) at a world which stands before it ready for cognitive inspection, but rather [3] existent Dasein. Dasein: that means an event of disclosure, a happening of truth, which lets the world emerge and so lets entities emerge in their worldly being. From the start, from an origin which has no beginning but is all along in place, Dasein is "in the truth," disclosing the world in this way or that: as the sphere of needed tools, of other persons, or of scientific objectivity. Dasein is radically, inescapably, in the truth. Skepticism is refuted by the very dynamics of Dasein's Being, by its very being-in-the-world, which is a happening of truth.[1]

But this being which lets the world appear, which opens the space within which entities emerge, has always and already been delivered over to this world. Dasein's disclosive life never gets a clean start. Dasein is already caught up in and carried along by an understanding of the world of which it is not the author but the heir. From the start, from a moment that I do not remember because it was transacted for me without my consent, I am delivered over to a language and a history. I am immersed in an understanding in which I grow up and which I can never outgrow. Thus this being which understands the world itself stands under a world which is not of its own making. If Dasein is in the truth it is because it is thrown into the truth, because it seeks the truth out of the pre-givenness of a language, a history, a tradition. To have a tradition (*Überlieferung*), that means to be handed over in advance to a certain understanding of things which antedates and constitutes my own understanding.

The project of reinserting knowing within the pre-givenness of the world, of keying understanding to being, is called by Heidegger the "hermeneutics of facticity."[2] In the hermeneutics of facticity understanding is an event of *factical Dasein,* of a being which finds itself concretely situated in an historical and cultural world. Hermeneutics is rigorous philosophy because it rigorously enforces the rule that the act of understanding labors under the conditions which are imposed upon it by its being-in-the-world. *Intelligere sequitur esse.*

In a text which I very much cherish, which takes its point of departure from the passage in the *Nicomachean Ethics* (1106 b 28ff.) in which Aristotle remarks upon the difficulty of hitting the mark of virtue, Heidegger describes the hermeneutics of facticity as an effort we make to restore to life its original difficulty.[3] It is as if Heidegger thought that in the past philosophy has been too much inclined to make things easy for itself, too much inclined to let the ties which lace understanding to being go slack. Philosophy tends too often to drift into free-floating constructions – about the pure *eidos,* or the pure *cogito,* or pure transcendental reason – as if it were possible for Dasein to cut itself loose from the conditions imposed upon it by its mode of being. Hence the task of this new hermeneutics of facticity is to hold understanding to the fire of being and to expose the [4] illusion of an unconditioned thinking, which is above all the dream of Cartesian modernity, *la songe de Descartes.* The dream of philosophy has too long been to relieve Dasein of the conditions which make understanding possible in the first place. To relieve Dasein of its language and its tradition, of its concrete situatedness, to sever understanding from the very being upon which it is founded – that is the essence of the Cartesian gesture.

It follows that in *Being and Time* skepticism is an absurdity, an ontological perversity, which would deny the disclosiveness of Dasein, even as absolutism is a dream which would deny the facticity of Dasein. Skepticism is refuted before the sceptic so much as forms a proposition, by the very being of the sceptic as being-in-the-world. Dasein thus moves in the intermediate space defined by the impossible extremes of absolute unconditioned truth, a truth not subject to the conditions of facticity, and absolute untruth which would, *per impossibile,* shut down the very disclosiveness of Dasein. Because it is bound to *being,* skepticism is impossible; because it is *bound* to being, absolutism is impossible. The disclosiveness of Dasein opens up the space between absolutism and skepticism, the space of concrete, historical, factical truth.

Now it is precisely the binding of understanding to being which leads Heidegger to the identification of understanding with interpreting (*Auslegen*). We understand always and only from the situation in which we find ourselves, from the perspective which we do not so much adopt as inherit. The conditions under which understanding works are set by the horizon of our being-in-the-world. Understanding is bound by the framework imposed upon us by being, by the boundaries of our being-in-the-world. There can be no question of getting free of this interpretive horizon, of slipping outside the hermeneutic net, for that would be to close down the whole operation of understanding altogether and so altogether to misunderstand our being. It is never a question of loosening the loop of the hermeneutic circle but rather of casting it forth in more adroit and felicitous ways so as to capture more and more about our world and about ourselves (*Being and Time,* §§31-2).

To define understanding as interpreting is to set forth the limits of understanding. But let us be clear about this. The inescapability of interpretation, which is the mark of finitude upon understanding, does not make us "prisoners" of our own "fictions" but provides us rather with our only access to the world, as Gadamer has so admirably shown. To interpret is to

51

have a bias: that is true, and it is a true limit, but it is a productive limitation, a limit which produces understanding. To interpret is to have what Gadamer calls a *Vorurteil,* not a prejudice in the negative sense, but an orienting direction, an angle or slant on things.[4] To have an interpretation is to have an angle of entry, a perspective, a frame of reference, a horizon. [5] These are categories of vision, not of blindness. For it is not those who have perspective *(per-spectare)* who cannot see but those who lack it. A perspective enforces a certain narrowing of vision but it does this precisely in order to give focus, to produce sight and not blindness. Interpretation, perspectivity, give us an angle, but it is an angle of entry. The condition of perspectivity, which I am calling here the hermeneutic condition, "constrains" us rather the way our grammar constrains us: by obeying the constraints of grammar we are enabled to speak; by obeying the constraints of hermeneutics, we are enabled to have a world at all.

The hermeneutic claim, which identifies understanding with interpreting, is that understanding arises always from the situatedness of Dasein, from its concrete worldly concern with its own possibility to be in the midst of the hermeneutic situation, i.e., of the language, the tradition, and the world to which it has always already been given over. Understanding is always narrowed down to a determinate interpretation by the concrete conditions of our being. *Intelligere sequitur esse.*

Thus to speak of the inescapability of interpretation is not to attack reason but to redefine it in a more reasonable way and to rescue it from the Enlightenment distortion of rationality. For the Enlightenment subjected reason to the impossible ideal of unconditioned rationality and absolute indubitability, and then, in the hope of meeting such impossible standards, turned reason over to the rule of a rigorous method and systematicity. The Enlightenment sought to make reason absolutely transparent to itself, right down to its ground, and hence to abolish facticity and the conditioning of understanding by being. One way to look at the history of philosophy in this century is to see that we have learned to stop blaming reason for the failure to meet these standards and to start blaming the Enlightenment.[5]

That is why I am insisting that hermeneutics turns on a classical, pre-Enlightenment thesis which binds *intelligere* to *esse.* It has been said that Augustinianism is the philosophy of a sinner who repented and that Thomism is the philosophy of a man who had a reputation for angelic innocence. One of the temptations from which Thomas was mercifully spared – I do not know whether or not it was another reward for chasing that young woman out of his cell – was the lure of the Enlightenment project. As I have tried to show in *Heidegger and Aquinas,* everything in Thomas' thought was mobilized by a certain religious experience of God and of the world which was worlds removed from Enlightenment rationality. That is why St. Thomas subordinated *ratio* to *intellectus* and that is why, in my view, his entire metaphysical science of *esse* needs to be understood in terms of an ultimately religious and mystical impulse.[6]

It was perfectly clear to Thomas that the intellect operates under the conditions which are imposed upon it by *esse,* that the *modus intelligendi* is [6] measured by the *modus essendi.* For Thomas that means, and this was the boldness of his Aristotelianism, that the human intellect labors always under the conditions of its corporeal embodiment and in dependence upon sensuous givenness. But once again, and in accord with the law of a condition which both limits and enables, this constraint does not blind the soul but is rather the very condition of its insight and operation. Thus if the restraint of the body is lifted from the soul, if the soul is relieved of the condition of embodiment, the result is not to have liberated the soul but rather to have killed the man and to have cut off the intellect from its sensuous sources and its access to the world. Thus, according to St. Thomas, even if the intellectual soul survives the dissolution of the body to which it was united, and to which it remains always and already inclined, we will have a devil of a time – if I may be pardoned the use of such an expression in reference to an angelic doctor – explaining how the soul manages to get anything done in such a condition. For in such an ab-solute condition, such an un-conditioned condition, the soul has lost the conditions which enable and empower it.[7]

In Thomas's view, the sort of objects which the human intellect can know is cut to fit its kind of being, proportioned to its mode of being, received according to the mode of being of the receiver. What I am arguing here is that hermeneutics today pursues this classical axiom, but that hermeneutics has more fully and more searchingly determined the nature of these enabling and limiting conditions. Hermeneutics today continues to insist that the mode of understanding is measured by the mode of being, that nothing is received except according to the mode of the receiver, and that the human condition is one of inescapable embodiment. But these venerable motifs from Aristotle and St. Thomas receive a considerable shock when they are enlisted into the hermeneutic project. For Heidegger does not determine the Being of Dasein in terms of a what (*quid est*) but a who (*quis est*), not in terms of substantiality but of existentiality, and so for him the *modus recipientis* includes the modalities of language and history. Dasein is indeed the *zoon echein logon* but that means the living thing in whom language, history and world come about.

Let me put this as brazenly as possible. With much the same impulse that led St. Thomas to bind the human intellect to its sensuous and corporeal condition, let us say to its corporeal facticity, which was for Thomas the condition of its being, hermeneutics binds the understanding to language and history, which are for it conditions of its being-in-the-world. Hermeneutics extends and radicalizes the Thomistic and Aristotelian insistence upon the inescapability of embodiment. Linguisticality and historicality arise from corporeality; to have a body is to have a time and a tongue. The linguistic and historical turn, let us say the hermeneutical turn, are steps [7] taken in the aftermath of the turn to embodiment which Aristotle and Thomas forged in the classical world.

From Facticity to Textuality:
Postmodernism and the Hermeneutic Condition

If hermeneutics, as I have presented it, represents a certain extension and radicalization of the classical thesis of the primacy of being over understanding, postmodernism represents a certain extension and radicalization of hermeneutics. If hermeneutics insists upon the situated and factical being of Dasein, postmodernism argues that facticity is an even more complex and knotted matter than hermeneutics was prepared to admit. If hermeneutics claims that being is the measure of understanding, postmodernism claims that being is said in many ways, that it is profoundly pluralized, disseminated, even ruptured and split. In a word, postmodernism pushes hermeneutics to the edge. Were we to cast postmodernism in a motif from the tradition, we would say that the postmodernists insist, with a mercilessness hitherto unseen in past philosophers, that being is said in many ways, *ens dicitur multipliciter*.[8]

To be sure, postmodern writers are themselves quite severe in their judgment of hermeneutics. But in the view which I have been defending in my most recent work, and which I have called "radical hermeneutics,"[9] I take postmodern critique to be, not an outright destruction of hermeneutics, but a radicalization of hermeneutics which keeps it faithful to its most fundamental tendencies. If the hermeneutics of facticity is bent on restoring life to its original difficulty, postmodernism is out to see that hermeneutics itself does not get off too easily. Postmodernism wants to hold hermeneutics to the fire of an even more radical criticism. Indeed, on the reading which I am pursuing here, postmodern hermeneutics does not even jettison the idea of being but rather submits understanding to the conditions of being in an even more radical manner.

To illustrate what happens when you open up hermeneutics to postmodern critique, let us take up the deconstructionist notion of "textuality." In my reading, textuality is a radicalization of the notion of facticity. Textuality does not uproot us from the world but catches us up in the density of the world in a more radical way. The metaphor of "radical" here takes on the sense, not of a firm foundation, but of the "racinated," of a knotted root system, of a plant that has overgrown its container so that it is impossible to sort out one root strand from another.[10] On this reading, textuality does not represent the denial of being-in-the-world but the complication of it.

But is this not flatly to deny what deconstruction is all about? Is it not [8] precisely in virtue of this notion of textuality that Rorty can speak of a "world well lost?"[11] If everything in hermeneutics as we have been pursuing it here turns on "being-in-the-world," on the rootedness of the hermeneutic subject in a historical world, is not deconstruction precisely the denial of the world, of being, in favor of the affirmation of the free play of signifiers? Is it not well known that the fundamental gesture of deconstruction is to deny reference and to replace referring with deferring, so that one signifier simply leads to another signifier in an endless chain of signifiers with no hope of ever making contact with the world? Does not textuality send us slipping and sliding down an unending chain of signifiers whose defining feature is their purely internal differing from one another? Does not textuality indefinitely defer and delay contact with things? Differing and deferring: difference, *différance*.[12]

Furthermore, is it not the case that in deconstruction the world is not just lost, but it is well lost, because the loss of the world opens up the opportunity to frolic in the play of signifiers, to dance all the more light-footedly because the ontological weight of being has been lifted from our shoulders? God is dead and now everything is permitted. There is no transcendental signified, no real being or objective truth, to inhibit us, to anchor us down to this being or that, this truth or that. The transcendental signified has gone up in smoke, so now anything goes. The old God is dead and good riddance. Thus spoke Zarathustra, Derrida, and quite a few others.

Deconstruction then can hardly be taken as radicalizing hermeneutics. Rather it decimates hermeneutics or, as Derrida likes to say, disseminates it, scattering the seeds of hermeneutic truth to the four winds. Textuality does not extend facticity; it just shatters it to pieces.

Or so it seems.

For in my view that is a one-sided reading of textuality which is in part fostered by the excesses of deconstructionist literary critics (and even deconstructionist theologians) and is in part encouraged by Derrida himself whose strategies of disruption and whose irreverent utterances invite just this sort of reading. But it is not the point of textuality to deny reference but only to complicate it. Textuality does not aim at cutting us off from the world but at divesting us of a too easy assurance that what we have indeed is the world and objective truth and nothing else. The function of deconstruction is to restore to reference its original difficulty, rather in keeping with the young Heidegger's characterization of the hermeneutics of facticity.

It is not Derrida's point to *reduce* language to an internal system – that indeed is the very move he rejects in the structuralists – but to complicate the internal/external, interior/exterior distinction. It never happens in deconstruction that you can make a clean break and draw neat borders between the inside and the outside, and that goes for the distinction between [9] signifier and signified, referring and referee, language and world, words and things. Derrida does not deny the world and lock us "inside" a prison house of language; such a view, he says in an interview, is a sheer "stupidity."[13] What Derrida is denying is that you can ever extricate a signifier from the chain of signifiers to which it belongs and by which it is constituted, for the signifier is what it is in virtue of the way in which it differs from other signifiers in the same chain. Signifiers are not atoms; they operate under certain conditions which we cannot simply throw off.

Hence it is an illusion to think that by singling out a word, or a proposition, and by inhabiting its intentional momentum into the world – which it has and which deconstruction does not deny – we have made some sort of naked or uninterpreted contact with the world. While it is true that we have contact, it is not naked, but differentiated, contact. The signifier does not just vanish, does not just magically shed its embeddedness in its chain. We have seized upon the world in just the way the differential system permits.[14] The signifiers we deploy continue to belong to their differential chain, which cannot be reduced or left behind. That means every time we refer to the world by means of some signifying unit, the signifier continues to drag along with it the chain of signifiers to which it belongs. We never get to a point where we hit upon the thing without the signifier, upon the word's own thing, the one and only thing it can mean, or the thing's own word, the one and only way in which it can be "articulated" (which means fitted together, joined, jointed, linked). Deconstruction takes no small pleasure in pointing out to us all of the *other* things which we did not mean to say, did not mean to drag into the picture. We meant to say something neat and clean, sharply trimmed at the edges, and deconstruction delights in pointing out how much messier things are, how much violence is involved in trying to cut such neat margins, and how it is not up to us simply to legislate how these signifiers work or play (because there is no private language).

Textuality means the uncircumventability of signifiers, dependence upon substitutes and representatives, helpers and supplementers. It does not mean no reference, but rather no reference without deference, deferral and inescapable delay. In short, textuality means mediation. Textuality is the open confession of the necessity under which we labor of having the world mediated to us, the uncircumventability of signs, the inescapability of interpretation.

A lot of the rhetoric which invites the one-sided interpretation of textuality which I am rejecting arises from the fact that textuality functions in deconstruction as a critical notion. It plays a crucially important role in alerting us to and warning us against those who claim to have dispensed with mediation, which is pretty much what Derrida means by metaphysics. For the denial that we are subject to the constraints of mediation is [10] dangerous. We do not succeed in escaping mediation, but only in convincing ourselves and sometimes others, too, that we have. That is why Derrida tells us that he is just trying to alert us against those who "on the pretext of delivering you from the chains of writing and reading" proceed to "lock you in a supposed outside of the text: the pre-text of perception, of living speech...of real history...." Note the paradoxical expression, lock us up in the *hors-texte*: you see where the real prison is for Derrida, the real locus of police action and constraining confinement: in the claim to have gained access to an unmediated world, a world delivered without constraints, restraints, perspectives, interpretations. Derrida continues: "And it's also with supposed nontext, naked pre-text, the immediate, that they try to intimidate you, to subject you to the older, most dogmatic, most sinisterly authoritarian of programs, to the most massive mediatizing machines."[15] Once the illusion of un-conditioned understanding is in place, it becomes unconditionally violent.

That is why I situate a postmodern critique like Derrida's within the hermeneutic program, as a radicalization of it, and not as a simple destruction of it, and that is why I speak of radical hermeneutics. Radical hermeneutics is not engaged in a skeptical denial of truth but in pointing out, albeit in a rather more merciless way, the constraints under which the claims to being and truth must labor. It is not out to deny that the world is given, but only to insist that it is never given to us except under a reading, a construal, a *hermeneusis*. We go back to the claim of *Being and Time*. Dasein is always, already, inescapably in the truth. As soon as Dasein comes to be, there is world and truth. But truth is an occurrence of factical Dasein, and the postmodernists are exceedingly good at showing us just how factical we are. For an essential part of the facticity into which we are thrown is the textuality of a chain of signifiers of which we are not the author but the heir, which we do not project but to which we are delivered over. Textuality is part of the pre-givenness which antedates Dasein, part of that realm which has been negotiated for us in advance.

Faith and the Human Condition

I wish now to connect this entire argument with the notion of the human condition. By probing ever more searchingly into the conditions under which we must labor, by addressing the conditions which belong necessarily to human existence, we are addressing ourselves to the human condition. To pursue hermeneutics with such radical intentions is to pursue the human condition with a corresponding radicality. In short, the hermeneutic condition is just what defines and demarks the human condition, and radical hermeneutics is by that very fact a kind of radical humanism, if humanism [11] means concerning oneself with the condition of man – and woman too.

The main complaint that "hermeneutics" and "postmodernism" have had about traditional metaphysics is that the latter tends to make things too easy for itself. All of this talk about pure intuition, absolute forms, innate knowledge, transcendental standpoints, the absolute spirit, are ways we have found to bail out on the human condition, to take one sort of speculative leap or another right on out of existence. In this hermeneutics more radically conceived we keep insisting that we cannot get off that easily; that life does not provide such guardrails and safe passages, that we do not have sure fire Cartesian certainties to fall back upon. But the point of all this is to sharpen the sense of our own condition, not to make life impossible or to abandon ourselves to the wolves of irrationality or nihilism.

But have we not again come into direct conflict with a central idea in postmodernism, its rejection of humanism? Does not all this talk of the human condition show that we are trying to resurrect humanism, trying to exhume one of the old gods? But humanism is over and man is dead! Everybody from Nietzsche and Heidegger to Foucault and Derrida knows that. This is the age of the end of man. Once again, in my view, the critique of humanism which has been going on in recent philosophy has been understood in a much too one-sided and even hysterical way. For the humanism which is criticized these days is really subjectivism, the rule of the ego cogito, the notion that man is the measure and the master of the earth. Indeed it is just such "humanism" which has and is provoking ecological and political disaster – we grant ourselves infinite license over the earth and its latent energies and in the process court self-destruction. What is criticized under the name of humanism is a lot like what the Bible calls pride and greed, and it is not far from the will to dominate which results in the exclusion of the divine. What is criticized under the name of humanism in Heidegger's work is replaced by *Gelassenheit,* a gentle letting be of earth and gods.

The meditation on the human condition for which I am calling here arises precisely from the overcoming of subjectivism and of the illusion of human domination and hence represents a certain acknowledgement of a more properly human and mortal state. You can just as easily call what I describe here as "radical hermeneutics" an "ec-centric humanism" (to borrow an expression that William Richardson used some time ago), one in which human beings have gotten over the pre-Copernican illusion that everything revolves around themselves.

We get a sense of the way radical hermeneutics addresses the human condition by seeing how it can be brought to bear upon the question of Christian faith. For the upshot of hermeneutics is not to divest us of our faith but to sharpen our sense of what faith involves. Faith operates always under the [12] conditions of mediation and Christianity is above all the religion of *mediation,* for it proclaims that God spoke to us in Jesus, the mediator of the Father. Now the problem with mediation is precisely that it is never immediate and unambiguous, never a naked, unmediated happening, but rather something which, in virtue of its mediating character, demands a rendering, a reading, a *hermeneusis.*

Thus the power of the Father which is invested in Jesus defers itself so that for the Christian Jesus poses the most decisive hermeneutic issue of all. The first disciples are not distinguished from the rest of the tradition by the fact that they simply saw naked divinity in the raw, for that would lead to the "grotesque conclusion," as the Catholic theologian Walter Kasper writes, that they were distinguished by the fact that they had no need of faith.[16] What they saw was a man who was mediating divinity. What we have always honored in the early disciples is not the fact that they were above faith, but precisely the excellence of their faith, i.e., the remarkable *hermeneusis* which they were called upon to make. When, in the gospel of Mark, Jesus turns to the disciples and asks, "but you, who do you say that I am?" he puts a question which Simon and the twelve had asked themselves a thousand times, which keeps reverberating across the Christian epochs, which is definitive of the Christian tradition. And Simon got to be Peter, the rock, just because of his hermeneutic boldness.

Indeed the hermeneutic question which Jesus put to the disciples was also a question which he evidently put to himself. For we are told, in what is nowadays called Christology from below, that Jesus, being truly man, wrestled with the problem of his own identity, with his own self-interpretation.[17] The question which Jesus put to Simon is thus one which he also put to himself and over which he himself had many times prayed and meditated. In such a view, the mediator is mediated even to himself.

It is a mistake to construe faith as if it has to do with an uninterpreted fact of the matter, a pure given which releases us from the inescapability of interpretation, from the constraints of the human condition as I have described them here. On the contrary, faith does not erase these constraints, but it sharpens them. We reach here a moment, not of being relieved of the human condition, but of being solicited all the more profoundly by it. To stand in the tradition of Christian faith is to come under the sway of layers of interpretations, centuries of commentators, theologies upon theologies, in a complex web, a complex textual system. Back at the beginning stands a powerful and compelling book to read, indeed not one book but a complex of books, of narratives and letters and even an apocalyptic vision. Behind those texts, shrouded in the mist of history, an enigmatic figure, a scandal and a stumbling block, a man who transformed the lives of those who came in contact with him, the occasion of a tremendous hermeneutic disturbance, [13] whose death left his disciples with an enormous hermeneutic task. Jesus does not come to bring the peace of no more hermeneutics but the sword of the most radical hermeneutical act of all.[18]

In sum, what I call radical hermeneutics, a hermeneutics more radically pursued, which takes into account the conditions and constraints under which human life must labor, does not cut us off from the world and leave us to frolic in a play of signifiers; nor does it proclaim the end of man in the sense of indifference to the human condition; nor does it announce the death of God and of religious faith. Radical hermeneutics does not leave us worldless or selfless or godless. The idea is always to restore the difficulty in things, the difficulty of gaining access to the world, to God, to human existence, and to cut off the sort of pretentiousness which tends to overtake those who think they speak for the things themselves. After all, the motto of phenomenology, "back to" (*zu*) the things themselves (*Sachen*) suggests that the latter are elusive and slippery targets. Radical hermeneutics just reminds of the difficulty of hitting the mark.

Notes

[1] I take this analysis from Martin Heidegger, *Being and Time*, trans. Edward Macquarrie and James Robinson (New York: Harper & Row, 1962), §44(b-c).

[2] *Being and Time*, 490, note i.

[3] *Gesamtausgabe* B. 61, *Phänomenologische Interpretationen zu Aristoteles: Einführung in die Phänomenologische Forschung* (Frankfurt: Klostermann, 1985), 108-10.

[4] Hans-Georg Gadamer, *Truth and Method*, ed. G. Barden and J. Cumming (New York: Continuum, 1975), 238 ff.

[5] The delineation of a post-Enlightenment concept of rationality is the principal task of Richard Bernstein in his *Beyond Objectivism and Relativism: Science, Hermeneutics, and Praxis* (Philadelphia: University of Pennsylvania Press, 1983).

[6] John D. Caputo, *Heidegger and Aquinas: An Essay on Overcoming Metaphysics* (New York: Fordham University Press, 1982), Ch. 8.

[7] See how Thomas distinguishes the human soul from an angel in S.T., I, 74, 7, in particular his response to the third objection.

[8] Using both Scotus and Spinoza, Gilles Deleuze argues that the univocity of being is its equivocity, viz., that it always means something different. See *Différence et Répetition* (Paris: PUF, 1981).

[9] John D. Caputo, *Radical Hermeneutics: Repetition, Deconstruction and the Hermeneutic Project* (Bloomington: Indiana University Press, 1987).

[10] Jacques Derrida, *Of Grammatology*, trans. G. Spivak (Baltimore: Johns Hopkins University Press, 1974), 101–102.

[11] See the essay by that title in *Consequences of Pragmatism* (Minneapolis: University of Minnesota Press, 1982), 3–18. [14]

[12] See *Of Grammatology*, 158–59.

[13] *Dialogues with Contemporary Thinkers*, ed. Richard Kearney (Manchester: Manchester University Press, 1984), 123–24. For a text of Derrida which is clear about reference, see *Limited Inc. a b c*, trans. Samuel Weber, Glyph 2 (1972), secs. q and r, pages 193 ff. See also Christopher Norris, *Derrida* (Cambridge: Harvard University Press, 1988) for a sensible presentation of Derrida on this and other points.

[14] A similar account of the relation of signifier and signified is to be found in Peirce, whose semiotic theory Derrida discusses in *Of Grammatology*, 48 ff. See also the contributions of John Deely, Ralph Powell, and Richard Lanigan elsewhere in this volume.

[15] Jacques Derrida, *The Truth in Painting*, trans G. Bennington and I. MacLeod (Chicago: University of Chicago Press, 1987), 326–27.

[16] Walter Kasper, *Jesus the Christ,* trans. V. Green (New York: Paulist Press, 1976), 139.

[17] The best example of such an approach is Edward Schillebeeckx, *Jesus: An Experiment in Christology*, trans. H. Hoskins (New York: Crossroad, 1979); see e.g., his account of Jesus' attitude towards his approaching death, 298–312.

[18] For an excellent exercise in putting hermeneutics and postmodern critique to work in understanding religious faith, see David Tracy, *Plurality and Ambiguity: Hermeneutics, Religion, Hope* (San Francisco: Harper & Row, 1987).

HUSSERL AND DERRIDA

5

DERRIDA, A KIND OF PHILOSOPHER:
A DISCUSSION OF RECENT LITERATURE

[In *Research in Phenomenology*, 17 (1987), 245–59]

Rodolphe Gasché, *The Tain of the Mirror: Derrida and the Philosophy of Reflection*. Cambridge: Harvard University Press, 1986. 348 pp.

Irene E. Harvey, *Derrida and the Economy of Différance*. Studies in Phenomenology and Existential Philosophy. Bloomington: Indiana University Press, 1986. xv & 285 pp.

John Llewelyn, *Derrida on the Threshold of Sense*. New York: St. Martin's Press, 1986. xiii & 137 pp.

[245] The name "Derrida" has become a red flag at the mere sight of which many philosophers today charge. And the charges come from many directions. The Anglo-Americans were sure all along that continental philosophy was bound to come to grief in just such an excess of non-sense which makes no apologies for, indeed which celebrates, its very non-sensicality. The success that Derrida has enjoyed in literature departments only proves what they have been saying, that continental philosophy is metaphor and closet poetry. But the Derrida affair is not simply one more round of Anglo-American/continentalist hostilities. For not a few shots have been fired in Derrida's direction by those who remain faithful to the "classical" continental tradition – Husserl's transcendental phenomenology, the Heidegger of *Being and Time* (and even of the *Letter on Humanism*), the French phenomenologies of Sartre and Merleau-Ponty, and the hermeneutics of Gadamer and Ricoeur.

Something appears to snap when it comes to Derrida, something that sets tempers flaring. Derrida appears to go too far, to embrace happily and without compunction a kind of frivolous nihilism which mocks even the very attempt to distinguish the serious and the frivolous. He appears to say a good many outrageous things, and there is no short supply of [246] outrageous things said about him. If, as he says, auto-biographies are oto-biographies, if what Derrida writes is bound up with how it is heard, Derrida is in trouble. For a good many philosophers, people of learning and good will, hear a great deal of non-sense. It is widely held that he denies reference and locks us inside a "textualist" world of signifiers, that he is a sceptic, that he denies intentionality, communication, subjective agents, truth, and so on. The dissonances of nihilism, anarchism, relativism, and irrationalism are ringing in a good many ears.

In the midst of this brouhaha several sensitive Derrida readers have appeared on the scene to lend Derrida a hand by lending him a more favorable ear. Harvey and Gasché serve notice on the literary deconstructionists that they have missed the tip of Derrida's stylus. If literary critics want to pursue Derrida's work "seriously" they had best brush up their Hegel, Husserl and Heidegger, for there is no access to Derrida which does not pass through this formidable triple-H club of German philosophy. Knowing that this will not reassure Anglo-American philosophers, Llewelyn defends another front with an insightful account of Derrida's relation to Frege, the late Wittgenstein, Quine and Goodman.

Now all of this sounds a lot like what is called in Paris a "classical philosophical gesture." Derrida's work is serious (there is a serious/frivolous distinction), and you have to understand it properly (there is a distinction between understanding and misunderstanding, proper and improper understanding), as do these authors, who speak with sensitivity and familiarity about Derrida, who are close to Derrida (there is also a distinction between inside/outside, internal/external criticism). Finally, there is a serious disciplinary distinction between philosophy and literary criticism, and understanding Derrida requires solid philosophical training; that sounds a lot like professional turf protecting, like a warning against trespassing on the philosopher's field. If so, Gasché is the biggest offender, writing as if Derrida is a very technical philosopher, still fresh from the womb of structuralism, engaged in a relatively straightforward debate with German Idealism. Gasché's version of Derrida will sound the strangest to the Derridean, while Llewelyn's will have the ring of truth – if truth is a Dionysiac. But Gasché's book has a chance of reaching a larger audience and may indeed reshape the image of Derrida in the United States, while Llewelyn's work frequently sounds like more Derridean cant.

Now just because all of these writers know their Derrida exceedingly well, and know Derrida "personally," *in persona propria,* they also know that these distinctions have been made questionable by Derrida himself. In one way or another, they all focus on the deconstruction of inside/outside distinctions, which Llewelyn emphasizes by choosing the "threshold" [247] motif for his title, while Harvey's "economy" refers to the exchange and borrowing that takes place between philosophy's inside and outside.

The problem all three authors face is this: How do you defend Derrida as a philosopher when Derrida puts philosophy and its instruments of defense into question? How do you argue that Derrida is a philosopher without embracing the purism, professionalism, and rigorism which Derrida deconstructs? They all want to argue the same point: that Derrida is a subtle and sophisticated philosopher who repays the patient reading he demands (and gives to others). But they all appreciate the methodological treachery of this enterprise, that they risk domesticating deconstruction, turning it from philosophy's *other* to *philosophy's* other. They all understand that it will require a certain light-footedness and agility to steer themselves through such treacherous waters.

In general the common strategy they pursue looks something like this. They argue that, far from being illogical, Derrida gives a radical account of the conditions of possibility of what philosophy calls *logos,* of the realm of logical meaning, conditions which are not only enabling but also limiting or delimiting (somewhat in the manner of a Kantian critique.) Far from being an irrationalist, Derrida pursues a rationality which does not issue from philosophy's *logos*. In short, we should take Derrida seriously, as a philosopher of the first rank, who addresses complex and technical issues.

But, they all agree, Derrida is more than that, or less than that, not exactly that. Derrida is a philosopher because he works on the margins of philosophy, nibbles at its edges, neither inside nor outside, because he "borrows" from philosophy, as Harvey likes to emphasize, without buying permanent stock in the undertaking. Derrida is concerned with the "conditions" under which philosophy works, which are somehow anterior to philosophy without being outside philosophy. Derrida is thus, to adapt an expression which Mackey uses of Kierkegaard, "a kind of philosopher."[1]

Llewelyn's title is helpful here. Llewelyn situates Derrida on the "threshold" of sense. He does not try to counter the charges that Derrida's work is non-sense by showing its sense, but by showing the way in which it sets forth the conditions under which sense emerges – only to fall into complicity with its opposite. He argues, not that Derrida makes sense, but that Derrida is concerned with how sense is made and unmade (how things are done and undone with words) so that Derrida himself inhabits, not a logically prior sphere, but a sphere prior to *logos*, which is why Gasché says that *différance* is "pre-logical." Llewelyn wants to situate Derrida on the border line between the classical oppositions of sense and non-sense, sensible and super-sensible, inside and outside, philosophy and non-philosophy, in short, on the slash inserted between all the binary [248] schemes on which metaphysics feeds. And that place is of course neither (wholly) inside nor outside of philosophy, which means that it is (in part) both inside and outside philosophy. This undecidability principle is Derrida's answer to the Sheffer stroke. Like Gasché, Llewelyn argues that Derrida is a philosopher in the sense that philosophy and its schemes are the issue Derrida wants to philosophize about, not by situating himself *above* philosophy in some meta-philosophical site, but on those margins, edges or thresholds where philosophical structures emerge on the scene.

Gasché and Harvey are more boldly transcendental about this whole thing. Derrida's concern with the conditions under which philosophy works is a concern with the "conditions of possibility" of philosophy. Now what marks this off from philosophy in the straight sense is that these conditions are also shown to be conditions of impossibility as well, that is, limiting conditions. By "limiting" they do not simply mean that philosophy remains finite, which hardly anyone ever denied, but rather that these conditions *undo* philosophy, rob it of its prize, take away what it desires, including "transcendental" attempts to provide "conditions of possibility" or even to distinguish the transcendental and the empirical. That is why Gasché fine-tunes his description of Derrida to "quasi-transcendental."

The idea is not so much to carve out a space for Derrida as it is to show that he does not *have* a space, that he has no place to call his home, that he has nothing *heimlich*. Rather, he rents the space of the philosophers and borrows their tools and their logic in order to show how that logic arises and how it is doomed to fail. We might be tempted to call this meta-philosophy, except that would be precisely to set up a space *beyond* precisely in the manner of philosophy itself which has always turned on the gesture implied by the "meta-," the reflective distance, the judicial separation, looking on from on high, writing from above. Nor would it do to say that these authors are trying to find a voice for Derrida. Rather they argue that Derrida settles into the discourse of philosophy and uses its tongue in search of the conditions which have brought it about that philosophy has never lacked for voice, has never failed to voice its opinion, to let its voice be heard, and hence also to privilege (its) voice. If there is a voice at all for Derrida, it is the middle voice. If there is a ground, it is a middle ground, or a groundless ground, neither inside nor outside.

Now there is a Hegelian ring to all this that has to be sorted out, because it sounds something like a project of mediating between philosophy and anti-philosophy, sense and non-sense. It sounds as if Derrida is trying to mount a Hegelian fence between the binary opposites and that "undecidability" is a *tertium quid*, a third thing midway between antitheses. And that is another common feature of all these works; they all insist [249] that Derrida's relation to Hegel goes to the heart of the issue, that *différance* is not a neutral third value, midway between identity and difference, or a higher sublated unity, and that everything depends on seeing how it is not and why it is not.

I want now to highlight the distinctive feature of each book and to show how each author develops the general argument I have been sketching.

Reflections. Gasché's achievement is the most impressive and, I believe, could lay to rest a good deal of the gross misunderstanding of Derrida which is so prevalent today. A tour de force of technical argumentation, it is, nonetheless, thoroughly faithful to Derrida and does not assimilate him into metaphysics. One might object that Gasché wants to make Derrida "respectable" in the academy – which is Derrida's critique of Marxism and why Derrida thinks that in the end Marxism only reenforces the university and its power structure. I would say, however, as Derrida says at the end of "The Principle of Reason," that any critique of the university must first prove itself according to the standards of the university, and that Gasché shows conclusively that Derrida is "rigorous" in a sense which is widely ignored today. While Llewelyn's flippant and playful style is more in the spirit of Derrida, that may well undermine his attempt to speak to readers of Wittgenstein, Quine and Goodman. No such objection can made to Gasché.

Gasché situates Derrida in the context of the problem of "reflection." Starting out in Descartes as the ego's self-certainty, the philosophy of reflection culminates in the Hegelian conception of reflexivity as a feature of being itself. In Hegel, "absolute" reflection means that the object which the subject reflects is the subject's own other, its alienated, and hence mirrored self (21) which is recaptured by the reflecting (mirroring) self and thus returned to itself. There is a "play of reflections" in Hegel, but one that is regulated by the absolute's goal of self-unification and totalizing self-return. The strong point of absolute reflection is its capacity to assimilate its opponents. Having assumed a comprehensive, totalizing form, it regards its "other" as a moment in its own life. Kierkegaard, Marx, indeed all the critics of absolute spirit, are already anticipated, already part of the life of the Spirit, negative moments which, by being assimilated, urge it on toward completion. Absolute reflection is a machine fueled by its own critics.

Given that any frontal attack upon absolute reflection will be consumed by the system, the question is whether there can be anything "beyond" reflection, anything sufficiently "other" or "heterologous" to reflection. Dilthey, Nietzsche and Heidegger all set out on such a path. Derrida's strategy is closest to

Heidegger's: not to refute reflection head on [250] but to show that reflection is a founded mode – possible only in virtue of conditions which simultaneously limit it, making reflection impossible in the very terms which it sets for itself. But Derrida puts his finger on conditions which are "truly ultimate" (G 88),[2] and hence truly heterologous to what they found – the metaphysics of reflection as a totalizing system. Derrida alone posits a difference which is not simply the opposite of identity (that will be dialectically assimilated by the system) but which is *prior* to identity/difference, which is "older" than everything which is merely negative, which slips down beneath the identity/difference distinction.

Derrida is in search of "ultimate foundations," not in the metaphysical sense, but in the sense of those conditions which necessitate (and ultimately defeat) metaphysics' search for foundations. Like Heidegger, Derrida feels around for what is *unthought* in metaphysics, not, however, for its unthought "themes" but for its unthought syntax (G 127–8). Derrida looks for faults on the level of *logos,* not in order to mend them on a higher level (Hegel) but in order to expose their deeper structural inevitability. He shows that philosophy is inevitably victimized by these structural faults and is both possible and impossible because of them. The reason for this is that all rational discourse is made possible by a differential matrix in virtue of which philosophical concepts are what they are by being entered in a concatenated system of concepts. No concept is an atom. Every concept is marked by every other, and each member of a binary pair has inscribed within it a reference to its opposite, thus bearing within itself a trace of its opposite. Such features of philosophical discourse are not logical but pre-logical. Because they occur below the surface of its discourse, Gasché calls them, following Derrida, "infrastructures."

Thus while philosophy is interested in what is happening on the stage of meaning, deconstruction is interested in the staging. Philosophy grows out of these infra-structures but can never dominate them or get them within its reflective control. Philosophy can never ground itself upon them, as they operate below the level of philosophical discourse. The infra-structures thus are: (1) pre-logical conditions of philosophical logos; (2) synthetic powers which produce the oppositions on which philosophy nourishes itself (sensible/supersensible, etc.); and (3) economical structures which supply the minimum explanation possible (G 148–54).

But then is Derrida a structuralist? Is infra-structuralism a variant structuralism? Not so, Gasché contends, because the grounds which the infra-structures supply are non-grounds. They are not essences which give the system closure, but interventions on structures which open the system up to its own outside, denying it closure. It is precisely in virtue of the [251] infra-structures that philosophical systems cannot cohere, or close. They are not grounds because they describe the "space" in which the ground/grounded distinction is drawn. They mime the grounding process and taunt it by drawing their names from the empirical correlates with which they most "communicate," which is always the excluded partner of the pair – like writing, supplementation, etc.

But this last point explains the uneasiness that Derrida readers will feel with Gasché. For in the binary pair of system/fragment, Gasché does not side with the devalorized member, "fragment," but with its more prestigious partner, system. Gasché uses the language of the establishment, of science and system. He wants to set out the arche-*system* and its arche-*structures*. He does not speak of "generalized fragmentation" – which would be very close to "dissemination" itself – but of generalized system. There is a tension between Gasché's and Derrida's formulations which will set some Derridean hair on ends. Gasché has, however, good strategic reason for proceeding thus, viz., the hearing ("ear") that Derrida has been getting in the United States. Besides, this generalized system is "beyond Being." The chain of infra-structures is inherently pluralized, composed of multiple, "equi-primordial" origins no one of which dominates, organizes, centers or closes the (non-)system, thus preventing the infra-structural network from being formalized. The infra-structures are irreducible to one another; they change with changing needs; they are not aspects of a primordial unity.

There follows a careful presentation of a series of infra-structures: arche-trace, *différance,* supplementarity, iterability, (re)mark (G 177ff.). E.g. an origin is what it is by reason of its opposition to the trace which faintly copies it. But that means that the two terms require each other, that an origin is unintelligible without its polar opposite, and that the "trace" of each is to be found in the other. This arche-trace is the name neither of an origin nor of a trace but of the oppositional system in virtue of which every signifier is what it is by reason of the trace which its other makes upon it. The arche-trace is a prior tracing which renders itself invisible in favor of the oppositional schemes to which it gives rise. The infra-structures always "withdraw" (Heidegger) in favor of the structures which they make possible.

These analyses are to my mind the heart of the book and they are too rich for me to summarize here. I can only urge readers to examine them for themselves because they amount to the best presentation of Derrida's views that I know. They chart the field of the original spacing in which semiological systems are inscribed; the original iterability in virtue of which unities of meaning are built up (and down, *ab-bauen*). They explain how unities are both possible and impossible, constituted and destructible, [252] and always in virtue

71

of the mutual implication and complicity of the terms of the oppositional schemes with each other.

Now we come back to the problem of reflection and the rather inscrutable title of Gasché's book (225–239). The infra-structures describe a field of originary doubling (or re-petition, re-marking, reproducing etc.) in which the produced effects of metaphysics – the binary pairs – play themselves out. Derrida describes a kind of originary mirroring which gives rise to the play of reflections which reflect one another because each is marked by the other and comes to be what it is by reason of its opposition to each other. Dialectics tries to master this mirror-play by regulating it according to a principle of original and copy, while Derrida says that it cannot be dominated, that every identity is just its difference from others. The infra-structures thus provide the conditions of duplicity, of doubling, which both generate identity and make its doubling back on itself impossible, thus prohibiting any form of self-presence or absolute reflection. The system of infra-structures is the tinfoil (tain) on the back of the mirror which generates the reflections. Philosophy feeds off the play of reflections which is thus generated and it consists in a futile attempt to chain them down, to center and dominate them. The infrastructures explain how philosophy is possible/impossible.

The undecidability of the infrastructures is not semantic or syntactic, not a matter of wavering meanings or an uncertain grammar. It belongs on the level of an arche-grammar of spacing or differentiating which makes all semantic and syntactic effects possible. By marking each with the other (originary re-marking), it links them all to one another so that none can ever achieve atomic independence, autonomy, self-presence. None can ever make a perfect reflective return upon itself. Each remains inscribed in a system of reflections-of-one-another. This arche-grammar cuts deeper than Husserl's pure logical grammar, although it is a continuation of that project which reinscribes logic itself within its space and supplies the conditions under which the syntax/semantic cut can be made. Only the infra-structures provide us with a heterology which is truly other-than-logos and other than philosophy.

The last part of Gasché's book consists in a bit of finger-wagging at American literary critics (although no one is singled out in particular) who speak in Derrida's name. It is a relatively stern rebuke aimed at breaking the bad news to them that writing, text, and metaphor in Derrida are not what they think but rather infra-structures not be confused with their "empirical homologues."

"Writing" is a "quasi-transcendental synthesis" (274) formulated by Derrida in a debate with Husserl which has nothing to do with saying that philosophy is literature, that everything is just a form of writing. "Text" is [253] not the premise of some new form of textualism, or textual idealism, which locks us inside the prison house of language (which, ironically, would give the signifier a fixed, decidable referent, viz., the inside). Textuality does not deny reference (G 280–81) – a point which needs the greatest emphasis these days – but only that signifiers are atoms, that they ever seize upon a referent so wholly and fully as to detach themselves from the chain of signifiers by which they are defined. Belonging to a debate with Heidegger's "*es gibt*," it means to say that even Being itself is granted only within the "text" (the infra-structures).[3] Finally, Derrida is not trying to say that everything is hopelessly metaphorical or to dismiss the difference between philosophy and literature. He is not siding with metaphor in a debate with the proper but seeking out the space prior to both which organizes the debate between concept and metaphor. "Quasi-meta-phoricity" belongs to the metaphysical debate about the analogy of Being, but it cuts deeper than any doctrine of analogy, which is always a theory of "meaning."

So, then, are the literary critics to keep their hands off Derrida? No, this whole discussion is meant to clear the way for a genuine confrontation of Derrida and criticism – by sending the literary critics back for a crash course in Husserl and Heidegger. Gasché wants to enforce a distinction between philosophy and literature as a propaedeutic – a rather "purist" propaedeutic – to understanding the claim that Derrida works at a level prior to this distinction. He leaves little doubt, though, that this prior level "communicates" more with philosophy in the narrow sense than with literature. That, I think, is a general impression which most of Gasché's readers will have. I might add that one would like to get some minimal idea from Gasché of what genuine literary deconstruction would be like – to round off this long philosophical preamble about the technical sense of Derrida's words. In any case, his point is clear and well taken: it is a mistake to think that Derrida is spearheading a campaign to turn everything into literature and to turn literature into chaos.

Economy. 1986 was a tough year for deconstructionist literary critics. For the scolding continues in Irene Harvey's *Derrida and the Economy of Différance* – a dissertation co-directed by Derrida – which begins with three open letters: to literary critics who are upbraided for ignoring the philosophical underpinnings of deconstruction; to philosophers who are chided for dismissing Derrida out of hand; and interestingly to Derrida himself who is told that, whether he likes it or not, and whatever his *vouloir-dire* (meaning/desire) there is a "philosophy of textuality" brewing in his works. For there is a transcendental philosophy of sorts – Gasché would say a quasi-transcendentality – in Derrida which feels around for conditions of possibility. That means that Harvey has to do the same

[254] balancing act as Gasché: to show how there is something philosophical about Derrida's work on the margins of philosophy; a kind of dipping into the jar of philosophy without getting his hand stuck. Like Gasché and Llewelyn she insists that Derrida operates on the slash or the border between metaphysics and non-metaphysics, that he is both (and neither) inside and outside. The "economy of *différance*" of which she speaks regulates the exchange between inside and outside. It describes the conditions of the possibility and impossibility of metaphysics in virtue of which meta-physics never succeeds in making the hyphen stick, in excluding what it means to exclude, thereby making its favorite children – consciousness, presence, etc. – into orphans and enigmas.

Given this quasi-transcendentality, it is not surprising that Harvey begins by pointing out the similarities of the Kantian and Derridean projects. Both thinkers delimit the illusions of metaphysics and show their origin in desire. But, she points out nicely, Kant wanted a closed system of pure reason which returned each concept to its "proper" place, thus securing a transcendental science and transcendental truth. Derrida on the other hand produces a critique of this critique which denies that metaphysics can be delimited in the name of intuition and science, of truth and proper uses (H 14–20).

Harvey makes a great deal of Derrida's critique of Husserl and de Saussure in which, she thinks, the nub of Derrida's views are to be found. Here, she thinks, Derrida's methods are out in the open, for the attempts made by Husserl and de Saussure to exclude and purify, to reduce to pure essence, fail precisely in virtue of their own accounts of purity and essence. Singling out these essays on Husserl and de Saussure raises an interesting methodological problem for Harvey, because she rejects the method of "exemplification" as turning on a Platonic notion of exemplarity (H 56). But what else are her own favorite examples of Derridean analyses? She tries to swerve around this by calling them "case studies" (37–38). But are they not favored, privileged, exemplary case studies? Furthermore, how else is one to proceed? Is not exemplification just one more borrowing, one more stealthy raid on the goods of metaphysics which deconstruction is forced to make in order, once inside, to blow the whistle on metaphysics?

Harvey itemizes nine such "borrowings" or tools which deconstruction rents from metaphysics – e.g., the notion of conditions of possibility, the distinction between chance and necessity, the metaphysical form of the question, etc. (H 24ff.) Deconstruction makes use of these metaphysical ideas but in a non-metaphysical manner, always in such a way as to intervene on metaphysics and put its results in question (e.g., to show the [255] conditions of possibility of a metaphysical system is also to show its impossibility.)

74

Harvey then undertakes a series of analyses which make the following points. Derrida's critique of metaphysics is not based upon a monolithic or totalizing concept of "metaphysics;" that would commit him to the notion of an ahistorical essence which manifests itself over time. Instead Derrida is just picking up on certain "exclusionary gestures" which are repeated again and again in Western thought, like the exclusion of writing. Indeed, such gestures – like the notion of the transcendental signified, or of a presence without signs – are built right into our ordinary belief systems (Ch. 3). *Différance* is a way of accounting for metaphysical discourse which cannot be named except by analogy. Furthermore, it is so inconspicuous, it so much keeps out of sight, that the effects it produces look like origins and it "itself," the (non-)origin, looks like an effect or, as she says, the post-script looks like a beginning (Ch. 4). This is followed by an analysis of writing which closes with an interesting reflection on the inhuman basis by which our humanity is inhabited – madness, animality, divinity, abnormality – which blurs the lines of the "human" and exposes us to the abyss.

All of this is meant to lead up to a concluding chapter on the structure of *différance* in which Harvey proposes that Derrida is trying to insert the structure of repeatability into the texture of thought and reason, not to throw reason to the wolves, that he means to delimit reason by situating it in terms of the "economy of *différance*." This economy is an open system of transformations, of exchanges between presence and absence – like the exchange which takes place in the logic of supplement (addendum/substitute). That economy infiltrates all of the transactions of philosophy, of social, political and ethical life, and of daily life, for that matter. This economy, which is in a sense the tip of Derrida's stylus, injects a tragic quality into our existence for it shows how we are "thrown ... into the text of life itself and the tragedy of "one's own indestructible and mortal desire" (H 214), a point which, taken in conjunction with Harvey's remarks on the inhuman in chapter 5, is one of the most interesting suggestions in her book. In sum, she suggests, Derrida is engaged in a (quasi-) transcendental aesthetic, which has to do with the originary spacing and timing of arche-writing, an aesthetic which provides the conditions of possibility/impossibility of the intelligible itself.

Thresholds. As I indicated above, the title of Llewelyn's book encapsulates a strategy shared by all three of these authors. The charges of non-sense directed at Derrida fall wide of the mark, for Derrida is situated on the slash between sense and non-sense, in that region in which meaning [256] is formed and de-formed. The irony is that in a book which argues quite doggedly and with

75

considerable insight against this inside/outside distinction there is so much in-talk. Llewelyn's treatment of Derrida is often brilliant, but it is just as often dense and gnomic. And that is a pity, given that the Anglo-American philosophical audience that it means in part to address will more likely be discouraged than helped by such Derridean acrobatics.

Llewelyn's procedure is to follow Derrida's principal critical readings – of Hegel, Husserl, Heidegger, etc. – which he construes as a series of "semiologies" – dialectical semiology," "transcendental phenomenological semiology," etc. Derrida's work is presented as a take-off on these semiologies, not in such a way as to offer a competing semiology, but as a critical disruption of semiology's claims to coherence and unity, hence as an "ana-semiology." A semiology is a classical theory of signs which turns on the unity of meaning, while ana-semiology, by bringing deconstructive pressure upon the fault lines of the classical systems (L 95), leads to their breakup (as in ana-lysis). Thinkers from Hegel to the major contemporaries on both sides of the Atlantic offer variant philosophies of meaning. Derrida, on the other hand, attempts not to step back into another region, but to edge off toward the margins or thresholds where meanings take shape. And this is another way of describing what Gasché and Harvey call his (quasi-)transcendental posture.

Llewelyn begins with four mercilessly terse and at times epigrammatic presentations of Derrida on Hegel, Husserl, Heidegger and structuralism. Like Gasché and Harvey, Llewelyn tries to lay to rest the misunderstanding that Derrida's differentialist notion of signifiers commits him to a denial of reference. Derrida is only denying that we ever get to what the positivists called a "protocol" statement, that is, a statement which escapes the chain of substitutions and is defined not in reference to other statements but in reference to the things themselves, in naked reference (L 57). That it seems to me is a felicitous way to put it, and a salutary warning to those critics of Derrida who have been shocked by the declaration that there is nothing outside the text – for neither is there anything inside it.

In chapter five on "rhetorological semiology" (speech act theory construed as a theory of signs), Llewelyn continues to set the record straight on some of the more outrageous things of which Derrida has been accused. He shows that the upshot of Derrida's encounter with Austin and Searle is not to deny communication, intentionality, standard use, promises, or signatures, but only to point out that we have an exaggerated idea of their prestige. Again and again we hear from these commentators: Derrida is showing that the conditions that make meaning or reference, [257] subjects or objects, *possible – ab esse ad posse valet* – also put them on the skids, that is, delimit them. Thus there is no hard semiological distinction between use and mention because use is already mention, that is, use requires a systematically repeatable code which makes it possible in the first place and makes mention possible as the repetition of a use. (And the same thing goes for texts/commentary.) And this, Llewelyn claims, sheds some light on the relation between Derrida and the late Wittgenstein. For in switching from a theory of ideal meanings to meaning determined by public use, Wittgenstein, like Derrida, brings essentialism under fire but, unlike Derrida, not the primacy of meaning itself. That is, by falling short of a theory of iterability, Wittgenstein's position remains logocentric (L 68–69).

Derrida is on the lookout, not for an identifiable third thing, not some sort of *Aufhebung,* but a space of undecidability which engenders (and limits) the (apparently) decidable oppositions upon which metaphysics feeds. Undecidability is not a third value but the breakup (ana-) of value in a Heraclitan flux – a metaphor which Llewelyn favors (L 85, 113, 115), as do I. This structure of being "third" is carried by the middle voice, which is the voice of *différance,* and the subject of one of Llewelyn's most suggestive discussions (L 90–94). The middle voice does not express what speakers do or have done to them, but how someone or something gets involved in a process which is happening to them. This third thing is not an intermediate value but an anteriority, *antre, entre,* a prior milieu in which oppositions arise, a spacing or interval which makes both semantics and syntax possible. The fact that words too often have antithetical meanings is not a piece of bad luck *(malchance, méchance)* but reflects the complicity of oppositional terms, the way they belong to the same system, so that terms are "structurally" dependent upon what they attempt to exclude.

That gives us a better fix on the difference between Wittgenstein and Derrida, which is also a very valuable contribution of this little book (L 100-109). Like Derrida, Wittgenstein is interested in undoing the whole foundationalist project and hence in pulling the plug on the certainty/skepticism debate, which he does by determining meaning as use. But while Wittgenstein thinks that a pragmatic theory of meaning puts this whole issue to *rest,* so that his only advice is stay within the limits of the language game. Derrida is interested in pressing the issue that such language games are but effects of the force of repetition. Both deny that language is inscribed in ideal space; that it is governed by hard laws. For both, language obeys rules whose status is somewhere between necessity and chance, rooted in the practice of actual speakers, where what is ruled in or out remains to be seen. But Wittgenstein is trying to console those [258] who are made nervous by the loss of necessity, while Derrida tenders no one any solace.

The discussion of Quine is also very illuminating. Quine is looking for acquiescence in the mother tongue and wants to take words at their face value. Because the home base language is just given, because the game is just played as it is, it harbors its own inscrutable ontology. Now the real difference between Derrida and Quine is that Derrida is not willing to call this ultimate inscrutability an ontology (L 111). That move, Derrida thinks, is too much like Heidegger's archi-maternal language (early Greek discourse) which is taken to harbor a deep ontology, or Wittgenstein's forms of life, or Goodman's entrenched discourse.

The real value of Llewelyn's book is to be found in its last chapters on Derrida and Anglo-America. The rest of it makes good reading for Derrida lovers, for anyone in search of precious nuggets to encapsulate favorite Derridean insights. My hope is that all this preciousness does not bury the useful discussions at the end and the considerable insight scattered throughout the text. I hope the book does not discourage the very audience which it is seeking to persuade that there is more to Derrida than an artful teaser of words without philosophical import.

The task that faces serious readers and expositors of Derrida's thought is both clear and urgent – if you pardon the apocalyptic tone. It has to do with Derrida's "good name" which has been considerably blemished by serious misunderstandings of what he is up to. It has to do with laying to rest the unsavory images of nihilism and irrationalism which his work provokes. One has the sense that something has gone wrong in the debate over Derrida, that this is not the usual sort of disagreement that philosophers have among themselves. The time has come to show with some patience that Derrida is engaged in a critical project which is deeply in accord with the critique of metaphysics which has marked continental philosophy throughout this century, which began with Husserl and was given a more radical form in Heidegger, particularly in his later period.

The task then, here and now, beginning where we are, is for more clear-headed renderings of Derrida which, by demonstrating the power and subtlety of his analyses, and their continuity with Husserl and Heidegger, will raise the level of the debate a notch or two. My guess is, if I may prognosticate for a moment, that Gasché's book will do the most to set the record straight – although I do not mean by this to say that I do not appreciate the contributions of Llewelyn and Harvey. Gasché's book is long and difficult but it is technical and precise and it gives Derrida the sober and sobering rendering which is at present so badly needed. It is a stunning and remarkable achievement. At another time, one might have objected that he has domesticated Derrida for the academy, sold him down the river. But not here, not now.

Notes

[1] [259] Louis Mackey, *Kierkegaard: A Kind of Poet* (Philadelphia: University of Pennsylvania Press, 1971). Actually, this was an expression Kierkegaard used to describe himself.

[2] I will use G, H, and L followed by page numbers to refer to the books by Gasché, Harvey, Llewelyn respectively which I am her reviewing.

[3] Like most Derrideans, Gasché (and this holds also of Harvey and Llewelyn) misses the fact that as early as the Marburg lectures Heidegger too was moving "beyond Being" and that by *Ereignis* Heidegger meant something which grants Being and presence, meaning and truth, proper and improper, while remaining "itself" prior to or older than them, rather like the infra-structures described by Gasché. I argue this point in "Cold Hermeneutics: Heidegger/Derrida," *Journal of British Society for Phenomenology,* 17, no. 3 (October 1986); and in *Radical Hermeneutics* (Bloomington: Indiana University Press, 1987), chapter 6.

6

THE ECONOMY OF SIGNS IN HUSSERL AND DERRIDA: FROM USELESSNESS TO FULL EMPLOYMENT

[In *Deconstruction and Philosophy*, ed. John Sallis (Chicago: University of Chicago Press, 1987), 99–113]

[99] In the *First Investigation* (§15) Husserl gives two examples of nonsense – "Green is or" (*Grün ist oder*) and "Abracadabra."[1] These are dangerous expressions for Husserl, indeed not expressions at all, but examples of a wild grammar which defy the rules of pure logic. Husserl wants to banish them, to escort them to the edge of the city, to exile them from the *polis* of meaning and sense, of *logos* and language. Derrida, ever alert to the rights of those who are excluded and denied privilege, comes to their rescue. For these signifiers are illustrative indeed, not of non-sense, but of the deeper work which signifiers do, the deeper formality of the signifier, a structural formality which Husserl both recognizes and represses. By means of this blatant agrammaticality, Derrida thinks, we gain access to the freedom of signs, their liberation from intuition. Their banishment by a priori grammar is in fact a liberation from an oppressive regime.

But Derrida is interested not only in the liberation of signifiers, here represented by these jarring examples, but in finding them a job. He is interested, not only in battling for their freedom, but in defending their right to work. For even the signifiers which Husserl admits into the *polis*, those which bear a meaning and a possible relation to intuition, are declared useless, *zwecklos*, without purpose. They are "unproductive" members of society; they make no contribution. So Derrida's task is to show what they can do, the work of which they are capable, the contribution they can make.

My task in this paper then will be to follow the case study of "green is or" and "abracadabra," to see if they have been denied their rights, to see how Derrida comes to their defense and what sort of work he finds for them to do. I will proceed in three steps. (1) In the first section, I examine Derrida's arguments against the "uselessness of signs" in Husserl's *First Investigation,* which is the central [100] deconstructive thread in *Speech and Phenomena*. (2) In the second, "the freedom of signs," I pursue the liberation of "green is or" and "abracadabra," which results in what Derrida calls the "freedom of language, the candor of speech" (VPh 100/89).[2] And it is here, I will argue, that the impact of Derrida, the pointed tip of his stylus, can best be felt. (3) In the final and concluding section, entitled "the productivity of signs and the economy of full employment," I try to show that the very productivity and indefatigability of signs, the full employment which Derrida gains for them, produces a phenomenological result which goes against Derrida's intentions, even as his contention that presence is a constituted effect produces a deconstructive result which goes against Husserl's intentions. Here I consider the question of *die Sache selbst, la même chose.*

The Uselessness of Signs

Husserl has two arguments against allowing indicative signs to play a role in solitary life. First, any such interior dialogue of the self with the self is purely pretended and imaginary – there is no genuine, effective, real communication of anything to the self by the self. Second, these are ultimately without purpose (*Zwecklos*) in the monological sphere. In soliloquy, in the life of the ego with itself, Husserl thinks, the instrumentality and mediation of indicative signs would be quite useless (...*solchen Anzeigen hier ganz zwecklos wäre*) [§8]).

Derrida argues each point in turn. Against the first, he delimits the claim of real communication to be real and effective – inasmuch as it must rely upon the representative power of indicative signs to produce its effect. That is to say, there can be no naked contact, no immediate presence of mind to mind, in actual communication, but only a work of mediation carried out by signs and representations. Against the second, he shows that signs are not useless, that there would be a role for them to play were they allowed back into the city, and that it is precisely Husserl himself who establishes this role. It is with this second argument that I concern myself here.

With the momentous discovery of the reduction, Husserl isolates an operation which is at once the fundamental gesture of philosophy and the undoing of the classical role of philosophy to provide foundations and assured presence. The reduction is the name of philosophy's critical power, its impulse to get beyond naiveté and already constituted products. Derrida does not quarrel about the reduction, does not question its possibility, does not want to short-circuit its critical operation. He only want to see that it is carried out far enough, that the work of [101] critique is not subverted in advance by a teleology of presence and fulfillment. He wants thus to carry out what Husserl set in motion, to extend the work of reduction, but to do so ruthlessly, without pity, with the hardness of heart of Zarathustra. For in Husserl himself the reductive impulse is cut short. Phenomenological vigilance is not enough. It is satisfied with presence, intuition, self-showing – when that is precisely what needs to be questioned. The teleology of fulfillment obscures Husserl's achievement and causes us to lose sight of Husserl's discovery of the genuine reduction, let us call it here, the semiotic or semiological reduction.

Signs are useless in solitary life, according to Husserl, because there can be no need to indicate mental acts to oneself. This is because "the acts in question are themselves experienced by us at that very moment" (§8). *Im selben Augenblick*: there is not the blink of an eye between the ego which speaks and the ego which hears itself speak. Nothing intervenes in this diaphanous medium of pure, inner voice. There is no opacity, no thickness to divide the ego from itself.[3] Yet that is a view which has been effectively undermined by Husserl's own account of inner time-consciousness. For the now is not altogether now, is not all together, is not a self-identity, pure and simple. Instead, in virtue of his own doctrine of retention, Husserl insists that now must be continuously compounded with now (VPh 72/64), presence with nonpresence, in order to make up (constitute), to make up for (supplement), the present in the wider, more pregnant sense, which is a protential-retentional synthesis. That means that the present depends upon the function of representation, of retentional making present again. If retention is a representational modification of the now (which is the present in the strict, narrow sense), nonetheless the genuine and living present (in the wide, pregnant sense) is an effect, a product, of the work of retention. In the living present, now is woven together with now to produce a more complex fabric/text. Here representation makes presence possible; presence is the effect of representation. The metaphysical prejudice that representation is a modification of presence is rooted out.

Husserl realizes the disruptive potential of this admission and hence takes great pains to contain it by insisting on the distinction between retention and reproduction. Phenomenologically, there is an essential distinction between the tones which have just lapsed in the melody which is still sounding, or the syllables which have just lapsed in the multisyllabic word which is still being uttered, and, let us say, a melody we heard yesterday, or words spoken an hour ago. Different sequences of *Erlebnisse* have intervened in the meantime, the intentional stream has been inhabited by different objects. Yet what is the [102] difference *in principle,* Derrida asks, between what is just lapsed and what has been lapsed for some time now? What is the difference in principle if – and this is a constraint which Husserl imposes upon himself – one demands absolute self-presence, perfect immediacy, *im selben Augenblick*? A moment cannot be qualified as just a little bit past, just a little lapsed. The present in the pregnant sense cannot be just a little bit pregnant! That is not a difference in principle. Retention and reproduction are but variant degrees of representation, different only in virtue of the extent to which they are distanced from the simple now-impression.

But if retention is necessary, signs are *not* useless:

> The fact that nonpresence and otherness are internal to presence
> strikes at the very root of the argument for the uselessness of
> signs in the self-relation. (VPh 74/66)

There *is* a role for signs to play. For the work of protention and retention is a work of *tenere,* tenancy, place-holding, a work which is facilitated by the *pharmakon* of signs, the remedy which will provide a supplement for memory. Indeed would it be "humanistic" and "anthropomorphic" to compare what Husserl calls *animalia,* which have no recourse to signs, with the tremendously enhanced powers of the beings whose conscious stream is supplemented by signs, which aid it in the work of compounding now with now, of holding together presence with non-presence, strengthening it with the tenaciousness of retention and protention?[4] Signs are not useless. They make consciousness stronger, more tenacious. Indeed they make consciousness in the pregnant sense *(con-scire)* possible.

Husserl takes consciousness to be a diaphanous life which operates by means of the pure voice. The voice is not spatial and mundane. The voice is heard and understood as soon as it speaks, in "absolute proximity" to the speaking subject, in perfect auto-affection:

> My words are "alive" because they seem not to leave me: not to
> fall outside me, outside my breath, at a visible distance. (VPh
> 85/76)

The worldly body of the voice fades away at the very moment it is produced. That at least is how it *seems.* For Husserl's phenomenology operates in a naivete generated by the invisibility of the voice and the phonetic sign, even as it is the task of the semiotic reduction to make signs conspicuous. Husserl's reduction is waylaid by a natural attitude, not about language, but about the transparency of sound which leads him to think that language is not productive, that it merely [103] reproduces the pre-expressive stratum. Husserl carries out a reduction *of* phonetic signifiers, not a reduction *to* them. His transcendental phenomenology operates in a naive belief in the works which have been wrought by the phonetic signifier. But this reduction of language is never quite complete, the subjugation

84

of the reduction to this phonological metaphysics never quite succeeds. An uneasiness pervades his text:

> because an underlying motif was disturbing and contesting the security of these traditional distinctions from within and because the possibility of writing dwelt within speech, which was itself at work in the inwardness of thought. (VPh 92/82)

The analysis of internal time-consciousness betrays the realization that presence is infiltrated with non-presence, that presence is a constituted effect, that the primordial comes to be under the hand of the trace. The production of presence is the work of retention. But how can the work of retention be carried out without the labor of signs? ("Doubtless Husserl would refuse to assimilate the necessity of retention and the necessity of signs…" (VPh 74/66].)

With that, the role of signs is made conspicuous. The opacity of writing infiltrates the pure medium of the voice. The *cogito* is thick with time, as Merleau-Ponty said, differentiated and extended in a temporal continuum. And just so it is also thick with writing, whose work it is to weave the stream of *Erlebnisse,* of *tenere,* tenancy, into the unity of a text, *texere,* textuality. A lingering naivete is rooted out. The reduction is radicalized, transformed into a semiotic reduction which discovers the work of the signifier and its anonymous productivity.

The Freedom of Signs

Now I want to turn to Derrida's strategy for liberating "green is or" and "abracadabra," these two refugees from pure grammar. Even if signs are necessary to the work of retention, why must that implicate us in such non-sensical signs? Why does Derrida insist on keeping such unsavory company?

When Husserl identified the structural capacity of the sign to operate in the absence of its object he isolated the essence of the sign as such. The sign is *für etwas.* It plays the role of *tenere,* tenancy, standing in and holding the place for something, just when what is present, *für sich,* is not to be had. More importantly, and this is the essential point for Derrida, for it is the more treacherous situation, the sign stands in [104] for and holds the place for something even when it is to be had, even when it is present. The sign, on Husserl's own accounting, implies non-plenitude, the power to function without fulfillment. And this is structurally necessary to it as a sign. Derrida writes:

> The whole originality of this conception lies in the fact that its ultimate subjection to intuitionism does not oppress what might be called the freedom of language, the candor of speech, even if it is false and contradictory. One can speak without knowing. And against the whole philosophical tradition Husserl shows

85

that in that case speech is still genuine speech, provided it obeys certain rules which do not immediately figure as rules for knowledge. (VPh 100/89–90)

Speech is still good speech when its object is absent, when it is true but not fulfilled – as when I speak of Madrid, the capital of Spain, even though I have never been there. It is still good speech when it can be fulfilled imaginatively (the golden mountain). It is good speech even when it cannot be fulfilled at all, because it is false or even because it is contradictory (the circle is square). Even the *Widersinn* is not an *Unsinn*. Speech is not impaired when it has neither object nor consistent meaning.

But here the series of reductions breaks off. Despite the "boldness" of pure logical grammar, Husserl loses his nerve. He senses that he is skirting dangerously close to the edge of the city, risking exile, and so he takes care. The wandering signifier must be contained. He calls upon the police to establish law and order. Rules of a prioiri grammar, combinatorial rules governing the forms of meanings, are put into effect, limiting where one may travel.[5] He takes measures to contain wild grammar – "green is or" – and wild articulate sounds – "abracadabra." But why are these signifiers wild and dangerous? Because they declare their absolute independence of all possible intuition. Unlike "the circle is square," they are not even of a form such that, were one to replace them by other signifiers of the same form, intuition could result. They are absolutely defiant; they practice absolute civil disobedience.

Yet Husserl himself has shown that it belongs to the very structure of the sign to operate without fulfillment, in the absence of its object. That is Husserl's own view. But on that accounting "green is or" and "abracadabra" represent the isolation of this structure and hence a welcome liberation from the rule of intuitionism, a liberation which is in fact made possible by the reduction of the rules of a priori grammar. Pure logical grammar, because it measures meaning in terms of [105] intuitability is not formal enough to resist the semiotic reduction, to survive as a semiotic residuum. This reduction – the one which is in place when we write "green is or" and "abracadabra" – liberates the signifier from the oppressive regime of intuitionism and its unfair demand that every signifier lead to Being, presence, objectivity, even when such demands cannot be met. Intuitionism exacts a tax which no one can pay.

"Green is or," "abracadabra" are thus the first utterances of free speech, wondrous examples of the "freedom of language, the candor of speech" (VPh 100/89), of "the emancipation of speech as non-knowing" (VPh 109/97). "Green is or" is free and licit sign-making, no less than anything of the form "S is P," indeed more so. It represents the weaving together of a text, an interweaving of signifiers which produces an effect, an odd, obscure effect which tantalizes us, but an effect nonetheless, one we could spend some time pondering and unraveling. There is sign-making here even where there is what metaphysics regards as *Unsinn*, where there is no possible relation to an object. Indeed Derrida even suggests that there is a *Sinn* here, a *Sinn* which has been rewritten in a wider nonmetaphysical sense, which does not promise knowledge, truth, or objectivity, for the latter are so many unjust restrictions of the civil rights of *Sinn*, so many attempts at intuitionistic conscription.

Thus, by means of "green is or" and "abracadabra," we are able to isolate the pure form of the signifier, the formal system of signifiers, the repeatable code. We liberate the form of writing, not writing in the narrow sense, but arche-writing, *différance*. We make reduction of a logico-grammatical form, which is still heavy with the matter of metaphysics, in order to make reduction to the pure power of signs to produce their effects, to generate their products.

But Derrida warns us not to conflate the two examples, that they are different:

> (and Husserl links up these last two examples somewhat hastily;
> he is perhaps not attentive enough to their difference).... (VPh
> 110/98)

What is the difference? What difference can there be between two examples of non-sense? Does non-sense come in degrees? Are they not both equally non-sensical? In fact, "abracadabra" is not non-sense.[6] In the first place, it serves as an example of non-sense, and hence, as Derrida points out in "Signature Event Context,"[7] performs a meaningful, repeatable function which is to be found in any respectable dictionary. Furthermore, "abracadabra" is an old name, an old cabalistic word: *abra*, *cad*, and then again *abra*, and hence structured around a form of repetition. [106] Meant to be written in triangular form – *abra* at the right and left hand angles, *cad* at the apex – it functions as an invocation of the Holy Trinity (for which it is likely an acronym) in order to drive out a malaria-like disease.[8] "Abracadabra" is an incantation, a power of producing effects with the aid of signs alone. One need only utter the words, to invoke the signifier (under certain circumstances, the village Austinian would insist), and the effect is produced. "Abracadabra" thus is a performative utterance, while "green is or," is constative, or tries to be.

But on my reading "abracadabra" is not just an exotic example of a performative utterance; it is the very form (albeit a formless form) of any utterance, indeed of any signifier at all. It is a way of signaling the productive power of signs as such. It is not so much a signifier as a way that the very act of signing is itself signaled, signified. Its preeminence is not semiotically "ontic," if we may say so, not to be a particular signifier, but "ontological," because it awakens us to the productive power of the semiotic system as a whole. "Abracadabra" is an old name which points to the power and productivity of signs, impresses upon us that signs are not useless but magical performatives, which, like all magic, know how to hide behind their effects, so that you see only the effects, the products.

What else is magic than to have command of occult powers, to be able to produce mysterious effects? How can the trace – let us prescind from its substance, let it be phonic or graphic – do such things? How can signifiers name things which are not there? How can the word "I" function when he/she is not there, continue to produce effects when I am dead? Is this not necromancy and black art? How can signifiers operate in the absence of things? How can these signifiers walk on water like this? Signifiers work like magic. They are powerful forces which produce extraordinary effects – and this by uttering a formula. They have the power to traffic with things which are not present, to produce results with signs. For it is the very function of the sign, its structural necessity, to be able to operate in the absence of its object. The semiotic reduction *releases* the power of signifiers to work their magic, lets them be what they are, magical performatives.

Consider the first example, "green is or." Against Husserl's intentions, this produces an effect, in German or English, no less than in French where, when spoken, it sounds like a question about where (*où/ou*) we are to look for the green, or for the glass (*vert/verre*) (*Marges* 381/320). Indeed this example produces exactly the opposite result of the one Husserl intends, for it shows that signifiers retain their powers even in the absolute absence of intuition, and that it is impossible ever [107] to deploy them in such a way as to produce *no* effect. "Green is or" illustrates the "abracadabra." The agrammatical example points to a power which we cannot repress, extinguish, one capable of producing grammar itself. Husserl's example – against his intentions – defies us to create a string of signifiers which has no product, which leaves no comet's tail trailing behind it. It belongs to the very magical power of signifiers to produce effects. The Husserlian-Derridean reduction lets a genie out of the bottle whom we cannot master and control.

Signifiers are magical performatives which produce a staggering array of amazing results: science, art, outright fictions, graffiti, metaphysical systems, ethical exhortations, mythologies, scriptures, insults, commands, baptisms, poems, political constitutions, public prohibitions, curricula, colloquia, soliloquies, logical systems, normal and abnormal discourses of all sorts, and on and on. We can liken this productivity to the power of the "imagination" in

German Idealism. For here, too, we have to do with *Ein-bildungs-kraft*: with an inexhaustible power to engender form, to produce formed effects. This is not to say that the power of *différance* is a subjective faculty. The energy in question is not the energy of a subject but the power of the differential system to generate new effects indefinitely.

Indeed Husserl himself had a glimpse into this abyssal power of productivity, albeit one which was couched in the language of transcendental subjectivity and transcendental freedom. He describes this for us in §§47–49 of *Ideas I* in terms of "the annihilation of the world," in a discussion aimed at showing the "constitution" of the world. The world around us is radically contingent, he says. The actual world is but a special case of a multitude of different, possible worlds. Things take shape for us as the correlate of a factual sequence of experiences, and we can imagine that these sequences would be different, would change. We can imagine that clouds would turn into monstrous animals and sweep down upon us in a wave of anger, that the seas could begin to boil, that all sorts of Kafkaesque transformations would transpire. There is a radical contingency in the make-up of things, for consciousness has the resources to constitute the world in a multitude of alternate ways, and even to survive the total breakdown of all meaningful configuration, so that it would be left to rule alone over a Dionysian flux.

Now what is the upshot of all this? What has Derrida wrought by this defense of "green is or" and "abracadabra"? That is embedded in the rhetoric of "liberation" which I have employed throughout this essay. The story of the "liberation" of "green is or" and "abracadabra" – about their banishment from the *polis* of good grammar, [108] about the police work of a priori grammar – all of this is an allegory about liberation at large. Liberation is what I think Derrida is all about, the impact his work has, the point of his writing, the tip of his pointed stylus. He is interested in a long list of liberations. "Green is or" and "abracadabra" are only the first beneficiaries, which includes the liberation of literature and of every kind of discourse: scientific, political, ethical, institutional, religious, discourse within and discourse without the university, *intra muros* and *extra muros*.

What Derrida has done above everything else, in my mind, is to expose the primal and unsettling contingency which lies not far beneath the surface of our creations. He alerts us to the danger of falling into subjugation by created things, contingent unities of meaning.[9] He keeps his transcendental-semiotic reduction in place so as to keep everything open, to show the revisability, contingency, reformability, rewritability of whatever has achieved hoary prestige and the look of irreformability. He interrogates entrenched authority, the established powers that be, which pretend to be, which pretend to be present. He solicits the people of substance, *ousia*. Such authorities, as he likes to say, have not dropped from the sky; they are contingent formations, constituted products. He gives the critique of metaphysics – hitherto understood only in terms of *Gelassenheit* – a socio-political cutting edge, pointing it in the direction of a politics of liberation.[10] He is interested in producing a Socratic effect.

The Productivity of Signs and the Economy of Full Employment

I want now, if I may say so, to philosophize a bit with this critique of Husserl, and in so doing to see if phenomenology does not reemerge under the hand of Derrida's critique, rewritten, reproduced, repeated, this time under the sign of the sign.

Derrida knows that it is not enough just to liberate signs. For if we do not find them gainful employment, give them honest work to do, they will roam the streets aimlessly and risk confinement and incarceration. But this produces a curious result. In defending the right of signs to useful work – against Husserl's intentions – Derrida likewise defends the rights of the things themselves – against his own intentions. He concludes this essay – which is essentially an essay on retention – by writing that the thing itself always steals away: *la même chose se dérobe toujours*. But by the very terms of his own analysis of Husserl, that can hardly be. For signs are not useless; he has himself put signs to work in the indefatigable labor of saving things from such a fate. That is part of their magic, part of what results when one insists that they are not [109] useless. The thing itself always sticks around! Though, doubtless, Derrida would resist this assimilation of the necessity of signs to the necessity of the things themselves.

Presence is, he argues – against Husserl's intentions – a constituted effect. For signifiers have work to do, not only in the absence of their object, but even when the object is present. Here, too, the signifier intervenes, producing the effect of presence as something constituted, compounded with absence, dependent upon signs, structured and textualized. Derrida warns us against the seductive "effect" of presence and the cleverness of signs which, by making themselves transparent, lead us to believe that they are not productive, that they are useless. But Derrida has found gainful employment for them, which is the labor they expend in the production of presence. The work of signs is to produce presence in the pregnant sense, where presence is impregnated with absence, presence in the supplemented sense, where presence is supplemented by signs, sustained, maintained (*maintenant*) by protention and retention. Presence is not fallen from the sky; it is generated by constitution, engendered by repetition. It is a work wrought by signs which produce the effect of the things themselves: *die Sache selbst, la même chose.*

Yet Derrida has written, has meant to say, the thing itself always steals away:

> And contrary to what phenomenology – which is always phenomenology of perception – has tried to make us believe, contrary to what our desire cannot fail to be tempted into believing, the thing itself always steals away. (VPh 117/104)

La même chose se dérobe toujours? But how is that possible? Are signs useless? Can they not do an honest day's work? Have we not given them a job? Can they not make themselves useful? Indeed. That is what Derrida has shown. They have been hired to do the work of retention, *tenere,* employed because of their tenaciousness, to hold on to the thing itself before it slips too far, before it sinks away (*herabsinken*) altogether. Derrida has shown, not that there is no retention, but that retention is the work of signs, which stand for, hold the place for, what is sinking away. That is why signs are productive, not useless. That is the work which Derrida finds for them to do, how he gets them off the unemployment line.

The thing itself steals away. But what is the thing itself for Husserl? It is not some absolute being, for it is only the conscious flux – and not Being in the sense of existence of reality – which is absolute for [110] Husserl. It is not some thing-in-itself, absolutely independent of conscious life, for that, too, is a phenomenological error (*Ideas I*, §43), the Husserlian equivalent of the "transcendental signified." That steals away indeed. And good riddance.

Rather, the thing itself is the *phainomenon*, which is to say, precisely that which has been released by the reduction from the conditions of absolute presence and absence, from the constraints of real being, which is free to be the compound product of presence and absence, or even to be hallucinatory. It is precisely because the living present is a fabric of presence and absence that Husserl finds it necessary to withdraw the authority of real being, of absolute presence, by means of the reduction. The thing itself is *phenomenal* being, a structure of *appearance,* which Derrida has shown to be, not an illusion, but dependent upon the work of signs. If signs are not useless, then what phenomenology regards as the thing itself, the phenomenal living present, does not sink away, but is, rather, shown to be a textured product, a woven fabric which is always and already brought forth by the play of signifiers. For Husserl, the thing itself is a phenomenal *system,* a systematic interconnectedness of *noemata,* and Derrida has shown that such a system cannot be woven together without the work of signifiers, of *texere.*

91

The productivity of signifiers is the power of weaving together the noematic system, the protentional, retentional system of phenomenal being. Derrida, thus, not only finds employment for signs, but he has them working night and day, in the absence and the presence of objects, around the clock of internal time-consciousness, in a top-security job at the heart of the phenomenological industry. The one form of plenitude that Derrida does not object to is the economy of full employment for signifiers, whose right to work full-time he always defends.

But if that is so, then the final sentiment of *Voix et la Phénomène* – *la même chose se dérobe toujours* – must be held in tandem with, must be supplemented with, another more phenomenological principle, one which Heidegger borrows from Stefan George: *Kein Ding sei wo das Wort gebricht:* no thing may be where the word breaks off. That is to say, failing the intervention of the signifier, the thing itself slips away. The magic of signs is also the magic of the goddess in George's poem who saves things from loss by the word.

> She sought for long and tidings told:
> "No like of this these depths enfold."
> [111] And straight it vanished from my hand
> The treasure never graced my land....[11]

The work of signifiers is retentional, preservative; they keep the world from vanishing altogether. The task of thinking is to learn to think these two sentiments about the things themselves *together,* to learn to say them, if not at the same time, *im selben Augenblick,* at least in rapid succession. In this way alone can we gain access to the work of *différance* in all its productivity.

The productivity of the pure signifier, its power to produce effects, prodigious and irrepressible, draws near to the power of poiesis in the sense described by Heidegger. This Derridean-Husserlian reduction liberates the power of world-making, the magic of creation. It makes contact with what Heidegger and Husserl alike call *Stiftung,* institutive creating, a making which gives origin to. The productive power of the signifier is the power of *Stiften* which, in "The Origin of the Work of Art," Heidegger associates with *Dichten* and *Dichtung.*[12] It is the primal poetic power of words, the *poiesis,* the power to create, to weave worlds out of signs, the magic, the incantation. There is no way to suppress the ongoing institution of the world.

Indeed, that is hardly the problem. The danger is not that we will run wild in creativity, in rewriting and rereading. The danger is the scales on the dragon, thousands of years old. And that, as we said above, is what Derrida is after, to slay the dragon with his magic, to rid us of idolatry before graven images, to remind us of the radical continency and reformability of things, the graveness, the createdness, of whatever is brought forth, produced, constituted, un-concealed. And that is at the same time to recall us to the power of poiesis, of making anew, of bringing forth anew thing and world.

The thing itself always steals away.

Where the word fails no thing may be.

The thing itself steals away if signs are useless.

Where the word fails the thing itself steals away.

The power of the signifier, the work it does, its ultimate art and magic,[13] its ultimate economy of full employment and triumph over uselessness, is the *poiesis*, the *Stiften,* which brings forth the things themselves.[14] The things themselves are woven products, brought forth, engendered by the work of signs.[15] That is the matter for thought, *die Sache des Denkens.* Is the thing itself, *das Ding,* Heidegger's jug, half empty or half-filled?

Abracadabra. *A-letheia.*

Notes

[1] All reference to the *First Investigation* will be to the appropriate section and enclosed in parentheses in the text. See Husserl, *Logische Untersuchungen,* vol. 2, pt. 1, 5th ed. (Tübingen: Niemeyer, 1968); *Logical Investigations,* trans. J. N. Findlay, 2 vols. (New York: Humanities Press, 1970).

[2] VPh: *Le voix et le phénomène* (Paris: PUF, 1967). The pages following the slash are from the English translation *Speech and Phenomena,* trans. David Allison (Evanston: Northwestern University Press, 1972).

[3] J. N. Mohanty suggests ("On Husserl's Theory of Meaning," *Southwestern Journal of Philosophy* 5 [1974]: 240), that Derrida's argument fails because it neglects Husserl's theory of reference and focuses entirely on the theory of meaning. But nothing is changed by switching from sense to reference. For in referring, consciousness would still, on Husserl's account, claim to know that it refers and what it is referring to, and to know it in the self-same moment of referring; it would still claim to carry out the act of referring prelinguistically, self-presentially. It is not solipsism that Derrida objects to but the theory of prelinguistic self-presence. See also Mohanty, *Edmund Husserl's Theory of Meaning* (The Hague: Nijhoff, 1969), chapter 2. For a defense of Mohanty's position see Susan Ruth Carlton's dissertation at the University of Michigan, "On Authors, Readers, and Phenomenology: Husserlian Intentionality in the Literary Theories of E. D. Hirsch and Jacques Derrida" (1984), chapter 3.

[4] Derrida regards this attempt to set humanity off as something higher than animals as a hallmark of metaphysics. Yet he will certainly agree that the human use of signs is vastly superior to that of animals. His point is that this superiority is a difference in degree rather than a neat, categorical difference, without overlap or partial convergence.

[5] This is the point of the *Fourth Investigation,* on the idea of a pure grammar. For more on the relationship between Derrida and Husserl which takes its point of departure from the theory of pure grammar, see the writings of Rodolphe Gasché, in particular his contribution to the present

volume [i.e., *Deconstruction and Philosophy*, ed. John Sallis (Chicago: University of Chicago Press, 1987) –Ed.] and "Deconstruction as Criticism," *Glyph 6* (Baltimore: Johns Hopkins University Press, 1979), 177–215. It is interesting too that Heidegger's habilitation dissertation dealt with the *Fourth Investigation*. See my "Phenomenology, Mysticism and the '*Grammatica Speculativa*': A Study of Heidegger's 'Habilitationsschrift,'" *Journal of the British Society for Phenomenology* 5 (1974): 101–17 [This essay appears in Volume 1 (chapter 6) of this series, *Collected Philosophical and Theological Papers* –Ed.].

[6] That is why Mohanty modifies the example to "abcaderaf" (*Edmund Husserl's Theory of Meaning*, 36).

[7] In *Marges de la philosophie* (Paris: Minuit, 1972), 365–93; *Margins of Philosophy,* trans. Alan Bass (Chicago: University of Chicago Press, 1982), 307–30.

[8] See the entry "abracadabra" in the *Oxford English Dictionary.*

[9] I do not mean that Derrida criticizes only the contingent and not the necessary, but that he shows the contingency of this very distinction, that it is a produced effect; "contingency" is thus another case of Derridean paleonymy for me.

[10] In discussions from the floor Derrida resisted this suggestion only to the extent that it implied optimism, utopianism, some kind of metaphysics of the future in which all will be free. I do not mean anything of the sort by liberation, but only a kind of local strategy to be put into place wherever possible.

[11] Martin Heidegger, *Unterwegs zur Sprache* (Pfullingen: Neske, 1965), 220; *On the Way to Language,* trans. P. Hertz (New York: Harper & Row, 1971), 140. Heidegger also emphasizes that it is the *Wort* which holds and sustains *(hält)* the thing in Being [113] (appearance); the *Wort* gives things their *Unterhaltung:* sustenance, maintenance; see *Unterwegs*, 176–77, 187–88; *On the Way*, 73, 82. Thus the *Wort* in Heidegger plays the role of "tenancy'" isolated by Husserl – in accord with the Derridean demand for a role for signs to play.

[12] *Gesamtausgabe,* vol. 5, *Holzwege* (Frankfurt am Main: Klostermann, 1977), 58-66; "The Origin of the Work of Art," in *Poetry, Language, Thought,* trans. A. Hofstadter (New York: Harper 8c Row, 1971), 71–78.

[13] There is something of this same magic of productivity in this passage from Merleau-Ponty: "It [language] appears as mere sign only once it has provided itself with a meaning, and the coming to awareness, if it is to be complete, must rediscover the expressive unity in which both signs and meaning appear in the first place. When a child cannot speak, or cannot yet speak the adult's language, the linguistic ritual which unfolds around him has no hold on him, he is near us in the same way as is a spectator with a poor seat at the theatre; he sees clearly enough that we are laughing and gesticulating, he hears the nasal tune being played, but there is nothing at the end of those gestures or behind those words, nothing *happens* for him. A story is told in a children's book of the disappointment of a small boy who put on his grandmother's spectacles and took up her book in the expectation of being able himself to find in it the stories which she used to tell him. The tale ends with these words: 'Well, what a fraud! Where's the story? I see nothing but black and white.' For the child the 'story' and the thing expressed are not 'ideas' or 'meanings,' nor are speaking or reading 'intellectual operations.' The story is a world which there must be some way of magically calling up by putting on spectacles and leaning over a book. The power possessed by language of bringing the thing expressed into existence, of opening up to thought new ways, new dimensions and new landscapes, is, in the last analysis, as obscure for the adult as for the child. In every successful work, the significance carried into the reader's mind

exceeds language and thought as already constituted and is magically thrown into relief during the linguistic incantation, just as the story used to emerge from the grandmother's book" *(Phenomenology of Perception,* trans. Colin Smith [Atlantic Highlands: Humanities Press, 1962], 401).

[14] For a delimitation of the Husserlian notion of the "things themselves" from Derrida's point of view, see John Sallis, "The Identities of the Things Themselves," *Research in Phenomenology* 12 (1982): 113–26. See also the contribution of Rudolph Bernet in the same issue devoted to "Husserl and Contemporary' Thought."

[15] Since completing this paper, I have come upon a comparable reading of Derrida which I recommend: Joseph O'Leary. *Questioning Back: The Overcoming of Metaphysics in Christian Tradition* (Minneapolis: Winston, 1985), 36–48.

7

THE AGE OF REPETITION

[In *The Southern Journal of Philosophy* (1993) Vol. XXXII, Supplement, 171–77]

[171] A question of central importance to understanding Derrida's interpretation of Husserl is Husserl's "reduction" of "indication" in the *Logical Investigations*. This so-called reduction attempts to reach the sphere of pure soliloquy or monological interiority in which signs are useless. At that precise point, that point of the now-point, Husserl says, signs are not needed because the ego's own intentions are immediately manifest to itself, in an instant, at that very moment, *im selben Augenblick*. Derrida's well-known argument against Husserl's view is that such a moment of perfect self-presence is impossible because the presence of consciousness is never simple. Like everything else transpiring in time consciousness, self-presence is an effect of synthesis, of the compounding of *Erlebnis* with *Erlebnis*. Because it is not simple, Derrida concludes, signs are not useless.

This debate turns on the interpretation of Husserl's notion of "retention," in virtue of which the *Augenblick* is constituted by a *Blick-zürück*. The "moment" for Husserl is never an unextended atomic instant, like a mathematical point, but always rather a *Dauer,* a continuous duration, an extended, enduring flow in which whatever transpires "now" is never merely now but always also just-now (*soeben*) and just about to be now. The now is always a part of the *Erlebnisstrom* in which *Erlebnis* is continuously blended with *Erlebnis*, in an originary flow, a flux of originary impressions. With the flowing off of the primal or originary impression there is, in Husserl's view, no loss of originality. Far from being lost, the origin is precisely preserved – or "retained" – in the flow, joined immediately to the primary impression so as to widen, extend, or fill out the primal impression, thus constituting the fullness of the living present. Retention is not the past of originary experience, but the originary experience of the past, in the sense of the just lapsed. Its noematic correlate is a past lived-experience. Retention is the consciousness in which the past is given; it is a perception which is essentially different from a representation.[1]

Accordingly, and seemingly contrary to Derrida's interpretation, there is nothing about the fact that the living present [172] is compounded, or non-simple, that would undermine its originariness. Experience may be both complex and originary, an originary compound, a synthesis that preserves its originariness throughout, despite Derrida's contention that the non-simplicity of the living present threatens the whole of Husserl's argumentation.[2] Nor should there be anything surprising about a complex origin because we have already seen something like it before in Heidegger's notion of "equiprimordiality" (*Gleichursprünglichkeit*) in *Being and Time*. Heidegger points out that something might be both primordial and multiple, which is precisely the case with the multiple strewing (*Streuung*) of the constitutive items of being-in-the-world, viz., of projection, thrownness, and fallenness, each of which is equally originary, that is, "underivable" (*unableitbar*) from the other.[3] On this reading, the primal impression and retention, *jetzt* and *soeben,* belong together equiprimordially, viz., as nonidentical but equally originary items in the originary synthesis, analogously to the way thrownness and projection belong together in the Being of Dasein.

There is, however, a crucial disanalogy in this analogy – however useful it may first appear to be – that vitiates the essence of the analogy. Retention is not truly equiprimordial with the primal impression just because retention is precisely *derivable* from the primal impression. Retention is with good reason described by Husserl as a "modification" (*Husserliana X,* §11) of the primal impression, as a non-independent (*unabhängig*) moment that draws the totality of its content from the primal impression, i.e., which derives from it. The retention modifies the primal impression by prolonging, extending, or continuing the impression, allowing just this same impression to last as present even though it has just lapsed. Now one could conceive (but not imagine) that the internal time-flow would cease, that we would find ourselves in a *nunc stans,* which would be a primal impression without retention, but one can neither imagine nor conceive a retention without primal impression, i.e., a retention that would not be the retention of a prior impression. This disanalogy is important from a Derridean point of view. The notion that retention is a "modification" goes to the heart of the place assigned to "repetition" in Derrida's analysis, or better, to the age of repetition, for repetition in Derrida's view is always older than presence.

For Derrida, the work of constitution is a work of "spacing" between the now-phases, a work of imprint and trace, of a primal impression that retains the trace of just-now, so that the now is not an isolated now but carries with it a comet's tail of impressions that are just-now, just-just-now, etc. The now is necessarily, structurally marked or traced by the just-now. The [173] living present is a comet's tail, a trail of impressions, a now traced by a just-now, by a trace, an after-trace, a trail of traces, that fill the now in, that provide it with magnitude, continuity, and extension. By the same token, and on its other side, the now is marked by a certain anticipatory tracing, an advance sketch, a tracing out beforehand, a pre-tracing (*eine Vor-zeichnung*), that fills the now in on its other side, its anticipatory or protentional side. This produces the effect not of a tail or trail, but rather, one might imagine, of a certain parting of the waters ahead before an advancing ship, or of doors opening in advance of one's arrival.

In Derridean terms, the living present then is a composite (*eine Verbindung*), a compound effect, of primal imprint, after-trace, and fore-trace, a certain play or spacing of traces. Lived experience has continuous magnitude, endurance or perdurance (*Dauer*), a flowing character, rather than an interrupted, atomic, or staccato quality. Imagine not a drawing with distinct lines and definite borders around objects, but rather a sketching that produces a total Gestalt effect by shadings, where the darkest shading corresponds to the primal impression and the lighter shading to the protentional and retentional traces. Now imagine the drawing changing before our eyes, so that darker passes over into lighter as it is displaced by new impressions, new prints. The living present is an impressional continuum, a continuity of imprints, a print, a trace, or play of traces. That is why Derrida says that the living present is the effect of *différance,* that is, of differential spacing and tracing. He says this, I think, not merely, not primarily, not at all, as *a critique* of phenomenology, as a polemical attempt to defeat its claims, but as a way to read and understand phenomenology. (A good deconstruction is just a very good reading, a reading that underlines something that might otherwise be lost or repressed by the dominant or received reading.)

Derrida's account turns on whether retention is rightly described as "repetition," on whether repetition is "older" than presence. In one sense, retention is clearly not repetition. Retention is not reproduction in the Husserlian sense; it does not make something present *again*. Retention does not re-produce or re-peat or re-stage its object, because its object has never left the scene, never dropped from view. The presence of the object has never subsided but has been precisely sustained or retained, allowed to endure or perdure without interruption. As there is neither rupture nor interruption, but the smoothness of a continuous flow, there is no need to restore or reproduce or repeat. That much is clear and it belongs, I would say, to the elemental insights of Husserl's phenomenology.

But in another sense, in the sense that interests Derrida, retention is repetition, for the work of holding-back (*re-tenere*), [174] of not letting the primal impression lapse, is a work of "asking back" (*re-petere*). Retention is no less a work of asking back (*zurück*) than of looking back (*blick zurück*). The *re-* in retention and repetition refers to the "back" (*zurück*). The "back" does not mean "again" (*wieder*) – which is, I think, precisely what is misleading about the word and what arouses such fierce resistance among orthodox Hussserlians. Repetition-as-*différance* does not mean presence, followed by absence, followed by a renewed presence, which is precisely the work of secondary memory (*Wiederinnerung*), whose distinction from retention is elemental for the Husserlian. Rather, retention as the sustaining of presence is the productively repetitive maintaining – in the synthetic unity of the *maintenant* – of the primal impression. What interests Derrida, and everything in Derrida's view turns on this, is the necessary "supplement" supplied by retention, the "additional" work that must be supplied or added on, without which the primal impression would not "fade" but be obliterated *without a trace*.

Repetition in the Derridean sense is not reproduction in the Husserlian sense but rather a way of identifying and underlining the supplemental operation by means of which the primal now is prolonged, extended, or continued beyond the *absolutely* primal now-point so as to include the just-now in the living present. Repetition seeks life, asks for more life (*re-petere*), for the primal impression, which begins to die off in the same moment in which it occurs. Repetition seeks and gives more life to the fading note whose dying off belongs to the very structure of the melody. For the retentional modification goes hand in hand, Husserl says, with a "weakening" (*Schwachung*) of the primal impression (*Hua* X, 31). This preservation of the fast fading tone, this lending strength to a weakening tone, this dying or fading away, this death, belongs to the life of the living present. The living present (*lebendige Gegenwart*) is thus an *Urgegenwart* that requires a supplemental life, an enlivening supplement, a supplement which, if it cannot be called *Vergegenwärtigung* in the Husserlian sense, is nonetheless a modification of the *Urgegenwart*. This modification is an alteration – from the now to the just-now – and this alterity is what Derrida wants to capture under the title of "repetition." It is an alteration, not of noematic content, but of its mode of givenness. Only the now-point, the *Urimpression* or *Urgegenwart,* is absolutely unmodified, while the living present is a synthesis, which means, in Derridean terms, a tissue of difference, a weaving and interweaving of prints, a tracing. Derrida does not deny the "living present"; he seeks to understand its constitution. He does not regard it as a "specious present," a fictional effect, in the empiricist sense of William James, but a living present. He is interested, however, in the way that the living present is the work of a supplement, a [175] work in which a little something extra has been supplied.

That is why, even in the terms of a strict Husserlian orthodoxy, retention is connected with reproduction – even though the two are distinguished – inasmuch as retention is the basis of reproduction and the legitimating ground of reflection. For no subsequent act of reflection, in which an *Erlebnis* is directed at the very stream to which it itself belongs, would be legitimate, whether absolutely or relatively, would even be possible, without retention. It is only in virtue of the unbreakable line between retention and reproduction that reflection and secondary memory are possible, that whatever is imprinted *originaliter* is not lost forever in the flow of the *Erlebnisstrom*. It is only in virtue of retention that a primal impression is able to be retrieved, returned later, to the stage of consciousness. Re-taining and re-producing belong to the same generic operation of saving the appearances from loss, of supplying a saving supplement, which is what repetition means for Derrida. That is why signs are not useless for Derrida, for the function of the sign is to supply a supplement wherever plenitude fails, wherever primal presence, the *Urgegenwart,* is in need of help.

Now, one might argue that Derrida's analysis holds for external perception, for the perception of the temporal object, but that it does not hold for consciousness of internal time, which is perception in a "completely different sense."[4] In internal time consciousness, one *Erlebnis* is given to another with such originariness and immediacy as to have the force of a perception, not a non-perception. The retained primal impression has the immediacy and immanence of a sensation, not the contingency and transcendence of an object. Accordingly, primal impression is joined with the retained impression as perception with perception, and not, as Derrida would have it, as perception with non-perception.

But I do not believe it is possible to insulate interiority from exteriority in this way and to attribute an immediacy to inner time consciousness that one denies of transcendent temporal objects. At least, it is not possible in such a way as to make interior monologue or soliloquy possible, and this because of the relatively high level or complexity of the stratum of expression. For nowhere is the work of supplementation – and repetition – more required, nowhere is the sign more unavoidable, than in the work of constituting expressive meanings, where the unities in question are complex noetico-noematic formations. It may be that there is an elemental, immediate retention or supplementation at work in prelinguistic perception, which seems a plausible, if speculative, way to interpret the perceptual life of infants and animals, but

101

that does nothing to explain the possibility of soliloquy. The higher order work of constituting meaningful [176] expressions requires a higher order, more powerful supplement, a supplementation by signs that are able to operate in the absence of the signified.

Soliloquy or interior monologue for Derrida – and I think Derrida is right about this and Husserl is wrong – is a certain miniaturization, privatization, or reduction to the sphere of the private, of the essentially prior intersubjective operation of communication and indication. Soliloquy is a kind of mentally whispered indication; it is a parasitic function of intersubjective linguistic systems because the unities of meaning in which inner consciousness trades have already been carved out by the preconstituted system of differences – by the systems of repetition – in which signs acquire values. If there is a certain immediacy of contact between the retaining act and the retained now, such contact is, in the case of soliloquy, a contact transacted in the sphere of constituted meanings, for which signs are not useless. It is a contact in which I signify meaning to myself but in just such a way as to depend essentially on the prior constitution of meaning that the linguistic system makes possible in the first place. I signify to *myself* with a certain immediacy – I do not need to dial a telephone, speak loudly enough, or otherwise get someone else's attention – but *what* I signify is a highly mediated, constituted, synthetic unity of meaning, for which signs, far from being useless, are completely essential. The interior ego draws upon the resources of the pregiven linguistic system into which it enters, upon the treasure of meanings constituted prior to the privacy of individual consciousness, upon systems of repetition that are older than the ego, in virtue of which it is able both to discover and invent what it thinks.

I might add, by way of a conclusion to these remarks, that the sense that "repetition" has in Derrida's interpretation of Husserl bears a fruitful comparison with Kierkegaard's use of this word.[5] For Kierkegaard, repetition has the sense of "repeating forward," that is, of producing something by the repetition, of producing what is repeated. On the Derridean/Husserlian scheme, presence is the effect of "representation in the widest" sense, i.e., the effect of the trace in the sense we have explained. Repetition produces (constitutes) what it repeats, produces presence, rather the way Constantius says that the self is produced by repetition forward. For unity is always the effect of repetition, not conversely, whether one forges ahead in the stream of life, thus forging the unity of a self, or forges ahead in the stream of consciousness, thus forging a unity of meaning. Repetition produces what it repeats, producing by reproducing, according to the principle that unity is always the effect of

102

synthesis, that unity is preceded and made possible by difference, or that repetition is older than presence.

Notes

[1] [177] Didier Franck, "The Extension of the Concept of 'Non-Presence' in Derrida's *Speech and Phenomena*," (Paper delivered at the 12th Annual Spindel Philosophy Conference, Memphis, Tenn., 1 October 1993).

[2] Jacques Derrida, *Speech and Phenomena*, trans. David Allison (Evanston: Northwestern University Press, 1973), 61.

[3] Martin Heidegger, *Being and Time,* trans. John Macquarrie and Edward Robinson (New York: Harper & Row, 1962), 170.

[4] Franck, "The Extension of the Concept of Non-Presence' in Derrida's *Speech and Phenomena".*

[5] For a fuller comparison, see John D. Caputo, *Radical Hermeneutics* (Bloomington: Indiana University Press, 1987), Chapter 2.

HEIDEGGER

8

MODERNITY AND THE END OF PHILOSOPHY IN *BEING AND TIME*

[In *Hermeneutic Phenomenology: Lectures and Essays*, ed. Joseph Kockelmans (Washington, D.C.: Center for Advanced Research in Phenomenology / University Press of America, 1988), 81-90]

[81] Heidegger always had a penchant for "ends," for adopting the standpoint of the end of the history of ontology, or the end of philosophy. When he wrote a history, he began at the end. This tendency has acquired a particular importance today because of the way the "end of philosophy" has caught on in Paris where it has spread out to include the end of just about everything else too (man, history, etc.) I think that a lot of the clout which the later Heidegger has, a lot of the leverage he gets into what he says, arises from the way he manages to speak from "out of the experience" (*aus der Erfahrung*) of the end-state (*eschaton*) into which the Western, Greco-European world has been driven, that extremity into which we have been pushed by the age of the *Gestell*. The power of his thought is in no small measure due to his ability to make the present into an end, the final unfolding of the implications of metaphysical thinking.

I want to argue two points in connection with this eschatologism. (1) I want to demonstrate that the thought of the end is not an innovation of the later work, but rather is already in place in *Being and Time*. I will show that in *Being and Time* it does not issue in eschatological and anti-modernist warnings about the illusion of technique. On the contrary, it champions the advances made in modernity which have made it possible now, more than ever before, to catch sight of the temporal meaning of Being. Thus if the talk about the end of philosophy in the later writings is post-modern talk, in *Being and Time* it is of an entirely modernist sort. And if Heidegger's turnabout on modernity belongs to the turning (*Kehre*) in his thought, his affection for the standpoint of the end (*Ende*) remains one of his constants.

(2) But then I want to argue that Heidegger's penchant for giving the "end" historical instantiation – whether that is conceived as the advances made by the

transcendental turn or the trouble we are in because of the fury of the *Gestell* — is a distortion of his [82] insights. The historical values which Heidegger gives to the "end-point," I will hold, represent a certain "mythological" turn in his thought. I will claim that "end" ought to be conceived as "delimitation" and that it ought to have a strictly "structural" character, not an historical one. What Heidegger means by the "meaning" (or later "truth") of Being cannot have historical instantiation, because it is a theory about the history of metaphysics, not a theory which could ever appear within it. Heidegger offers an account of how one "meaning" of Being after another comes about. He does not propose the latest or best "meaning of Being." I will confine myself here to *Being and Time*, but I have argued elsewhere that the same point can be made about the later Heidegger as well.[1]

In §6 of *Being and Time* Heidegger proposes the task of "the destruction of the history of ontology." The history of ontology is to be deconstructed down to its roots, by showing that, regardless of the sort of things it says about Being overtly, it is covertly committed to a temporal account of Being. Dasein has grown up in a tradition to which it has fallen prey so that the "primordial sources" of that tradition have been blocked off. Thus this tradition must be destroyed "down to" (*auf*: SZ, 22/BT, 44)[2] its original experiences. The destruction is to be carried out backwards, beginning with Kant, and that is because it was Heidegger's constant view throughout the Marburg years that it is only lately, in modern times, that the clue to the "meaning" of Being gets ferreted out.[3] The existential analytic shows that the meaning of Being is to be [83] determined in terms of time, that the temporality (*Zeitlichkeit*) of Dasein provides the clue to the temporality (*Temporalität*) of Being. The clearest case where that clue was followed up, however imperfectly, is Kant's doctrine of the imagination. But Kant's discovery operated unquestioningly within the traditional sense of Being (as what is present) and time (as the succession of now's). The work of Kant is the best effort yet, the closest metaphysics has yet come, to putting its finger on the temporal meaning of Being. But Kant was waylaid by the weight of the tradition, by the traditional ways of conceiving Being and time.

The reference to "primordial sources" ought not to mislead us into thinking that there is already in *Being and Time*, as there would be in the later writings, a primal epoch with a privileged experience of Being which has subsequently been covered over by a history of ever deepening oblivion. On the contrary, it is only recently that we have begun to awaken to the temporal sense of Being and hence have been in a position to see what is really going on in the tradition. Heidegger wants to read the history of ontology backwards because he takes his bearings from the modern problematic, from the transcendental determination of time, which is but a heartbeat away from the determination of Being in terms of time. The "historical destruction" is meant to loosen the grip which the tradition exerts upon us and which tends to block off a discovery which is breaking through in modernity. Heidegger wants to agitate and solicit that tradition which kept Kant "from working out the phenomenon of a 'transcendental determination of time' in its own structure and function" (SZ, 24/BT, 45). In this "going back which destroys" (*destruierendes Rückgang*) into the history of ontology, the aim is to loosen the grip of ancient ideas on modern ones. Thus the first version of "destruction" or "deconstruction," far from being post-modern, is formulated precisely from the standpoint of the advantages of modernity.

Accordingly, Heidegger promises to go back from Kant to Descartes and to show how Descartes conceives the *cogito* in the most traditional manner, indeed in medieval terms, as *substantia* and *ens creatum* or *ens finitum*. It is these "fateful prejudices" which are tying the hands of later generations (*die Folgezeit*: SZ, [84] 25/BT, 46). Nor does Heidegger think, at this point, that medieval metaphysics distorts Greek philosophy. On the contrary, the categories of Greek thought are "tailor made" (GA 24, 16B/BT, 118) for the Christian idea of creation. The two belong together in a metaphysics of making (*Herstellen*), of form and matter, essence and existence, in which beings are conceived as products made in accord with ideal designs, as forms put into matter or made to exist outside the divine cause (*existentia* means *sistere extra causas*).

But it is only when we get back to the Greeks that we get to the bottom of the traditional prejudices. Here is where the trouble starts. For it is with the Greeks that the decision is made for the first time – they are the beginning of the tradition – to take Being in terms of world-time, i.e., of both world and time. The Greek decision harbors a two-fold prejudice: a cosmological prejudice and a presential prejudice. And this will explain why the subsequent tradition has, until recently (the advent of the transcendental turn), both (1) privileged the world over Dasein in a way which remains blind to the disclosive work of Dasein, and (2) privileged the time of things, i.e., of the presence of what is present, the presence of the present-at-hand, *ousia*. The result of this Greek decision is to block our access to time altogether. For (1) genuine time is primordially a phenomenon of Dasein itself, and things are in time because they are temporalized by Dasein, that is, given temporal determination by Dasein's own temporalizing understanding. And secondly (2), insofar as things are taken to be "present," we tend to lose sight of their temporal qualities altogether and to treat them as stable, motionless, and timeless. The genuine concept of time requires the absential moment of futurity and having-been which is preeminently characteristic of the temporality of Dasein.

Thus the Greeks made a fateful decision which we have all been living with, and suffering from, ever since. And it is only in modernity that we have begun to recover from it, for Kant has turned our attention (1) back to the subject instead of naively taking the world for granted, and (2) back to the temporality of the subject, although unhappily he determined both the subject and time in the traditional way. The work of this destroying regress is carried out only when, going back to the Greeks, it puts its finger on this decisive move and catches the Greeks at that very point where they made this fateful slip. In so doing we can free up the work of those [85] who come lately, *wir Spätlinger* (GA 5, 326/EGT, 17),[4] who up to now had been working in the blind about time and the subject.

For this, Heidegger says, the word *ousia* can function at least as a clue. *Ousia* means the stable presence of things which are truly and enduringly present, not merely passing away. But *ousia* functions by means of a concealed time-clue: the present. Presence (*Anwesenheit*) is a function of the present (*Gegenwart*). The stable presence and substantiality of things (*ousia, substantia*) is a function of the presential "now" which belongs to Dasein's temporalizing. The presence of things is conceived on the basis of a concealed temporal function. The temporality of Dasein – its experience of what is now – operates behind the back of the ancient ontology.

Hence the Greeks have an ambiguous status in this going back which destroys: as the beginning of all the trouble they are important to its solution. It is with them that the attempt to get to the bottom of the confusion stops – for they are where it starts. *The destroying regress then is an exercise in trouble-shooting.* It wants to know why Kant's attempt at a "transcendental determination of time" was waylaid, and it locates the trouble, first in Descartes, then in Plato and Aristotle. It is in Plato and Aristotle that we see where the move was first made to which everybody else just consented without question. This makes Plato and Aristotle very important but in an ambiguous way. Something very important happened in and with them: they raised the question of Being for the first time. They let Being break out in all its wonder,[5] and they did so in terms of time. But they themselves missed the temporal clues which were functioning behind their back. Hence they got as far as the question of Being, but not as far as the *temporal meaning* of Being – which can only be flushed out in a hermeneutical reflection on ontological theory-building. The Greeks illustrate quite well – for us moderns – the crucial role that temporal clues play in [86] the conception of Being, even though such clues remain implicit. The Greeks operated within a temporal conception of Being but, because they failed to see the clues they were using, they in fact defended a view of Being as timeless presence:

> Yet the Greeks managed to interpret Being in this way [in terms of time] without any explicit knowledge of the clues which function here, without any acquaintance with the fundamental ontological function of time or even any understanding of it, and without any insight into the reason why this function is possible. On the contrary, they take time itself as one entity among other entities and try to grasp it in the structure of its Being, though that way of understanding Being which they have taken as their horizon is one which is itself naively and inexplicitly oriented towards time. (SZ, 26/BT, 48)

The ambiguity of the Greeks is to stand at the head of our tradition, to be its founding act, and to determine Being and time in a way which is positively fateful for the rest of us. But that means that if we go back to them we can find out not only how the whole tradition managed to get off the ground in the first place but also what went wrong with the tradition subsequently, for what went wrong with the tradition first went wrong with them. Their importance lies in being both the source of the tradition and the source of the trouble – and it is for that reason that they are so instructive about the meaning of Being. They wrestled with the things themselves in a struggle among the giants (*gigantomachia per tes ousias*: SZ, 2/BT, 21) which brought "Being" out of misty obscurity and into the light of thematic clarity, and they even thought Being in terms of time, *but* they did not realize the temporal clues they were using. The determination of Being in terms of time came about *in* them, but behind their backs, unwittingly, so that what they explicitly said suppressed the implicit time-clues they deployed. While they thematized Being, they did not thematize the temporal clues *in terms of which* (*woraufhin*) they thematized Being. They got to Being, but not to the *meaning* of Being.

Accordingly, it is only we modern ones, we late-comers, who can see what is going on in the history of ontology, which is why our [87] destruction goes backwards, starting from the standpoint of Kant's discovery of the temporality of the subject, looking back into what blocked Kant's success. We read from the privilege of modernity's insight into the temporality of the subject which is but one step removed from an insight into Being's "meaning."

(2) However, the privilege which modernity enjoys in *Being and Time* requires reexamination. For there can be no moment in the history of ontology where what Heidegger means by the "meaning" of Being could ever have historical

instantiation. Plato and Aristotle produced an interpretation of Being (*Seinsauslegung*) which was not alert to the temporal clues (*fungierende Leitfaden*) which were functioning in it. They did not see that time performs a fundamental-ontological function, and that time is not just a being, or sphere of beings (temporal being vs. eternal being). It is all this talk of temporal "clues" "implicitly functioning" in "explicit" notions of Being which is important for my thesis. For such talk implies a movement of "delimitation" which gets beyond this or that idea of Being to the functioning ingredients in the idea, i.e., to the structural item or items which produce the particular historical sense of Being.

In other words, when Heidegger talks about the "meaning of Being" in *Being and Time* he intends this in a "functional" sense, not in an historical sense. It is not his purpose to find the one true theory of Being which has been brought forth in the history of Being, or to add it himself if it is missing but rather to put his finger on what is at work in any given theory of Being. He wants to show how ideas of Being are *constructed* – he wants to isolate their structural make-up but not to come up with another idea of Being himself. He does not want to get into the competition about Being which constitutes the history of ontology but to de-construct that history just in order to show how it was put together in the first place. One has to dismantle the sedimented, historically accumulated notions of Being, which now take on an air of authority and self-evidence, just in order to see where they were taking their clues – which Heidegger locates in time-functions.

And this means that Heidegger has an unusual idea of meaning, i.e., a functional one, and not one of a more ordinary sort – which is precisely what a close reading of *Being and Time* shows. For when Heidegger discusses "meaning" he does so in terms of a distinction between the "Being" of a thing and its [88] "meaning." This is a distinction between what he calls the "primary projection" of a thing in its Being, and that "upon which" (*Woraufhin*) the projection is carried out, which is the hidden "function" which organizes the Being-structure (*Seinsverfassung*). He writes:

> What does "meaning" signify? ...meaning is that wherein the understandability (*Verstehbarkeit*) of something maintains itself (*hält sich*) – even that of something which does not come into view explicitly and thematically. "Meaning" signifies the "upon which" (*Woraufhin*) of a primary projection in terms of which something can be conceived in its possibility as that which it is....

> To lay bare the "upon which" of a projection, amounts to
> disclosing that which makes possible what has been projected....
> Taken strictly, "meaning" signifies the "upon which" of the
> primary projection of the understanding of Being.... All ontical
> experience of entities...is based upon projections of the Being
> of the corresponding entities – projections which in every case
> are more or less transparent. But in these projections there lies
> hidden the "upon which" of the projection, and on this, as it
> were, the understanding of Being nourishes itself (*nährt*). (SZ,
> 323–24/BT, 370–71)

Heidegger thus distinguishes the more or less overt projections of Being –
entities are projected here, in science, in terms of *Vorhandensein*, and there, in
everydayness, in terms of *Zuhandensein* – from the hidden function which is at
work in these projections, "sustaining" and "nourishing," that is, organizing
them. This hidden function is the *Woraufhin*, the implicit clue which explicit
accounts of Being are always following without paying them any heed.

But such a theory of meaning puts a distance between *Being and Time* and
any theory of Being which actually makes an appearance in the history of
ontology, any particular historical account of Being. It puts Heidegger in the
position of standing back from the fray in order to isolate the functional
element which [89] organizes, sustains, and nourishes any such projection of
Being as does get put forward in the course of that history. The "history of
ontology" discussed in *Being and Time* operates on the primary level – of the
primary projections of Being. But *Being and Time* itself operates on the
fundamental-ontological level of the destruction of these projections; it aims at
putting its finger on the implicit clues which are being followed in the history
of ontology. That is, *Being and Time* operates on a structural level, ferreting out
the hidden functions in the actual historical formations.

Perhaps one reason why Division III, First Half ("Time and Being") was
never written was that it has no work to do apart from the history of ontology
– apart from feeling around for the temporal clues at work in the historical
projections of Being which actually have been put forth from Plato to the
present. *Being and Time* has no business getting into the history of ontology or
privileging some moment within the history of ontology. It is rather a theory of
the history of ontology. To find the "meaning" of Being is to locate the function
which is performed, or the clue which is followed, every time some projection
of Being or another appears on the scene. The business of finding a "meaning"
is an entirely functional one. This meaning never has and never can assume
historical form in some theory of Being. The quest for the meaning of Being is

a deconstructive one which dismantles historical theories in order to find out what makes them work. So the answer to Brentano's question about the manifold sense of Being is that there are only the manifold senses of Being – unless you want to add to this the hermeneutic account of the functions by which they are constructed. But that is not one of the historical senses that Being has been given in the history of ontology.

The same point can be made about the later writings. To think Being as *Ereignis* is think that which grants the history of Being, that which sends the various epochal shapes and destinies of Being as presence. It is not to assimilate *Ereignis* into Being, or the history of Being, and to make it the latest and best word about Being (SD, 22-23/TB, 21-22). The thought of the epochal dispensations cannot take on epochal form itself, cannot be clad in historical costume or have an historical form of life. Despite an intractable tendency to tell a story about the history of Being, what Heidegger has in fact accomplished is to "delimit" that history, to think its structural limits. The real power of Heidegger's thought [90] can be unfolded only when if it is first released from its mythological, story-telling tendencies.

What Heidegger has discovered is not a story which began in the early Greeks and culminated in modernity, but an essential delimitation of metaphysical thinking which is always in place and which does not allow the privileging of any epoch, whether at the beginning (the later Heidegger) or the end (the early Heidegger). The end of philosophy is the delimitation of metaphysical thinking which is always already at work and which plays no historical favorites. What he thinks is the sheer unfolding of *a-letheia*, the happening of the epochs as constrictions of the open expanse. What he thinks can never take the form of an epochal structure in that history but must always be understood as the very happening of that history, its sheer historicizing, in a play which plays without why.

But I said at the beginning that the power of Heidegger's thought has been in no small measure due just to his story-telling, to the sense of urgency that he summons up by his ability to make the present into a crisis and an end-state. We must never underestimate the power of a good story, the grip that a powerful tale can exert upon us, to make a point. Demythologizing must inevitably be followed up by remythologizing. Perhaps the genuinely "poetic" character of Heidegger's thought is narratival, its ability to construct powerful narratives which make a telling point about the "delimitation" of metaphysics. Like Foucault, Heidegger tends to write a history of the present which tells us how we have gotten into the current crisis, which shows us how what is happening now, all around us, is the unfolding of something which has been all along. The epical/epochal character of thinking gets its leverage from its ability to carry out this delimitation by showing that we are now, in the present, also at the "end."

Notes

[1] See my "Demythologizing Heidegger: Aletheia and the History of Being," *Review of Metaphysics*, 41 (March 1988): 519–46.

[2] I use the following abbreviations to the works of Heidegger:

BP: *The Basic Problems of Phenomenology*, trans. A. Hofstadter (Bloomington: Indiana University Press, 1982).

BT: *Being and Time*, trans. E. Robinson & J. Macquarrie (New York: Harper & Row, 1962).

EGT: *Early Greek Thinking*, trans. D. Krell (New York: Harper & Row, 1975).

GA 5: *Gesamtausgabe*, B. 5, *Holzwege* (Frankfurt: Klostermann, 1971).

GA 24: *Gesamtausgabe*, B. 24, *Die Grundprobleme der Phänomenologie* (Frankfurt: Klostermann, 1975).

SD: *Zur Sache des Denkens* (Tübingen: Niemeyer, 1969).

SZ: *Sein und Zeit*, 10. Aufl (Tübingen: Niemeyer, 1971).

TB: *On Time and Being*, trans. J. Stambaugh (New York: Harper & Row, 1972).

[3] Even as a young student, Heidegger wanted to "go back" to scholasticism from the standpoint of "modern logic." See my *Heidegger and Aquinas: An Essay on Overcoming Metaphysics* (New York: Fordham University Press, 1982), Ch. 1.

[4] In "The Anaximander Fragment" this expression signifies the decline of modernity while, in the Marburg period, late-comers have the advantage.

[5] In *Gesamtausgabe*, B. 45, *Grundfragen der Philosophie* (Frankfurt: Klostermann, 1984), 30-39, Heidegger gives an excellent account of the greatness of the Greeks whose destiny it was to experience the upsurge of the being into appearance and whose fundamental mood (*Stimmung*) was wonder (*thaumazein*) at the emergence of the being – whereas the wonder for us today is that we are not thinking. I examine this more carefully in "Demythologizing Heidegger" (n. 1).

9

HEIDEGGER AND AQUINAS: DECONSTRUCTING THE RAHNERIAN BRIDGE

[In "Heidegger and Aquinas: Deconstructing the Rahnerian Bridge," *Philosophy and Theology* (1991), Disk Supplement]

In a recent issue of *Philosophy Today*, Prof. Robert Hurd offered a sensitive and intelligent critique of my *Heidegger and Aquinas: An Essay on Overcoming Metaphysics* for which I am quite grateful.[1] Hurd's treatment is singularly free of the reactionary and partisan polemics which unfortunately plague the Heidegger-Aquinas debate. Indeed his study is, just as it claims to be, a partner in the dialogue of Heidegger and Aquinas which my book intends to promote, not to close off by way of pronouncing the final word. Hurd is not concerned with defending a party line but with thinking through the matter of thought, the question of Being which, he and I agree, is the only point of undertaking a confrontation of Heidegger and Aquinas. There are other, and important, points of agreement between us which I hope to bring out in my response to his perceptive reading of my book, but none so important as our common commitment to the *Sache des Denkens*, to a reading of texts which aims at retrieval and not merely at exegesis, and our common aversion to barren polemics.

The matter to be thought, Prof. Hurd and I agree, is the question of metaphysics, more precisely, the question of whether metaphysics is, as Heidegger says, something to be overcome (whence the subtitle of my study). For Heidegger, "metaphysics" signifies what he calls, somewhat misleadingly and in shorthand, the "oblivion of Being." Clearly, everything in this debate turns on what one means by metaphysics and just what overcoming this oblivion would look like. Hence I begin these remarks with a characterization of what metaphysics means for Heidegger, and the reasons he has for speaking of metaphysics as an oblivion. Then I will take up Hurd's insightful account of another – Rahnerian and transcendental – reading of St. Thomas in order to dispute his claim that it is not necessary to "overcome" metaphysics in the Heideggerian manner, but rather to reconstitute it in the transcendental mode in order to meet Heidegger's critique of metaphysics. As Prof. Hurd puts it,

"Rahner's transcendental analysis…reaches into the same dimension of the Being-process that Heidegger's *Seinsdenken* does" (120).

On the contrary, I want to show, transcendental Thomism is an unexceptional, and in some respects a salient, example of the oblivion of which Heidegger speaks, although it is not an example which I examined in *Heidegger and Aquinas*, as Prof. Hurd rightly protests. I want, then, unhappily, to dismantle Hurd's "Rahnerian Bridge" between Heidegger and Aquinas, not with the deconstructive delight of a demolition squad, but precisely in the service of preserving the matter to be thought. It is not, I maintain, by any reworking of Thomistic metaphysics, whether in an existential or transcendental mode, that one finds the point of contact between Heidegger and Aquinas, but only by locating that point in St. Thomas's work where the metaphysical itself is surpassed, a point which I myself situate in what I would call the mystical element in St. Thomas's work. Hurd is right to object that I gave a privileged hearing to the existential reading of St. Thomas – which stresses the primacy of *esse* – but I want to show now, thanks to his study, that transcendental metaphysics – which gives renewed emphasis to the unity of *esse* and *intellectus* – fares no better. In the light of Heidegger's critique, metaphysics, whether transcendental or existential, is something to be overcome.

Heidegger's Critique of Metaphysics

"Metaphysics" for Heidegger is constituted by what I might call the "will-to-ground," the will to supply reason and ground, explanation and foundation, for the realm of beings.[2] In metaphysics, beings are taken as lacking ground, and Being is taken as their founding basis and primal source. Whence the family of terms which signify the metaphysical archeological project of returning beings to their primal ground: *Grund, principium, ratio, causa, logos, archē*.

Metaphysics seeks to give beings a stable ground, to make them secure, to firm up their foundations. It thinks in terms of ground and grounded, foundational and founded. In keeping with its name, meta-physics treats the world in terms of a binary opposition between entities (*ta onta, ta physika*) and their transcendent ground (*meta-*). Thus Plato sought to secure shadowy appearances on the firm foundation of the true *eidos*; Aristotle sought to ground changing and mobile being on the ground of true *ousia*. The medieval philosophers demonstrated the foundation of the *ens creatum* on the creator; and modernity tried to show the grounding of all "objects" on the transcendental subject, on the thinking subject as *fundamentum inconcussum*. Finally, and most tellingly of all, Nietzsche undertook to say that every entity is a function of the will which posits it, and with this move, Heidegger thinks, metaphysics shows its hand. In Nietzsche a metaphysics is put forward which confesses openly what metaphysics is: the will to power, the will to know, the will to found and ground.

Ever since its beginnings in Parmenides metaphysics has had a certain oneiric quality, dreaming of the well-rounded circle, of Being without seam or gap, of the unity of things, of the convergence of thought with being. Metaphysics dreams of fullness and plenitude, perfection and intelligibility, of completed drives and fulfilled aspirations. It will allow no vacuum or void, no discontinuity or disruption. All differences are regulated by identity, all distinctions are graded into hierarchies; multiplicity is governed by order; discord by a deeper harmony; all movement is ruled by a dialectical principle of progress towards the *telos*. Beginnings are pointed towards ends. Every intention is fulfilled, every gap plugged up, every being has a cause and a reason. Everything is traversed by an archeology which points back to a beginning and first cause, and by a teleology which draws it forward to its end so that all things are knitted together in an archeo-teleological system. Shadows point to the Sun, time to eternity, change to the unchanging, ignorance to knowledge, death to life, dynamisms towards their fulfillment, objects to subjects and subjects to objects. Being is an onto-logical, theo-logical, teleo-logical, archeo-logical order, in which unity prevails over multiplicity, and intelligibility rules over unintelligibility.

A great deal of what Heidegger means by metaphysics is captured in Derrida's critique of what he (Derrida) – the expression is not Heidegger's – calls the "metaphysics of presence" and its "dream of presence."[3] It practices a hermeneutics of comfort, seeking to put things on secure grounds, to relieve what Derrida calls the trembling in things, to arrest the play. The Being/beings schema is a net of intelligibility which metaphysics throws out over things, a map by means of which it hopes to keep track of things and keep them on track, a web in which it hopes to catch them. It provides a ground for what needs grounding; it stabilizes the flux, arrests the trembling. Metaphysics wants to bring all things under the sway of the *principium, archē, prima causa*, to give all things a ground in keeping with Leibniz's *principium rationis*.

Now it is Heidegger's project to think metaphysics through, and in so doing to think through metaphysics. He asks what metaphysics is, what comes to pass in metaphysics and as metaphysics. And in thinking it as the will to ground, his own thinking ventures out into the realm beyond metaphysics and its grounds, beyond *principium* and *causa*. Hence it moves beyond Being-as-ground, beyond the ground of Being.

119

The real matter for thought for Heidegger was never Being, but rather what gives Being, what grants Being, the "truth" of Being, and even as early as *Being and Time*, the "meaning" of Being. His thought was always on the way "beyond Being," as he says in one of the Marburg lectures, to that which grants Being to metaphysics.[4] Hence his question about metaphysics was already a question going beyond metaphysics[5] to that which gives metaphysics to think, and to that which it is given to think.

It was never Heidegger's intention to issue one more view about Being, to take his place in the forum of metaphysical views about Being with a view which would surpass the others by its breadth and depth.[6] When he sought to determine the "meaning" of Being in *Being and Time*, that did not mean that he was about to set down the final determination of what Being means in the conventional sense of "meaning." It is rather an attempt to find the implicit rule which is at work in the history of metaphysics, which gives rise to the successive determinations – or "meanings" – of Being by which that history is constituted. It is not a question of coming up with a competing theory of Being, but of finding the phenomenological clue to the organization of the theories of meaning which populate the history of ontology. Once that clue is found we will have launched a deconstructive critique of the history of ontology which will show how that organizing center has been systematically repressed. And that clue of course is "time." *Being and Time* undertakes to offer a reading of the history of the theories of Being to show how at a critical point metaphysics has recourse to time in order to project beings in their Being.

In other words, and this is a point to which transcendental Thomism is systematically blind, there is already a deconstructive critique of the metaphysics of Being at work in *Being and Time*. There is already an attempt to go beyond Being as the ground of beings to the "upon which" which organizes and makes that ground possible. Time as the transcendental horizon – the meaning, the "upon which," of Being – is already the disruption of the primacy of Being as horizon. The transcendental horizon of which *Being and Time* speaks is not Being, but time. The history of metaphysics is a history of the various Being/beings, ground/grounded schemata or grids which metaphysics puts forth in order to draw an adequate ontical map. The history of metaphysics is the story of the changing projections, the horizonal shifts, which mark its course. It is not Heidegger's intention to get into this fray, to give the latest and best projection, but rather to locate the hitherto anonymous rule, or unruly rule, by which all such projective arrangements have been guided.

It is of the utmost importance to see that the "step back" out of metaphysics is a *ternary* and not a *binary* gesture. It moves not only from beings to Being –

that is the move of metaphysics, the act of transcendence which constitutes metaphysics as such, which erects a projective arrangement of beings in their Being – but it moves back still further to the "upon which" of the projection of beings in their Being (in *Being and Time*), to that which "gives" Being (in "Time and Being"). The ternary structure of Heidegger's thought became progressively clearer as his work developed. And that development largely consisted in an adequate way to characterize and to think this *ekstasis* beyond Being. He ceased referring to this third thing as the "meaning" of Being immediately after *Being and Time* appeared. By 1929, in *Vom Wesen des Grundes* (*The Essence of Reasons*) he was speaking of the "ontological difference" between Being and beings, in which what interested him was neither Being nor beings but the *difference* between them. This term, stripped of the qualification "ontological," made its way into the later works which spoke of the *Unter-Schied* or the *Aus-trag*, the differing, what brings about the difference, between Being and beings in a given age, and has attracted a good deal of attention because of Derrida. In the Thirties and Forties Heidegger began to distinguish the "truth" of the Being of beings. There were also some attempts to save the word "Being" by distinguishing beings from the metaphysical projection of their "Beingness" (*Seiendheit*), and at one point he tried even to cross out the word ~~Being~~ to name what he had in mind. Finally, he settled upon "*Ereignis*" to name the process by which metaphysics does it work of projecting beings in their Being, spreading them out against the horizon of Being.

I will show below how Rahner's metaphysics remains entirely confined to the program of seeking a particular horizonal arrangement of beings in their Being, entirely contained within a most traditional metaphysical and binary grid. I will argue that Rahner misuses the key notion of the "upon which" of the projection of Being and so lapses into a Being/beings schema of the most traditional sort, "oblivious" of the "meaning" of Being just as Heidegger could have predicted. In a parallel way, I will contend that Prof. Hurd mistreats Heidegger's critique of transcendental-horizonal thinking.

The question of Being, which is always a question beyond Being, the question of metaphysics, which is already underway to overcoming metaphysics, vows to do without the comforts of metaphysics. It must even renounce the language of metaphysics – an undertaking which is of course impossible in any thorough-going way[7] – in order to speak in a non-metaphysical way of an experience of things which is prior to the intervention of metaphysical conceptuality. It is much less impressive than transcendental metaphysics, with much less to say. It does not achieve transcendence, does not surpass beings for their Being, but tries to listen, patiently, quietly, to what Heidegger calls the splendor of the simple.[8]

This is an undertaking of the most extraordinary austerity, for it must do without all the instruments of metaphysics, all its conceptual resources, its whole arsenal of concepts and principles and proofs, the whole grip of ground and grounded. It ventures out into the desert where it is without aid or resource, without comfort or recourse, where there is no proving or disproving, where there is only the naked simplicity of thought. It is helpless, exposed to every objection of arbitrariness, without defense before the weaponry of metaphysics, before its searing cross-examinations. It ventures into the abyss where there is no ground or grounding, where the epochs of metaphysics simply unfold as they do, in a manner which Heidegger simply calls a play, the play which plays without why:

> The play is without "why." It plays for the while that it plays.
> There remains only play: the highest and the deepest.[9]

Being means ground, and beings mean what is grounded, and so the movement *beyond* Being is a movement beyond ground, beyond the diverse grounding/grounded schemata, into the abyss, the non-ground, the groundless play of these diverse schemata. All that remains for a thinking which is so austere as to have let go of every metaphysical comfort, every metaphysical accounting and grounding, is to admit itself into the groundlessness of the play of metaphysical schemata and accounts. The history of metaphysics is the play of such epochal configurations, the perhaps endless succession of proposals about the ground and the grounded, the ceaseless historical effort to arrest the play and to bring it to an accounting, to map it out on some new version of the old Being/beings grid. The thought of Being – that is, the thinking which is directed towards the Being-process, to the history of the diverse ways in which the Being/beings opposition unfolds – exposes itself to the groundlessness of this play, experiences the comfortlessness of a play which plays without ground, without why.

The "oblivion of Being" is a misleading expression. Metaphysics is not oblivious of Being, for that is all it ever talks about – in one way or another – whether as *eidos*, *ousia*, *esse* or subjectivity. Metaphysics is rather an oblivion of the third thing, of the *meaning* of Being, the *truth* of Being, the *difference* between Being and beings, the *Ereignis* which is at work, at play, in the unfolding of the history of metaphysics. Metaphysics is too busily involved in arranging one Being/beings schema or another to stop its work and meditatively to think what – in virtue of its very simplicity – keeps eluding it in the history of such schemata and scheming. Metaphysics is oblivious of what is happening *in* metaphysics and *as* metaphysics.

Now I want to turn to Prof. Hurd's commentary on *Heidegger and Aquinas*, and I want to argue that Rahner has proposed a metaphysics of the most traditional sort, which does not at all depart from the metaphysics which Heidegger wants to think through, and which does not begin to "reach into the Being-process that Heidegger's *Seinsdenken* does." Or rather, it does begin such an effort, for it is clearly touched by Heidegger,[10] but it remains an incomplete gesture which soon lapses back into the most traditional metaphysical determination of Being.

Deconstructing the Rahnerian Bridge

Prof. Hurd makes two central claims in his study: (1) "a transcendental hermeneutic of Aquinas is not only a genuine possibility but a necessity" (115); (2) Thomistic metaphysics, transcendentally retrieved by Rahner, attains to the thought of Being and overcomes the oblivion of Being criticized by Heidegger (124). I am prepared to accept, indeed I have always welcomed, the first claim; it is a point on which Prof. Hurd and I agree. But I deny the second claim.

(1) Transcendental Thomism, as Hurd presents it (115–16), amounts to an *Aufhebung*, a raising up and joining together in a higher unity, of classical objectivism – with its emphasis on *ens reale* – and modern transcendentalism, which has discovered the inescapable role of the subject in the constitution of the object. But it is an *Aufhebung* which is effected by returning to the suppressed transcendental motif in classical philosophy itself which runs through the Platonic-Augustinian tradition and makes its way into Thomas himself. Such a return overcomes the principal defect of modern transcendentalism, viz. its neglect of a metaphysics of a real being in favor of an exploration of the transcendental life of the subject. Transcendental, let us say at once, means the investigation of the conditions in the subject which allow for the knowledge of the object. But a transcendental retrieval of classical metaphysics is prepared to accept the claims of real Being and does not run the risk of modern subjectivism. As such, transcendental Thomism will prove to be an *Aufhebung*, not only of classical and modern philosophy, but, within classical philosophy itself, of both the Platonic-Augustinian and Aristotelico-Thomistic traditions.

The transcendental motif in Thomas Aquinas himself centers on the doctrine of the agent intellect which "coordinated Aristotle's illuminating intellect with the Platonic-Augustinian transcendent Light in a way calculated to offer an orthodox alternative to Arabian Aristotelianism" (117). For Thomas, the agent intellect, while formally a power of the soul, is "a participation of the divine light" (S.T., I,12,a,11). To understand is to understand by means of a light which is itself but a share – an intrinsic, but finite share – in the Divine Light. In Rahner's view, this transcendental theme in St. Thomas is organized around what Thomas calls the *excessus* (118–24). From the point of view of the divine being itself, the *excessus* signifies the infinity with which God's Being "exceeds" the capacity of the soul to comprehend it; and subjectively, or from the point of view of the soul which seeks to know God, it means the aspiration, dynamism, or reaching out of the soul towards God, a tendency which is never fully actualized but remains always a *Vorgriff*, an anticipatory fore-grasping of the divine being, of the Light in which it sees light.

It is at this point that the Platonic-Augustinian motif which is alive, if latent, in Thomas is wedded with, or has recourse to, Heidegger's projective theory of Being in *Being and Time*. For Heidegger the interpretive understanding of any particular being is made possible by a prior grasp – which in Heidegger's own vocabulary includes not only a *Vorgriff*, but also a *Vorsicht* and *Vorhabe* (*Being and Time*, §32) – of the Being of that being. Beings are manifest only on the grounds of a prior understanding of Being. Ontological knowledge makes ontic knowledge possible. Now for Rahner this ontological knowledge, this prior grasp of Being, is the soul's participation in the divine light. This participation constitutes an implicit, preconceptual understanding (but not a conceptualization) of God, as the fullness of Being and light.

Now all of this shows, as Hurd rightly argues, that Thomistic metaphysics is susceptible to, and profits from, a certain transcendental rounding-off; that the metaphysics of the object gains something from, and can indeed even be organized around, a metaphysics of the subject (119). And he is right to complain that, in *Heidegger and Aquinas*, I tended to represent Thomistic metaphysics in the traditional manner as a metaphysics of the object, of *ens reale*.

On the transcendental reading, *esse* in St. Thomas does not only, does not even primarily, mean *esse reale*. Thomas is not only concerned with Being (*esse*) as the process by which things come to be real, *extra causas*, but with the process by which they come to be manifest, *esse manifestivum*. It is a mistake to take material being – which lacks intrinsic manifestness and self-knowledge – as paradigmatic for Being in general. One ought to look at the higher instances of Being, at the Being of spirit, to see that for Thomas, Being in its higher registers is always equiprimordially knowing; in God, *esse* and *intelligere* are identical.

That does not mean that we are to deny Being of material things, but rather that we must rethink the analogical meaning of Being in St. Thomas, reformulating it, not in terms of *actualitas*, but of what Rahner calls *Bei-sich-sein*, the internal unity, self-possession or self-presence of Being to itself. This is clearly realized most perfectly in God, in whom *esse* and *intelligere* are identical, and then in angels who are identical with their own *intelligere* but not with their *esse*, and least perfectly in material objects, which are an internal unity of matter and form possessing only a minimal interiority. Man, of course, is to be inserted in the middle of this hierarchy, on the edge of the sphere of spirit, and on the edge of the sphere of the material world, as Spirit-in-world. Drawn out into the world by the bodily *ecstasis*, man is capable of the return, the reflexive grasp of self, but this only in virtue of the *conversio ad phantasma*, which is the subject of Rahner's dissertation, subsequently published in 1939 as *Geist in Welt* (*Spirit in the World*). (That dissertation was, unfortunately, turned down by its director, Martin Honecker, who expected a straight, objectivistic version of St. Thomas, and not a retrieved, transcendental version.)

Now once we have recognized this much, once we have seen that Being means *Bei-sich-sein*, Hurd argues (120–24), then it makes no sense to criticize Thomism as objectivistic and to deny it an "alethiological" status, that is, to fail to treat it as a philosophy of the way things come to presence, come to appear, emerge into appearance. Clearly, one can find in St. Thomas an "alethiological" conception of Being, one that meets Heidegger's critique of metaphysics.

At this point one can raise an exegetical objection to Rahner's reading of St. Thomas. For Thomas, *esse* and *intelligere* are identical in God because God is subsistent *esse* (S.T., I,14,4,c). Hence there is a definite subordinating of *intelligere* to *esse* in Thomas. God understands because God exists; God does not exist because God understands.[11] And God is God's understanding, and the perfection of understanding, because God is God's own *esse* and the perfection of *esse*. *Intelligere* belongs to God because the *plenitudo essendi* belongs to God, not conversely. And more generally, the interiority and self-possession of beings in general is a function of *esse* and the fact that *esse* is always, to a greater or lesser extent, *unum*. A being has unity to the extent that it has *esse*. Everything in Thomas is organized around *esse*, not *intelligere*. The *verum* is defined in terms of *esse*, not conversely. And that is why Thomas puts *esse manifestivum* third and last in enumerating the senses of truth, a text about which Prof. Hurd is understandably silent.[12]

The response to this objection is clear: it addresses the explicit, historical actuality of the Thomistic text, whereas Transcendental Thomism speaks to the latent, implicit possibility which can be opened up in this text by a reading bent on retrieval, not merely exegesis. Since this is the hermeneutic rule which guides my own reading of St. Thomas in *Heidegger and Aquinas*, I can hardly quarrel with it. It is rather a point on which Prof. Hurd and I agree fully and which makes his response to my study in many ways agreeable.

Furthermore, this objection is, from the point of view of the Heideggerian project of overcoming metaphysics, strictly an in-house metaphysical dispute. It matters not a whit to the Heideggerian critique whether one organizes everything around the unity of *esse* and *intelligere*, as the transcendental Thomists do, or around *esse* itself, as the existential Thomists do, or around *essentia* as Suarez and the classical manual tradition tended to do. I was myself, in *Heidegger and Aquinas*, mainly taken up with the claims of the mainstream existential Thomists and with rebutting their much-heard claim that once the primacy of *esse* over *essentia* is recognized, there can be no more talk of *Seinsvergessenheit* in the Heideggerian sense. Now, with Prof. Hurd's excellent defense of Rahner in hand, I must extend that argument to transcendental Thomism and Hurd's parallel claim: that once the unity of *esse* and *intelligere* is recognized in the notion of *Bei-sich-sein*, there can be no more talk of *Seinsvergessenheit*. Prof. Hurd's critique forces me to extend my argument in a way which I neglected in *Heidegger and Aquinas*, and for that I am grateful.

I would say that Hurd's presentation of Rahner provides us, not with an "alethiological" thought of Being,[13] but rather with a fuller and more perfect representation of the metaphysics which Heidegger criticizes. Transcendental Thomism is not merely a metaphysics of objectivity but of subjectivity as well; not only of real being but of manifest being. In Thomas, objectivism is completed, balanced and complemented by transcendentalism. That gives Transcendental Thomism a status like Hegel's, where the truth is both substance and subject, where all the essential tendencies of metaphysics are spelled out, or like Husserl's, as the secret longing of modern philosophy. But if we accept Transcendental Thomism as a more perfect, fuller, balanced metaphysics, then this only shows it to be even more fully entrenched in the history of metaphysics – as its *Aufhebung* and fulfilling gesture – which Heidegger wants to overcome. Heidegger's critique of metaphysics is not affected in the least by any attempt to bring metaphysics to fulfillment in a gesture which unites Plato and Aristotle, Augustine and Aquinas, classical objectivity and modern transcendentalism. Indeed, the better one makes metaphysics, the more one strengthens and fulfills and balances its claims, the worse things get from Heidegger's point of view. One makes metaphysics clearer, but one leaves the thought of the Being which is addressed by metaphysics unthought, in oblivion.

Let us believe Prof. Hurd and hold that Rahner, like Hegel, constitutes the fulfillment of the onto-theo-logical nature of metaphysics, exploiting everything that metaphysics means by Being, everything that metaphysics has to offer. Nonetheless, on Heidegger's terms, Rahner, like Hegel himself, would leave the question of Being as a question beyond Being, of metaphysics as a movement of overcoming metaphysics, in essential oblivion.

(2) All of this amounts to saying that I accept Hurd's first step – that a transcendental hermeneutic of St. Thomas is both possible and necessary. That should be obvious from my own enthusiasm for Rousselot, whom I regard as a great figure in the history of the Neo-Thomist movement whose work I take myself to be extending, albeit in a non-metaphysical direction, even as Rahner extended it in a metaphysical one. But I deny his second step, that this Rahnerian transcendental hermeneutic "speaks the language of both Heidegger and Aquinas and so [can] moderate a conversation between them" (124). I will first spell out my reasons for this denial in the most direct manner possible, and here I will have recourse to the first section of this paper. In the next section I will take up Hurd's discussion of "horizon" around which he organizes his argument against the charge of *Seinsvergessenheit*.

For Heidegger, as we have said, metaphysics is grounding (*Gründen*), ground-seeking and ground-laying (*Grundlegung*), spreading beings out against a horizon of ground, on a grid of ground and grounded, Being and beings, horizon and horizoned. Summoned by the call to deliver a sufficient reason (*principium reddendae rationem sufficientem*), metaphysics always delivers the goods, i.e., the grounds for what needs grounding.

Far from putting this program of ground-laying in question, far from questioning Being as ground, Prof. Hurd shows us that, transcendentally interpreted, Thomism is even better at it that we supposed. The projection of Being-as-ground in Thomistic metaphysics is wider than we portrayed. For it is not only a projection of Being as the ground of real beings, but it is also the ground of manifestness. Not only is Being as ground in St. Thomas pure actuality (*actus, actualitas*) but it is also light (*lumen*).[14] On the transcendental reading, Thomas extends the reach of the projection of Being as ground, and of beings as grounded, by showing that Being is not only a real cause (*causa essendi*) but also the cause of intellection (*causa intelligendi*), the light in which all light is seen. Thomism is not only a philosophy of objective Being but also a transcendental metaphysics of subjectivity. The true in Transcendental Thomism is both substance and subject.

But this extension of the metaphysical sweep of the notion of *esse* in Thomism leaves intact everything essential in Heidegger's critique of metaphysics and his charge of *Seinsvergessenheit*. Metaphysics continues to move, indeed moves even more impressively and with a grander sweep, within the parameters of Being and beings, ground and grounded, horizon and horizoned. Being in Transcendental Thomism means everything the metaphysical tradition, ever since the time of Parmenides, says it means: plenitude, intelligibility, perfection, divinity. This transcendental metaphysics is still the attempt to think this out, to draw a still more perfect onto-theo-logical grid, one which brings together everything of which metaphysics is capable. Hurd argues that the traditional metaphysical ground means both *lumen* and *actualitas*, both reality and light, and he objects to treating the metaphysical ground as one-sidedly realistic, objectivistic. Hurd shows that Transcendental Thomism is more deeply, more perfectly, metaphysical than I let on, more fully entrenched in the ground/grounded schema, than I made it out to be. But that only makes things worse.

It not only leaves the essential determination of Being as ground untouched, it reenforces it. And it leaves unasked, unquestioned, the essential thing that Heidegger wants to ask: How is it that this whole binary meta-physical schema – of ground and grounded, Being and beings, transcendent and transcended, infinite and finite, perfect and imperfect, cause and effect, eternal and temporal, subsistent and participant, light and illuminated – how does such a schema arise? What sets it into motion? Whence does it arise? What is at work in it? What comes to pass *in* metaphysics, *as* metaphysics? What is metaphysics? And what "is" (*west*) it which metaphysics calls Being, ground, light? Far from reaching into the very process of asking this question, far from asking about this Being-process, Rahner's metaphysics leaves it untouched, unquestioned, rock-sure and indubitable. Rahner does not put this into question; he moves about freely within it and argues about how best to arrange its furniture, how best to exploit all its resources. Rahner does not put into question this Being-process – this whole history in which we are given to think and speak and to organize our world in such binary, hierarchical terms. He does not make the history of this tendency the matter to be thought. He moves about within it, within the traditional understanding of Being, and claims to have the best, the most parousial *Aufhebung* of everything that metaphysics means by Being.

For Rahner, Being means unity, intelligibility, self-presence – the *unum* and *verum* which is convertible with *ens* in classical metaphysics, and within whose scope modern metaphysics continues to operate, albeit in an altered form and with different emphasis.[15] But these are the most traditional of assumptions and predeterminations of Being which leave the Being-process, the coming-to-pass (*Wesen*) and event (*Ereignis*) of Being itself, unthought and unquestioned. Rahner takes Being to mean what Being has always given itself out to be, what it has always been taken to be, and hence, from Heidegger's point of view, has been taken in (*eingenommen*) by Being, pulled in by its withdrawal, which is what oblivion means. For Heidegger, to question Being is to question into this very process and event of Being by which it gives itself out to be the stable ground, the secure foundation, the source of light, the unifying unity. Heidegger wants to think Being's very coming about, that very process by which Being gives itself out to be in the way that Rahner and metaphysics generally takes it to be. He wants to think beyond Being as ground, as unity, as overarching identity and self-presence, to set thinking loose into the dark abyss, the simple play of epochs, of the coming to pass of Being in the successive epochs. He wants to think into the *Spiel*, the *an-archē* of the child-king,[16] not the principium of the self-thinking thought, the self-presence of *Bei-sich-sein*.

Rahner does not venture out into the desert. Rahner does not ask what is happening in metaphysics; he just keeps on doing it. He asks the question of Being, but in the traditional sense, which takes the first step – from beings to Being, from the finite to the infinite, the ontic to the ontological, transcended to the transcendent, the ground to the grounded – but not the second, and more radical step, which is to ask why we are driven to think things in terms of Being and beings, ground and grounded, light and illuminated. *He does not ask what the world would be like were we to let go of this kind of thinking and try something else*, take up another kind of thinking. My argument in *Heidegger and Aquinas* is that the one place I see St. Thomas "let go" is at the end, in the *non possum*.

Then, at that point, where we let go of such thinking, we lose our security, our footing, our groundedness. Things no longer point securely to a transcendent ground, *realia* no longer point to an *ens realissimum*, nor acts of finite intellection to an infinite *intelligere*. Then, at that point, we experience the abyss, the *ébranler*, the trembling, the play. I do not see any trembling in this "metaphysics of finite knowledge." Instead of the groundlessness of mortals I see a finitude caught up in the binary metaphysical opposition of finite/infinite, where it is already underwritten and made safe. Instead of the radical contingency of *kinesis* I see a teleologically regulated dynamism steaming ahead towards the *parousia*. I hear the endless metaphysical refrains of Being and beings, ground and grounded, infinite and finite, horizon and horizoned. Everywhere grids, foundations, teleologically monitored aspirations, infinite resources for finite effects, infinite assurances. But no groundlessness.

To take Being as *Bei-sich-sein* is not to put into question the history of metaphysics and what it calls Being. It is to try to sum it up, exploit all its resources, to say everything it has meant to say and to leave wholly unquestioned, to assume from the start, the authority of the metaphysical project. It perpetuates the division of the world into binary – meta-physical – pairs, setting unity over multiplicity, interiority over exteriority, spirit over world, infinity over finitude, light over darkness, the self over the other, identity over difference, subject over object, presence over absence (and, of course, in the traditional manner of metaphysical dialectics, to say that these opposites have a deeper identity.) It is a salient example of the metaphysics of presence in which the classical metaphysical assumption of the priority of presence and of self-presence is not questioned but invoked at every turn. There are everywhere metaphysical assurances in Rahner – do they arise from faith? – which are altogether denied to a thinking which ventures out beyond metaphysics, everywhere hope, confidence, faith in natural order, in a great chain of Being, a momentum towards unity.

But the thought of Being, the thinking which puts this metaphysical undertaking into question, has no such assurances, no such firm foundations, no clear maps. It is cut adrift, more humble than metaphysics, with less to say. It lives by way of renunciation – the renunciation of the conceptuality of metaphysics, of the assurances of onto-theo-logic, of all grounding. It lacks the security of having a fixed position set by a horizon; it is horizonless, adrift, with no stars to guide it, decentered. Its best name is the old name that Meister Eckhart gave it long ago, *Gelassenheit*, letting be, letting go. If it thinks Being, God, world, then that means for it to let go of the apparatus of metaphysics and to let God, to let the world, to let Being be, to let them rise up with a simplicity which eludes all conceptual sophistication and which reminds us of the responsiveness of the poet, on the one hand, and the austerity of the mystic, on the other. I pray God to rid me of God, Meister Eckhart said, to rid me of these metaphysical-theological constellations, and that meant of *ipsum esse subsistens*, of *Bei-sich-sein*, and of all the chatter of metaphysics. *Sicut palea*. And it was Meister Eckhart who described the naked Godhead as a desert.[17]

Horizonality and the Open

I want to return now to the text of Prof. Hurd's response to show the point of breach between Heidegger and Rahner, the point where, in my view, Rahner and Hurd alike back off from the radically Heideggerian, deeply deconstructive gesture. It concerns the question of horizons. Hurd wants to make light of the gesture beyond Being – to the meaning, truth or *Ereignis* of Being – and to treat it as a matter of vocabulary, since whatever one would call this ternarial term, this third thing, one would certainly have to mean Being-as-horizon (otherwise metaphysics would be confounded!). Now since Being means horizon in Rahner, and since the claim of the second step in Hurd's argument is that Rahner is the bridge between Aquinas and Heidegger, then it is a matter of some embarrassment to see Heidegger explicitly renounce transcendental-horizonal thinking, as he does in *Gelassenheit*. Hurd therefore offers us a metaphysical reading of this text (127–28) which is not a retrieval of the text but a retreat from it, in which he robs it of its deconstructive import by subsuming it within the ready-made metaphysical concept of dialectical unity or identity-in-difference (127). It is the one place in his excellent study where I think he has mishandled a text, but it comes at a crucial juncture.

Heidegger wants to show that a "horizon" of Being is a certain determinate way Being is sent, an epochal configuration, one of the circumscribed, delimited, determinate faces which Being wears. By means of a "horizon" we draw a line around entities, project them in their Being in a determinate way, make them manageable (intelligible), shrink them down to size. Heidegger wants to say that while such transcendental-horizonal thinking is the practice of metaphysics, the task of thought is to think the horizon through, to think through the horizon, to that of which the horizon is the circumscription and contraction. And since horizons close off – that is, they open up precisely by closing off, by erecting a frame of reference, a horizonal schema, a configuration of Being within which we can situate beings – then that of which they are the circumscription is best called "the open." The horizon, Heidegger writes, "encircles the view of a thing – the field of vision" (G, 3B/65).[18] It opens up a field of vision by giving it determinate boundaries. Transcendental thinking transcends the individual entity to the transcendental horizon which makes it possible. But that is always only the first step for Heidegger; the second step, the step back from meta-physics, consists in thinking that which lies behind the horizon or projection of Being, which is here called the Open. Everything in thinking depends upon making that step. And so Heidegger writes:

> *Teacher*: What is evident of the horizon, then, is but the side facing us of an openness which surrounds us; an openness which is filled with views of the appearances of what to our representing are objects.

That is, a horizon is a constriction, side or face of the Open. He continues:

> *Scientist*: In consequence the horizon is still something else besides a horizon. Yet after what has been said this something else is the other side of itself, and so the same as itself. You say that the horizon is the openness which surrounds us. But what is this openness as such if we disregard that it can also appear as the horizon of our representing? (G, 39–40/64)

That is, given that the horizon is the horizonal contraction of the Open, then what is that Open itself, apart from its contraction in the horizon? The horizon and the Open are not two different things – Heidegger does not have a two-worlds theory; rather the horizon is a transcendental-metaphysical determination or contraction of the Open. And so Heidegger wants to know what it would be like to set sail in the Open without the guidance of a metaphysical-nautical horizon. Terminologically, in this essay, he calls the openness of the open a *"Gegend,"* which is translated as "region:"

> It strikes me as something like a region, an enchanted region where everything belonging there returns to that in which it rests.

The region is quickly qualified – in a phrase which Hurd excises in his citation (127) – as "enchanted" (*Zauber*). That is, region does not refer to a metaphysical-causal system, a grid of intelligibility, but a sphere of releasement (*Gelassenheit*) where things "rest," where we let them be, where we do not stretch them out against the horizon, confine them within the fore-structure of some metaphysical arrangement or another. The word *Gegend* in particular is aimed at deconstructing the metaphysical term *Gegenstand*, object, that which stands over and against us as soon as we have erected a horizon within which it can make an appearance or acquire a standing. The idea of a *Gegend* is to think that which is coming to pass *in* horizonal thinking, but unknown *to* horizonal thinking, viz., that the Open gives itself and withdraws in and through the successive horizons. The essential matter for thought is to think the Open which is always in concealment behind the horizon and forgotten by horizonal thinking.

There are two points to Heidegger's critique of transcendental-horizonal thinking:

(1) Horizons are not man-made but granted, or sent to us, by the Open. The history of metaphysics is not the history of human thinking, but the history of the ways Being gives itself to be thought, which means, the way Being keeps giving itself under one face, horizon, projection, or another – *eidos, ousia, esse, Gegenständlichkeit, Subjektität*, etc.

(2) While all along holding itself back in essential concealment, the Open is that in which this whole succession of epochal faces happens, but of which we are oblivious, and so the essential thing is to think that withdrawal of the Open itself, to get beyond or behind horizonality to the Open itself, which we get by disregarding the horizon.

Now Hurd embraces the first point – the horizon is not the project of the subject but granted by Being – because it sounds like transcendental Thomism's effort to wed classical realism with modern transcendentalism (126). That is hardly Heidegger's point, of course. He means to say that any metaphysical theory of Being is a way Being has of withdrawing on us while leaving behind an epochal, horizonal face or configuration. In fact, then, the first point enmeshes Transcendental Thomism in the "history of Being," making it one more epochal mittence.

But Hurd tries to dull the deconstructive edge of the second point (127–28). Heidegger is speaking about making our way to the Open, or the Region. But that suggests that we could somehow or another not be in it, so that the task for thinking would be to find a way to book passage to it. But that is manifestly absurd: we are always and already in the Open – even when we are engaged in transcendental-horizonal thinking, for transcendental-horizonal thinking arises precisely when and as the Open conceals itself: "…it [the Region] conceals itself as the horizon" (G, 51/73). Thus, even though we are taken up with transcendental-horizonal thinking, we are still in the Open, for transcendental-horizonal thinking is but the self-withdrawal of the Open. But insofar as we fail to recognize this, insofar as we remain oblivious of this – and this is the point of speaking of *Seinsvergessenheit* – we are still not in it, in the sense that we do not recognize the withdrawal as *a withdrawal.* Hence Heidegger writes:

> …we are in that-which-regions when, re-presenting transcendentally, we step out into the horizon. And yet again we are still not in it, so far as we have not released ourselves for that-which-regions, as such. (G, 51/73)

We are never outside the Open, but we rarely manage to think the Open which encompasses us and which conceals itself behind the horizonal schemata which populate the history of metaphysics. But Hurd draws from this situation of ambiguity in which we are always caught up – we are always *in* the Open, but we do not grasp it *as* the Open – this surprising conclusion:

> …the symbol of the opening in Heidegger is functionally equivalent to the symbol "horizon of Being" in Rahner's transcendental hermeneutic…. The convergence of the transcendental symbol of the horizon of Being with the alethiological symbol the "opening" should not surprise us. What would the symbol opening mean if not horizon? (128)

After Heidegger's painstaking differentiation of the horizon from the Open as its self-concealment and contraction, Hurd concludes to their "functional equivalence" (128), their "substantial equivalence" and then proceeds thereafter to confound Heidegger's point by speaking of "opening/clearing/horizon" (129), by saying that horizon and *Ereignis* are "equivalent symbols" (132) and in general by conflating horizon and opening. Heidegger's point is not that horizon and opening are equivalent symbols – if anything that is the point he is rebutting – but rather that there is a certain sameness between transcendental horizonal thinking and dwelling in the Open inasmuch as one who is held captive by transcendental-horizonal thinking, who is not released from it, nonetheless is held in the grips of something which is the Open itself in the mode of its withdrawal. The horizon is the Open as the self-withdrawal of the Open. But thinking in terms of horizons, without further ado, without thinking horizonality as a withdrawal, is precisely oblivion of this withdrawal, that is, of the Open, that is, of Being, and hence direct confirmation of what *Seinsvergessenheit* precisely means.

Hence Prof. Hurd can claim that Transcendental Thomism has the same reach as *Seinsdenken* only by excising the second, deconstructive, step back out of metaphysics taken by *Seinsdenken*, and reducing it to transcendental-horizonal thinking. He wants to deprive the notions of the Open, the Clearing, *Ereignis*, of their precise sense in Heidegger. The whole power of these expressions is to open thought to that realm in which the various figures and structures of metaphysical thinking arise. This is the sphere beyond the creatures of metaphysics – ground and grounded, horizon and horizoned, cause and effect, transcendental and transcended, etc. – in which we are released from their spell and able to let things be, let them rest in themselves, where not only we but the things themselves are released from the projective, horizonal scheming of metaphysics. Rahner's "metaphysics of finite knowledge" is woven wholly out of such creatures, moves entirely within the traditional metaphysical framework, and as such is an unexceptional piece of metaphysics. It does not attempt to renounce the metaphysical project and makes no gesture aimed at thinking that realm of openness beyond any horizon of Being or Being-as-horizon.

Rahner's Theory of the "*Woraufhin*"

There is a move, parallel to Hurd's, in *Spirit in the World* where Rahner likewise dulls the edge of Heidegger's movement beyond the horizonality of Being, and hence divests the apparatus of *Being and Time*, of which he makes so much use in *Spirit in the World*, of its critical-deconstructive point. This concerns Rahner's use of the term *Woraufhin*.

There is an important distinction in *Being and Time* between the Being of a being and the meaning of that Being, a distinction which turns, it seems to me, upon an implicit distinction between the primary and the secondary phases of the work of projection. The being is projected in a first and preliminary way upon its Being, and then in a second and determinative way upon the meaning of that Being. Heidegger writes:

> What does "meaning" signify? In our investigation, we have encountered this phenomenon in connection with the analysis of understanding and interpretation. According to that analysis,

meaning is that wherein the understandability (*Verstehbarkeit*) of something maintains itself – even that of something which does not come into view explicitly and thematically. (SZ, 323–4/370–71)[19]

Meaning is not merely the object of understanding, what is understood by the understanding, but, more exactly, the organizing component in what is understood, that upon which the understandability depends, around which it is organized. Thus we see a distinction between understandability and the organizing center of the understandability. He continues:

"Meaning" signifies the "upon-which" (*das Woraufhin*) of a primary projection in terms of which something can be conceived in its possibility as that which it is. (SZ, 324/371)

The organizing principle or center of reference in the understandability is called the "upon-which" of the "primary" – or first phase of – projection. We are thus to distinguish in the projective understanding of any being the initial projection – of the being in its Being – from that upon which the projection was carried out, that upon which it maintains itself, that which organizes and structures the projection. He adds:

Projecting discloses possibilities – that is to say, it discloses the sort of thing which makes possible. (SZ, 324/371)

When we have determined the meaning (the upon which, the second, determining element) of the Being (the primary projection, the initial or provisional determination) of a being, we will understand that which makes that being possible as a being:

To lay bare the "upon which" of a projection, amounts to disclosing that which makes possible what has been projected. (SZ, 324/371)

We can thus distinguish among:

(1) the being which is to be understood or projected, which is however never a bare fact and never makes an appearance apart from a determinate projection;

(2) the projection of that being in virtue of a certain initial determination of its Being;

(3) that upon which the projection was carried out, that which guided and organized it, albeit in an implicit and prethematic manner.

This is to distinguish: the being; its Being; the meaning of its Being. Or again: the being, the projection of that being upon its Being; that upon-which the projection was carried out. Here, already in *Being and Time*, we encounter a ternary and not a binary structure, a movement beyond the Being of beings to its meaning. Nor do we have here two different projections, but rather two different phases of one and the same projection: an initial or provisional phase and a final or radical phase. Heidegger thus concludes:

> All ontical experience of entities…is based upon projections of the Being of the corresponding entities – projections which in every case are more or less transparent. But in these projections there lies hidden the "upon which" of the projection; and on this, as it were, the understanding of Being nourishes itself. (SZ, 324/371)

Thus, in the existential analytic, the Being of Dasein was determined in terms of care, and the "upon which" of that projection was worked out in terms of "temporality." The projection of the Being of Dasein is nourished by time. And in that movement we see the argument of *Being and Time* generally: the "upon which" of the way Being has always been projected in the history of ontology is time. Time is the "meaning" of the way "Being" is projected.

But in Rahner this critical distinction between the projection and its "upon which" – in which the movement beyond Being is carried out – is effectively repressed.[20] Rahner begins with the judgment – which is already to be taken-in by the traditional primacy which metaphysics assigns to the theoretical standpoint. It is to "begin" with assertions whose derivativeness is clearly demonstrated in §33 of *Being and Time*. Presumably, spirit is in the world long before it is moved to form explicit judgments about worldly entities. In any case, every judgment has a thematic object about which some predicative assertion is made, an object which is determinate and limited. But, Rahner argues in the best "transcendental" style – in *Being and Time*, incidentally, one would say "hermeneutic," not "transcendental" – such a thematic operation is itself dependent upon and made possible by a pre-thematic pre-understanding of the range, horizon or Being of that being.

To judge that a thematic object bears a certain predicate – that such-and-such is a work of art – presupposes an understanding of that predicate as a whole – what art is. The thematic object is always a limited case of something which is relatively illimited. The limited, thematic object is explicitly grasped (*gefasst*); the illimited horizon is implicitly co-grasped (*mitgefasst*). Thus Rahner offers an interesting account of the work of the agent intellect: it is able to "abstract" a form from signate matter inasmuch as it preunderstands the separability of form from matter, which means that it has an understanding of its relatively illimited character, that is, of its possible range which is wider than its present instantiation. And that gives a Heideggerian ring to the theory of abstraction: to understand a meaning is to understand possibilities.

If the explicit grasp of the nature of a particular sensible object (*tode ti, hoc aliquid*) is dependent on a preunderstanding of the (relative) illimitability of form, the explicit grasp of the form is dependent upon a preunderstanding of the absolutely illimited character of *esse*, since the form always is a principle of the limitation of *esse*. Whence every judgment is ultimately dependent upon a preunderstanding of the *esse* of any particular *ens*, of the Being of beings. This pre-understanding is referred to by Rahner as *Vorgriff*, which in *Being and Time* is but one member of a tripartite articulation of the pre-understanding (which also includes *Vorhabe* and *Vorsicht*) and which, terminologically, is subordinated to what Heidegger calls the *Entwurf*, or projection of the being in its Being.

What then of the "upon which" (*Woraufhin*)? In the same way that Rahner simply collapses *Vorhabe*, *Vorsicht* and *Vorgriff* into one, he also effectively collapses the *Woraufhin* into the *Vorgriff*. Inasmuch as the *Vorgriff* is a prethematic, and not a thematic, object, inasmuch as it is only implicitly understood, Rahner says, the *Vorgriff* may be taken as pointing in a certain direction, towards (*auf*) a certain implicit object, which is the *Worauf*. That is why *Worauf* is translated as the "whither" of the *Vorgriff* in *Spirit in the World*, whereas it is translated as the "upon which" of a projection in *Being and Time*. Once we make explicit the reference or content of the implicit preunderstanding we have named the *Woraufhin*. The *Worauf* is nothing more than the implicit reference of the *Vorgriff* now explicitly stated.

Thus the critical movement beyond the primary projection of the Being of beings is cut short. The first step, the movement of transcendence from beings to Being, from horizoned to horizon, is carried out; but the second step – the step back out of the projection to what is at work in the projection, what is happening in it – is omitted. It is enough to gain the Being of any being, to effect transcendence, to make a transcendental-horizonal determination, to have a transcendental meta-physics. The more radical question, the deconstructive probing, the question of the meaning of that Being, that is to say, of the organizing component in the projection which "nourishes" it, which makes that projection possible, is never raised, is left in "oblivion."

Once Rahner determines that in the Thomistic metaphysics of knowledge, a being is knowable because an "*ens*" is grasped in its "*esse*" he ought then to have asked what is the meaning of *esse* in the sense of its "upon which". Of course Rahner does determine the meaning of *esse* in the conventional sense of meaning, as *Bei-sich-sein* – which ultimately implies the unity of *esse* and *intelligere* – but that is simply to remain within the projection of the Being of beings as *esse* and to determine its concepts more explicitly, to say more about what *esse* involves, to determine its content fully and in a way that traditional Thomism

137

did not suspect and modern transcendentalism missed. It is one more effort to propose the master-name for Being, to make a proposal about Being which will be able to compete in the arena of other metaphysical proposals – because of its innovativeness in fusing the classical and modern projections. (The survival value of such master names is measured by their greater or lesser originality in rearranging metaphysical furniture.)

But there is no gesture in *Spirit in the World* corresponding to Heidegger's movement beyond the projection of Being to its meaning, its *Woraufhin*, and which asks, why do we think the world, think God and creatures, in terms of *esse/ens*. By what are such projections "nourished"? Such a question would not result in another, more or less original metaphysical proposal – the Being of beings is *Bei-sich-sein* – but a meta-meta-metaphysical determination of why this metaphysics thinks as it does, what the clue is to this organization of the world, what rule it follows in articulating the world as it does.

In *Being and Time* this question led to time as the transcendental clue to the way the projections of Being are organized and nourished in the history of ontology. In *Basic Problems of Phenomenology* (§§11–12) Heidegger defended the view that the scholastic projection of Being was organized and nourished by a conception of *Herstellen*, of human making. Carried out resolutely enough, as it is in his later works, it would begin to lead in other directions. To a consideration of language and its metaphysical deposits: to what extent is the *esse/ens* schema the metaphysics of the Latin language, or of the Greco-Latin, or of the Indo-European family of languages? To a consideration of history: to what extent is such a grid an inherited Greco-European framework? To everything which Heidegger tries to evoke with the word "*Ereignis*," which is not the new master-name for Being, but an attempt to think what is at work in the metaphysical drive towards, the will-to, master-names which lay claim to define Being.

In the end, such a question, begun haltingly in *Being and Time*, would lead into the abyss. That is, it would find itself in the groundlessness which results from putting into question the whole constellation of ground-laying work which defines metaphysics throughout the ages. It would find itself cut adrift in the nakedness of a thinking which wants to locate that point, that juncture, where metaphysical conceptuality intervenes, and from there to find what lies on the other side of the juncture, to think things more simply than metaphysics allows, to call off metaphysics and let things be.

Conclusion

Seinsvergessenheit, the oblivion of Being, does not mean to fail to have a theory of Being, to fail to make a proposal about Being's master-name because of one's preoccupation with beings, which is, unhappily what it sounds like, and the way Heidegger too often explained it early on.[21] On the contrary, it is precisely to be preoccupied with theories of Being and to fail to ask what is concealed by all such metaphysical undertakings. It is not the failure to effect transcendence, to achieve a transcendental posture vis-à-vis beings, but the failure to ask what is happening in all such transcendental metaphysics. To seek to get beyond *Seinsvergessenheit* is to seek out that point of juncture where metaphysical conceptuality intervenes, to try to get behind that movement of transcendence, or better, to experience things before we have run them through our transcendental grid.

That is why, in looking for a deconstructive retrieval of Thomas Aquinas, I look for that point where Thomas appears ready to let go of metaphysical theology. We know that moment has some kind of biographical correlate in the events surrounding the end of his life. The *non possum* is precisely what I was seeking. For the *non possum* is a declaration of the break-down of metaphysics, not simply its crowning in a mystical theology which would necessarily have recourse to some metaphysical projection of Being or another. It signifies break-down, shattering, the experience of helplessness, inability to go on, surrender. But given the enthusiasm of medieval friars for making the best possible case for one of their own in the canonization process, and given certain medical considerations, that evidence could be nothing more than a pointer back to the texts themselves. It directs us to feel around for a seam in the text which, if unfolded, would open up another reading, for some point in the text itself which indicates a readiness, or at least the possibility, that Thomas would indeed have considered the *Summa* as so much straw, something in the text which suggests the undoing of the text.[22]

In such a search I enlisted the indispensable help of two guides: Pierre Rousselot and Meister Eckhart, each of whom performs a different service. Rousselot isolates the point of breakage in Thomistic metaphysics by his explication of human intellectuality in terms of what Thomas calls the *debilitas luminis intellectualis* (S.T., I,56,3,c). That puts all of the accomplishments of metaphysical intelligence into question. No matter how subtle or inventive, any metaphysical schema arises as a compensation for our weakness. Every metaphysical account is a but a "symbol" – a word which Prof. Hurd himself wisely employs to describe the reach of metaphysical insight – which arises as a substitute for a deeper experience. Given that point *in* the metaphysics, the

139

question *of* the metaphysics is raised. On the very terms of the metaphysics, the metaphysics itself can only get so far, can be, as Rousselot says, but a symbol and a supplement for what eludes metaphysics.[23]

Meister Eckhart – one of the direct successors of Thomas in the Dominican chair at Paris, thus enjoying an historical relationship to Thomas and something of a Thomistic pedigree himself – makes that metaphysics as questionable as anyone in the Thomistic tradition. It is in Eckhart's astonishing sermons that the "breakthrough" beyond all the creations of metaphysics is effected. It is Eckhart who recognizes that even the best names of Trinitarian theology are so many facades, porticoes, antechambers for the truly divine Godhead behind God. When Eckhart says "I pray God to rid me of God" we reach not some kind of metaphysical peak or summit, but a regressive, deconstructive backtracking which seeks to situate itself at that point of juncture where metaphysical conceptuality arises, and which tries in earnest to let go of metaphysics, which wills not to will, which understands that we do not understand, which experiences the shattering of our symbols, their splitting asunder (*supra*, n. 16). If Rousselot tells us that metaphysics is a tissue of symbols, Eckhart reminds us of their contingency.

Thus I do not want to make Rousselot the basis of a new metaphysics, to make of him one more resource for erecting and defending a new master name for Being, a source for the metaphysics of *Bei-sich-sein*. I see in Rousselot a recognition of the brittleness of metaphysics and the need for another kind of thinking.

One gets nowhere in coming to grips with Heidegger's critique of *Seinsvergessenheit* if one does not see in it a call to the desert, to the abyss. It is not Heidegger's intention to lay foundations for us, but to pull them out from under us, to disabuse us of the illusion of foundations, to restore to us a sense of helplessness, to bring the sword to metaphysics, not to establish peace in the quarrel between the ancients and the moderns. Nor is this so much nihilism. It is rather the attempt to let (what metaphysics calls) Being be, to let the matter for thought speak for itself. It is only in the shattering of human creations and of metaphysical conceptuality that the matter begins to be heard from. It is only when one enters the dark night, denuded of one's security, that Being and God can hold sway.

That is why I do not think that the "metaphysics of finite knowledge" represents either an adequate retrieval of Thomas or an adequate vehicle for a dialogue between Aquinas and Heidegger. But if it is not a sufficient instrument of retrieval, Rahner's metaphysics is I think itself a suggestive object of retrieval. That is, there is a point in Rahner's other writings where a seam can be found, a point of possible breakdown, and that I locate in his own recurrent emphasis on mystery, and his express declarations that "the *Woraufhin* of our transcendence" – which is absolute *esse*, God – is present only in the mode of absence and denial, distance and silence, unnameability.[24] It would after all be surprising were this not a central motif in a thinker who stands so close to Thomas, Rousselot and Heidegger.

But so long as such assertions are encased in a metaphysics of knowledge which makes them safe, they do not touch the point which Heidegger makes. They must be set loose in their full deconstructive power, so that the *"Woraufhin* of our transcendence" is seen to be so much metaphysics, a symbol to be broken up. For the truly divine Godhead is concealed by such metaphysical enframing and conceptuality; the truly divine God is more hidden than that because God is closer than that. The mystery is not in fact far, but rather its mysteriousness derives precisely from its being so close and so elusive of metaphysical conceptuality. The mystery is simple and that is why it is so difficult. Our transcendence keeps overshooting it. We keep burying it every time we set out in search for it. And it is only when we experience the breakdown of our transcendence that we can ever establish contact with it, a contact which is not the effect of a triumphant transcendental achievement but of the simple releasement which finally understands that we already are in the midst of the mystery. It is not a question of going out, of going over, in a grand gesture of metaphysical transcendence, but of staying home, as both Heraclitus and Meister Eckhart agree, where the gods already dwell.

Notes

1 Robert L. Hurd, "Heidegger and Aquinas: A Rahnerian Bridge," *Philosophy Today*, 28 (Summer 1984): 105–37. See John D. Caputo, *Heidegger and Aquinas: An Essay on Overcoming Metaphysics* (New York: Fordham University Press, 1982). For more on this debate I recommend Thomas Sheehan's *Rahner: The Philosophical Foundations* (Athens: Ohio University Press, 1987) from which I have greatly profited.

2 Heidegger characterizes metaphysics in these terms throughout *Der Satz vom Grund* (Pfullingen: Neske, 1965); see especially, pp. 185 ff.; see also "The Onto-Theological Constitution of Metaphysics" in *Identity and Difference*, trans. Joan Stambaugh (New York: Harper & Row, 1969).

3 Derrida's essay "Différance" in *Margins of Philosophy*, trans. Alan Bass (Chicago: University Press, 1982), 1–29 is a good place to see how Derrida appropriates Heidegger's critique of metaphysics.

[4] Heidegger, *Gesamtausgabe*, Vol. 24, *Die Grundprobleme der Phänomenologie* (Frankfurt: Klostermann, 1975), 402–443; *The Basic Problems of Phenomenology*, trans. Albert Hofstadter (Bloomington: Indiana University Press, 1982), 284.

[5] *Was ist Metaphysik?*, 9. Aufl. (Frankfurt: Klostermann, 1965), 43; "What is Metaphysics?" in *Existence and Being*, trans. W. F. C. Hull and A. Crick (Chicago: Regnery Gateway Books, 1949), 349–50.

[6] See *On Time and Being*, trans. Joan Stambaugh (New York: Harper & Row, 1972), 21–22, 40–41.

[7] One of the merits of Derrida is to emphasize a point which is not always stressed by Heidegger, viz., that there is no clear break from a metaphysical to a non-metaphysical discourse, that every attempt to deconstruct metaphysical discourse is always more or less subverted by metaphysics, that the best one can do is to be "vigilant" about this state of affairs.

[8] See Martin Heidegger, *Poetry Language and Thought*, trans. Albert Hofstadter (New York: Harper & Row, Colophon Books, 1971), 7.

[9] Heidegger, *Der Satz vom Grund*, 188.

[10] See Karl Rahner, "The Concept of Existential Philosophy in Heidegger," trans. Andrew Tallon, *Philosophy Today*, 13 (Summer 1969): 126–37 and Rahner's tribute to Heidegger in *Martin Heidegger im Gespräch*, ed. Richard Wisser (Freiburg: Alber, 1970), 48–49 in which Rahner says that he had many a good professor (*Schulmeister*) but only one whom he reveres as a "teacher" (*Lehrer*).

[11] Meister Eckhart was conscious of departing from his predecessor ("brother Thomas") when he wrote that he no longer holds that God understands because he is, but that God is because he understands. See my discussion of this text in "The Nothingness of the Intellect in Meister Eckhart's Parisian Questions," *The Thomist*, 39 (January 1975): 85–115. [Essay also appears in *Collected Philosopohical and Theological Papers*, Vol. 1, chapter 9. –Ed.]

[12] Aquinas, *De ver.*, 1,1; *Heidegger and Aquinas*, 202–3.

[13] In *Heidegger and Aquinas* I tended to oppose alethiology – the experience of Being as a-letheia – to objectivism – the experience of Being as objective presence. That is misleading, and I have misled Prof. Hurd by it, for he rightly objects that transcendental metaphysics is an alternative to objectivistic metaphysics. Hence I oppose here both transcendental and objectivist metaphysics to alethiology, which is a non-metaphysical experience of the matter to be thought, prior to the intervention of metaphysical categories of any sort.

[14] I pointed out this possibility only in passing in *Heidegger and Aquinas*, 203.

[15] Kant, for example, remained within the traditional metaphysical persuasion about the convertibility of *ens* and *unum*, but he shifted it to the side of the subject by centering everything on the unity of apperception as the highest condition of possibility of objectivity.

[16] *Der Satz vom Grund*, 188.

[17] For an account of this side of Meister Eckhart see my *The Mystical Element in Heidegger's Thought* (Athens, Ohio: Ohio University Press, 1978; rep. New York: Fordham University Press, 1986), 127–34.

[18] G = *Gelassenheit*, 2. Aufl. (Pfullingen: Neske, 1960); the pages following the slash refer to *Discourse on Thinking*, trans. J. Anderson and E. Freund (New York: Harper & Row, 1966).

[19] SZ = Martin Heidegger, *Sein und Zeit*, 10. Aufl. (Tübingen: Max Niemeyer, 1963); the pages following the slash refer to *Being and Time*, trans. John Macquarrie and Edward Robinson (New York: Harper & Row, 1962).

[20] For what follows on Rahner see *Geist in Welt: Zur Metaphysik der Endlichen Erkenntnis bei Thomas von Aquin*, 3. Aufl. (München: Kosel Verlag, 1964), 153–56, 163–66; *Spirit in the World*, trans. William Dych (New York: Herder & Herder, 1968), 142–45, 174–79.

[21] *Was ist Metaphysik?*, 7–23; "The Way Back into the Ground of Metaphysics," trans. Walter Kaufmann in *Existentialism: From Dostoevsky to Sartre* (Cleveland: Meridian Books, 1956), 206–21.

[22] Caputo, *Heidegger and Aquinas*, 252–56.

[23] That is why Gerald McCool argues in a forthcoming study of the history of the scholastic movement that there is an inherent movement within scholasticism itself, centering on Rousselot and his followers, towards pluralism and hence towards the breakdown of the intentions of *Aeterni Patris* to establish a single, univocal expression of Catholic metaphysics. [Ed. Note: Gerald McCool, *From Unity to Pluralism: The Internal Evolution of Thomism* (New York: Fordham University Press, 1999)].

[24] Cited by Vincent Branick, *An Ontology of Understanding: Karl Rahner's Metaphysics of Knowledge in the Context of Modern German Hermeneutics* (St. Louis: Marianist Communications Center, 1974), 143n79 (from *Theologische Schriften*, IV, p. 72). See Branick, 143–47.

10

SPIRIT AND DANGER

[In *Ethics and Danger*, eds. Charles Scott and Arleen Dallery (Albany: SUNY Press, 1992), 43–59]

[43] I shall speak here of spirit and danger, and likewise of what Jacques Derrida, in *De L'esprit*,[1] calls the law of the quotation marks.

Two by two, Derrida says, these little marks stand guard over the word *Geist* in Heidegger's *Being and Time* and prevent its entry. Or again, like little hooks, Derrida says, they hold up a curtain that is half-opened so that the word is still visible under the marks, only partly erased. Then, at a certain point, just six years later, this curtain is suddenly lifted. Onto the stage strides the impressive figure of *Geist,* well clad in full military uniform, in blazing, flaming color, and (if we are to believe Hugo Ott) with no little display of academic pomp and circumstance.[2] We can hardly believe our eyes. This is not the same figure we thought we saw through the partly opened curtain. Maybe it is just a ghost. But it is a "terrifying" moment, Derrida says, not a little intimidating to the spectators (OS 31).

I shall speak here of two things. First, of the fearsome figure which is cut by *Geist* when it enters the stage in Heidegger's rectoral address and in *An Introduction to Metaphysics*. I will take my lead from a remark of Derrida's, in which he speaks of the "proportion" between "spirit" and "danger" (OS 45), and then extend and reinforce his analysis, proceeding, let us say, as much in the spirit of *De L'esprit* as in its letter. Second, I wish to say something about the law of the quotation marks, about the operation of the stage machinery, about the lifting itself, and hence about what was set aside in order to [44] allow the striking figure of *Geist* to make its appearance. I shall show that the law of the quotation marks makes use of what I call the law of the "economies" (to use Derrida's term) that govern the deployment of individual words like *Geist*.

As soon as Heidegger lifts the ban that was in place on *spirit* in *Being and Time,* as soon as he suspends the law of quotation marks which caused the feet of *spirit* dangle in the air (of mention) above the ground (of use), as soon as *Geist* gets its feet on the ground, something very dangerous breaks loose. As soon as spirit is in the door and let on stage, something inflammatory flares up, a fiery spectacle occurs on stage (the stage that is also the scene or place of Being's comings and goings) (OS 32). This is not an innocuous and merely immaterial blaze which does not really burn. This fiery figure, this very German *Geist,* is dangerous; indeed, it can be defined by its dangerousness, or by its love of danger, its willingness to endure fiery pain.[3]

In the 1930s, danger is the flame of the spirit.

In *De L'esprit,* at the end of chapter 5, which is devoted to Heidegger's rectoral address and *An Introduction to Metaphysics,* Derrida remarks that "the experience of spirit appears proportional to 'danger'," that for the Heidegger of the 1930s "the most spiritual people" is the "most endangered" (OS 45). Although the thematic of danger is not a dominant one in Derrida's own discussion, I want to show just how right Derrida is. The entire problematics of the *Entmachtung* – the enfeeblement – of the spirit, which Derrida discusses in chapter 7, is a function of the question of danger, for the power of the spirit is measured by its love of danger.

Derrida is referring to the famous pincers passage in *An Introduction to Metaphysics,* in which Heidegger speaks of the menace of having too many neighbors; it is, Heidegger says, very dangerous. Heidegger wants to keep his neighbors at a distance. As fond as he is of nearness and of what is nearby, he likes his neighbor to be at least a good walk down the road, as far away as it takes to smoke a pipe (*Being and Time,* §23). He does not like crowded neighborhoods – or crowded continents. The nearby neighbor ought to be kept at a safe distance; otherwise it is dangerous.

In *An Introduction to Metaphysics,* the Germans are called – this is their vocation as the most endangered people – to be the most [45] spiritual people. They have been situated by the "geopolitics" (OS 44) of Being in the middle. This is a destiny (*Schicksal*) that has been sent the Germans' way, not by Being's history but by Being's geography. It is this people's unique vocation (*Bestimmung*), their destiny, to struggle in and from out of that middle. We are certain of this, Heidegger says; there is no doubt of it (*derer wir gewiss sind*).[4]

That is very interesting. In a book devoted to making everything questionable, one that wants to expose everything to the question of Being, that makes everything tremble with the possibility of its non-being, which exposes it to the abyss of asking why-it-is-rather-than-not, Heidegger seems to think there is no need for questioning why *this* should be so rather than not. It does not fall within the domain of the question of Being to wonder whether Germans have this destiny rather than not, whether they are the center of the map, whether there are not other maps on which they are not the center, whether even the center is the privileged place rather than not, or whether any place at all should be privileged (which is what one might have thought if all there really is, is the *es gibt* which gives without why). It does not occur to Heidegger to wonder whether this is not all a massive "tautology," as Derrida says, rather the way that you can only think *Sein* and have *Geist* in the German language (OS 71-72).

Be that as it may, Heidegger is saying that the certain destiny of the Germans is to rise up out of that middle, to let all of the great spiritual power of what is German unfold and spill over from that middle, and this in virtue of Germany's endowment as the metaphysical people par excellence. In that way, this middle, metaphysical, spiritual people will be able to push itself – and thereby Europe – out of this cramped middle and back into the originary sphere where the powers of Being prevail (EM 41–42; IM 38–39). For Europe is Germany's responsibility, and this people seems to be certain of this, too, and eager to assume this responsibility.[5]

We see now all the terms of what Derrida calls the "proportion" between danger and spirit. Our people (*unser Volk*) is the most overladen with neighbors (*das nachbarreichste Volk*), which makes it the most endangered people (*das gefährdetste Volk*), and this most endangered people is the most metaphysical people (*das metaphysische Volk*). The measure of this *Volk* is taken ultimately by its metaphysicality, which is itself what uniquely endows it with the ability to deal with danger, and danger is just what has been assigned to it by Being's geography or "geopolitics." It is in virtue of being the most metaphysical people that this spiritual people can rise to the danger of the neighbor. This most spiritual of all peoples has been [46] granted the destiny of being the most metaphysical people in one and the same granting in which it has been granted the destiny of being endangered by its neighbors.

Now let there be no misunderstanding. Heidegger is not complaining. This is not a piece of bad luck. He is not lamenting the fact that Russia or the United States, who have fewer neighbors, have it easy and therefore are better off. On the contrary, in matters of the spirit, danger is a gift of destiny, and the lack of danger is dangerous, the highest and deepest and most perilous danger of all. Those who have been given danger have been given a great gift – which is the gift of spirit itself. It is not a question of bad luck but of destiny, for in matters of destiny resoluteness drives out everything accidental (*Being and Time*, §74). This people has been granted a destiny; they have been given greatness, singled out by destiny in order to fulfill an historical role. That is why Heidegger's rhetoric in the early 1930s turns on a call for danger, a call to danger, a warning

147

about the danger of dangerlessness, of being unendangered (*ungefährdet*) (EM 160; IM 151). Complete safety would no doubt distress Heidegger very much.

We see this for the first time in 1929-30, in *Die Grundbegriffe der Metaphysik,* where the Germans are warned – for this is dangerous – about the distress (*Not*) of lacking distress (*Notlosigkeit*). Speaking in 1929, in Weimar Germany, Heidegger says that there is a deep and pervasive boredom besetting "us." (Who is this "us"? And how does Heidegger know this about "us"? Is this a matter of sociological fact or a kind of essential intuition he has?) This boredom cuts more deeply than any or all of the multiple problems which are all around us today: "contemporary social misery, political confusion, the impotence of science, the hollowness of art, the groundlessness of philosophy, the debility of religion."[6]

But, one might ask Heidegger, what about all the parties, groups, and associations that are organized to meet these needs and have programs aimed at offsetting these ills? Heidegger's rejection of such undertakings could not be more complete. Such ventures, he thinks, are worse than nothing, for they serve only to cover over the real need, need as a whole, to consign to oblivion a more profound void.

What truly besets and oppresses us, Heidegger thinks, is the fact that we are cognizant only of particular needs and that we do not feel more deeply beset and oppressed. The real need is found in the "absence of an essential oppression of our Dasein as a whole" (GM 244). There are many bureaucrats administering one program or another but no "administrator of the inner greatness of Dasein [47] and its necessities." We have nothing to make us great, because the only way to be great is to face up to an "inner terror" (*innerer Schrecken*). This absence of distress is the most distressing of all and lies at the basis of the void of boredom. These bureaucrats are trying to induce in us "a generally complacent comfort in dangerlessness" (GM 245). Heidegger continues:

> This comfort in the very ground of our existence, despite all the multiple needs, leads us to believe that we have no more need to be strong [*stark*] in the ground of our existence. We trouble ourselves about teaching skills. The present is full of pedagogical problems and questions. But by heaping up skills we will never replace power and might [*Kraft und Macht*]; if this sort of thing does anything at all, it will only choke them off. (GM 245)

The liberal institutions of the Weimar state, of bourgeois democracy, lack inner greatness and power because they are concerned with making life comfortable,

148

with meeting our needs, with curing our ills. They are making us soft. Presumably, then, we need something to make us hard.

We have forgotten, Heidegger warns, that it is only by putting one's shoulder to the "ownmost burden" of existence (GM 248), by bearing the unbearable heaviness of Being, that we can restore weight to things and to our human being (cf. EM 9; IM 11). Dasein, Heidegger says, is not like a car one can take for a relaxing cruise: "But because we are of the opinion that it is no longer necessary to be strong and to have to resist danger, we have all of us together snuck out of the danger zone [*Gefahrzone*] of Dasein, and so relieved ourselves of the need to take over Dasein" (GM 246-47).

What, then, to do? What does it mean to shoulder one's existence? Just this, to procure genuine knowledge (*Wissen*), which will enable us to be ourselves. But how is that possible? Only by letting ourselves be overtaken by this void, by letting it transfix our existence, and by *not taking action against it*. (What would that actually mean? Would we abandon every program to help society's most helpless?) In Heidegger's view, the trouble is that we multiply our efforts to fill up this void with one quick fix after another and with hastily conceived programs instead of pushing Dasein into its extreme condition. We have buried deep boredom under an avalanche of depth psychology and psychoanalysis. Heidegger does not seek piecemeal reforms, to undertake local action here or there, but rather to make everything turn on a radical, inner – let us say spiritual – [48] transformation. Only a revolution can save us. This will be possible only if we let things drift into their most extreme destitution and thereby test the mettle of our Dasein against inner terror, putting it to the test of the greatest difficulty and danger. Hard and dangerous is the great.

Spirit needs distress. Spirit needs to be needy. Neediness (*Notdürftigkeit*) is necessary (*notwendig*) for spirit. It is our fate, our necessity (*Notwendigkeit, anankè*) and we need it We must have it. It is not safe to lack danger; we can never be saved if we are safe.

The saving and the safe are dangerous. The danger is in the safe. Where the safe and saving are, danger grows. We see here the original Jüngerian form of the later and better-known Hölderlinian formula – where the danger is, the saving grows. The latter formula is the mirror image of the Jüngerian motif and the result of a remarkable *Kehre*. In the 1930s, that is, in the economy of spirit there is no talk of moving beyond danger to the saving. On the contrary, in this Heideggerian-Jüngerian economy, the movement is exactly the opposite, from the saving, the safe, the unendangered, to the danger. Furthermore, Jünger's formula implies an active nihilism, a voluntary pushing of humanity into extreme destitution, which Heidegger seemed to accept in the early 1930s, while the Hölderlinian version of the formula expresses acceptance of the drift towards the extreme state as a movement beyond human control.[7]

That is why in his rectoral address, delivered just a few years later in 1933, Heidegger issues a call to danger in and as the call to spirit:

> If we will the essence of science understood as the *questioning, unguarded holding of one's ground in the midst of the uncertainty of the totality of what-is, this* will to essence will create for our people its world, a world of the innermost and most extreme danger, i.e., its truly *spiritual* world.[8]

For spirit is danger; thus a spiritual world is one filled with the spirit of danger. Now to pique the spirit, to raise it to its highest peak, the German people must submit itself to its Greek beginning and return to the Promethean insight that knowing (*Wissen*) – Heidegger's translation of *techne* – is far weaker than necessity (*ananke, Notwendigkeit*). Among the Greeks there was no flight from neediness and necessity, no attempt to soften the hard necessity of life, no attempt to make things easy. The Greeks knew the one thing necessary, which is that knowing should fling itself against necessity [49] and let itself shatter in a defiant display of creative impotence (*schöpferische Unkraft*) (SdDU 11; SGU 472). Knowing knows that it will be overwhelmed by the overwhelming power (*Übermacht*) of its destined fate, that it will fail before it. But that is precisely what makes it strong and gives it its truth.

Knowing, for the Greeks, is no cultural ornament but the willingness to persevere against impossible odds, against the insuperable, unalterable concealment of Being. Knowing is a willingness to pit oneself against, to do battle with an unfathomable abyss. Science is no safe (*gefahrlos*) occupation, without danger. On the contrary, it is unguarded exposure (*ungesetzten Ausgesetzsein*) before the uncertainty of Being's own abyssal questionability (SdDU 13; SGU 474). For "us," knowing is no academic game, not a matter for schoolteachers or conferences, no occasion for careerism. "But for us this knowledge is not the settled taking note of essences and values in themselves; it is the most severe endangerment [*Gefahrdung*] of human being [*Dasein*] in the midst of the overwhelming power of what is" (SdDU 16; SGU 477). Knowing is self-endangering; it throws away all the security and safety of life and casts itself into an abyssal danger, the danger of the "questionability of Being."

That is why, Heidegger insists, we must rouse these professors out of their academic sleep and push them out ahead of the student body which is already awake, already on the march. The students started marching before the professors. They are already ahead of the faculty, which is no way to conduct an academic procession or a military march. The professors must not think they have a safe profession, behind the front, for theirs is a call to battle (*Kampf*), even presumably without helmets (uncovered), a battle over, with, about Being (*Kampf um das Sein*: EM 114; IM 107). We must challenge the teaching body to assume these most dangerous posts (*äusserste Posten der Gefahr*: SdDU 14; SGU 475), for we have learned from Plato that greatness is always attended by the storm. The greatness of the spirit is its readiness for the storm, its readiness for danger.

In *An Introduction to Metaphysics*, Being itself is the storm. For Being is determined, following Heraclitus (fragment 53), as *polemos,* which Heidegger translates sometimes as *Auseinandersetzung* (strife, confrontation) and sometimes as *Kampf* (battle). This is, of course, no human war but the aboriginal conflict among the elements which gives all things their unity (*logos*) and order of rank. Still, this aboriginal *Kampf* if it is not outright war, nonetheless communicates with concrete human Dasein. It is the origin of the human creators – the poets, thinkers, and statesmen – who continue the *Kampf* and [50] carry it on (*tragen*). These human creators are as it were a barrier, a block, a bastion – but ultimately a futile and impotent one – against the overwhelming power (*überwaltigendes Walten*) with which they must contend. When the creators are gone from the nation, when their authentic *Kampf* ceases, when the hand they lend to the aboriginal *Kampf* grows still, then we are left only with decline, decay, the loss of the world (EM 66-67; IM 62-63). What does not battle and grow stronger can only weaken; when things are soft and safe, the real danger sets in.

In *Antigone,* the aboriginal *Kampf* of Being is determined as *deinon. Deinon* means, on the one hand, the terrible itself (*das Furchtbare*) in the sense of the overwhelming power that compels terror and anxiety; on the other hand, *deinon* means the one who wields or uses power (*Gewalt-tätig*), who contends violently (*gewaltig*) with the overwhelming. Thus *deinon* names alternately the terrible power of Being itself and the terrible one, human being, who deploys his power against Being. Such a man the poet calls *to deinotaton,* which Heidegger translates as "the most uncanny one" (*das Unheimlichste*), not in order to hide his violence but in order to accentuate it. "We understand the *Un-heimlich*," Heidegger says, "as that which casts out of the 'home-ish,' i.e., the homey, the customary, the familiar, the unendangered [*Ungefahrdeten*]" (EM 160; IM 150-51). The violent, uncanny one, the one who leaves the warmth of the hearth, the comforts of the familiar, is one who renounces safety, who wades into the danger, who does not shrink from impossible odds, who embraces the danger of the *Kampf* with appearance, the battle to wrest Being from appearance. The great Greek poet, whose formula in *Antigone* gives us "the authentic Greek definition of man" (EM 160; IM 151), that is, the authentic definition *simpliciter,* wants to give us

151

back our danger, wants to see to it that man does not suffer from the neediness of lacking need. He sees to it that man will be exposed to the danger that constitutes Being-there: uncovered exposure to the abyss of the terrible power of Being.

On Heidegger's reading, the violent one ventures, sets out, breaks out upon (*Aufbruch*) the stormy sea in order to subdue it; he disturbs the tranquility of the earth by breaking into it (*Einbruch*) with mighty plows; he violently snares the peaceful animal with his net (EM 163; IM 154). With his wind-swift understanding he has learned to rule over cities and to subdue even the elements of unpropitious weather.

So this *techne* that pits itself against the overwhelming has all the marks of the *Gestell* but with this one difference – that such *techne* [51] serves the flame of the spirit, *this* spirit, which is marked by its love of violence (*Gewaltsamkeit*) and struggle. No tender tending of the earth, no letting be and letting in (*einlassen*), but rather breaking in and breaking up. (This too reflects the earlier, Jüngerian economy.)

But however far the uncanny, violent one ventures, he is always thrown back on the paths he himself lays out: "All violence shatters against *one* thing. That is death.... Here there is no breaking-out or breaking into, no capture or subjugation" (EM 167; IM 158). With the power of his *techne* the uncanny one wrestles with (*erkämpft*) the overwhelming, trying to subdue and stabilize it in his works, his art:

> Yet he can never master the overwhelming.... Every violent curbing of the powerful is either victory or defeat. Both, each in its different way, fling him out of home, and thus, each in its different way, unfold the dangerousness [*Gefährlichkeit*] of achieved or lost being. Both, in different ways, are menaced by disaster. The *violent one,* the creative man, who sets forth into the un-said,...stands at all times in risk and venture [*Wagnis*] (*tolma*). (EM 170; IM 161).

Such a shattering against death is not a lesson in *Gelassenheit* but a test of courage. Without home or hearth, risking death and disaster, the creative one wrestles with the overwhelming power, only finally to shatter against it. He holds up the barrier of his work – statue or state, text or temple – which for a passing moment gives the appearance of stability, only to go under in the mighty rolling wave of the overwhelming power. The uncanny one dares all, risks all, and finally loses all.

Now that is spirit – that's the spirit – and we should get it (OS 125-27n8). That's hard, tough spirit; no tender spirit this. The violent one flings himself against the terrifying and shatters against it. He is tough, "bad," a lover of dangerous seas and wild game, a violent knower/doer (techne), a being of danger, risk, hazard, who in the end is torn to shreds, dispersed by the overwhelming, a victim of the insuperable odds of fate. But that is what makes him great. For if he is indeed crushed by the aboriginal *polemos,* which is no human war, he will be a fearsome opponent in the purely ontic wars with his neighbors ("but who, Lord, is our neighbor?")[9] in which he must be engaged, for this is a point of honor for the *Geist.*

We would say in English that such a fearsome figure "does not know the meaning of danger," which means of course that he really does know it, where *Wissen* is *techne,* where knowing is doing. Indeed that is the very greatness of his spirit

[52] **The Law Of The Economies**

Now I return to the law of the quotation marks. I want to identify the lever that operates this curtain, that lifts it up and down, the machinery that lets the word *Geist* dangle in the air or get a footing on the ground. That law I will call, invoking a notion of which Derrida often makes use, the law of the "economies." That law governs the following proposition, the defense of which I can only sketch here: the spirit of danger is and is not Nazi talk. This is a dangerous way to talk. I admit it. But everything I like and everything I dislike about Heidegger – both at once – are contaminated by this talk of danger, flirts with the danger of this danger, is and is not dangerous, is and is not a Nazi danger.

The "spirit" of "danger" *is* Nazi talk – but it is talk from a philosopher who has set out to make the meaning of "is" tremble, to make it waver in instability.

The "spirit" of "danger" *is* Nazi talk – but it is being read by a philosopher (for Derrida is a "certain" kind of philosopher) who reads through the lens of undecidability.

The "spirit" of "danger" *is* Nazi talk, but I am commenting upon it, for I have signed my name to this piece, and I am speaking of Heidegger and Derrida, of *Geist* and *De L'esprit,* as one who does not believe in essences, as one who thinks that Derrida has shown that we cannot reduce a word or a work to a fixed, identifiable, essentializable meaning. (This also has a profound effect on my reading of Heidegger's discourse on the *Wesen* of this or that, not only of truth, but also of pain when the spirit returns in the Trakl essay.) With Derrida, I do not think that a word has a meaning "in itself," that its sense is fixed and fitted inalterably in one direction or another, and this certainly holds for the words *danger* and *spirit.* For Derrida, words do not have meanings but, rather,

153

they belong to changing economies, and everything depends upon the economies into which they are entered.

All of this is another way of saying that there are no words about which we can comfort ourselves that just by using them, by protesting loudly that we are on their side and that we stand with them, we can thereby show *we are in the right*. There is no assurance that we are in the right just because we say we are against danger, or against struggle, or against the strength of the spirit, or against the spirit of danger. For there is no danger "in itself" no spirit "in itself." Conversely, there is nothing about *national* or *socialism* that proves that we or anyone else are in the wrong.

[53] The economy of spirit and power in the 1930s is very detestable. I have tried to make it as detestable as possible, that is, to let everything detestable about it stand out without mask or disguise – something I have been doing recently with regard to other texts of Heidegger, to the dismay of many old friends, and it is hard to see where it will stop![10] But I want to conclude this chapter by pointing out (and this is by no means to be construed as a full-fledged demonstration) that this discourse on danger and hardness is not without a *history* in Heidegger's texts and hence that it has been subject to a number of economic shifts. That means that it has taken other forms, has belonged to other economies, has had other senses.

On the one hand this discourse has had a prehistory that goes back to Heidegger's earliest interest in Aristotle and Kierkegaard.[11] Towards the beginning of *An Introduction to Metaphysics* Heidegger says that "philosophy by its very nature never makes things easier, only more difficult" (EM 13; IM 11). He adds that "making things difficult gives the weight [*Gewicht*] (the Being) back to things, to beings." To take things lightly, to make life easy, is to rob things of their weight, to expose them and oneself to the unbearable lightness of Being, to let everything float away in ontological weightlessness. In *An Introduction to Metaphysics* this whole notion of difficulty is immediately tied to the origin of everything "great," which is itself tied to the "destiny" of an "historical people." In short, it is entered into the economy of the spiritual danger that we have just rehearsed, which is, I say, detestable. For that is what lets *Geist* enter in full military garb through the opened curtains.

But that represents a change, a fundamental transformation of Heidegger's standpoint that could not have developed before the late 1920s and had already gotten a foot in the door of *Being and Time,* especially in §74. For one who has been reading the work of the early 1920s this invocation of the thematic of "difficulty" is a reference to Aristotle. In fact it is practically a translation of the text in the *Nicomachean Ethics* (1106b28ff.) where Aristotle observes that there

154

are many ways to miss the mark of virtue but only one way to hit it and that therefore the former is easy but the latter is difficult. Heidegger thought that this Aristotelian notion, to which he attached, in my view, a very Kierkegaardian significance, was just the thing he needed.[12] For Heidegger was trying to shake philosophy loose from the spell of Husserlian "neutrality" and to shift it into the mode of difficulty and struggle, for which he even used the word *Kampf* some four years before *Mein Kampf*. *Kampf*, struggle, difficulty, venture, all stand there, in that economy, in differential opposition to transcendental neutrality.

[54] In this Aristotelian, Kierkegaardian, even Lutheran economy, Heidegger was striving with the bloodless subject of transcendental philosophy and seeking to reinstate the rights of what he called in those days "factical life." He was talking about the difficulty of factical living, of the "danger" of simply drifting along with the downward pull of daily existence, of the struggle in which we are all engaged to hit the mark. He had in mind, too, the "danger" that genuine philosophizing about factical life would be suffocated by its academic setting.

Now that is not a detestable economy. In fact, I would say it hits the mark.

But somewhere in the mid to late 1920s this discourse underwent a momentous and ominous economic shift – very likely under the impetus of the encounter with Ernst Jünger[13] – from Aristotle and Kierkegaard to Nietzsche. These economies are complicated: for even as this had been a very Kierkegaardian Aristotle, so too this would be a very Jüngerian Nietzsche. With that shift, "difficulty" became "danger" and the lever that controls the lifting of the quotation marks was pulled, allowing this fiery German figure of *Geist* to make its entrance.

But even as the discourse on the spirit and danger had a prehistory, so too does it have a subsequent history. *An Introduction to Metaphysics* raises the question of Being with a radicality that is such as to make everything tremble, including and above all itself, a radicality that it itself compromises, that it indeed betrays. Thus this fiery figure of *Geist* turns out to be nothing less than the question of Being in military uniform – after it has been turned over by Heidegger himself (one would have thought him its most trusted admirer) to the military authorities. The question of Being withdraws the security and comfort of Being from beings, letting them waver in uncertainty and insecurity. But Heidegger tried to draft this question into the army, to deck it out in a shining, blazing uniform, to enlist it into one of the three services of the rectoral address. Nonetheless, the power of this question twists free from this domestication, nationalization, and militarization – shall we say it goes AWOL?

155

– and ultimately troubles all of Heidegger's own discourse about *Geist, Volk, Dienst, Kraft und Macht,* and *Gefahr.*

Indeed, in the later works the *Gefahr* became the danger that we are not thinking, a very salutary, saving danger, and the whole movement between saving and danger is reversed, with the goal of moving beyond the danger to the saving. This is not to say that I am not profoundly troubled by what I have elsewhere called the later [55] Heidegger's "phainesthetics" or about the place of the "victim" and the meaning of "evil" in the history of Being.[14] Nor do I think that they are adequately addressed by pointing to the phenomenon of errancy (*die Irre*) in Heidegger. Errancy is not evil. These are serious issues and grave problems for me, and they have (irreversibly, I fear) affected the way I will henceforth think about Heidegger. But nothing Heidegger has said or failed to say manages to suppress the enormous power of the question of Being and the questioning of the history of metaphysics that irrupts in his later writings.

For me, the most powerful pages that Heidegger has written occur at the end of the last lecture in *Der Satz vom Grund,* where Heidegger writes that Being is "without why,"[15] a formula that invokes both the rhythms and the vocabulary of the Rhineland mystical tradition. Being plays because it plays. There are – *es gibt* – only the various epochs of Being, the comings and goings of Being's multiple economies, whose only law is play without why. Here Heidegger formulates the law of the economies.

There is – *es gibt* – and that is all. It gives because it gives. And that is all.

It is our exposure to this groundless ground, to the loss of principles and of primordial assurances, of overarching stories and reassuring essences, that constitutes the originary difficulty of life.

Shall we not call that also the danger of the "postmodern" fix we are in, and can we not say, this time in English, that we need the spark, the nerve, the spirit, to come to grips with it? May the spark of that spirit return! *Viens, revenant!*

Notes

[1] Jacques Derrida, *Of Spirit: Heidegger and the Question,* trans. G. Bennington and R. Bowlby (Chicago: Univ, of Chicago Press, 1989), hereafter "OS"; translation of *De L'esprit: Heidegger et la question* (Paris: Galilee, 1987).

[2] Hugo Ott, *Martin Heidegger: Unterwegs zu seiner Biographie* (Frankfurt am Main: Campus, 1988), 171–72. Likewise, it is Ott's documentation of Heidegger's fondness for matters military, and not just during the rectorship, that prompts the militarizing of the figure of *Geist* in the present essay.

[3] Ernst Jünger, "Über den Schmerz" (1934), in *Werke* (Stuttgart: Klett Verlag, 1960-65), 5:149–98. Incidentally, the original version of Heidegger's remark in the 1942 lectures, cited by Derrida (OS 4), in which Heidegger [56] says, "Tell me what you think about translation and I will tell you who you are" (Heidegger, *Hölderlins Hymne "Der Ister,"* GA 53 [1984], 74), is to be found on the first page of Jünger's essay: *"Nenne mir Dein Verhältnis zum Schmerz, und Ich will Dir sagen, wer Du bist."*

[4] Martin Heidegger, *Einführung in die Metaphysik,* GA 40 (1983), 41; abbreviated "EM." Translations are mine, but they closely follow the English translation; compare *An Introduction to Metaphysics,* trans. Ralph Manheim (New Haven: Yale Univ. Press, 1959), 38 ("IM").

[5] See Martin Heidegger, "Letter to the Rector of Freiburg University, Nov. 4, 1945," in Karl A Moehling, "Martin Heidegger and the Nazi Party: An Examination" (Ph.D. diss., Northern Illinois University, 1972), 265.

[6] Martin Heidegger, *Die Grundbegriffe der Metaphysik,* GA 29/30 (1983), 243; abbreviated "GM."

[7] For more on the Jünger-Heidegger link, see Michael Zimmerman, *Heidegger's Confrontation with Modernity: Technology, Politics, and Art* (Bloomington: Indiana Univ. Press, 1990).

[8] Martin Heidegger, "The Self-Assertion of the German University: Address, Delivered on the Solemn Assumption of the Rectorate of the University Freiburg," trans. Karsten Harries, *Review of Metaphysics* 38 (1985): 470–80, p. 474; abbreviated "SGU." Compare *Die Selbstbehauptung der deutschen Universität* (Frankfurt am Main: Vittorio Klostermann, 1983); abbreviated "SdDU."

[9] That there might be a biblical alternative to the question of neighbor and friendship is suggested by Derrida in "The Politics of Friendship," trans. Gabriel Motzkin, *Journal of Philosophy* 85 (1988): 632–44, p. 644.

[10] John D. Caputo, "Heidegger's *Kampf:* The Difficulty of Life," *Graduate Faculty Philosophy Journal* 14:2–15:1 (1991): 61–83; "Heidegger's Revolution: An Introduction to *An Introduction to Metaphysics,*" in *Heidegger toward the Turn: The Texts of the Thirties,* ed. James Risser (Albany: State Univ, of New York Press, 1999); "Heidegger's Scandal: Thinking and the Essence of the Victim," in *The Heidegger Case: On Philosophy and Politics,* eds. Tom Rockmore and Joseph Margolis (Philadelphia: Temple University Press, 1992), 265-281; "Thinking, Poetry, and Pain," *Southern Journal of Philosophy* 28, Supplement, *Heidegger and Praxis* (1989): 155-82. [Editor's Note: These papers were published in John D. Caputo, *Demythologizing Heidegger* (Bloomington: Indiana University Press, 1993.]

[11] See John van Buren, "The Young Heidegger, Aristotle, Ethics," in *Ethics and Danger,* eds. Charles Scott and Arleen Dallery (Albany: SUNY Press, 1992), 169–86.

[12] More specifically, Aristotle held that the practice of virtue became easier with time and habit (*hexis*), but Kierkegaard always resisted that side of Aristotle, insisting on the need to reenact from moment to moment the choice of the good. Kierkegaard regarded settled practices as a lulling to sleep of the will, and in its place he put decisive choices in the existential moment. [57] See George Stack, *Kierkegaard's Existential Ethics* (University Park: Univ, of Alabama Press, 1977). This view depended on an Ockhamistic-Cartesian conception of time in which being must be created from moment to moment by divine freedom instead of being steadily conserved. Kierkegaard's reading of Aristotle was decisive for Heidegger in *Being and Time,* who, on this point, interestingly enough, is using a more Christian and Cartesian conception of time and not a Greek conception at all. See John D. Caputo, *Radical Hermeneutics: Repetition, Deconstruction, and*

the Hermeneutic Project (Bloomington: Indiana Univ. Press, 1987), 18. It seems grossly ungrateful of Heidegger to complain about the Christian distortion of the Greek experience of Being and time when it is just this Christian conception which he is using to challenge Greek parousiology.

[13] I take the appearance of Jünger's "Die Totale Mobilmachung" (*Werke*, 5:123–47), which appeared in 1930 in a collection entitled *Krieg und Krieger*, to be a significant date in this history.

[14] See Caputo, "Heidegger's Scandal." For an account of Heidegger in terms of errancy, see William J. Richardson, "Heidegger's Truth and Politics," in *Ethics and Danger*, 11–24, and my response to Richardson in "Thinking, Poetry, and Pain," 176–80.

[15] Martin Heidegger, *Der Satz vom Grund* (Pfullingen: Neske, 1957), 187–88. Compare "The Principle of Ground," trans. K. Hoeller, *Man and World* 7 (1974): 207–22.

11

KIERKEGAARD, HEIDEGGER, AND THE FOUNDERING OF METAPHYSICS

[In *International Kierkegaard Commentary*, Vol. 6: *"Fear and Trembling"* and *"Repetition"*, ed. Robert Perkins (Macon, GA: Mercer University Press, 1993), 201–224]

[201] Heidegger's assessment of Kierkegaard's weight as a thinker, that is, as something more than a religious polemicist, is severe. He takes the frequent comparison of Kierkegaard with Nietzsche to be a popular misconception. He is eager to keep the two apart on grounds that Nietzsche moves in the same orbit as Aristotle, as a great thinker, one who thinks in terms of Being itself, who is not confined to a merely "ontic" region such as the sphere of the religious. Aristotle and Nietzsche move about in the realm of the Open itself whereas Kierkegaard debates a particular ontic issue, namely, the difference between speculating about Christianity and becoming Christian. At best, Kierkegaard's significance is that his is a particularly timely, if narrow, protest against the reigning metaphysics of the day:

> But the time has come for us to learn to perceive that Nietzsche's thinking, although it must display another mien when judged historiographically and on the basis of the label assigned it, is no less possessed of matter and substance and is no less rigorous than is the thinking of Aristotle.... The comparison between Nietzsche and Kierkegaard that has become customary, but is no less questionable for that reason, fails to recognize, and indeed out of a misunderstanding of the essence of thinking, that Nietzsche as a metaphysical thinker preserves a closeness to Aristotle. Kierkegaard remains essentially remote from Aristotle, although he mentions him more often. For Kierkegaard is not a thinker but a religious writer, and indeed not just one among others, but the only one in accord with the destining belonging to his age. Therein lies his greatness, if to speak in this way is not [202] already a misunderstanding.[1]

Kierkegaard is a timely writer with something to say about the controversies of his day, an important writer because his polemics *respond* to then-current "destining" (*Geschick*) of Being, the omnipresent Hegelianism, but not one to think his way through this Hegelianism, to step back from it and think the destining of Being itself:

> By way of Hegelian metaphysics, Kierkegaard remains everywhere philosophically entangled, on the one hand in a dogmatic Aristotelianism that is completely on a par with medieval scholasticism, and on the other in the subjectivity of German Idealism. No discerning mind would deny the stimuli produced by Kierkegaard's thought that prompted us to give renewed attention to the "existential." But about the decisive question – the essential nature of Being – Kierkegaard has nothing to say.[2]

I want to argue against Heidegger's severity towards Kierkegaard on just this point, by showing that Kierkegaard's religious writings have ontological weight and that his impact on Heidegger goes right to the heart of Heidegger's ontological project. I want to show that Kierkegaard's influence on Heidegger cannot be circumscribed in the way Heidegger attempts, by confining it to the existential side of *Being and Time*, while being declared "forgetful" of the deep ontological question.

One could argue this point by showing that Kierkegaard's influence on *Being and Time* decisively shapes Heidegger's determination of the "Being" of Dasein, and not merely certain "existentiell" issues.[3] It is not confined to the analysis of "anxiety" but goes right to the essence of what Heidegger means by "care" (*Being and* [203] *Time* §42). It is essentially bound up with Heidegger's determination of the "temporality" of Dasein (§65); and finally – and here *Repetition* is immensely important – the entire published text of *Being and Time* culminates and is gathered together in a grand, italicized crescendo, in the historical determination of the temporality of Dasein in terms of historical repetition (§74). That is to say, the essential point the published section of the first half of *Being and Time* reaches, the grand summation and consummation of its argument, is articulated in terms of *Wiederholung* (repetition), the word used as the German translation of Kierkegaard's *Gjentagelse*, which had appeared in 1909.

It could further be pointed out that in none of these places does Heidegger manage to cite Kierkegaard, although his analyses are in a quite straightforward manner directly dependent upon Kierkegaard. Indeed, were one to peruse the German translations of Kierkegaard that Heidegger was reading one would find there, in addition to *Wiederholung* itself, a good deal of the central vocabulary of *Being and Time* – *Angst, Stimmung, Gerede, Levellierung, Augenblick, Entschlossenheit*, for example – along with a systematic lack of acknowledgment in the notes of the origin of this vocabulary in Kierkegaard's writings. To some extent, such an argument has already been made, though with no notable success in persuading the Heideggerians.[4]

[204] But instead of arguing that Kierkegaard's influence extends to the heart of the ontology of the published sections of *Being and Time* – as it does, despite Heidegger's notorious parsimoniousness in the matter of footnoting Kierkegaard – I want to argue an even more forceful point, that Kierkegaard's influence extends to the *unpublished* project of *Being and Time*, that Kierkegaard was *beyond Being and Time* and not just a more or less clear anticipation of it. I want to argue that Kierkegaard had already undertaken "the destruction of the history of ontology," the project of the *unwritten* second half of *Being and Time*, that he was already well underway towards the delimitation of metaphysics and humanism, that he had already set out the limits of existential subjectivity. Kierkegaard had already seen the "end of philosophy." He was not, as Heidegger said, working on *this* side of the ontological, in some narrow ontic region, but rather on the *other* side of ontology, on the "foundering" of metaphysics and ontology. He was not interested in a renewal of ontology, as was the Heidegger of the Marburg period, in a new phenomenological, ontological science, but in precipitating the foundering of metaphysics and in bringing it to grief, in a disruptive, unscientific transgression of metaphysics.

Far from being a pale, ontic adumbration of the deep ontology of *Being and Time* Kierkegaard was already at work on making metaphysics waver like the late Heidegger and, after him, Jacques Derrida. In a manner profoundly comparable to Nietzsche, and on a point in Nietzsche that Heidegger missed, as Derrida has shown,[5] Kierkegaard was at work on a disruptive, transgressive "deconstruction" of metaphysics. Kierkegaard took faith to be the transgression of metaphysics par excellence, a transgression that made metaphysics' head spin and threw it into confusion.

Contrary to Heidegger's attempt to dress down Kierkegaard, it took Heidegger's famous "reversal" to get to the point that [205] Kierkegaard had already attained. Like those who want to get beyond Socrates and Abraham but who do not manage to get quite that far, Heidegger had trouble enough getting as far as Kierkegaard – and on a point which could not be more central, namely, the delimitation of the essence of metaphysics, the central project of the destruction of the history of ontology. Kierkegaard not only decisively influenced the first half of *Being and Time*, he was already at work on the second half. That is why there is growing interest in Kierkegaard from the standpoint of the work of Jacques Derrida,[6] a figure well known for his critique of the residual metaphysical element in Heidegger himself and of Heidegger's metaphysical reading of Nietzsche. Kierkegaard did not merely anticipate Heidegger's *Being and Time;* he had moved beyond it and was pressing the deconstruction of the metaphysics of presence.

That is the thesis of the present study. And *Repetition* is a text particularly well suited for this undertaking. In *Repetition* Kierkegaard *thinks* the history of metaphysics as a whole, effects a certain "closure" of it as it reaches its "end," and helps to precipitate the "foundering" or "coming to grief" of metaphysics. This ontological thematic is written all over *Repetition*, at the very beginning and all along the margins as Constantin tells the story of the travails of his young friend. Both the farcical story of Constantin's return trip to Berlin and the serious story of the young man are set within a pervasive "ontological" framework; they are made to register on an ontological scale.

This is not to say Kierkegaard is arguing *for* an ontology, an Aristotelian one, for example (although that is what he appears to be doing a good deal of the time), but rather that Kierkegaard is arguing for the "deconstruction" of ontology, the way ontology founders and comes to grief when it raises the question of repetition: "Repetition is the *interest* of metaphysics and the interest upon which metaphysics comes to grief" (R, 149).[7] As Heidegger [206] *is* in *Being and Time*, Kierkegaard is *not* simply trying to wrest loose the best fruits and most originating insights of Western metaphysics (which is mainly what the "destruction" of the history of ontology meant at that point[8]), but in bringing metaphysics to grief, in forcing it to "step aside" (CA, 18), in precipitating its foundering. He understood that metaphysics is always implicated in the metaphysics of presence, and he took repetition to be the gesture which transgressed metaphysics and forced its desire for presence into the open.

I will argue for this in three steps: (1) by showing that repetition involves a confrontation with movement and *kinesis* for which metaphysics has no appetite; (2) by a reading of the story Constantin tells in terms of this critique of metaphysics; and (3) by addressing the question of the foundering of metaphysics as such.

Repetition and "*kinesis*"

The question of repetition is fundamentally an Eleatic puzzle. The farcical problem Constantin poses – whether he can repeat a vacation to Berlin – is conceived on analogy with, and humorously juxtaposed with the hoariest and most sober philosophical problem of them all: whether movement is possible. Constantin is the modern-day counterpart to Diogenes:

> When the Eleatics denied motion, Diogenes, as everyone knows, came forward as an opponent. He literally did come forward, because he did not say a word but merely paced back and forth a few times, thereby assuming that he had sufficiently refuted them. When I was occupied for some time, at least on occasion, with the question of repetition – whether or not it is possible, what importance it has, whether something gains or loses in being repeated – I suddenly had the thought: You can, after all, take a trip to Berlin; you have been there once before, and now you can prove to yourself whether a repetition is possible and what importance it has. (R, 131)

[207] The real question for Kierkegaard is whether and how the individual can get on the move, whether he can make existential progress, forge ahead in the process of becoming a self. For a good many of us manage to pass our days not making a stir, idling away the time that is the substance of our life, avoiding the exertion of existential *movement*. But that is deeply out of step with Christianity. Indeed it is a pagan and immanentist view of life. It is what the philosophers, who have not reached the point of transcendence, think that Being is: always somehow immobilized, mummified, frozen, motionless. Philosophy is scandalized by movement and has always argued in one way or another against it.

Philosophy (speculation, metaphysics) opened its doors with the problem of movement. When Heraclitus affirmed the flux, the Eleatics and Plato came rushing in, trying to arrest the flow. Thus the first great philosophical theory, the opening gesture in the history of metaphysics was the doctrine of recollection, which attempted to skip out on the flux, to make one's excuses to life and take an early departure. As soon as philosophy found itself confronted with time and movement, it started looking for a back door. Thrust into existence, speculative thinking wanted to know how to reverse gears and back its way out. If existence and life flow forward, thought tries to move in reverse. Philosophy is *metaphysics*, the attempt to get beyond *physis*, whose most characteristic feature is *kinesis* (motion, movement), according to Aristotle (the one philosopher in antiquity with a taste for the flux, and hence with the heart for a good fight). Philosophy means meta-physics, the attempt to suppress movement, arrest the flux, stabilize the rush of existence.

Indeed philosophy is only possible *as* meta-physics. That is its principal condition of survival. Like Medusa, philosophy has to turn its objects to stone, still them, for if it looks movement in the face it will perish. It cannot withstand the face of the flux, cannot keep its head in the swirl, cannot manage all that movement. The desire of philosophy is to bring the flow to a halt in the *system*, to confine the rushing river within the fixed borders of its categories, to lay a systematic grid over it to contain its movements and allay our fears. Pure movement would send philosophy to an early grave.

[208] Thus *Repetition* begins with an insightful account of the difference between recollection, the way of philosophy, and repetition, the way of the existing individual, as literally opposite courses. Repetition is the affirmation of becoming and time, while recollection, having found itself situated in time, looks for an honorable way out. Recollection is a movement but, as a movement backwards, of a rather odd sort. It is really a kind of un-movement, or undoing of movement, reversing its course, trying to get *back* to the point prior to the movement. After all, there would be something perverse about saying of an army that it is on the move, when what is meant is that it is in retreat, or of a financier that he is on the move, when what is meant is that he is going bankrupt. Recollection takes one look at the flux and retreats. Repetition, on the other hand, presses forward. It has the courage for the flux, the will to press ahead. It knows the prize lies ahead and is given only to those who fight the good fight, who can forge their identity amidst the ravages of time.

Recollection and repetition are movements in opposite directions because they turn on the same point, eternity. They both concern the transition the individual makes from time to eternity, but they follow opposite courses. Recollection is the way of immanence. It takes eternity to be a lost possession and time to be the source of the loss. It looks back, sadly, nostalgically, upon the time before the fall, the time before time. But for the Christian, for the existing individual, eternity is the promise of the *vita ventura*, the life to come; it is the light held out like a beacon that calls us forth.

Thus as a mode of being in time recollection is turned towards the past, while repetition is futural and hence genuinely temporal. Recollection wants to undo time, while repetition is through and through temporal. Indeed "temporality"[9] arises at that point – the moment – where eternity touches time, where it intersects with it and charges it with its energy.

> The moment is that ambiguity in which time and eternity touch each other, and with this the concept of *temporality* is posited, whereby time constantly intersects eternity and eternity constantly pervades time. (CA, 89)

[209] Genuine time is futural, and the genuine future is the *vita ventura*, a Christian not a Greek conception. For the Christian, the eternal hangs in the

balance as a possibility, something is at stake every moment, something momentous, something *eternal*. Properly speaking, therefore, the Greeks, by putting eternity behind them, likewise deprived themselves of time:

> The future in a certain sense signifies more than the present and the past, because in a certain sense the future is the whole of which the past is part, and the future can in a certain sense signify the whole. This is because the eternal first signifies the future or because the future is the incognito in which the eternal, even though it is incommensurable with time, nevertheless preserves its association with time. Linguistic usage at times also takes the future as identical with the eternal (the future life – the eternal life). In a deeper sense, the Greeks did not have the concept of the eternal; so neither did they have the concept of the future. (CA, 89)

The Greeks lacked the deeper concept of time as futural, and of the futural as the eternal. Furthermore, it is only in virtue of understanding the moment as turned towards the future that it is possible adequately to conceive the past:

> The moment and the future in turn posit the past. If Greek life in any way denotes any qualification of time, it is past time. However, past time is not defined in its relation to the present and the future but as a qualification of time in general, as a passing by. Here the significance of the Platonic "recollection" is obvious. For the Greeks, the eternal lies behind in the past that can only be entered backwards. However, the eternal thought of as the past is an altogether abstract concept, whether the eternal is further defined philosophically (a philosophical dying away) or historically. (CA, 89-90)

The Christian lives in authentic temporality. But for the Greek, time is but a "passing-by;" this is the minimal, negative sense of time as the mere absence of eternity from which we ought to extricate ourselves as expeditiously as possible.

Repetition requires the strength of soul to stay with time, from day to day, in an accumulating process of growth and inner development. Repetition forges the self in time; it produces self-identity [210] and continuity by its own resolute, tenacious grip.[10] Recollection takes one look at time and starts to make excuses: it does not hail from this place; it was sent here by mistake; it is too dark and shadowy here for its eyes. Repetition simply puts its hands to the plow and presses forward.

But whatever the failings of recollection, it does have the virtue of honesty. It has no taste for movement and it does not try to throw dust in its eyes or ours about that fact. Classical Greek philosophy understood that movement is not its element and so it just denied that movement had ultimate ontological standing. That is greatly to be preferred to modernity which raises a considerable fuss about "mediation" and makes itself out as the friend of movement – only to sell it out in the end. Philosophy opened shop with the denial of motion and the attempt to beat a hasty retreat from it. But philosophy reached its climax in modernity with a more cunning attempt to befriend motion/movement and hence to bring it under conceptual restraints. Thus if philosophy does not simply deny movement, it must find a way to subvert it, for philosophy is always meta-*physis*.

There really are only two sensible approaches to movement: to affirm it in repetition, or to deny it in recollection. "If one does not have the category of recollection or of repetition, all life dissolves into an empty, meaningless noise" (R, 149). The one really muddled thing to do with movement, however, is to try to interpenetrate it with thought, to constrain its motions with logic, and to produce the confusion of "mediation:"

> "Mediation" is a foreign word; "repetition" is a good Danish word, and I congratulate the Danish language on a philosophical term. There is no explanation in our age as to how mediation takes place, whether it results from the motion of the two factors and in what sense it is already contained in them, or whether it is something new that is added, and, if so, how. In this connection, the Greek view of the concept of *kinesis* corresponds to the modern category "transition" and should be given close attention. (R, 149)

[211] Mediation makes real movement impossible because real movement means moving forward, just as real time means what is coming, and that means that something new really happens.

All that happens in mediation is that a certain logic unfolds. Here is a time made safe by logic, underwritten by necessity, and that moves in preestablished grooves. It is a mere show of motion which is no more real than the ride children take on those cars in amusement parks that run on rails, so that no matter how wildly the children steer the car always follows the same safe track. Nothing new really happens. Nothing can go wrong. We never really get anywhere. We keep tracing the same course. It would be better, like the Greeks, simply to deny that we can digest movement and novelty and be done with it. The worst thing is to invent such fraudulent, logic-driven movement that can never make a wrong turn, and then proclaim, like children to their parents, that we have learned to drive a car.

In Hegel, time and becoming are insulated from the one thing that gives movement its sting: its contingency, the possibility of going wrong, and hence also the exhilaration of having steered the course and pressed ahead to the victory. This is not time and movement; it is a fraudulent metaphysical substitute for it.

Against the doctrine of recollection Kierkegaard insists that repetition moves forward, is futural; against the doctrine of mediation Kierkegaard insists that repetition is free, that it produces something new, that it is ever exposed to contingency so that we cannot say with assurance how the movement will turn out. Thus the Aristotelian category of *kinesis* is thought by Kierkegaard in Ockhamistic, Protestant terms as *freedom*. "The change of coming into existence is actuality; the transition takes place in freedom.... All coming into existence occurs in freedom, not by way of necessity" (PF, 93). The contingency of natural movement is the natural analogue to the movement of human freedom. Both are non-necessitarian processes and both are images, each in their own way, of the absolute freedom of God in creating the world and then of conserving it from moment to moment. Repetition is movement in the eminent sense – futural, free, productive – even as God's creative act is a primordial repetition.

[212] But instead of the robust pressing forward of repetition, Hegelian mediation is a noiseless, anemic counterfeit:

> In logic, transition is movement's silence, whereas in the sphere of freedom it becomes. Thus, in logic, when possibility, by means of the immanence of thought, has determined itself as actuality, one only disturbs the silent self-enclosure of the logical process by talking about movement and transition. (R, 309)

The only noise Hegelian mediation makes is to be found in all the chatter it inspires among the Hegelian professoriate. This noiseless hush of mediation itself is no more than a silent shifting of concepts. In repetition something new irrupts: a breakthrough into the novel is achieved; the walls of immanence are broken. "In the sphere of freedom, however, possibility remains and actuality emerges as a transcendence." (R, 309-10) Something new, something genuinely transcendent to the *terminus a quo* is brought forth, whereas mediation consists in a hushed unfolding of already implicit potentialities. There is genuine *Potenz* and *dynamis* and hence a genuine emergence of actuality (*energeia*) and real work (*ergon*) getting done only in freedom's movement.

The highest case of freedom and repetition is the case of the most profound qualitative shift, when the individual emerges as something new, a new person, in the transition from sin to atonement. Atonement is repetition in the highest sense (*sensu eminentiore*) (R, 320). Sin can only be forgiven, not mediated. This transition is a genuine movement of transcendence in which a prior state is totally transformed. And that transition shatters the categories of metaphysics. It is a scandal to recollection and a stumbling block to mediation. Such a repetition, in which the individual gets himself back, is a matter of pressing forward, not backward, and not in virtue of a logic of necessity and immanent reason, but in virtue of the absurd. Here the individual can make a move only in faith (R, 313).

Thus without stacking the deck in advance, without providing for an assured result that does not risk real movement, repetition is the way the individual survives the flux and establishes himself as a self. Repetition is the way freedom forges the self as a self or, in the end, allows itself to be forged by God, so that the self does not just go up in smoke, dissipated by the flux:

> [213] In the individual, then, repetition appears as a task for freedom, in which the question becomes that of saving one's personality from being volatilized and, so to speak, in pawn to events. The moment it is apparent that the individual can lose himself in events, fate, lose himself in such a way that he therefore by no means stops contemplating but loses himself in such a way that freedom is taken up completely in life's fractions without leaving a remainder, then the issue becomes manifest, not to contemplation's aristocratic indolence, but to freedom's concerned passion. (R, 315)

No matter how great the "dispersal" (R, 320) it is in virtue of repetition that the individual maintains his identity. There is always a "remainder" no matter how much the flux of existing in time "subtracts."

In sum, time and the flux are a whirl that threatens to dissipate the self, to scatter it to the four winds. Recollection appreciates this and tries to make its excuses in order to make an early departure from existence. Mediation puts on a great blustery show of movement when all along it is stationary and it is only the scenery behind it which is in motion. But repetition takes a deep breath and wades into the wind.

Constantin and the Young Man

The text of *Repetition*, the story of Constantin and his young friend and correspondent, is woven across an ontological frame. The story is an imaginative illustration, a work of art that works out in the concrete, not an ontology but the breakdown of ontology, not a metaphysics but the way metaphysics comes to grief. The ontological question is always what is at stake.

The question as to whether repetition is possible is also the question as to whether metaphysics is possible. Metaphysics and repetition are inversely proportional to one another. If metaphysics is possible, repetition is useless, for life can be insulated from the flux. But if we require repetition, that is because we understand that metaphysics is building a house of cards, a make-believe world of concepts.

Repetition comes to pass in the element of the flux, and metaphysics is an attempt to get beyond the flux and to subvert it with thought. Metaphysics, from beginning to end, from Plato to Hegel, systematically searches for a way to arrest the play and allay our [214] fears, whereas repetition is ready to face the worst. Heidegger took Kierkegaard to address ontico-existentiell issues by means of an implicitly Hegelian ontology, that is, a dialectic which, while it transferred its interest from logic to existence, turned on Hegelian distinctions. In fact, Kierkegaard was engaged in the undoing of ontology, its deconstruction. Kierkegaard was trying to bring metaphysics to grief, to stop it in its tracks, to say that when things literally get interesting, metaphysics has nothing to say. And he had the good sense not to try to do this in ponderous Germanic tones but in deft artistic strokes.

He raises the most sober of philosophical questions, the question of the flux upon which, as he thinks, metaphysics founders, by way of a farcical story. The farce Constantin attends in Berlin contains the central thrust of the book, which is Kierkegaard's booming laughter at onto-theo-logic and its ineptitude in the presence of a woman. The deep alliance of Kierkegaard and Nietzsche that Heidegger never saw, because he never saw this point at all, is their invocation of laughter in the face of metaphysics, not only their own enormous wit, but their appreciation for the fact that truth is a woman, a light-footed dancer upon whose feet ponderous German metaphysicians and dogmatic philosophers of all stripes are always stepping.[11] They both reject the deadly serious conceptuality of metaphysics and they both understand its clumsiness in the face of the flux. They know that only the light-footed can keep their balance in the swift currents of life. They know that onto-theo-logic is refuted only by the laughter of the shepherd in Zarathustra's vision, by the laughter of the mocking self-concealing author who produces texts of a dizzying ironic complexity that knock our onto-theo-logical feet from under us.

Kierkegaard was not, as Heidegger thought, a dissident Hegelian tinkering with the system in order to make it produce results in the sphere of existence. Kierkegaard's target was philosophy, metaphysics, speculation itself. He already understood what we today, after Heidegger, call the "end of philosophy," and he had already set about the work of deconstruction. The real difficulty with the fact that Heidegger gave *Wiederholung* [215] a central place in the conceptual architecture of *Being and Time* is not that he failed to acknowledge his source (although he should have done so), but rather that he was taken in by the ruse. He thought repetition was a concept that could assume its rightful place in an existential-analytic with pretensions to being phenomenological science. He took an image that Kierkegaard was bouncing off a mirror and stabilized it in a concept (indeed with a lengthy italicized formulation which reminds us of Climacus's ironic definition of truth [CUP, 182]).[12]

The fact is that in *Repetition* Kierkegaard creates a character who does not exist – Constantin – who also creates a character who does not exist – the young man – all in the service of an imaginative exercise, a psychological thought-experiment, meant to show whether and how repetition is possible. The whole thing is another Kierkegaardian hall of mirrors, a *mise-en-abîme*, meant to give the issue between recollection and repetition imaginative form. We do not find repetition in the first part of the book (Constantin's experiment fails) nor do we find it in the second part (the young man becomes a poet), the part called "repetition" which repeats the first part and repeats the title. There is no repetition in *Repetition*.

Where then is repetition? Not in this book, not in any book, including *Being and Time*, which meant to be a book, a big book of phenomenological science. Not in philosophy, which is metaphysics. But, if at all, only in the flux itself, in *physis*. As soon as one turns to philosophy one takes one's leave of the flux and begins making excuses. No philosopher is ready for the whirl and the dispersal of the flux. They are all looking for a way to calm the storm, to arrest the play.

The farthest the young man gets is when he turns to Job rather than to the fables of the metaphysicians who are always looking for a way to bail out on the flux, sometimes directly (recollection), and sometimes by boasting that they love stormy seas while all the time they stay below deck (mediation). The point of *Repetition* is not to make it a conceptual centerpiece in a ponderous treatise, even with a footnote, but to see to it that one is driven to Job for advice (or to Abraham, since one has to buy both books together). [216] The young man is making progress when he turns for guidance not to Plato or Hegel but to Job:

> The issue that brings him to a halt is nothing more nor less than repetition. He is right not to seek clarification in philosophy, either Greek or modern, for the Greeks make the opposite movement, and here a Greek would choose to recollect without tormenting his conscience. Modern philosophy [Hegel] makes no movement; as a rule it makes only a commotion, and if it makes any movement at all, it is always within immanence,

170

whereas repetition is and remains a transcendence. It is fortunate that he does not seek any explanation from me, for I have abandoned my theory, I am adrift. Then, too, repetition is too transcendent for me. I can circumnavigate myself, but I cannot rise above myself. I cannot find the Archimedean point. Fortunately, my friend is not looking for clarification from any world-famous philosopher or any *professor publicus ordinarius* [regularly appointed state professor]; he turns to an unprofessional thinker who once possessed the world's glories but later withdrew from life – in other words, he falls back on Job. (R, 186)

Job is a teacher of repetition, of taking-again, because he knows that giving and taking belongs to the Lord. And he repeats the prayer of repetition, of giving and taking, again and again. But, to our astonishment, the movement of repetition must go not only beyond metaphysics but even beyond Job. Even this master of rough seas and difficult times, even this genius of disaster and misfortune, Job, is still on the outskirts of repetition. One would think there is no one more able to cope with the flux, no one with better advice to give, than Job who suffered every imaginable reversal and who still managed to regain his feet and take back (*gjen-tagelse*) his life.

But even Job will not do. *Repetition* in the highest sense, *eminentiore sensu*, is not in Job or Job's *Book*. For Job's loss is merely an ordeal, a temporary test which, when it is over, can be replaced. But the radically inner advance Christianity demands cuts deeper than that and requires a more fundamental renunciation that can move ahead only in virtue of the absurd.

Where then is repetition to be found? In *Repetition* the closest we come to it is when the young man is ready to give up, when he thinks he cannot take another step forward, when the sea is so stormy, the wind so bad, that he cannot see how he can go on. "I [217] am at the end of my rope. I am nauseated by life; it is insipid – without salt and meaning" (R, 200; see 200-201). Then he makes himself ready for God's action, throws his finite hands up in a healing despair in human resourcefulness and utters his fiat: let this repetition be carried out in me, he says in effect, for I cannot go on. There, at that point, repetition is possible. There, when one is ready for the thunderstorm, when one quits the illusion that a man can make himself whole by his own powers, then a healing power from without can intervene, a transcendence can come thundering down on him from the outside, knitting up the rent garment of his life, making one again what had been dispersed and disseminated by the wind of the flux. Then repetition is atonement. When one gives up, when one surrenders oneself, then one gets oneself back on terms one has never negotiated:

> All I know is that I am standing and have been standing *suspenso gradu* [immobilized] for a whole month now, without moving a foot or making one single movement.
>
> I am waiting for a thunderstorm – and for repetition....
>
> What will be the effect of this thunderstorm? It will make me fit to be a husband. It will shatter my whole personality – I am prepared. It will render me almost unrecognizable to myself – I am unwavering even though I am standing on one foot....
>
> In other respects, I am doing my best to make myself into a husband. I sit and clip myself, take away everything that is incommensurable in order to become commensurable. (R, 214)

This is the Archimedean point of *Repetition*. We know Kierkegaard altered the text after this point, having gotten the thunderstorm from Copenhagen that Regine was engaged (see R, xx). In the story, the young man suffers a relapse back into recollection; for, upon hearing the news that the girl is married, he resolves upon the life of a poet. Now he belongs to the Eternal Idea of love, not to the real love, which belongs in time, not to the hard work of making love last a lifetime, to the task of putting it into practice from day to day for the rest of one's days. He takes the easy way into eternity. The young man excepts himself from the universal, from marriage, not in the name of the religious but in that of the poetic idea.

The poetic thus functions in *Repetition* on an analogy with metaphysics, for in both cases the real is displaced by the ideal,[218] time by eternity, the bumps of existence by the smooth surface of pure Being. To poeticize is to weave a web of gossamer beauty, even as the metaphysicians weave a yarn of over-arching conceptuality and world-historical meta-narratives. The turn to poetry is conceived here as an escape, a way around the difficulties that existence poses, an idealization in which the ruggedness of existence is allowed to vanish. The poet is not treated as one who suffers from life, who is larger than life, who gets beyond the abstractions of metaphysics for a deeper insight into life, but as one who eases himself out the back door of life to luxuriate among fictions. The poet is the counterpart of the Hegelian metaphysician. Poetry and metaphysics are alternate ways to not-exist.

The young man's turn to poetry, however, gains a "religious resonance" (R, 228) and constitutes, if not another farce, at least an allegory for real *kinesis* and movement, namely, "the transition to the truly aristocratic exceptions, to the religious exceptions" (R, 228). The first part of the book is a farcical caricature of repetition, the second part a more serious allegory of it. In the first part, aesthetic repetition founders on the impossibility of reproducing all the fortuitous circumstances that make an esthetic delight possible. In the second part, religious repetition succumbs to the lure of the eternal and thus avoids the travails of the temporal.

There is no repetition in philosophy, which can exist only so long as it denies movement. Nor is there repetition in Constantin and the young man. Even in Job and Abraham it is but adumbrated and foreshadowed. Even they are still on the outskirts of repetition. Where then?

Repetition, Constantin says – now he steps from behind the scenery and owns up to having invented the young man (R, 228) – has become a kind of "inexpressible substratum" (R, 229), nothing we can find in a book. We do better by exercising a constant vigilance about our inability to express it conceptually than to enshrine it in a system, even an anti-system, an unscientific postscript.[13] Rather than putting it in the center of a conceptual [219] articulation of the Being of Dasein, even with the italics and the footnote, Constantin defers saying anything more. He who is incapable of repetition himself – it is too transcendent – is at least a good sideline observer of all the ruses that are tried in undermining movement, in sidetracking its progress, in devising counterfeit forms of repetition.

We get to repetition only when everything human and subjectivistic shatters against the difficulty of repetition, only when the wind of the flux is howling, when we cannot go on, when the currents are too wild and we seem certain to be destroyed. Then, in a moment when eternity intersects with time and charges it with its energy, when the transcendent bursts upon the scene of immanence, in a transition philosophy cannot conceive, in a movement meta-physics would suppress, which Abraham and Job only foreshadow – then repetition is possible.

The Foundering of Metaphysics

Repetition supplies a central piece of the architecture of the published sections of *Being and Time*. But even had Heidegger been willing to acknowledge this, the "existential analytic" would still fail to get as far as *Repetition*. For Kierkegaard was really at work on the project Heidegger had sketched for the second half of *Being and Time*. In the last page of *Being and Time* Heidegger said the importance of his treatise is not so much in what it has accomplished but in what it sets in motion, that the essential thing is that it is *unterwegs* (underway, on the way) towards a more radical thinking of what "metaphysics" sets out to think. My argument is that Kierkegaard was farther down that way than *Being and Time* appreciated, that he had already set to work on the more radical "deconstruction" of metaphysics that emerges only in Heidegger's later writings and in the French, poststructuralist appropriation of Heidegger.

While Heidegger was importing extensive and unacknowledged discussions of Kierkegaard into the first half of *Being and Time*, Kierkegaard was at work on the second half. While Heidegger was working through the existential analytic, Kierkegaard was exploring the breakdown of the existential subject and the shattering of the powers of subjectivity. And when Heidegger [220] allowed that Kierkegaard had any importance for him, he dressed him down as an existentiell and ontic writer, as one who had not yet made the step back from the ontic to the ontological, whereas in fact Kierkegaard was writing on the other side of ontology, beyond metaphysics, at the limits of metaphysics, where metaphysics comes to grief.

Kierkegaard understood clearly that metaphysics cannot function except in the element of presence (and hence that it is always implicated in – to use Derrida's words – a "metaphysics of presence.") He saw that Platonism simply denied time and becoming, and that Hegelianism made a fraudulent show of affection for it, one that made sure it was perfectly safe before it entered the stream. He knew that metaphysics, both in its inaugurating gesture in Plato and in its consummating gesture in Hegel, is always *meta-physis*, always looking for a way to extricate itself from the flux, always looking for a way to still its play, calm its winds. Metaphysics for Kierkegaard begins as a disinterested, disengaged *nous* (knowledge, reason) looking on at the spectacle of *eidos* (sense perception) and ends as a phenomenological "we" that claims to have situated itself above the flow so as to observe serenely the forms of life through which everyone *else* passes (itself presumably having gotten beyond life, that is, having died).

But repetition lacks the resources to find the high ground above the stream. It is caught in the element of actuality, in the flow of existence and time, situated firmly in and amidst the rush of things. The existing spirit exists (*esse*) in the midst (*inter*) of time, caught in the interstices and corners of actuality. Repetition does not understand how recollection and mediation do not get their coattail caught in the door of actuality whenever they try to make their way out. Repetition has never managed to slip out the back door, to make the speculative leap that lands it on the other side of the flux. The existing spirit exists in the midst of the flux. Its *esse* is *inter-esse*; its being is being-between, being-in-the-midst-of. (Heidegger would later say that the Being of Dasein is "care," by which he obviously meant "interest" in this Kierkegaardian sense.)

That is why Constantin says, in a passage that has oriented this entire study:

174

> If one does not have the category of recollection or of repetition, all life dissolves into an empty, meaningless noise. Recollection [221] is the ethnical [*ethniske*, pagan] view of life, repetition the modern; repetition is the interest [*inter-esse*] of metaphysics, and also the interest upon which metaphysics comes to grief; repetition is the watchword [*Løsnet*] in every ethical view; repetition is the *conditio sine qua non* [the indispensable condition] for every issue in dogmatics. (R, 149)

Discounting mediation as a confusion, Constantin thinks there are really only two sensible alternatives in the face of the stream: either deny movement and make one's way out of time and becoming as gracefully and expeditiously as possible, or take one's stand courageously in the flux. The first is the way of the Eleatics and the theory of recollection; the second the way of repetition. The first tries to maintain itself in disinterest; the second affirms that the existing spirit is always interested.

Thus if philosophy wants to be faithful to actuality it must do so in terms of repetition; but as soon as it takes repetition into account, it runs aground. Everything metaphysics, ethics, and theology want to say depends upon repetition, but as soon as repetition is introduced, they begin to founder. Repetition thus effects a threefold delimitation: of metaphysics, ethics, and theology, which is to say, of everything that Heidegger meant by "onto-theo-logic" and "humanism." This is made clear by a commentary on this central passage by Vigilius Haufniensis:

> The first statement has reference to the thesis that metaphysics as such is disinterested, something that Kant had said about esthetics. As soon as interest steps forth, metaphysics steps aside. For this reason, the word is italicized. In actuality, the whole interest of subjectivity steps forth, and now metaphysics runs aground. (CA, 18n)

Metaphysics can make its way only by keeping its head above the flux, by having commerce only with fixed essences and the rule of law which stabilizes the flux. But as soon as it allows itself to take account of actuality – movement and real change – it runs aground. As soon as metaphysics turns to the real world and turns aside from its own constructions, then it comes to grief. Metaphysics cannot survive in the element of *physis*. If it permits the interests of the existing spirit to come into play, its whole project comes to grief. Its vision is blurred by real transitions and it is at a loss to account for how things really change – how the world [222] came to be, how natural objects move – without reducing them to the unfolding of necessity. Above all, it is confounded

175

by how the existing individual can be made new again in faith and so can say with St. Paul "Behold, all things are become new" (2 Cor 5:17).

For that reason ethics too is in the same bind. Ethics cannot get beyond an immanent logic of moral life, a development according to moral laws that provide for continuous transitions from one moral state to the next. It is at a loss to explain religious repetition, for the discontinuity by which the individual passes from corruption to grace, from sin to atonement:

> Either all of existence comes to an end in the demand of ethics, or the condition [faith] is provided and the whole of life and existence begins anew, not through an immanent continuity with the former existence, which is a contradiction, but through a transcendence. (CA, 17n)

Ethics is bound within the sphere of immanence. It is nonplussed by the idea of a transcendent intervention that pushes the individual beyond anything immanence could reasonably expect. Religious repetition confounds ethics and breaks its grip on existence. "If repetition is not posited, ethics becomes a binding power. No doubt it is for this reason that the author states that repetition is the watchword in every ethical view" (CA 18n).

Kierkegaard thus had a much clearer sense of the limits of subjectivity and of ethical humanism than is to be found in *Being and Time*. He had already written his "letter on humanism" and his delimitation of the sphere of ethics. Heidegger's well-known reversal consisted largely in discovering what Kierkegaard had already known about the limits of existential subjectivity and willing. Rudolf Bultmann's central criticism of *Being and Time* consisted in arguing this Kierkegaardian point, which Heidegger later on conceded, that the transition from inauthenticity to authenticity is not something effected *by* man but rather something effected *in* man by a saving grace.[14]

Finally, repetition is required by all theology ("dogmatics"), [223] and is the rock upon which theology founders. Theology turns God and the world into fixed essences and subordinates them to the rule of reason. But if theology allows faith its say it must permit the most astonishing irregularities and unpredictable divine action. It is at a loss to explain God's way with men, though that is its sole reason for being: "If repetition is not posited, dogmatics cannot exist at all, for repetition begins in faith, and faith is the organ for issues of dogma" (CA, 18n). Repetition effects the delimitation of the whole range of onto-theo-logic, humanism and subjectivity, which is to say, the entire range of issues that Heidegger's project of "overcoming metaphysics" addresses. Repetition causes a tremor in "metaphysis" that metaphysics cannot calm. Repetition wrests free from the constructions of metaphysical reason and drags

176

nous down into the rush of the world. It insists on keeping company with time and change and transition. It lives in an element where metaphysics cannot breathe and, instead of looking for a way out, it wants only to press forward.

Among the metaphysicians, repetition's chief ally is to be found in the Aristotelian doctrine of *kinesis* (and, among the moderns, in Leibniz, a neo-Aristotelian of sorts). There, Kierkegaard thinks, philosophy attempts to account for the real world, for change and becoming, without reducing the world to *presence*. Metaphysics is comfortable only with a world of presence and absence, with Being and its negation. And it has always had the greatest difficulty in focusing on what is *between* them, on that movement which neither is nor is not but somehow fluctuates between the two. Metaphysics is constantly *resolving* movement into being or nonbeing, pushing it into the extremities of a binary oppositional scheme where it can work with it, where it can either declare it nothing at all (since it is not being), or a mere imitation of something (since it is not non-being). It has always had the greatest difficulty in recognizing it for what it "is," on its own terms and in its own right.

Aristotle at least undertook such a venture, as Derrida points out in a famous critique of the concept of time in *Being and Time*).[15] [224] In fact, of course, Aristotle too was under the spell of *metaphysis*, and he too subordinated movement to *ousia*, to the stability of what is permanently present. Aristotle too belongs to the history of metaphysics that stretches from Plato to Hegel. In the end, metaphysics must always take its leave of the flux if it wants to remain metaphysics.

Although Kierkegaard was not a historical thinker, he had already sketched out in *Repetition* a destruction of the history of ontology as the metaphysics of presence. In *Repetition* he cut off the two fundamental strategies of metaphysics: either to deny movement outright and claim that only presence is real; or, posing as the friend of movement, to subvert it by reducing it to the rule of logic and necessity, a kind of presence-in-motion in which movement is always kept safe and "maintained" (held by the hand, held in place, governed by the now). Kierkegaard understood the desire of metaphysics to arrest the play, and he took faith to be the great transgression of metaphysics, the frustration of that desire, flushing out its ruses, cutting off its escape routes, forcing it to face the flux. It is true that he said repetition is eternity, but that only had the effect of burying the existing spirit in time.[16]

Heidegger's parsimonious references to Kierkegaard in the published sections of *Being and Time* are not the main problem. The more astonishing thing is how profoundly Kierkegaard had both anticipated and set in motion the deconstruction of the history of ontology that Heidegger had not yet addressed.

It would take more than a footnote on Heidegger's part to fix his relationship to Kierkegaard. It took the full force of his turning in his later writings to get as far as *Repetition*.

Notes

[1] Martin Heidegger, "Nietzsches Wort 'Gott ist tot'," in *Gesamtausgabe* 5, *Holzwege*, (Frankfurt: Vittorio Klostermann, 1971), 249; English Translation [ET]: "The Word of Nietzsche: 'God Is Dead'," in *The Question Concerning Technology and Other Essays*, trans. William Lovitt (New York: Harper & Row/Colophon, 1977), 94.

[2] Martin Heidegger, *Was Heisst Denken?* (Tübingen: Niemeyer, 1954), 129; ET: *What is Called Thinking?*, trans. J. Glenn Gray and Fred D. Wieck, (New York: Harper & Row, 1968; Harper Torchbooks, 1972), 213.

[3] Cf. Martin Heidegger, *Sein und Zeit* (Tübingen: Niemeyer, 1963); *Gesamtausgabe* 2, 1977), 235n.6; 338n.3; ET: *Being and Time*, trans. John Macquarrie and Edward Robinson (New York: Harper, 1962), 494n.vi; 497n.iii.

[4] See especially Calvin O. Schrag, "Heidegger on Repetition and Historical Understanding," *Philosophy East and West* 20 (1970): 287–95; and *Existence and Freedom* (Evanston IL: Northwestern University Press, 1961). Some quite excellent work has recently begun to appear from John Edward van Buren whose dissertation (McMaster University, 1988) "The Young Heidegger" repays study; see Van Buren's "The Young Heidegger: Rumor of a Hidden King," forthcoming in *Philosophy Today* and "The Young Heidegger and Phenomenology" forthcoming in *Man and World*. See also Dan Magurshak, "The Concept of Anxiety: The Keystone of the Kierkegaard-Heidegger Relationship," 167–95 in *The Concept of Anxiety, International Kierkegaard Commentary* 8, ed. Robert L. Perkins (Macon GA: Mercer University Press, 1985); Michael E. Zimmerman, *Eclipse of the Self: The Development of Heidegger's Concept of Authenticity* (Athens: Ohio University Press, 1981); William Spanos, "Heidegger, Kierkegaard, and the Hermeneutic Circle: Towards a Postmodern Theory of Interpretation as Dis-closure," *Boundary* 2/4 (2) (1976): 455–88. In French, the numerous writings of Jean Wahl established the general relationship between the early Heidegger and Kierkegaard; see "Heidegger et Kierkegaard," *Recherches philosophiques* 2 (1932–1933): 349–70; *Études Kierkegaardiennes* (Paris: Aubier, 1938; Paris: Vrin, 1974); and, in English, Wahl's *Philosophies of Existence: An Introduction to the Basic Thought of Kierkegaard, Heidegger, Jaspers, Marcel, Sartre* (New York: Schocken Books, 1969).

[5] See Derrida's reading of Heidegger's reading of Nietzsche in *Spurs: Nietzsche's Styles*, trans. Barbara Harlow (Chicago: University of Chicago Press, 1979); cf. my "Three Transgressions: Nietzsche, Heidegger, Derrida," *Research in Phenomenology* 15 (1985): 61–78. [Also in Caputo, *The Collected Philosophical and Theological Papers*, Vol. 1, chapter 25.]

[6] See the work of Mark C. Taylor and the series edited by Mark C. Taylor, Louis Mackey, and Eugene Kaelin, "Kierkegaard and Postmodernism," especially, Sylviane Agacinski, *Aparté: Conceptions and Deaths of Søren Kierkegaard*, trans. Kevin Newmark (Tallahassee: Florida State University Press, 1988).

[7] The old translation, "upon which metaphysics founders," is worth preserving; see Søren Kierkegaard, *Repetition*, trans. Walter Lowrie (Princeton NJ: Princeton University Press, 1946), 34.

[8] Martin Heidegger, *The Basic Problems of Phenomenology*, trans. Albert Hofstadter (Bloomington: Indiana University Press, 1982) 22–23.

[9] *Being and Time*, §65.

[10] In Derridean terms, repetition is productive and recollection is reproductive. I have discussed this at some length in my *Radical Hermeneutics: Repetition, Deconstruction, and the Hermeneutic Project* (Bloomington: Indiana University Press, 1987), chapters 1 and 5 in connection with Kierkegaard, Derrida and Husserl.

[11] This is the argument of Derrida's *Spurs*. See my *Radical Hermeneutics*, 155–60.

[12] *Sein und Zeit*, 385; ET: *Being and Time*, 437.

[13] See the line of interpretation of the pseudonymous authorship pursued by Josiah Thompson in *Kierkegaard* (New York: Knopf, 1973) and in his anthology *Kierkegaard: A Collection of Critical Essays* (Garden City NY: Doubleday, 1972).

[14] See Michael Zimmerman's treatment of Bultmann and Heidegger in *Eclipse of the Self*, esp. 144–45, and in "Heidegger and Bultmann: Egoism, Sinfulness, and Inauthenticity," *Modern Schoolman* 58 (1980): 1–20.

[15] Jacques Derrida, "*Ousia* and *grammé*: Note on a Note from *Being and Time*," in *Margins of Philosophy*, trans. Alan Bass (Chicago: University of Chicago Press, 1982), 29–67.

[16] See the criticism of Kierkegaard's notion of repetition by Gilles Deleuze, *Différence et Répétition* (Paris: PUF, 1981), 12–20, especially 16–20, and 126–27, 377. For a Kierkegaardian reaction see André Clar, "Médiation et Répétition: Le lieu de la dialectique Kierkegaardienne," *Revue des sciences philosophiques et théologiques* 59 (1975): 38–78, esp. 77n.87.

12

PRESENTING HEIDEGGER

[In *American Catholic Philosophical Quarterly*, 69:2 (1995), 129–33]

[129] I am pleased to present to the readers of *American Catholic Philosophical Quarterly* this special issue on the work of Martin Heidegger (1889–1976). Arguably the most important and easily the most controversial European philosopher of this century, Heidegger has never ceased to shape the direction of the philosophy of our time. With the appearance of *Being and Time* in 1927 Heidegger became almost overnight a figure of international importance even as his post-war writings have shaped contemporary debates about the "end" of philosophy, or of metaphysics, or even the "end of man" in recent French thought. With the ongoing publication of his *Gesamtausgabe*, which contains the many lectures Heidegger gave over the years, the impact of his work continues to be felt.

Heidegger has, moreover, deeply influenced Catholic thought in this century – his name is forever linked with that of Karl Rahner, for example – and, by the same token, the Catholic tradition was an important part of his own early years. Writing in a conservative Catholic journal, the young thinker once said, citing a leading German Catholic philosopher at the turn of the century, "Dig deeply enough and you will strike Catholic ground." Even as late as 1921, he described himself as a "Christian theologian." That is not of course what we recognize as "Heidegger" today; a thorough account, however, of Heidegger's tangled but unbroken relationships with the Christian and specifically Catholic tradition, and with the Aristotelianism of that tradition, goes a long way towards explaining who Heidegger is and how he became "Heidegger." That in one way or another is the topic of the several papers gathered together in the present collection, which represents the work of some of the most distinguished American and European Heidegger scholars of our day, and a few younger voices as well.

The most important development in Heidegger studies in recent years is the emergence of the "First Freiburg period" (1919-1923) and the pre-*Being and Time* period generally as a distinct object of inquiry. [130] That is the crucial period when the young philosopher, just home from World War I, having turned away from both Catholicism and scholasticism, began his inquiries into the "hermeneutics of factical life" by way of a series of extraordinarily original interpretations both of Aristotle's ethics and the life-world of the *New Testament* communities. Thus it is no accident that more than half the studies in this issue take up that exciting period.

The opening essay by Freiburg historian Hugo Ott, whose *Heidegger: A Political Life* is at the center of the present debate over Heidegger's involvement with National Socialism, gives us an insight into the Catholic world in which the young Heidegger moved, and explores the reasons why Heidegger left the Catholic faith, carefully examining the now famous letter to Engelbert Krebs in 1919. The next two essays are by John van Buren and Theodore Kisiel who together have virtually staked out the terrain of this new field of investigation. Van Buren's *The Young Heidegger* (1994), and Kisiel's *The Genesis of Heidegger's Being and Time* (1993), which are repeatedly cited in the present collection, are surely among the most important, groundbreaking studies of Heidegger to appear in many years in any language. Van Buren here provides a lucid account of the central methodological notion of "formal indication," which represents Heidegger's attempt to find a philosophical structure that is trimmed to the wind of the immediacy of pre-philosophical, factical life. Continuing this analysis, Kisiel deftly interprets the "breakthrough" Heidegger made in 1919 to his fundamental project as the discovery of the language demanded by philosophy if philosophy is to bring immediacy to words – as opposed to Heidegger's earlier logical investigations into a pure grammar, when he was still under the influence of the Scotistic speculative grammar of Thomas of Erfurt and Husserl's notion of a pure a priori grammar.

In an exhaustive study of the relevant materials, Istvan Feher, the distinguished Heidegger and Hegel scholar from Budapest, whose comprehensive study *Martin Heidegger* Feher is currently rewriting and expanding in English for Fordham University Press [note: this edition never appeared –Ed.], makes a fascinating case for the meaning of Heidegger's "methodological atheism" in the 1920s, as philosophy's requisite silence before God, a position Heidegger held, on Feher's view, throughout his entire life. Beyond Heidegger's influence on theology, Feher shows how Heidegger's own thought arises from an attempt to come to grips with the theological questions that first set his work into motion, including a project to get back to the world of primitive Christian experience free from the distortions of Greek philosophy, the mirror opposite of the project of his later studies of the early Greeks.

William Richardson, S.J., is the dean of American Heidegger scholars, generations of American students having cut their teeth on his [131] *Heidegger: Through Phenomenology to Thought*, which itself generated Heidegger's important letter to Richardson. In "Heidegger's Fall," Richardson defends his thesis (against an impudent admirer) that Heidegger's errant political choices are explained best of all by Heidegger's own notion of *Irre*. In the course of this deep and probing study, which shows the way Heidegger lays the ontological foundation for understanding any ontically determinate evil, Richardson takes us through the 1921–22 Freiburg course, *Phenomenological Interpretations of Aristotle* (GA 61), in which the first sketches of "fallenness" are made, some crucial texts on evil in the later writings, and along the way through an interesting excursus on the problem of original sin.

Frank Schalow, who has written widely about Heidegger, Kant, and ethics, shows that the notion of conscience in *Being and Time*, which goes to the heart of Heidegger's destruction of the Cartesian subject down to the existential subject, is best understood by considering the linkage between *praxis* and *logos* in the early lectures on primal Christianity, and hence that there are religious and not only Aristotelian sources for Heidegger's notion of conscience.

The next two pieces explore Heidegger's revolutionary readings of Aristotle in the 1920s. Thomas Sheehan, whose *The First Coming* earned him the wrath of more traditional Christologists, and whose pieces in *The New York Review of Books* on Heidegger's Nazism and on the Derrida interview in Wolin's *The Heidegger Controversy,* earned him the wrath of Heideggerologists and Derridaologists, here tries to stir up trouble by way of some recommendations as to how and how not to translate Heidegger. Sheehan offers a subtle, suggestive microanalysis of Heidegger's difficult language and, by focusing on the Aristotelian sources of the notion of *Zeitlichkeit*, makes the startling proposal that, having been too much attached to "having been" as a translation of *Gewesen,* we need something new. In a careful and insightful study, M. T. Kane shows that when the young Heidegger first undertook his analysis of Aristotle's notion of time he found not the corruption of the Christian notion of *kairos* as the moment of choice and truth, but "a fundamental insight into *kairos* and this before Christ" in the *Nicomachean* Ethics – along with a levelling of that insight in the *Physics.*

The remaining essays turn to Heidegger's later writings. In a beautiful and evocative piece, which is a wonderful introduction to the later work, *ACPQ* Editor, Robert Wood, a distinguished student of the interaction of the tradition and contemporary continental writers, sketches six Heideggerian figures, not static types but six Heideggerian ways to be, which play and interplay like so many leitmotifs in a musical composition, which co-play and collaborate in opening the Clearing, the "*Da.*" If, in the first Freiburg period, Heidegger sought to find a Christian experience undistorted by Greek philosophy, then, after 1930 [132] Heidegger's project was exactly the opposite. Robert Bernasconi, from whose searching studies of Heidegger, Derrida, and Levinas we have all learned so much, addresses Heidegger's resolute insistence in the later work that philosophy is Greek in origin and essence as well as his resistance to the idea of Christian philosophy, not to mention Asian or African philosophy. This is to be understood, Bernasconi holds, not as a short-sighted or neglectful history of philosophy but as a carefully thought out philosophical program, rooted in a certain "law of exclusion," which turns on the idea that the only way to release what is unthought in Being's history, and hence the possibility for "another beginning," is to return to the early Greeks (linked through the war years with the Germans) as an absolute first beginning in a way that effaces both the sources of the Greeks themselves and the later Christian renderings of the Greeks.

By taking the historicality of the work of art as a paradigm, distinguished Notre Dame theologian and long time student of Heidegger's works Thomas F. O'Meara argues that a careful reading can find an alternative in Heidegger's history of Being to the usual theological options for interpreting the history of doctrine. Instead of thinking of history as progress, decline, or stasis, Heidegger's notion of cultural "disclosure," of revealing-concealing, gives each epoch a certain *sui generis* validity, its own disclosive power and limitations. A theology belongs to an epoch the way a work of art does, as a disclosure of it, the result being a plurality of cultural periods each with an integrity of their own that permits change without succumbing to historical relativism. If van Buren has shown how the young Heidegger's thought was inspired by a theology of the cross, Matthew A. Daigler, making his publication debut, shows in an insightful study how the later Heidegger's thought of Being's shining splendor resonates with von Balthasar's theology of the glory of the Lord. Referring to the work of Marion, Daigler says that the two ways part, however, over the issue of the gift, for Being's beauty is an impersonal, anonymous giving, whereas for von Balthasar the world is the gift of love, of God's creative act, so that it is love that divides the parties to this lover's quarrel.

Is Heidegger's "a-theism" real or methodological, real or a way that philosophy observes silence before God? Is Heidegger an atheist or does God play a central if elusive role for him? Is his thought set in motion by the earliest texts of the *New Testament* or by the earliest texts of the Greeks? Is his thought tuned to the *theologia crucis* or to the *theologia gloriae*? Are his Catholic beginnings a stage that is decisively left behind or do they come back to him from the future? What relevance does Heidegger have for theology? What relevance does theology have for understanding his thought? What lies behind the systematic exclusion of Christian thought from the truth of Being? How are we to understand [133] his Nazism? Can it be understood in terms of his own thought? Has he himself explained the possibility of erring better than anyone today? In trying to break through the crust of scholasticism's Aristotle, did he discover a more radical Aristotle or an Aristotle made over in his own image? Do his several attitudes towards Christianity and theology reflect the dynamics of the "path of thought"?

These and other questions are addressed by the distinguished contributors to the present volume in a series of probing and imaginative studies that I am honored to present.

13

GIVING PHILOSOPHY THE LAST WORD: LEVINAS AND THE YOUNG HEIDEGGER ON PHILOSOPHY AND FAITH

[In *Annäherungen an Martin Heidegger: Festschrift für Hugo Ott zum 65. Geburtstag*, ed. Hermann Schäfer (Bonn: Haus der Geschichte, 1996), 209-231]

As Hugo Ott has shown, the question of Heidegger's Catholic beginnings and of the changing and complex relationship Heidegger maintained with Catholicism over the years is central to understanding the full trajectory of Heidegger's *Denkweg*.[1] Ott's careful and detailed work throws light on the work that is today being done to understand Heidegger's first Freiburg period, from 1919 to 1923, a field of research that has emerged into prominence with the publication in Heidegger's *Gesamtausgabe* of the lectures from those years. It is quickly becoming clear that some of Heidegger's most original and groundbreaking work took place in a period of which we have up until recently known next to nothing. Both Heidegger and the heirs of his literary estate were initially less than forthcoming about these lectures – they were not included among the projected volumes when the *Gesamtausgabe* was first announced – perhaps because they reveal a Heidegger in intimate dialogue with Christian theology, a Heidegger who even described himself at one point as a "Christian theo*logian*."[2] But the fact stands that Heidegger's most creative breakthroughs occurred in the course of a close and insightful dialogue with the Christian faith, with a hermeneutics of the factical life of faith, without which *Sein und Zeit* would have been unthinkable. This work, which trims the sails of philosophy close to the winds of factical life, is, in my view, of more enduring significance than the dangerous myth of Greco-Germania that is embedded in the notion of the *Seinsgeschick* around which his later work is organized.[3]

The essence of the young Heidegger's project lay in returning philosophy to its pre-philosophical sources. Philosophy, he argued, stands in need of a relentless exposure to life in order to renew its logic and its categories. For philosophers, when they move at all, are likely to move about preestablished grooves, disputing the order of rank of the same old concepts, and generally managing only to rearrange the furniture on the conceptual deck, while the ship itself keeps a steady course. Philosophy needs to be shaken by life – by a certain hermeneutic violence – systematically exposed to what is not yet philosophy and returned to its non-philosophical or pre-philosophical soil. That gives philosophy the difficult, in some ways, impossible task, which does not make philosophy less interesting, that of saying something philosophical about what is not philosophy, about life, which is prior to or older than philosophy, but to do so without turning life back into philosophy. Philosophy, according to the program of the young philosopher, must somehow gain access to the life that is led before philosophy arrives on the scene, letting life speak for itself, while yet managing still to be philosophy.

The interesting thing that was almost entirely suppressed by Heidegger's work after *Sein und Zeit* and that Hugo Ott has helped bring out into the open is that the young Heidegger numbered religious faith, in particular the faith of the early New Testament communities, among those central pre-philosophical sources upon which philosophy should draw, with which philosophy must maintain constant contact, without which philosophy is consigned to remain abstract and out of touch.[4] Heidegger did not seek to find a neutral, ahistorical metalanguage, some kind of autonomous discourse into which faith along with everything else must be translated, or before whose eye everything must pass in review for legitimation. He rejected the modernist, neo-Kantian model of an epistemological judge in favor of what he called a "hermeneutics of facticity," by which he meant a philosophical, or pre-philosophical discourse that will be marked by its respect for the idiosyncrasies of life.[5] The hermeneutics of facticity, like the wax of which Descartes speaks, bears the aroma of the honied hive from which it is drawn but which, unlike Descartes, will never yield to a conceptual distillation. Rather than a philosopher-judge subjecting life to judicial review, adjudicating life's hard cases, Heidegger thought of philosophy as leading us to the brink and abyss in existence, leading us to the point of the difficulties and aporias of life that can be worked out, not in or by philosophy, but only in the movements of existence itself.

Faith, the young thinker insisted, is a central pre-philosophical form of life, a leap situated on the side of life not of philosophy. Faith is a way to leap, while philosophy looks on in wonder from its *Lehrstuhl*. Faith does; philosophers attend conferences. Philosophy not only begins in wonder, it stops there too, wondering at all the things that life carries out, for which it itself lacks the heart. Still, philosophy's task is difficult enough, for it must avoid turning life into more philosophy, avoid making things like leaps look easy. Philosophy must avoid covering over the originary and intractable difficulty of life, of which

Aristotle spoke in the *Ethics* when he said that there are many ways to miss the mark of life, overshooting and undershooting, leaping too much and leaping too little, but only one way to hit it.[6]

Now it is a curious thing to me that both Heidegger and Levinas – truly very different thinkers – at least, a certain very young Heidegger and a young, middle-aged and likewise excessively old Levinas, understood philosophy in very similar ways. Both thinkers sought to return philosophy to its pre-philosophical resources in order to give philosophy a new start, and they both urged in particular a return to the Scriptures – to the New Testament and the Tanakh respectively – as especially rich pre-philosophical experiences. Heidegger would eventually drop the letters of St. Paul from his canon of pre-philosophical sources and would begin recommending the poetry of Hölderlin in their place, although it turned out, when he died, that he had arranged for Fr. Bernard Welte to read from *both* Hölderlin and St. Paul at his funeral (so perhaps it ended in a draw).[7] Still, Heidegger's idea of returning philosophy to the pre-philosophical, to something that philosophy could never master but only heed and serve, of keeping philosophy structurally exposed to something that exceeded philosophy, stayed the same. Levinas on the other hand was even more constant; he never stopped recommending the Book and all the little books that are built around the Book to protect it like a fence.

In the present essay I would like to examine the relationship between Levinas and the young Heidegger on just this point and, to the distress of the Levinasians, demonstrate the surprising result that it was in fact Heidegger – a certain very young Heidegger about whom we have only recently begun to learn – who showed the more sensitive appreciation of the alterity of the scriptures and the more resolute insistence on the limits of philosophical conceptuality vis-à-vis the idioms of biblical life.

Convincing the Most Difficult to Please

Levinas, whose work Derrida has recently described as a kind of nondogmatic doublet of dogma, as a certain philosophical repetition of religion without religion,[8] wants to let philosophy be instructed by its pre-philosophical sources. In "The Youth of Israel," Levinas writes, "Besides, I have never understood the radical difference one makes between philosophy and simple thought, as though all philosophies did not derive from non-philosophic sources."[9] All philosophy arises from pre-philosophical sources which it brings to the level of a certain conceptuality. There are many such pre-philosophical sources – the ordinary experiences of everyday life; limit experiences like birth and death; the products of high culture, like a national literature. But, above all, for Levinas, there is his life as a Jew in the midst of a world that is Greek, Roman, Christian, Russian, French, not very visibly Jewish, in which Jews are almost invisible. Levinas's special work, as Robert Gibbs has so nicely explained, has been to take the unusual idiom of "Hebrew" existence – of Tanakh, the Talmud and Midrash – and "translate" them into Greek.[10] So Levinas will produce a "Jewish philosophy," analogous in its own way to the "Christian philosophy" that Jacques Maritain and Étienne Gilson defended years ago, a philosophy autonomous in its own right but still rich and fragrant with the Hebrew honey from which it is drawn, with its own unique idiomatic aromas which only Hebrew sources can supply.

Now by translation he does not mean merely to translate from one language to another, since Levinas writes everything in French, and since there already is a Greek Septuagint. Rather, he has in mind a movement from one discourse to another, from one mode of thinking into another, as Gibbs points out. Translation is an inter-discursive movement, not a vertical top-down movement from faith up above to reason down below, but a lateral one from one discursive structure to another. But translation is a real passage, a movement of *universalization*, which starts from the unusual idiom of biblical and Talmudic discourse, from the idiomatic genius of a particular people (the pre-philosophical), and moves to a more common, universal, even a university or academic discourse (the philosophical), which is relevant to all people, Jewish or not, to anyone with a taste for honey, however difficult they are to please. Translation is a passage from Hebrew to Greek, not as national languages but as discursive structures. "Often, all one needs to do is define an unusual terminology with words derived from Greek to convince the most difficult to please that one has just entered philosophy."[11] As Gibbs remarks, the motivation of Levinas's "Greek" works – *Totalité et Infini* and *Autrement qu'être ou au-delà de l'essence* above all – is "rhetorical" or "apologetic," appealing to the Other One, which here means philosophers who hardly ever are to be found reading the Talmud, to lend all this an ear, on the grounds that it will do them some philosophical good. Gibbs adds, commenting specifically on this passage, "Levinas in 1970 explained that he used 'Greek' terms to convince objectors that he was doing philosophy while commenting on Talmudic texts."[12]

This is quite fascinating. Levinas is trying to slip a little Midrash into Parisian pockets so that, if these philosophers are questioned by the police of thought, they will have a hard time explaining what is in their possession. He is trying to infiltrate academic philosophy with a foreign substance, with a little taste of philosophy's other, a little Hebrew honey imported from Jerusalem which he has packaged in Greek wrappings. But Levinas does all this for the good of philosophy, in order to give philosophy a new start, in order to restart philosophy with a dash of Midrash. Levinas has no interest in declaring "the end of philosophy" but, on the contrary, in getting it started again; nor does he seek to bring philosophy into line behind faith as theology's trainbearer and *ancilla*. Levinas takes a surprisingly strong view of philosophy and he places surprisingly great faith in philosophy. The particular line that Levinas takes is that the Torah and the Talmud are good philosophy, good ethics, good thinking, which just require a little translation. He thinks the thought of the sages "is radical enough to satisfy the demands of philosophy. It is this rational meaning which has been the object of our research."[13]

There is nothing to prevent the translation of the God of Abraham into the God of philosophy, and there is no reason to believe that there is any opposition at all between them, as Halevy and Pascal would have had us believe: "Philosophical discourse therefore should be able to include God, of whom the Bible speaks – if this God has a meaning."[14] The thing is not to bring the meaning of God into Being's orbit, not to let God's meaning be predetermined by the meaning of Being, but to find a meaning and a philosophy, a philosophical meaning, that is otherwise than Being. For the God of Abraham makes sense so long as we have the sense to understand that the sense God makes is otherwise than the one Greek philosophy has put in place, which requires us to be sensitive to the distinctive sense that the biblical God makes.

Levinas thus is seducing the philosophers – "non-erotic *par excellence*"[15] – getting them to talk about what is otherwise than being while all the while talking the talk of philosophy and making philosophical distinctions like that between saying and the said. Levinas provokes philosophy by injecting something new, something different, into philosophy's hardened arteries, something a little Hebrew, with the intent of raising the metabolism of a sedentary breed. He has managed to crossbreed the incredulity of the postmodern with a soaring, sweeping prophetic *récit* that carries them all off to a land that is otherwise than Being, that has Derrida dreaming of the impossible, that has Lyotard suffering the pain of unrepresentable justice. Levinas has succeeded in getting bearded, elbow-patched philosophers, their pipes clenched in their teeth, who haven't read Genesis since grade school, reading papers to one another on absolute altruism to the widow, the orphan and the stranger. That is a bit of derring-do that no one else would have dared, that no pious priest or rabbi, however puffed up with erudition, could ever have pulled off.

Levinas focuses on the relationship to the neighbor in Hebrew thought which he has relentlessly, single-mindedly, one might even say obsessively driven home to contemporary philosophy. He has cast it in uncanny categories that sound seductively Greek but also oddly un-Greek, that are a little "Jewgreek," to cite Derrida's memorable citation of James Joyce.[16] He has taken a fundamentally prophetic conception and turned it into an almost common philosophical parlance, into an odd but omnipresent discourse that has, surprisingly, caught on, so that it is impossible to attend a conference on recent French thought these days without having "openness to the Other" drummed into your ear. He has seduced philosophers for their own good, for the good of philosophy, back to the Good, back to thinking unthinkable thoughts like absolute altruism and the utter Otherness of God. Moving about in a world where the only blasphemy is irreverence towards Nietzsche,[17] Levinas has gotten philosophers, right there in the middle of the *rive gauche* or Greenwich Village, to talk about a radical sacrifice of the *conatus essendi* to the neighbor who turns me into a hostage in the name of God. He has gotten large numbers of cold-hearted atheists discussing the paradoxes of the *me voici*, i.e., of the Hebrew *hineni*, see me here, of which the French provides a beautiful translation. Levinas cites Isaiah without quite citing him, almost without ever mentioning his name, even though it is Isaiah that is whispering in his ear – and Amos and Abraham and a whole library full of Midrash whispering into their ears – translating these texts into *je ne sais quoi* – Greek? French? Jewgreek? Franco-jewgreek? Russo-franco-jewgreek? But he does not (quite) acknowledge his sources, lest the auditorium empty before his eyes. For while these elbow patched academics are all astir about openness to the other, they do not want to hear about the alterity of Levinas's sources.

A Philosopher's Judaism

Thus far Levinas's apologetics, his rhetoric, his strategy, has been an unqualified success. He has seduced a whole generation of philosophers, pleasing the most difficult to please, and made wiser thinkers of us all, wise with the wisdom of love and wary of the love of what the *Aufklärer* call "pure reason" *sans* faith and of the religion kept prisoner within its limits.

Levinas, who goes so far as to say that he is giving philosophy the "last word,"[18] takes up the prophetic religion of Judaism, the prophet's concern for justice, and turns it into philosophy, into ethics, which is not the property of any particular religion, but is common to all. It is almost as if there could be One Bible common to all religions and all peoples, a universal consensus, for "ethical truth is common."[19] This "common book" runs throughout all the great books of the national literatures, but it is to be found above all in the Book of Books. This common book is nothing supernatural, but an account of the face of the Other which is nothing more than the translation of the prophetic sense of justice into Greek, that is, into thought.

But if the philosophers find themselves surprised and disconcerted by Levinas's strange Jewish idiom working its way into Greek, it is interesting for philosophers to see that this translation project has bought Levinas a certain amount of trouble from Jewish quarters as well, where they worry about the way Judaism is worked over by philosophy in Levinas. For, if Levinas's translation project can be carried out, if, as Robert Gibbs remarks, "the uniqueness could be translated entirely and hence lose its uniqueness, then 'Greek' would triumph in logical form over 'Hebrew'...." That is what leads André Neher to "argue against Levinas's reading of Judaism that it is a philosopher's reading and so must discover, to no one's surprise, a philosophical Judaism."[20] Then the honey of the Hebrew idiom would be destroyed by the heat of philosophical reason, according to which wax is a rational substance with or without the aroma. That is a serious charge for it touches on philosophy's greatest danger, that it turns everything it touches into philosophy, so that if philosophy takes up Judaism it will give us back a philosopher's Judaism.

By undertaking a project of translation, Levinas would have turned Judaism into something *catholic*, for it would have handed the particularity of the Hebrew over to the universality of Greek, thereby turning the Hebrew into a case, a *casus*, a fall and a casualty, of something universal, *katholou*, Greek. Even if the Hebrew succeeded for a time in instructing the Greek, even if the Greek remained all ears for this other, the spider would in the end consume its guest, philosophy would eventually regain its feet and its autonomy, and the doors of the dialectic would swing closed, having heartily fed once again on a feast of negativity. Then the Same would assimilate the Other and all this, ironically, under Levinas's own hand.

Beware of giving gifts to Greeks.

Then we would need to protect Levinas against himself, to restrain his enthusiasm for philosophy, to limit his propensity to overestimate philosophy's capacity to transport Hebrew into Greek. We would need to show that there is an irreducible residuum, a remainder, "an untranslatable core," that the philosopher cannot reach, the impossibility of which, of course, as Derrida argues, is what *drives* translation, for we always begin *by* the impossible. We would need to de-limit philosophy, to show forth its structural limits, not to overestimate philosophy. We need to avoid letting philosophy become autonomous, letting it acquire a life of its own, for philosophy is not supposed to live its own life but to be life's *ancilla*.

193

The idea is to avoid thinking that philosophy enjoys a certain conceptual mastery over life, and Levinas knows this well, as if it had an independent life, as an autonomous, independent discipline with its own vocabulary, problems, and technical resources. That is an illusion, brilliantly exposed by Richard Rorty, whose growth in Euro-America is greatly promoted by the academic greenhouse in which philosophy is quartered. There philosophers speak in philosophicalese to other philosophers about philosophy at philosophy conferences in order to acquire tenured positions teaching philosophy to would-be philosophers who want to do some day what the philosophy professors are doing right now.

Instead of philosophy pure and simple, instead of *reine Vernunft* and autonomous philosophy, instead of philosophy with a life of its own, we need a more contrite philosophy, a humble and unpretentious philosophy, even a wounded philosophy, a philosophy that is, just as the ancient sages said, an *ancilla*. But not of *theology*, God forbid. Theologians are every bit as tenure-driven, conference-racked, and elbow-patched as the philosophers, not to mention the authoritarianism of the churches, to safely house philosophy among them. Rather philosophy ought to be a certain *ancilla vitae*, a handmaid of factical life. As such, philosophy would serve the interests of life, pointing to the difficulties of life, trying not to make light of life, trying to keep the ear of its practitioners trained to life, bringing the difficulties and undecidabilities of life to light, to a certain philosophical light or twilight, in which life's joys and sorrows, madness and disasters are neither denied nor camouflaged by a conceptual net neatly draped over them. Philosophy's ancillary work would be to lead us all up to the point of confusion and ambiguity, of dissemination and undecidability, at which point, having done all that it can do, philosophy would quietly take its leave. Philosophy cannot dominate or assimilate life, master or manipulate life, control or resolve life, but simply point out certain features of life which life must work out for itself, in the living.

Viewed thus, Levinas's translation project of bringing Hebrew into Greek, that is, into philosophy, should at a very crucial point break down; it should breach at a point of maximum stress where too much has been asked. It would, it should, reach a point of possible confusion which philosophy could not possibly resolve. Philosophy must have a look of wonder, of a surprise mixed with chagrin, on its face if anyone would expect it to know how to proceed at such a point of complexity and undecidability, to expect it to deal with matters that are strictly beyond it. To decide in the situation of this undecidability, one would have take up something extra-philosophical or non-philosophical, something pre-philosophical or post-philosophical, that is, one would have to live, to exist. Philosophy's humble, handmaidenly work would simply to be point out the difficulty, to lead us up to the point of possible confusion, to lead us to the point at which philosophy breaks down, and this on the premise that we are better off knowing than not knowing the trouble we are in for – like a sign on a highway warning that there is trouble ahead, philosophy can at best indicate, *anzeigen*, when we are headed for trouble.

Formal Indication

It is at this point that Levinas can use a little help from Heidegger. Heidegger, as I indicated above, had a surprisingly similar *Ansatz*. In his early Freiburg period, Heidegger lectured on the phenomenology of religion, commenting in particular on Paul's letters to the Thessalonians (*supra*, n.4). Having just broken with his Catholic youth and with his student interest in medieval speculative grammar, a story that Hugo Ott has helped to tell,[21] Heidegger began work in 1919 on what he called a "hermeneutics of facticity." The point of his hermeneutics was to trace the genesis of logical categories back to the "facticity" of life, in contrast to the pure logical foundation of meaning and the categories he had previously defended under the influence of Husserl and late scholastic speculative grammar. Philosophy, the young Heidegger contended, is subverted from within by a systematic blindness to the genesis of its own terms. This failure is connected by Heidegger with the academic setting of philosophy, with the "hermeneutic situation" of philosophical activity in the "university." Philosophical questions can be raised only by also raising the question of the university and its discourse. Academic philosophy has no heart for the radicality of philoso*phizing*, for radical, revolutionary *questioning*. Philosophy is a normalizing, institutional discourse that is never disturbed by the debates, however lively, that transpire within this discourse. But philoso*phizing* is a living act (*Vollzug*), a personal form of life, in which the philosopher seeks for himself to make things questionable and to do so radically (GA 61, pp. 65–73).

Philosophy is institutionally and constitutionally blind to is its own pre-philosophical sources. Philosophical disputes occur in a space that has already been constituted by distilling the substance of "factical life" into a set of categorial "ghosts." The "hermeneutics of facticity" have a formidable, even paradoxical task, to make philosophy take into account the sphere of life before it is touched by philosophical conceptuality, to make it take heed of the region of *non*-philosophy or pre-philosophy. How to philosophize about the pre-philosophical without turning it into just more philosophy, without distorting and mummifying it, was the substance of the revolution the young philosopher had in mind.

The burden of leading this revolution fell to what Heidegger called "formal indication" (*formale Anzeige*). Unlike the traditional concept or category that purports to seize or comprehend its object, the formal indication is but a projective sketch that traces out in advance certain salient formal features of an entity or region of entities. Instead of a conceptual mastery of its material that reduces the individual to an instance of the general, the formal indication is related to the factical region as the imperfect to the perfect, as a schema or anticipatory sketch to the idiomatic fullness of concrete life. The formal indication is not a universal that "contains" "particulars" "underneath" it, but a sign pointing at a region where it itself cannot enter. Fully to "understand" the factical would require a certain act or engagement or giving oneself over to the factical matter at hand, which would no longer be the business of philosophy. That is where philosophy excuses itself and politely takes its leave, leaving life to face the worst.[22]

Heidegger identified two such pre-philosophical sources as particularly important to his project: the early Christian experience of time and the ethical experience of the Greek *polis*. To be sure, access to these "revolutionary" experiences could be gained only by means of the most traditional texts, the New Testament and the *Nicomachean Ethics*. Accordingly, such texts could not be approached by conventional academic reconstructions but required a new, more radical method Heidegger called "*Destruktion*." A "destruction" does not destroy but breaks through to the originary factical experiences from which the text arises, the term having been suggested to him by Luther's notion of a *destructio* through the crust of scholasticism to the life of the New Testament. Lecturing on the "phenomenology of religion," Heidegger analyzes the temporality of the *parousia* in Paul's letters to the Thessalonians. The "second coming of Christ" is not a "when" to be calculated but a "how" to be lived, not a matter of reckoning a definite time in the future, but of being ready, existentially transformed and radically open to an indefinite possibility that must be preserved in its indefiniteness.[23] Recast in terms of a relationship to one's own death, this analysis became a centerpiece of *Sein und Zeit*.

Now, Heidegger's philosophical hermeneutics of the letters to the Thessalonians can be of service to Levinas. Like Levinas, Heidegger thinks that philosophy is nourished, enriched, and renewed by its scriptural sources. But if anything Heidegger shows a greater distrust of the university and of the universality of its discourse than does Levinas. If anything Heidegger is more insistent on questioning and rethinking the traditional conceptuality than is Levinas. That is why Heidegger proposes a project only of indication, not of "translation," for translation seems unduly to trust philosophy and the discourse to which factical life will be handed over, unduly to trust the Greek, who on Heidegger's view reduced being and time to static presence. Rather, Heidegger wants to forge a new, let us say, a quasi-conceptuality, formed of "formal indications" which are related to the singularity of existence, to factical life, as imperfect sketches or anticipatory foreshadowings (*Vorzeichnung*) of a prior and irreducible excess, an excess that can only be "engaged" or entered into *existentially*, not grasped conceptually. For this, there are no formal rules but only formal schemata or indexes of a region of complexities, ambiguities, and undecidabilities that are resolved only in the doing.

The strategic move that Heidegger makes that can help Levinas out is this. In a formal indication, the individual, the singularity, is not taken as an *instance* of the universal, does not become a case or a *casus* that falls off the pedestal of Greek universality, a temporal specimen of an unchanging species. Rather, the singular is affirmed in all of its singularity, respected in all of the richness of its idiosyncratic *haecceitas*, this-ness. The singular is thought not as a particular under a universal but as an unrepeatable, irreplaceable individual. What better embodiment of such a kingdom of singularities than the biblical kingdom itself, where God has counted every tear and numbered every hair on our head, where God knows every secret nestling in someone's heart, where every least little nobody in the kingdom is precious beyond measure. A formal indication provides as much as it is possible, or desirable, to "conceptualize" of such a world. A concept on Heidegger's accounting is not a "universal" but a sketch, not a universal *con-capere* or *be-greifen* that comprehends the particular round about, not an essence that turns the individual into a contingent fact, but a finger (*index*) pointing at the moon. By the same token, the singular is not a fall (*casus*) from universality whose feet are soaked by the particularity of matter or potency, but an *excess* that cannot be contained. A concept, on that account, is but a certain precursive indicator or "pre-*cept*," a light sketch of a region that can only be entered, engaged, existed, leaving philosophy and its conceptuality back home in the security of its academic chairs.

In short, the hermeneutics of facticity is not a project of "translation," for the latter is exposed to a naive conception of language as some kind of relatively neutral or non-corrosive container, and assumes the possibility of shipping or transporting the contents of one discourse into another without suffering any major losses to one's cargo. A formal indication does not translate from one self-contained discourse to another but rather moves from factical life – but always through texts, like the letters to the Thessalonians and the *Nicomachean Ethics* – to a delimited discursive structure. It tries to bring the factical life embedded in excessively rich texts, like biblical texts, e.g., to a certain pale formal structure which remains beholden to life, which remains but a handmaiden to life, which at most, at best, issues an invitation to live life and to keep thinking in its place. Heidegger thinks that for the most part philosophers have merely rearranged their conceptual furniture without returning to sources. They keep operating with a more or less finished conceptuality, first handed down by the Greeks, which has taken on a life of its own, which has acquired an unquestioned authority, and which they at most reconfigure, modify, or from time to time touch up, but which they never radically question and expose to trembling. Philosophy requires the trauma of revisiting its sources, and a new humility about its own conceptuality, which needs both to be reforged on the basis of its exposure to factical existence and to be distrusted in terms of the extent of its reach, a reach which is never transcendental but at best "quasi-transcendental." Levinas, on the other hand, by aiming at a translation into Greek, seemed somehow to trust the Greek in a way that Heidegger did not. Levinas's project was to infiltrate the Greek like a spy, to put new notions into philosophy's head that had not been dreamt of in philosophy, but he continued to grant the Greek, to grant philosophy, a certain autonomy. He did not make philosophy the handmaiden of theology or life but he said that philosophy has the "last word."

But philosophy is a handmaiden and it *never* should be given the last word; it is a handmaiden of the density and complexity, the undecidability and unencompassable priority of factical life, of which philosophy can only make certain humble traces in the sand before it takes its leave.

Conclusion

This lead us to the oddest of results. It is Heidegger – the philosopher who is accused by Levinas of making ontology fundamental, of allowing the Other to be swallowed whole and assimilated by ontological categories – who sharply delimits the authority of the concept in the name of the primacy and idiosyncrasy of factical life, while Levinas, the advocate of the Other and the merciless opponent of the totalitarianism of the concept, seems to drift into the position of allowing the Greek to assimilate the Hebrew and of producing a "philosophical Judaism."

The risk that Levinas undertook, which I hear his Jewish critics rightly criticizing, is to try to translate the idioms of singularity to which he is so wonderfully sensitive into a universal structure. Such a structure, in an odd way, amounts to a new structuralism, an ethical structuralism, in which responsibility is inscribed in the deep structure of the subject prior to any conscious act, as an imprint of creation itself, like the "innate idea" of the Infinite. Levinas thus counters structuralism with structuralism, with another form of structuralism. He meets structuralism itself, let us say non-ethical structuralism, which dissipates "saying" and the speaking subject, whose "*Bonjour*" constitutes a recognition of the Other, on its own grounds by challenging it with a counter-structuralism, an ethical structuralism, which gives ethical responsibility itself the status of a deep structure that is older than the ego.

Instead of a mere formal indication which points to a region of excess, Levinas proffers a deep structure that cuts through to its diachronic depth. This structure – variously called substitution, responsibility, election, etc. – is said by Levinas to be so old that it is older than any act of consciousness, older than the flow of time and historical movement, older than the Book, and even older than faith itself. This structure is so deep that it leads Levinas to relocate "faith" itself on the surface of the flowing synthesis of time-consciousness, as an ego-act that is of too recent a vintage for the deep structure of substitution. On Levinas's accounting, the special "election" of the Jews, for example, becomes a universal structure of all humanity, Jewish and non-Jewish alike. But that is to affirm something that is functionally equivalent to Greek universalism, to most of what the Greeks ever meant by *katholou, ousia, eidos*, to most of what we mean today by universality, being and essence, *Sein und Wesen, l'être et l'essence*. That is to make historical Judaism into an historical *instance* of an ahistorical or ante-historical overarching structure, the clearest and most instructive example, perhaps, but an *example*, nonetheless.

That makes Judaism a religion within the limits of practical reason alone, a historical case of a transcendental structure, which is "a philosopher's reading" which produces "to no one's surprise, a philosophical Judaism."[24] That is what comes of giving philosophy the last word.

Instead of leading us up to that point at which philosophy would humbly back off, confessing that at this point things have gotten too difficult. Instead of turning things over to the dynamics of factical life, which occur in history, time, texts, traditions, and institutions, which is also where the dynamics of faith are to be found. Instead of letting philosophy sketch the conditions of undecidability in which historical human beings make their choices, faith among them. Instead of that, Levinas tries to cut through to a deep structure, to an ethical transcendental that is older than factical life, to make responsibility older than choice, election older than the Jews, and, in an oddly structuralist manner, to identify an absolute diachrony that is older than Abraham and the prophets, older than faith, and – one wonders! – older than God.

I do not believe that faith floats on the surface of conscious, synthetic time, that it simply enacts or instantiates in history and personal time a deeper diachronic structure that is older than time. I do not believe that any such transcendental structure is accessible to philosophy and philosophy's reason, even if you insist that philosophy must be guided by ethical substitution rather than the autonomy of consciousness, by ethics and practical reason rather than speculative reason. That just results in an ethical as opposed to linguistic structuralism, a practical transcendental as opposed to a theoretical one.

Philosophy can at best describe in frail and faint tones, in (at most) quasi-transcendental terms, the difficulty of life, the density and undecidability of life. On its best day, philosophy leads us up to the very point of undecidability, at which point it steps down from the podium, its lecture ended, its formal indications having reached their limits, and life reasserts its claims. Faith is a form of life of which philosophy may make a certain index – by pointing out the quasi-transcendental conditions of its possibility and its limits, the undecidability with which faith tries to cope, as it tries seeing through a glass darkly.

Levinas then will have *said* too much, will have allowed philosophy to say too much, while a certain very early Heidegger, one whom we are today only beginning to recall, thanks in part to the work of Hugo Ott, would have shown the greatest deference for the idiosyncrasies of factical life and for the irreducibility of faith. Heidegger, unhappily, abandoned these insights and allowed the hermeneutics of facticity to dissipate in a *wesentliches Denken* which left factical life in the dust, which turned Christian faith into an oblivion of the Ur-Greek, and which allowed itself to be implicated in a political ideology from which we are still today trying to recover, an unhappy story that Hugo Ott has been carefully documenting for some time now.

Notes

[1] Hugo Ott, *Martin Heidegger: Unterwegs zu seiner Biographie* (Frankfurt: Campus Verlag, 1988), 45–127; "Martin Heidegger's Catholic Origins," *American Catholic Philosophical Ouarterly*, 69 (Washington, D.C., 1995): 137–56.

[2] See Heidegger's letter of August 19, 1921, to Karl Löwith in *Zur philosophischen Aktualität Heideggers*, ed. Dietrich Papenfuss and Otto Pöggeler, Vol. 2, *Im Gespräch der Zeit* (Frankfurt: Klostermann, 1990), 27–32.

[3] John D. Caputo, *Demythologizing Heidegger* (Bloomington: Indiana University Press, 1993); see the German translation of the first chapter, *"Heidegger Entmythologisieren:* Aletheia *und die Seinsgeschichte,"* trans. Michael Elred, in *Twisting Heidegger: Drehversuche parodistischen Denkens*, Hg. Michael Elred (Cuxhaven: Junghans-Verlag, 1993), 66–91.

[4] *Phänomenologie des religiösen Lebens*, B. 1, *Einführung in die Phänomenologie der Religion* (Wintersemester 1920/21), Hg. Matthias Jung u. Thomas Regehly; B. 2. *Augustinus und der Neuplatonismus* (Sommersemester 1921), Hg. Claudius Strube, Gesamtausgabe, B. 60 (Frankfurt/Main: Klostermann, 1985).

[5] *Ontologie (Hermeneutik der Faktizität)*, SS 1923, Gesamtausgabe, B. 63, Hg. K. Bröcker-Oltmanns Frankfurt/Main: Klostermann, 1988).

[6] *Ethica Nic.* 1106 b 28 ff. For Heidegger's commentary, see *Phänomenologische Interpretationen zu Aristoteles. Einführung in die phänomenologische Forschung*, WS 1921/22, Gesamtausgabe, Vol. 61, Hg. W. Bröcker and K. Bröcker-Oltmanns (Frankfurt/Main: Klostermann, 1985), 108-110. Hereafter GA 61.

[7] Bernhard Welte, "Suchen und Finden," in *Christ in der Gegenwart* (Freiburg: Herder), Nr. 24, 28 (June 13, 1976), 188.

[8] Jacques Derrida, *"Donner la mort,"* in *L'Ethique du don: Jacques-Derrida et la pensée du don* (Paris: Métailié-Transition, 1992), 52–53. Derrida also thinks one might include Heidegger himself among such thinkers.

[9] See *Du sacré au saint: cinq talmudique lectures* (Paris: Minuit, 1977); I use the English translation from *Nine Talmudic Essays*, trans. Annete Aronowicz (Bloomington: Indiana University Press, 1990), 122.

[10] I am very much indebted to Robert Gibb's illuminating presentation of Levinas's project of "translation" in *Correlations in Rosenzweig and Levinas* (Princeton: Princeton University Press, 1992), Chapter 7.

[11] Levinas, *Nine Talmudic Readings*, 122.

[12] See Gibbs, 164.

[13] Levinas, *Difficult Freedom: Essays on Judaism (Difficile liberté)*, trans. Sean Hand (Baltimore: Johns Hopkins University Press, 1990), 68.

[14] "God and Philosophy" (*"Dieu et la Philosophie"*), in Levinas, *Collected Philosophical Papers*, trans. A. Lingis (The Hague: Martinus Nijhoff, 1987), 154.

[15] Levinas, "God and Philosophy," *Collected Philosophical Papers*, 165.

[16] Jacques Derrida, *Écriture et la différence* (Paris: Éditions de Seuil, 1967), 228.

[17] Emmanuel Levinas, *Otherwise than Being or Beyond Essence*, trans. A. Lingis (The Hague: Martinus Nijhoff, 1981), 177.

[18] Levinas, *Ethics and Infinity*, trans. Richard Cohen (Pittsburgh: Duquesne University Press, 1985), 24–25 (*Ethique et Infini*).

[19] Levinas, *Ethics and Infinity*, 115.

[20] Gibbs, 173.

[21] See Ott, "Heidegger's Catholic Origins," (n1).

[22] See GA 61, 33–34, 61 *et passim*; the notion of *formale Anzeige* is developed throughout GA 61. See the superb studies of John van Buren, *The Young Heidegger* (Bloomington: Indiana University Press, 1994) and Theodore Kisiel, *The Genesis of Heidegger's Being and Time* (Berkeley: University of California Press, 1993).

[23] See Heidegger, *Der Begriff der Zeit. Vortrag vor der Marburger Theologenschaft*, Juli, 1924, ed. H. Tietjen (Tübingen: Max Niemeyer, 1989).

[24] Gibbs, 173.

14

DARK HEARTS: HEIDEGGER, RICHARDSON, AND EVIL

[In *From Phenomenology to Thought, Errancy, and Desire: Essays in Honor of William J. Richardson, S.J.*, ed. B. E. Babich (The Netherlands: Kluwer Academic Publishers, 1995), 267–275]

[267] If, as Heidegger says, thinking is thanking, then one can offer a work of thought as a bit of gratitude. Derrida, on the other hand, repeats the warning of the circle of the gift according to which, in all gift-giving, something is always returned to the giver. The giver always gets a pay back, a return on the investment, if only (or especially) in the most oblique, the most indirect form, of gratitude. Therefore, the purest gift-gifting demands ingratitude, which does not pay the giver back and therefore pay off and nullify his generosity.

Since I am in the highest degree the beneficiary of William Richardson's work and friendship, and more grateful than I am permitted to say, I have undertaken to protect his generosity with a certain ingratitude, precisely understood, with an utterly ungrateful bit of disagreement, not only with him, but also with Heidegger, to whom I have accumulated a life-long debt. So I offer what follows in the spirit of the deepest and most loyal ingratitude, cognizant always of the unworthiness of my ungift, which comes in response to what in a simpler world I would call the richness of the contribution that William Richardson has made to philosophy in America.

In "Heidegger's Truth and Politics,"[1] Richardson makes a striking argument that in Heidegger's notion of *lethe* there is to be found, not exactly an accounting of moral responsibility, but a certain radical situating of moral responsibility. *Lethe* for Heidegger is not simply the concealment of Being but the concealment of the concealment; not simply Being's withdrawal, which Heidegger calls the "mystery" (*Geheimnis*) of Being, but the withdrawal of the withdrawal, which – since this is what leads us astray – Heidegger calls "errancy" (*die Irre*). Errancy is not a correctable fault or flaw in Being or in us but the very core or heart of *aletheia*, the un-truth that is embedded in the heart of unconcealment. Errancy is neither something we have done nor something that can be corrected but something that holds sway over us, essentially and all-pervasively, bending and distorting and deranging human action. Errancy is a not a thing but a realm, not an identifiable defect but a kingdom (*Irrtum*) in which we wander astray,[2] the heart of a darkness by which we are on every side encompassed, to invoke, as Richardson does, the very powerful imagery of Joseph Conrad's famous novel. Heidegger's errant [268] political judgment, then, may be seen as testimony to the *Irre* by which Heidegger was "victimized."

It is a mark of my almost perfect ingratitude toward William Richardson, from whom I have learned far more than I may say, not only about Heidegger, but about thinking earnestly, deeply, honestly, that I think this powerfully argued view is only partly right. It is certainly right insofar as it finds in Heidegger's analysis a probing meditation upon human finitude, upon the "ontological limits" – may one still today speak like this? – by which human being is always already incised. But it is not right, in my view, insofar as what Heidegger calls *lethe* does not reach as far as evil, does not extend all the way to the malice that had curled up inside the heart of Conrad's "Mr. Kurtz." In my view, Heidegger's nontruth is precisely not "essentially other than truth," although that is what Richardson and Sallis would like us to think.[3] On the contrary, nontruth constitutes truth's most inward reserve, its deepest heart, its purest core, from which truth itself incessantly draws and to which it always returns. Is it not the case, as Heidegger asks, that "self-concealing, concealment, *lethe* belongs to *a-letheia*, not just as an addition, not as shadow to light, but rather as the heart of *aletheia*?"[4]

The movement from *adequatio* to *aletheia*, and then from *Geheimnis* to *Irre*, takes place within *aletheia*, within the kingdom of Being's play of concealment and unconcealment, moving from truth's visible surface to its inner heart, from truth's outer skin to its inner core, sailing deeper and deeper down that dark river *lethe*. But *lethe* does not leave the land of truth, of concealment and unconcealment, to venture upon truth's other, upon what is older than truth, older even than the untruth of truth, upon what is otherwise than truth. Truth and untruth, concealment and unconcealment, however deeply they are thought – and who can think them more deeply than Heidegger? – belong essentially together. Even if one were able to take a step back, not only from *Geheimnis* to *Irre*, but from *Irre* to something else, to something deeper still, to God knows what – to something Greco-Germanic, no doubt – even that would not be enough. What is wanting in Kurtz's heart is altogether otherwise than truth and untruth. It does not have to do with the concealment (*lethe*) at the heart of truth. The heart of Kurtz's darkness is the darkness that Kurtz discovered in his own heart, which is the hardness that had overtaken his heart (*porosei tes kardias*).[5]

What had gone astray in Kurtz's heart has nothing to do with the concealment of Being, nor with the concealment of that concealment. As Charlie Marlow says of him, "his intelligence was perfectly clear – concentrated, it is true, upon himself with horrible intensity, yet clear."[6] Still, he had "gone mad." He had gone out into the wilderness and gone mad, not with the madness of a dark power that had overtaken him and led him astray, poor thing, but with the madness of a man who had come to believe that he was alone, that all human restraints had been lifted from him in that wilderness, that he was worthy of supernatural honors, that he had power over life and death, which he could dispense arbitrarily, as whim dictated:[7]

> [269] I had to deal with a being to whom I could not appeal in the name of anything high or low. There was nothing either above or below him, and I knew it. He had kicked himself loose of the earth.... He was alone. I saw the inconceivable mystery of a soul that knew no restraint, no faith, and no fear, yet struggling blindly with itself.

Kurtz's corruption was not a matter of the concealment of Being, of the loss of originary, emergent *physis* or of the gathering of the originary *logos*. It had to do with *faces*, with his utter nullification of the face of the other. His was the solitude of a man for whom there were no other faces, nothing above him, nothing to come to him from on high. Those black faces around him in the jungle were not faces that faced Kurtz down, that commanded his respect, but instruments of Kurtz's "plans" or obstacles to be removed in the most ruthless – shall I say the most "heartless?" – manner. Kurtz's house was landscaped with the heads of his victims, of those who opposed his will, whose severed heads were propped on poles and plunged into the ground around his house. Shamelessly exposed, unburied, mutilated, these heads are not events of world disclosure but of flesh, of obscenely, hideously mutilated flesh. "Food for thought," Conrad writes, not for *Denken*, but food for those who thought about defying Kurtz's power, and "food for vultures."[88] (Like Polyneices.) These faces were turned to the house, so that they greeted Kurtz with deathly smiles whenever he stepped out, which he must have done many times a day, day after day. These hideous visages to which Kurtz had become inured, hardened, do not speak to us of truth's darkened reserve but of a more hideous cruelty, of a heart hardened against mutilated flesh, which is the dark side of the heart of darkness. Only one face greets the visitor, which Charlie Marlow spies through his binoculars:

> ...there it was, black, dried, sunken, with closed eyelids – a head that seems to sleep at the top of that pole, and, with the shrunken

dry lips showing a narrow white line of the teeth, was smiling, too, smiling continuously at some endless and jocose dream of that eternal slumber. [9]

There was "no restraint" in Kurtz's soul, Marlow says. Kurtz was alone; there was no Other, no Law of the Other, which he respected. When he went out into that dark world, that wilderness that was devoid of the trappings of European civility, of its laws and institutions, Kurtz made himself into a kind of white god and a law unto himself. There were no other faces in Kurtz's world. The heart of darkness is Kurtz's dark heart, the heartless savagery he found within himself in that strange and remote land. The kingdom of darkness was in his own heart, not in Being or the Congo. The darkness is not Being's wily withdrawal but the dark cruelty he found within himself. The wilderness had awakened in him "forgotten and brutal instincts, gratified and monstrous passions."[10] The darkness was not a dark and savage continent that corrupted poor Kurtz and did him in. It was Kurtz himself who had become [270] the savage among these hapless people who were thoroughly terrified by this magnificent European specimen, half English and half French ("All Europe contributed to the making of Kurtz"[11]). The heart of darkness is not Being's concealment, not even the "concealment of concealment," not any degree of concealment, carried out to whatever higher coefficient of concealment that one has time and inclination to count, to concealment *ad infinitum*, if you like. What has gone astray in Kurtz, the dark river of degradation flowing within his soul, is not the dark core of untruth in truth, but quite otherwise than truth and untruth. If there is oblivion here, it is not the oblivion of Being's shining gleam, of Greek temples shining in the Aegean sun, of the *denkendes Dichten* of early Greek thinkers who poetized in tune with Being's silent call. If anything. Being's Greco-European splendor is something Kurtz had *not* forgotten, something that was still on his mind. Kurtz was an excellent poet and capable of lofty discourses on love. He had "plans," great plans for these savage "niggers," to cite the merciless discourse of the trading company that Conrad employs with powerful effect. Charged by the International Society for the Suppression of Savage Customs, he had written an eloquent and moving discourse which "began with the argument that we whites, from the point of development we had arrived at, 'must necessarily appear to them (savages) in the nature of supernatural beings...'" (to which he later appended a hastily scrawled "Exterminate all the brutes").[12] Kurtz's mission was to bring them European culture and civility, the finest ornaments of Western civilization, and perhaps teach them to read a moving discourse or two on a Greek temple, maybe even, this would be the crowning achievement, to read a little Greek. Kurtz was out

206

to save them, to bring them Being's word from the West. The Russian whom Marlow encounters, Kurtz's last disciple, persisted in believing that this murderous man was still a great man, just in virtue of his "plans." All this, of course, Kurtz offered for a small charge: for all the ivory he could accumulate, even if that involved the devastating rape of this land to which he and his European "company" were not, shall we say, invited.

The darkness here is not the darkness of Being but the darkness of dark skins and of faces from which the light of humanity had been extinguished, of black men who are not us, not Greco-European, who are not capable of *Dichten* and *Denken*, and the darkness of a heart which cannot see a human face looking back at him from behind these blackened skins, which is invulnerable to the violence of severed heads. It was not his unmindfulness of Being's gleam that had darkened Kurtz's heart. It was his oblivion of the Law inscribed in those faces, the darkness of a heart that saw nothing human, nothing worthy of respect, looking back at him from those black faces, that indeed saw no face at all in this land where anything is possible, where you could do anything. It was not the occlusion of Being that did Kurtz in, not the concealment of the concealment of Being, but something otherwise than Being's play of lights, otherwise than the play of concealment and unconcealment, an "excluded middle" between concealment and unconcealment.[13] Kurtz's degradation was not a function of having lost contact with the [271] originary splendor of the Greco-European dawn; it lay in another direction, otherwise than that.

Murder is not a matter of the concealment of Being. The movement from *adequatio* to *aletheia*, from Husserlian intentionality to the disclosedness of *Dasein*, from projective *Verstehen* to standing in the opening of Being, from the Truth of Being to *Ereignis*, from *Geheimnis* to *Irre* – none of this makes the move to something otherwise than truth. The step back to *aletheia* is "conceived in the philosophical tradition of the West as a modality of [meaning's] manifestation, a light 'of another color,' than that which fills the theoretical intentionality, but still a light."[14] What Heidegger has not shown, what he never wished to show, is that there is indeed something other than truth, other than truth more deeply thought, other than the movements of concealment and unconcealment, that is truly worthy of thought.[15]

Murder is otherwise than concealment and unconcealment. Murder is the progeny not of concealment but of in-vulnerability, in-sensitivity, im-pas-sivity – and I mean these terms in the most technical Levinasian sense – of an oblivion of the most radical diachrony and of the most immemorial law, an oblivion upon which Heideggerian *Andenken*, although it is structurally meant to be a thought of the forgotten, has never expended a thought.[16] The darkness of the murderous heart is its im-passivity, its hardened heartlessness. Murder and its prohibition belongs to an altogether different register, to the economy of the "neighbor" and the "approach," of "proximity" and "substitution." Murder belongs to an altogether different script than Heidegger's ancient Greek, older than Heideggerian *a-letheia*, even with the hyphen, even written in Greek script. Murder is the issue not of *lethe's* darkness but of the cold white of hardened hearts, of the impassive look of lust and greed illumined by the gleaming white ivory tusks of slaughtered elephants glistening in the tropical sun. The darkness of *lethe* is not old enough, not ancient and anarchical enough, to envelop murder. *Lethe* belongs to the economy of shining temples and emergent *physis*, of dammed up rivers and smelly smokestacks, of the silent fall of snowfall outside the cabin and tinkling cowbells, of the thinging of the thing and the coming of the gods who will call us into commune with *physis's* emergent power. *Lethe* is *Schwarzwald* black, not *Buchenwald* black; murder has to do with the blackness of decapitated "niggers," not the deep black that lets beings glisten in all their shining *Schönheit*.

To the extent that it touches human erring at all, *lethe* attributes erring to deep thinking and to the most exquisite sensitivity to Being's call, thus getting thinking – or thoughtlessness – off the hook. *Die Irre* made them all do it, sent them sailing down the dark river *lethe*, sent them after that ivory, gave them the technology to construct their firearms, put the guns in their hands, made them pull the trigger, made them all killers. Kurtz is the victim, the poor man, sucked in by Being's withdrawal, set apart by Being's suction.[17]

The horror is, on this telling, some dark power that was victimizing him; the horror is *die Irre*, not the darkness of his own soul, of his own lack of [272] restraint. "The horror, the horror," were Kurtz's dying words, his final judgment upon this life.[18] That, we are to believe, is Kurtz's complaint about *die Irre*, about being victimized by *die Irre*.

Like poor Heidegger, who is the "Mistah Kurtz" of Being's tale. It is not ultimately (essentially) the heads on the poles that are the victims – "Those rebellious heads look very subdued to me on their sticks," Marlow ironizes[19] – on Richardson's reading, not the slaughtered natives, but Kurtz/Heidegger. The more essential victims that this *Seinsgeschichte* picks out are Kurtz and Heidegger. They are the ones who fall afoul of *die Irre's* dark and wily ways:[20]

He himself, I suggest, fell victim to the heart of darkness.

We asked to "take seriously the hypothesis that Heidegger's political debacle (his outrage) may be understood in terms of victimization by the errancy inherent in *lethe* that stretches off into the heart of universal darkness." ("*Die Irre, die Irre!*," this Heidegger/Kurtz might gasp.)

That is asking rather a lot.

I am not in the least capable of judging what was in Heidegger's heart, of passing judgment on Heidegger's personal responsibility for anything he has done or not done in his life. That is not my *Sache* and above all none of my business. Nor is that in any way at issue in the present bit of ingratitude towards Heidegger and Richardson, who have given me many gifts. What I am contesting is the utter inadequacy of thinking that what Heidegger calls *lethe*, to whatever coefficient of concealment it is carried, has anything to do with murder. On the contrary, adopting the standpoint of *wesentliches Denken*, getting oneself purely in "the element of Being," learning to think in terms of *Wesen*'s comings and goings, learning to think deeply into the *Wesen* of what is going on all around us, is precisely what abolishes murder as a matter to be thought. "Essential thinking" erases as "inessential" the difference between murder and nonmurder. Essential thinking means learning to think on the *Wesen* of things, instead of being taken in by the superficialities that interest ordinary people, journalists, literary critics, scientists, theologians, political leaders – in short *everybody* except Heidegger, Heidegger's Hölderlin, a few other select, rare and deep Greco-Germanic poets and mystical poets, and an occasional Japanese. If we learn to think like that, then we will have acquired a standpoint which neutralizes the distinction between murder and nonmurder which, when they both stand under the essence of technology, are in fact in essence the same, and do not differ in their essence, which can communicate across the abyss that opens up before Marlow's binoculars when he espies the haunting smile on the face of the severed head.

That is why Heidegger can write:

> Agriculture is now a motorized food industry – in essence, the same as the manufacturing of corpses in gas chambers and the extermination camps, the same as the blockading and starving of nations, the same as the manufacture of atom bombs.[21]

What is essentially the same on both sides of this astonishing equation is the [273] technologization, the concealment of Being as aboriginary *techne* and shining *physis* and gathering *logos*, the concealment of the concealment (*und so weiter*), without regard to the murder. What matters to essential thinking is not the murder; murder is not the *Wesen* to which *wesentliches Denken* thinks through, not the issue, the *Sache*. What is essentially the same about technologized killing (for Heidegger's saying is "correct" as far as it goes) and technologized agrobusiness (which is also killing, chemo-carcino-killing) is not the killing, although both are killers, but technology's essence, the *Gestell*. The *essence* of technology is older than murder, more aboriginal than slaughtered flesh, more primordial than decapitated "niggers" or incinerated Jews, older than "*les juifs,*" wherever they are found, in Europe or the Congo. Essential thinking looks right through, thinks right past, the faces on the poles outside Kurtz's house, or the faces that have been turned into the foul smoke ascending from the camp at Auschwitz, none of which is essential, none of which would ever be visible through Heidegger's binoculars.

The prohibition of murder inscribed in the face of the Other, in the black faces in this dark land where everything is possible, that is the "essentially other than truth" which has never entered the head of *wesentliches Denken*. That prohibition is not *Denken*'s business (*Sache*). But that Law is older and more diachronous than *lethe*, belonging as it does to a past that cannot be the object of any *Andenken*. The murderousness that lay dormant in Kurtz's heart, which broke loose in this land outside of Europe's splendid buildings and venerable institutions, outside the *Seinsgeschichte*'s comings and goings, even as it breaks loose again and again inside the *Seinsgeschichte*, that is the heart of darkness and the heart of Kurtz's degradation. The horror that he pronounces as his final judgment on himself and his life, which constitutes a certain self-understanding he has reached of what lies within his heart, is the horror inside his heart, the heartlessness which is deaf as stone to the echoes of the most immemorial past of all:

> A past more ancient than any present, a past which was never present and whose anarchical antiquity was never given in the play of dissimulations and manifestations, a past whose *other* signification remains to be described, signifies over and beyond the manifestation of being.[22]

But it is precisely murder, which is the oblivion of this immemorial past, of which essential thinking is essentially oblivious and which is essentially otherwise than truth and untruth. Murder is precisely what essential thinking does not notice, precisely what it does not take to heart, what it does not regard as essential. According to the logic of essence, what is essential comes to presence with or without murder, whether you are feeding people or killing them. But murder belongs to another logic and another past that is otherwise than Heidegger's truth and manifestation, more primordial than *Geheimnis* and *Irre*, older than *lethe*.

At whatever coefficient of concealment it is counted.

Notes

[1] William J. Richardson, "Heidegger's Truth and Politics," in *Ethics and Danger: Essays on Heidegger and Continental Thought*, eds. Arlene Dallery and Charles Scott (Albany: SUNY Press, 1992), 11–24; on "situating" moral responsibility see 17–18. The background for the present argument is found in my *Against Ethics: Contributions to a Poetics of Obligation with Constant Reference to Deconstruction* (Bloomington: Indiana University Press, 1993) and *Demythologizing Heidegger* (Bloomington: Indiana University Press, 1993).

[2] See Heidegger's "On the Essence of Truth," trans. John Sallis, in *Martin Heidegger: Basic Writings*, ed. David Krell (New York: Harper and Row, 1977), 135–137.

[3] Richardson makes use of John Sallis, "Deformatives: Essentially Other Than Truth," in *Reading Heidegger: Commemorations*, ed. John Sallis (Bloomington: Indiana University Press, 1993), 29–46.

[4] Martin Heidegger, *On Truth and Being*, trans. Joan Stambaugh (New York: Harper & Row, 1972), 71.

[5] The perversity and ingratitude of the present study here reaches a certain peak, as I am here quoting the New Testament (Mk 3:5) against William Richardson, S. J. We Catholics are however free to disagree about who has the word of God on their side and free also to doubt that anybody has all, most, or even much of it. Be that as it may, I respectfully submit that evil has to do with what the Scriptures call hardness of heart, not the concealment of Being.

[6] Joseph Conrad, *"Heart of Darkness" & "The Secret Sharer"* (New York: Penguin Books, 1983), 144.

[7] Conrad, 143–144.

[8] Conrad, 132.

[9] Conrad, 132–133.

[10] Conrad, 143.

[11] Conrad, 123.

[12] Conrad, 123.

[13] Emmanuel Levinas, *Otherwise than Being, or Beyond Essence*, trans. Alphonso Lingis (The Hague: Martinus Nijhoff, 1978), 181.

[14] Emmanuel Levinas, *Otherwise than Being*, 66.

[15] In an interesting exchange, John Sallis suggests to Jacques Derrida that the un-truth of truth, *die Irre*, constitutes a contaminating untruth in Heideggerian truth, to which Derrida rightly responds, "It [the *Un-* in *Unwahrheit*] is still too pure, too rigorously delimited…the *Unwesenheit*, the *Unwahrheit*, are as pure as *Wesen* and *Wahrheit*." See Jacques Derrida, "An Outline of the Remarks to the Essex Colloquium," *Research in Phenomenology*, 17 (1987): 180.

[16] I refer the reader to Lyotard's argument in *Heidegger and "the Jews,"* trans. Andreas Michel and Mark Roberts (Minneapolis: University of Minnesota Press, 1990), which has a Levinasian point of departure.

[17] Insofar as Heidegger occasionally implies, in the texts that Richardson cites, that *die Irre* should be extended to include moral degradation and evil, that is simply a promissory note on

which Heidegger cannot deliver. For Heidegger's essentially *phainesthetic* discourse cannot be transformed into a discourse on the fate of flesh; for that it would have to turn itself inside out. These occasional texts of Heidegger are simply failed attempts to cross the abyss that separates the economy of concealment and unconcealment from the economy of good and evil, futile efforts to undo the essentialization of evil which turns the most hideous of evils into the loss of originary *physis*. When confronted with the fate of slaughtered flesh, Heidegger/Kurtz looked right past it. Kurtz at least seemed, at the end, to be horrified by this, which represented a certain truthfulness which Marlow was forced to admire.

[18] Conrad, 147.

[19] Conrad, 134.

[20] Richardson, 18.

[21] [275] I follow the translation of Thomas Sheehan, "Heidegger and the Nazis," *New York Review of Books* (June 16, 1988), 41–43. The German original is to be found in Wolfgang Schirmacher, *Technik und Gelassenheit* (Freiburg: Alber, 1983), 25. For a fuller commentary and interpretation, see my *Demythologizing Heidegger*, chapter 7.

[22] Levinas, 24.

THE DECONSTRUCTION OF ETHICS

15

A PHENOMENOLOGY OF MORAL SENSIBILITY: MORAL EMOTION

[In *Act and Agent*, ed. George McLean (Washington, D.C.: University Press of America, 1986), 199–22]

[199] The fully moral act has often been located in the purely rational element – in clear knowledge and unimpeded willing. Passion, moods and feelings are taken to be somehow *external* to the inner workings of the true man. Passion is at best a matter over which the rational principle rules, and its proper role is to be submissive to the leadership of the rational principle. At worst, the impulses of our so-called sensible nature are taken as a positive threat to reason, threatening to usurp its free, rational direction of human life and to turn life over to whim, caprice, and self-seeking – in a word, to "feeling."

The position which I will defend in this paper, however, is predicated upon a unitary conception of man, a conception which was best defended in the classical world by Aristotle, and which receives its sharpest contemporary formulation in the writings of the phenomenologists. Phenomenologists, and foremost among them Heidegger himself, have always recognized in Aristotle a precedent and antecedent, for it was he who wanted to return to the "things themselves," to hew the work of reflection as closely as possible to concrete experience. Whence the direction of the present inquiry is at once Aristotelian, phenomenological, and experiential. In such a view man is understood to be an essentially embodied agent so that feeling and affectivity enter into the very structure of the moral act. Hence, moral life is not conceived as a battle waged between warring metaphysical principles.

The pages which follow strive to set forth the positive role of feelings in a sound moral theory.[1] I shall do this in the name of what is termed here "moral sensibility," by which is meant the harmony between our sensible nature and moral values. The chapter will unfold in the following sequence: (1) I will show that, far from being external to the moral act, passion enters into its very fabric, so that failing passion no act is of any moral worth at all. This point will be established by following the Kierkegaardian analysis of passion. (2) Next I will show that, far from "blinding reason," passion or mood plays an essential role in the *disclosure* of our world, and that means the world of moral values. That point will be established in connection with a study of Heidegger's notion of mood and disposition. (3) Having secured our ontological bearings in the opening sections of the paper, I shall then shift to the specifics of a properly moral sensibility. The point of departure for this argument will be found in Kant's analysis of the "feeling of respect," a theory whose phenomenological implications have to be disengaged from its dualist moorings in Kant's metaphysics. (4) The feeling of respect will lead into a concrete phenomenology of the human person as the place of value or, one can say, as incarnate value. (5) And this will make it possible to formulate what is in fact the principal thesis of this paper, which is that our bodily and affective relationship to the other constitutes a "proto-ethics" upon which all moral reflection is based. Whence, instead of excluding the affective from moral life, it shall be argued that it is the spring by which all ethics is [200] nourished.

Kierkegaard's Concept Of Pathos

It was Kierkegaard more than anyone else who broke through the heavily encrusted structures of dualist ontology – who "deconstructed" them, to use a word whose day has come – and who cleared the way for a new ontology of the emotions. Kierkegaard saw that the fundamental distinction in human affairs is not between reason and the passions, but between the committed and the uncommitted, the engaged and the detached.

He considered the distinction between the rational and the emotive, soul and body, to be pagan and Platonic. Christianity was to draw a line between those whose faith is living, a vital and operative commitment permeating their whole lives, and those whom the Scriptures call "lukewarm" (CUP, 206).[2] In the New Testament, Kierkegaard thinks, the crucial distinction which emerges is that between those who are fully involved or "engaged" and the apathetic, between the *pathos* of a living faith and the apathy or non-pathos, of those who drift along in a comfortable, bourgeois Christianity. "I do not deny," he writes in bitter satire, "that it is comfortable to be a Christian, and at the same time be exempted from the martyrdom which is always present...."[3] The essential distinction is thus between passion or pathos and a-pathos. This discrimination flies in the face of the Greek distinction between the rational principle and the irrational principle which has dominated the history of metaphysics from Plato to Husserl.

On Kierkegaard's terms a genuine Christian is one who is passionately committed to his faith, whose passion so informs his actions that, lacking

216

passion, they are lifeless and rote.[4] Everything thereby is reversed: the informing principle is the pathos, which Kierkegaard also calls the "how," whereas the "what," the belief or creed or article (proposition) of faith, is but the content or matter. The creed is just a list of propositions, an external and lifeless content which comes to life only in the passion of an existing and believing Christian faith. To know that I am going to die and that I am promised in faith a life after death, is not a thought, Kierkegaard says, but a deed. It is not accomplished by pronouncing the words, but by an act of faith that sends a shock throughout our entire being.

If Kierkegaard does not distinguish passion and reason, he does distinguish a merely aesthetic pathos or passion from true, ethico-religious pathos.[5] In aesthetic pathos or aesthetic sensibility we are only partially transformed, and the transformation issues only in words, perhaps in verse. Our "taste" is struck by a thing of beauty, but our lives are not changed. Aesthetic pathos remains disinterested, looking on from afar.[6] But ethico-religious pathos means a total transformation of our whole life so that we are made over into a new man, reborn in the image of God. It issues not in words but in deeds, and it signifies that one has entered into an absolute relationship to the absolute goal or *telos*. One is wholly committed to the absolute, committed even unto the end, unto death.

This is not to say that Kierkegaard's religious man is continually heaving and sighing with religious fervor, or that he is uninterrupted in the performance of great and heroic deeds: continually exposed to the lion, always on the verge of martyrdom. On the contrary, he tends to keep his absolute commitment under wraps and to bear it unseen (incognito). He hides it under the mask of humor and irony[7] so that outwardly, as he says in *Fear and Trembling,* the knight of faith may lead so uneventful a life that if we met him we would find that he looks like a tax collector. The real meaning of this absolute religious pathos is that it is an abiding, constant passion:

> To relate oneself with existential pathos to an eternal happiness is never expressed by once in a while [201] making a great effort, but by persistence in the relationship. [...] What holy vows a man knows how to make at the instant of mortal danger! But when that is passed, the vow is so promptly and so completely forgotten.[8]

Hence, the distinction between the resolute and the irresolute, which is often mistaken as a distinction between a pure, steadfast "will" and transitory passions, is rearticulated by Kierkegaard in a revolutionary way. Instead of opposing the pure will to the passion of the moment, Kierkegaard distinguishes a deep and abiding existential pathos – a totally self-transforming pathos – from a fleeting, transient pathos. There is thus a difference in temporality between these two forms of pathos. The one is abiding, constant, sustained from day to day even under the most undramatic circumstances. The other is momentary and awakened only on great occasions: "When the earth quakes...how swiftly then and how thoroughly does even the dullest scholar...comprehend the uncertainty of everything."[9]

When the great occasion passes this pathos slips back into its customary complacency. Some men are moved by the thought of God only on solemn occasions, at weddings and funerals, say, or at official oathtakings; but others know how to bring the thought of God together with the task of taking a trip to the park. It is all a matter of the abiding *depth* of one's passion. Kierkegaard does not oppose pure will to bodily impulse, but deep passion to shallow passion, abiding, transforming passion to transient, momentary passions which merely result in occasional disturbances on a mostly placid surface. There is no question of getting outside or above passion, no question of standing on a higher, supersensible ground from which to control passion. That is the framework of Platonism and Greek metaphysics, of "recollection," not of "repetition."[10] In the categories of Christianity, it is a question of separating the wheat from the chaff, the fervent from the lukewarm, those who are with Christ from those who are against, the total pathos from the occasional and transient one, the deep from the shallow passion.

There is, I might add, a good deal of confirmation for what Kierkegaard says in the sorts of distinctions we habitually make in ordinary language without falling into Platonism. We speak of a "cold anger," which is not the passing anger of the moment, an angry outburst, but a deep, even, life-long anger such as the patriot's profound, implacable anger against the colonial power. The same can be said of a "mortal" hatred, revenge, envy, or any other destructive passion which is deep-seated and abiding; it is too cunning and deadly serious to give itself over to mercurial and passing expressions. By the same token the love of a man and a woman, of a country doctor for his patients, of the farmer for the soil, has the same quality of quiet depth and surface calm. Still water runs deep, we say, meaning that the essential thing is the depth of a passion and not its surface stirrings.

By taking his point of departure in the categories of religious and Christian life, Kierkegaard redrew the map that Platonic metaphysics had given us: contrary to the Platonic view, there is no moral action at all outside of passion. The lack of passion in moral life means the perfunctory performance of acts which lack conviction and dedication. Indeed it is passion which brings the agent into the moral sphere, which makes his actions committed and decisive. The lack of pathos does not mean that the way has been cleared for the pure rational will. It means that we are not acting at all, but merely thinking about acting, or else that our actions are performed by rote, that they lack the moral quality of decisiveness, that they are neither heartfelt nor committed.

Heidegger's Ontology Of Moods

But if Kierkegaard placed Platonic ontology into question, the task fell to Heidegger to formalize Kierkegaard's revolution. Heidegger proposed an ontological account of man in which affectivity was considered to be a primordial and irreducible structure of human existence.[11] Existence, he held, is constituted of three co-equal and equally radical structures which he called projection, disposition and fallenness. Inasmuch as he is "projected" man is always ahead of himself, cast forth into one course of action or another; by "disposition," the being which is cast forth is at the [202] same time already situated within pre-given circumstances; and inasmuch as he is "fallen," the being which projects himself ahead, from out of a given situation, is ever liable to give up his project and to sink back into complacency with present actuality. The three structures are transparently temporal in character, describing the way in which man runs forth into future possibilities in the midst of an oppressing actuality into which he has already been delivered (having been) which tempts him to remain content with the present. The ontology or understanding of reality which Heidegger developed in *Being and Time* completed the revolution which Kierkegaard had set in motion. For here was an ontology which drew the decisive distinction in human nature, not between "reason" and "feelings," but between the various temporal structures of man so that the problem of an act which is "free" of feeling, or "above" feeling does not arise.

To describe affectivity Heidegger used the word "*Befindlichkeit*", whose sense for him is drawn from the colloquial expression "how are you?" (*"Wie befinden-Sie sich?"*), "how are you found?", "how do things sit with you?" "how are you situated?"[12] It is probably best translated as "disposition." If disposition represents an ontological structure, then moods are the particular entities (or "ontic" structures) through which the basic ontological structure is *disclosed*. In contrast, the intellectualist tradition speaks of the "light of reason," but regards moods as blind and subjective. Brooks do not brood; we do. Grey afternoons are not somber; we are. But Heidegger rejects the idea that there is a subject here and an object there and focuses instead upon the interaction "between" subject and object. In that case, moods play an essential role in disclosing the structure of our world and of our experience.

Heidegger thus puts forward two basic theses about affectivity: the first concerns its *necessity,* and the second concerns its *disclosive* power. Let us examine each in turn.

The tradition treats moods as transient, mutable states which come and go and which do not enter into the stable, permanent essence of man. In contrast, Heidegger, following Kierkegaard, gives moods an ontological role and makes them essential structures of our Being. That means that everything in man is, as it were, "mooded." Moods are the way man is "tuned" to the world, and he is always in one state of attunement or another;[13] it is a mistake to think that we are or can ever get free of moods. It is indeed necessary at times not to be disturbed, but that means simply that at times we require undisturbing moods such as peace and tranquility. When Descartes speaks of getting free of his passions in order to undertake his meditations, he is mistaking the mood of tranquility with being in a mood-free state. And when Kant speaks of countering inclinations with pure will, that can only mean countering bad inclinations with good ones.

Secondly, Heidegger assigns to moods a disclosive role; this is a phenomenological point not brought out explicitly by Kierkegaard. On the phenomenological account, a feeling is not some kind of "subjective response" to an "objective stimulus," but is possessed instead of an *intentional* structure,[14] that is, it is a way of intending or turning to the world, of disclosing its make-up and the structure of our experience. It is nothing "inner" and subjective, but rather an intentional transcendence, a stepping outside (or *ek-stasis*), which reaches out to the world. According to Heidegger moods have a three-fold power of disclosure.

To begin with, and this is their most important function, moods disclose what Heidegger calls the "facticity," the givenness, of our Being. For Heidegger man finds himself situated within the world – within a society, a tradition, a family, etc. – prior to any possible consent on his part: that is, he is always "delivered over" (*überantwortet*) to his Being. Moods disclose how that being-delivered-over is experienced, whether as a burden or a weight pushing us down (de-pression), or as the lifting of a burden (elation). Whence they disclose the naked "fact" of being-in-the-world, which is what Heidegger means by "facticity," the naked "that-he-is-there" of man. Facticity is thus not a mere "matter of fact" in the manner of seventeenth- and eighteenth-century philosophy; it is rather a lived or existential fact, a disclosed or phenomenological fact: it is the lived through experience of being factically situated in the world.

[203] Thus it is not to be confused with the standard idea of "contingency," which is an objectivistic notion, referring to something which a disinterested speculative gaze observes to be there rather than not. Because facticity is something lived-through, it can be apprehended or disclosed only by mood. One can consider matters of fact with what the tradition calls intellect (*nous*) for as long as one wishes and never experience facticity. Facticity is disclosed only in that "tuning" which belongs to a being who is "thrown." Contingency is at best a distillate of lived facticity, its objectivistic correlate. One may thus give theoretical assent to the contingency of one's being without ever opening one's eyes moodfully to facticity. It would take an earthquake, Kierkegaard said, to bring some sleepy scholars to admit the uncertainty of things![15]

Moods also disclose the world as a "totality." This is explained in *What is Metaphysics?* which treats of the disclosure of the world in anxiety.[16] Through anxiety the world as a totality fades into meaninglessness, even as in joy it glows with charm. One is exposed to this anxiety even if one has an optimistic, theoretical account of things; contrariwise, one can experience Being in positive tones even if one has a pessimistic metaphysics (as seems to have been the case with Eduard von Hartmann, a Schopenhauerian pessimist who was happily married and professionally successful).

Finally, moods not only disclose the facticity of our Being and the Being of the world as a whole, they also disclose particular entities within the world in such a way as to let these entities "matter" to us, to let them be of concern to us *(angegangen werden sein)*. Whence it is only in the mood of fear that something can matter to man as threatening:

> Pure beholding, even if it were to penetrate to the innermost core of the Being of something present-at-hand could never discover anything like that which is threatening…. By looking at the world theoretically, we have already dimmed it down to the uniformity of what is purely present-at-hand.[17]

The fearsomeness of a fearsome object cannot be disclosed by pure beholding; fear indeed *is* this disclosure of the fearsome object as such. The mood of fear, like every other mood, discloses the world in a way which cannot be substituted for or improved upon. Thus, moods are not "blind," but insightful and disclosive. They tell us about ourselves and others in a way to which we otherwise have no access. They tell us long before reason has noticed that we are on the wrong track, that we have no business here, that so and so is not to be trusted, that we are being untrue to what we have all along believed. Socrates' celebrated "voice" was precisely such a preconceptual, moodful power of insight, a way of disclosing things long before his dialectic could summon up arguments one way or the other. If this be so then in Socrates, at the very birth of philosophy, we find moral affectivity or the mooded disclosure of value. This is the point we want to make in the following pages.

But before taking up this issue let us summarize briefly the results achieved thus far. From Kierkegaard we learned that, far from being something external or outside the properly human, passion is precisely what renders an act decisive, committed and authentic: outside of passion there is only the lukewarm, the apathetic. In terms of morality this means that it is passion which makes a moral agent an agent, someone who truly *does* something, who acts and who stands by his action. From Heidegger, we learned that the ontological structure of passion and mood is to disclose; and that moods, far from being blind or subjective, reveal the world to us in a way to which reason has no access. This means that they play a disclosive role in moral matters as well. In the same way that fear discloses the fearsome object, moral affectivity discloses moral value, or what the tradition would call the "good." We are thus at an extreme removed from the dualism of is and ought, a point which is made also by David Schindler in Chapter X below [such references are to the original publication –ed.]. On this account value belongs integrally to the structure of what "is," so long as "is" is understood in all its amplitude as a self-manifesting or self-revealing phenomenon (*phainomenon*), rather than being reduced to a mere matter of fact in the manner of seventeenth-century philosophy. The task now is to show how that is possible.

[204] The Feeling Of Respect in Kant's Ethics

To carry on Heidegger's metaphor, moral sensibility is the attunement of the moral agent to moral value, his sensitivity and responsiveness to value: moral sensibility is affective moral life. In search of help for a theory of moral sensibility, I shall turn to Kant, although he represents an extreme case of moral and metaphysical dualism. Kant wrestled with the question of moral feeling throughout his writings, and it is worth noting that in his earlier, pre-critical writings, he actually defended a theory of "moral sense."[18] His mature ethical position was, in fact, a reaction against a view that he himself once defended. Indeed, even after he had formulated his rigorous separation of pure will and empirical inclination, Kant himself concluded that the view as it stood was dualistic and needed to be reconciled with the sensibility.[19]

The metaphysical setting of this moral feeling in Kant is, in my view, beyond redemption. In Kant's theory this feeling is the sole feeling which arises, not from antecedent phenomenal causes, but from the will itself, pure noumenal will.[20] It is in a sense the inscription left by pure reason upon our sensible nature.

But Kant can hardly defend such a view if the moral feeling is indeed a feeling and not a metaphor. For if it truly belongs to our sensible nature then it is as rigidly predictable as the movements of the heavenly bodies and has nothing to do with the freedom of the will; Kant could deny this only by denying the uniformity of nature. Moreover, on Kant's own terms, it must be fully explicable in terms of our neuro-physiological make-up and the physical stimuli which cause one neuro-physiological reaction rather than another; it can have no more to do with moral value than does feeling pain in the presence of excessive heat. It is a piece of nature which has nothing to do with the intelligible world; it has to do with facts and not values. The whole notion of moral feeling is a futile attempt to back out of the worst implications of his own theory. What he needed was a wholly new theory of experience and affectivity, one which would break with the fundamental presuppositions of eighteenth century philosophy.

Although this was not possible for Kant himself, the importance of Kant's analysis did not go unnoticed by Heidegger a century and a half later when he wrote: "Kant's interpretation of the phenomenon of respect is probably the most brilliant phenomenological analysis of the phenomenon of morality that we have from him."[21] This suggests that, with the help of phenomenology, we can rescue Kant's theory from its dualist moorings and achieve thereby precisely what our argument requires, viz., a phenomenological analysis of the moral phenomenon which centers on an affective moral intentionality.

Kant was grappling with the notion which Kierkegaard would later make abundantly clear, that the will is not moved except through passion. The purely "impassive" will is motionless and never achieves the status of being an agent at all. But Kant's metaphysics makes it strictly impossible that anything other than the moral law itself should be the "incentive" or driving force (*Triebfeder*) of the will, lest the will be moved to act by non-moral motives. As the law alone must be the sole incentive, the cause of our action could not be the moral feeling of respect, but rather the effect upon our sensible nature which the law brings about. We do not obey the law because of the feeling of respect, but we feel respect because we are subject to the law. We are moved to act by the law, and insofar as the law is moving as an incentive it effects in us this moral feeling.

Now there are two moments to the feeling of respect. In the first place, the effect of the law upon our pathological nature is to thwart our inclinations which tend away from the law. The law checks the feeling of pleasure in something forbidden:

> Thus far, the effect of the moral law as an incentive is only
> negative, and as such this incentive can be known a priori. For

all inclination and every sensuous impulse is based on feeling, and the negative effect on feeling (through the check on the inclinations) is itself a feeling. Consequently we can see a priori that the moral law as a ground of determination of the will, by thwarting all our inclinations, must produce a feeling which can be called pain.[22]

[205] The law holds in check self-love, our selfish urge for self-gratification, and self-conceit, our misled tendency to think ourselves of worth independently of our conformity to the law.

But the law is not merely negative, it does not merely forbid, it is also a positive, an ideal of freedom and moral excellence. Accordingly the feeling it induces cannot be merely negative; its positive grandeur is thus a function of its negative power to humble our sensible nature.[23] The law subdues our pathological nature; it brings us into submission to reason; it asserts its priority over us and implants in us a sense of being a "subject" of the law. The law itself then emerges in its positive power, in its majesty, kingship and regal authority and overpowers us. The law has a power and might like the starry heavens above, a majestic sweep, a show not of physical but of moral force.

Heidegger recasts the analysis in phenomenological terms.[24] Respect is always "respect for," that is, it has an intentional structure in virtue of which it intends the moral law. For Kant the law is the ground of the feeling, not the feeling of the law; the feeling is simply the way in which the law is disclosed or made manifest to me as intentional object. For Heidegger the feeling of respect is not only a feeling for the law, but also a certain self-feeling in which I am disclosed to myself. For I experience myself as subject to the law and so as free and responsible before the law. Hence I experience myself as a being of worth or dignity (*Würde*). If I feel subordination or subjection to the law, the law also raises me up by disclosing my true dignity as a moral personality (*personalitas moralis*), a member of the intelligible world.

The feeling of respect is at the same time both an inclination and tendency towards it as the source of our true dignity. The feeling of respect thus resembles anxiety, which Heidegger explains elsewhere. Anxiety, too, is a shrinking back before the nullity which it discloses and at the same time a being drawn towards, inasmuch as anxiety breaks the spell in which we are held by beings and enables us to experience the upsurge of Being itself as against this nothingness.[25]

The moral feeling of respect is then precisely this affective attunement of feeling and the law whose possibility we projected in the first two sections of this paper. We are attuned to the majesty of the law the way our aesthetic sensibility is attuned to the majesty of the starry heavens; we respond as deeply to the worth of a moral deed as to the beauty of a work of art. Kant's metaphysics made it impossible for him to defend his theory of the moral feeling, but the soundness of his phenomenological account of this feeling belied the metaphysics it was meant to defend.

I have not yet discussed, however, the most important feature of Kant's analysis. "Respect," Kant says, "always applies to persons only, never to things."[26] That is a decisive qualification, for Kant's rationalist metaphysics often leads him to speak in terms of a hypostasized law or reason. But now Kant adds that respect is directed not at material objects, and by extension not at an abstract law, but always at a concrete person who embodies the law. I respect a person, not a thing, and I respect a person not insofar as he holds high office or exerts great power, but precisely inasmuch as he embodies the law. Whence Kant writes:

> Fontanelle says, 'I bow to a great man, but my mind does not bow.' I can add: to a humble plain man in whom I perceive righteousness in a higher degree than I am conscious of in myself, my mind bows whether I choose or not, however high I carry my head that he may not forget my superior position. Why? His example holds before me a law which strikes down my self-conceit when I compare my own conduct with it.[27]

When we witness an example of virtue which surpasses our own, our own shortcomings are exposed and our self-love and self-conceit are struck down.

Now the person bears a two-fold relation to the law. The person is both the alpha and the omega of the law, the origin and the sphere in which it is applied. The dignity of a man of concrete virtue is not only that he holds his sensuous impulses in check and responds to a supersensible principle. It is found also – and even more primordially – in that he is the author of this law, that the law arises autonomously from his own rationality and is not imposed upon him from [206] without. Hence the *law* as a purely formal principle is convertible with the *person* as the bearer of the law (as subject and legislator). This, of course, is the basis of the alternate formulations which Kant gives of categorical imperative in his *Foundations of the Metaphysics of Morals*: the first expressing the law as a purely formal principle, the second addressing its content or matter, and the last announcing the kingdom of ends as the synthesis of the first two. Without the person, the law would be a nonexistent abstraction. It would not "hold" because it would have no one to hold *for* and no one to be held *by*. But without the law the person would lack all dignity and would remain a piece of nature, a merely phenomenal being no better than a Cartesian automaton.

Whence the law insures the dignity of the person inasmuch as it is in virtue of the law that the person rises above the sphere of nature; while the person gives substance to the law, rendering it real and effective.

Now I maintain that Kant gives expression here, in the categories of a dualistic metaphysics, to a profound and genuine experience. In my view it is possible to rid this theory of its sensible-supersensible dualism and to give it the stamp of genuine phenomenological coin. This I would do in two steps. In the first place the categorical imperative is no dictum of "pure reason" over and above our "sensible" nature. As an "imperative" it is a mode of discourse, a linguistic formation in the form of a command. It takes shape in, and is possible only within the framework of, language and grammar. Hence it belongs to the sphere of "discourse" or the Being of man insofar as man speaks, what Heidegger calls *Rede,* in Greek *logos.* As a mode of discourse it is a call, indeed a call which issues from man himself, from the depths of his Being, and bids him to be the being which it is up to him to be. The categorical imperative is no supersensible law, but a call which only a being who speaks can utter – and hear. It belongs to the Being of man as incarnate, as speaking, as calling and hearing.[28]

The same result is even more forcibly visited upon us when we turn from the "form" to the "content" of the laws, from the mere form of an imperative to the moral person (an issue which is also discussed in Chapter IX below). What is the moral person? As Heidegger asks: "What is the ontological concept of the moral person, which is thus revealed in respect, of the *personalitas moralis?*"[29] The answer is found in what Kant's *Foundations* calls the person as an end-in-himself and not merely as a means.[30] Man is not good

> because he is good for something – he is not merely a commodity in the labor force, a purveyor of services – but a good in himself, for himself. He is not good because of what he can do – for himself or for others – but because of what he is, in his Being. The Being of this being is to be of worth, and the worth of this being is ontologically secured against anything which may be ontically disagreeable about him.

Now Kant expressed the dignity of man in the dualistic terms of the ability of our supersensible will to subdue our sensible appetites. I see this as an alienated formulation of a more profound phenomenological experience of the dignity of the person. Let us listen again to Kant's adaptation of Fontanelle's words:

> "I can bow to a great man, but my mind does not bow." I can add: to a humble plain man in whom I perceive righteousness in a higher degree than I am conscious of in myself, my mind bows

whether I choose or not, however high I carry my head that he
may not forget my superior position.

That, I suggest, is the phenomenological origin of Kant's moral philosophy. What animated Kant's thought from the start was his experience of the dignity of the person, his concrete encounter with men and women of simple nature who understood better than generations of philosophers Socrates' statement that it is better to suffer injustice than to commit it. Kant was moved to deny reason in order to make room for faith because of a profound and animating experience of the dignity of the human person, an experience so deep and heartfelt that it has all the characteristics of the "passionate inwardness" of which Kierkegaard spoke. It was no shallow passion brought on by a great occasion, but a deep and lasting reverence which animated the whole critical philosophy.

We are thus led by Kant to a formulation of the fundamental principle of moral sensibility: that the person is given to us in the feeling of respect as a being of intrinsic worth and dignity. The moral feeling of respect discloses the [207] concretely given person as an object of moral worth. The person is disclosed in moral affectivity as a being of dignity and worthy of respect. Lack of this moral sensibility, failure in this moral affectivity, would render us morally monstrous, coldly indifferent to the worth of others, perhaps even pathologically ill. One imagines the cold executioners of whom history provides an unfortunate list of examples precisely in these terms – as moral monsters, repugnant, repulsive, sickening. Here all the chords of our moral attunement are in discord. Our moral sensibility is in sensible, not mere metaphoric pain.

The Phenomenology of The Person as a Primordial Disclosure of Value

I have claimed that the Kantian thesis of the person as an end-in-himself is a metaphysical theory which can be converted directly into phenomenological coin. I want now to make good on that claim and to offer a phenomenological account of our experience of the person, the point of which will be to show that value is disclosed to us prereflectively, in the sphere of affectivity, long "before" reflective reason has a chance to put in a word of its own. There is a prepredicative moral experience which lies at the base of moral reflection, even as there is a prepredicative perceptual experience which lies at the base of theoretical assertions. We are claiming thus that the life of the moral agent is prepredicatively shaped and formed, and that the reflection of the moral philosopher must be directed at unpacking or explicating this prepredicative experience. In the present section I wish to unfold this prepredicative experience of the person as an affective disclosure of value, and then in the concluding section to discuss how this constitutes a "proto-ethics."

Phenomenologists like Heidegger and Merleau-Ponty have argued long and persuasively that the "world" is not *my* world but a shared world, a world with others ("with-world"); and hence that the other is not only an object on my screen, a being-for-me which can be situated on my horizons, but a being-for-himself, irreducible to me. Such a phenomenologically construed world is at the far remove from the Cartesian illusion of an *ego cogito* on the one side and a totality of objects outside me. For I am from the start "outside," drawn into the world and subject to its innumerable influences. I am from the start in a world which is not of my own making, but shaped and formed by historical and linguistic structures which are thousands of years old, which were created with imperceptible slowness by long forgotten generations. These structures are not, as in Sartre's neo-Cartesianism, threats to my freedom; rather they nourish and give shape to my world (see Chapter XI below). My world is filled with others, shaped by their contributions. I am indebted to their generosity and filled with their presence. My family, friends and colleagues, my tradition at large, is a constellation of benefactors who hand over to me the possibilities of my Being.

Now I want to show how my debt to the others reaches down to the depths of my Being, of my prereflective relationship to them. Long before I reach the stage of reflective thought I am already in a relationship to others; my Being is from the start Being-with. I owe my origin to others, my nurturing and growth. From its first moments my life develops in rhythm with others, at first in tune with the rhythm of the maternal heart-beat, and then in tune with the rhythm of the home with its cluster of smiling faces and noises and lights and aromas. The world to which I belong from the start is not a world of material objects with various sizes, shapes, and velocities. It is a profoundly personal world focused on other persons as on radiant points of energy or light, the way the evening sky is filled with stars. From these centers of energy are radiated influences which surround and envelope me so that, when they are present I am filled with them, and when they withdraw I feel their absence. Their very absence testifies to their presence. This enveloping personal world is constantly given to us, always and already pre-given. So true is this that Heidegger says that the so called "problem of other persons" is not the Cartesian pseudo-problem of proving that others are there – that we are not alone in the universe, as Descartes puts it so astonishingly – but rather of finding ourselves in the midst of their encompassing presence. Others, Heidegger argues, are not those whom I am *not,* as if the ego came first and others afterwards as the negation of the ego, but rather those among whom I *too* am.[31] And this [208] relationship to others, which could not be more profound, is borne witness to throughout the length and breadth of our intentional life. The whole range of our intentional acts stands under the influence of the presence of others.

Here I am concerned chiefly with the bodily and affective resonance of this relationship to others, with that affective intentionality which discloses the other to us as a being worthy of respect, and which is already at work before the *ego cogito* arrives on the scene. I wish to argue that bodily intentionality is already ecstatic, that is, already extended beyond itself, stretched out to others, responsive to others. Long before the child enters the universe of words he already intends the parents' look and touch. He has already grown accustomed to the cadence of their voices, the style of their gestures, the feel of their grip, the aroma of their bodies; to the colors and patterns of the nursery, the home; to the bustle and noise of his siblings.

Long before reflective life intervenes we are tied by our bodies and bodily life and the network of its passions, feelings and moods, to the personal world around us. As intentional life matures, as the intentional moves I make become more refined and differentiated, I learn to sort out the persons themselves from the array of objects over which their influence spreads. I learn to lead a distinctively different intentional life towards other persons than I lead toward things, that is, the objects which we together share and use, accumulate and discard. Such things lead out from, and then back to others. They are made by others, sold by others, given to us by others, belong to others or to us: they are there for others or for us. I can grasp, push, pull and otherwise manipulate material objects, but my actions towards others are inscribed with caution, care and courtesy. When they are not, this is understood immediately and by everyone as offensive in the highest degree.

I can stare steadfastly at a material object in order to determine what it is, but it would be unspeakably rude to treat a person likewise. I lean against walls and furniture, but I keep a careful distance between myself and others, and an inner alarm sounds as soon as someone without an invitation approaches too close to us or touches us. I can feel a material object with curiosity about its texture, listen to a noise to discern exactly what it is, sniff about to isolate an aroma, but my bodily intentionality towards others is held strictly in check. I do not stare, poke, or sniff. I am aware, in a prereflective, bodily way, of the life which streams out from the other, of the subjectivity which makes its seat there, of the horizons which the other is constantly throwing out around himself. I do not lightly intrude into that circle. My bodily life takes heed of the autonomy which is exercised there, that the other is no being-for-me, no object reducible to my proportions and locatable on my horizon. I have from the start a bodily recognition that the other is something in itself and not merely for me.

Here then is the phenomenological equivalent of the beings which populate Kant's metaphysical world. Long before philosophical reflection arrives, there is a bodily disclosure of the other as worthy of respect, an end in himself, as a being not to be reduced to the sphere of objects available for my use. Long before philosophical reflection erects a distinction between subject and object, I am already tied to others, and they to me: together we carry out our mutual duties towards one another. Our bodily and affective life already apprehends the eye and hand of the other as the mediation of a personal life which commands our respect.

We have now been brought, I believe, to the point for which we have been striving. The world in which we live does not decompose into real facts on the one side and ideal objects on the other. What is primarily given is instead the inter-personal world, the world of other persons, their words and deeds and the things which they have made. In this world everything centers on the bodily presence of the incarnate other. The incarnate other is value incarnate, the concretely given embodiment of worth and value. The centers of energy, as we described other persons, are centers of value, commanding our respect.

Long before the debates of moral philosophers arise it is already clear that we are all, always and already, tied into a life of moral interaction and that we intend others – prereflectively – in a profoundly different way than we intend objects. The value of the other is not discovered by reflective thought, but only articulated in the language of concepts and judgments, for it is already prereflectively manifest in a more primordial way to our bodily affectivity [209] We are always and all along mooded and tuned to the other, whether in harmony (*sym-pathos*), or in discord (*anti-pathos*), or even when we treat him with callous disregard (*a-pathos*) which is not mood-lessness but the mood of indifference. We live all along in a charged environment of affective being-with, a field of affective impulses, a field of pathos. Were the life of pathos to give out on us, were the energy of our passionate involvement with one another to go dead on us, were we indeed ever to attain a pure reason free of the affective substructure which sustains our life, then moral reflection would become as meaningless as a treatise on the psychological effects of colors to a person born blind.

The task of reflection is to articulate a moral life in which we are already enmeshed, to which we are all precommitted, not to hold court over it. Moral life and moral values are primordially disclosed to us prereflectively, affectively. Our prereflective attunement with one another is the spring by which moral reflection is nourished. Moral reflection simply gives conceptual shape to the prereflective moral life in which we are all along caught up.[32]

Conclusion: Affectivity as Proto-Ethics

I have argued throughout this chapter that the moral struggle is misconceived as a struggle of reason with inclinations, of the rational principle with the irrational principle. I have said in effect that moral strife must be reconceived as a discord within a single nature. It is a dissonance within our affectivity which is reflected in a tossing to and fro between competing reasons on the reflective level: we are affectively drawn in opposite directions, and we can give reasons on either side. By the same token, moral reform does not take the form of bringing the passions back into subjection to reason, but rather of reestablishing harmony and consonance. As moral strife is not a tug of war between opposing metaphysical principles but a discord within a single nature, we should reorganize the totality of our existential forces, both reflective and prereflective, and redirect them to new and fruitful ends. It is a matter of "retuning," of a tune-up of our affective life.

In my view acquiring moral character is not unlike acquiring aesthetic taste, and I do not reject the proximity of morals and aesthetics which the expression "moral sensibility" suggests. Moral life seems to me a matter of being properly sensitized morally, and moral education a matter of seeing to it that our children grow up properly sensitized in moral matters. That means that we want them to feel for the poor and the oppressed – and that is no metaphor: they must in fact feel for the poor. If they do not, they lack moral sensibility as surely as their taste for the standard fare offered on television represents a failure in aesthetic sensibility. We want them to feel more strongly for justice than for acquisitiveness or the amassing of more and more material possessions of their own; we want them to be truly repulsed by brutality, to be horrified by war and inhumanity; we want them to feel a sense of reverence for the physical world and to abhor the technological desecration of the environment and of biological life; we want them to feel pain at violence and injustice. In short we want them to feel the right things: to take pleasure in the right things, and to feel pain at the sight of evil, as Plato and Aristotle both insist.[33] If they are taught to feel well, if they are morally sensitized, then the reasons will come of their own, just as when they are taught to feel the wrong things they do not lack for reasons to rationalize their ill-feeling and ill-will. If they do not feel these things in their marrow, then they are merely paying lip service to what we teach and will throw it over at the first opportunity, for the rationales we make them learn will be a veneer over a hollow, a shell without a kernel. If they do not respond to virtue and vice from the marrow of their bones, if they do not resonate from the depths of their sensibility to these values, if they have not been affectively turned to moral matters, then our words of moral wisdom will be to them only so many tinkling cymbals.

But by reinstating affectivity to a central role in moral life, by insisting upon the centrality of moral affectivity, do we not turn everything over to whim and fancy and make everything a matter of taste? Do we not reduce the choice between justice and injustice to the level of the choice of our favorite color? That at least is the rejoinder of those who make everything turn on the old dichotomy between fact and value, is and ought, real and ideal, sensible and [210] supersensible. The senses tell us what is, but reason must decide what ought to be. Our tastes tell us what we like, but reason tells us what we ought to choose. The old dualism does not give up easily; its death is painfully slow. Such an objection proceeds from a grossly inadequate analysis of the nature of human experience, one whose roots are in Platonism but which extend well into modem philosophy. The one lasting achievement of phenomenology, in my view, is to have corrected this abstract and contrived idea of experience, and to have replaced it with a sound and holistic account of experience as it is really *lived.* That is what I have attempted by means of my presentation of a phenomenology of the person.[34]

I have argued that experience is value-laden from the start, that we meet up with value from the first moments of waking life, and even before that. Human experience, properly conceived in all its amplitude, is from the start an experience of value, in particular of the value of the human person. Values are not something which reason discerns while the senses stand about, stupefied, awaiting its deliberations, though metaphysics has always favored such juridical metaphors. On the contrary, human affectivity is already sensitive to the value of the other, already discloses it, long before reason can set up court. We are always and from the start attuned to the other. We do not need to reach the age of reason, to achieve the *cogito,* or to undertake transcendental reflection to know that: it is already inscribed in our prereflective being. We have already learned it, have all along been learning it, from the first moments of our life. Our being is a being-with, and our being-with is an attunement to the other. The other's presence is an omnipresence to which our whole affective life is attuned.

Hence, by turning things over to affective and prereflective life, we have not turned everything over to whim and caprice; we have not surrendered "reason" to "feeling." On the contrary we have found there the prereflective moorings of the principle to which Kant gave a famous conceptual formulation when he told us always to treat humanity, whether in our person or that of another, as an end and never merely as a means.[35] Here is a principle which is already inscribed in our prereflective and affective intentionality, a principle which makes its presence felt from the start.

Now everything depends upon seeing that the relationship between affectivity and thought is not, as in dualist philosophers, a matter of having a blind feeling on the one side and pure reason on the other, the former lacking insight as the latter lacks incentive. On the contrary, in our scheme, affectivity and thought are related as the implicit to the explicit, so that the work of thought always consists in unpacking our prereflective life, explicating it, and giving it explicit formulation.[36] Hence when Kant announced this principle, it is not as if this were something he had devised, a theory of his, some construction which he wanted to test out. As he himself argues, this law is exceedingly well known to the simplest man and the task of the moral philosopher is to say and to defend what everybody already knows. Kant misconceived this task when he took it to mean that the philosopher must "purify" this principle of any empirical origin. I have argued in the opposite direction, viz., to show as clearly as possible the experiential-affective *base* of any such principle, to show its birth certificate in experience adequately conceived.

This means that we must set aside the wooden and atomistic counterfeit for experience which empiricism offers us. For the texture of experience is complex, rich with meaning, a ripe fruit about to burst. The philosopher is one who stations himself at that critical juncture where this explosion of experience into meaning, of the prereflective into thought, will take place, so that he will be sure to be there. He must be ready, on the spot, and hence able to report everything just as it happens. This work of reporting the most intimate movements of our prereflective life is precisely what philosophy is.

Hence, when we turn to the prereflective, the affective, we do not turn to chaos and the irrational, but rather to that origin by which any principle is nourished. *Our moral affectivity is already a proto-ethics.* It is already possessed of proto-principles which are there, waiting to become explicit sense and meaning under the hand of reflective thought. [211] The moral agent is not a being of reason whose inclinations have been subdued, but a being of delicate moral sensibility who is attuned to the right things. Moral philosophy is not a metaphysics of morals which wants to preserve the rational purity of moral principles, but rather a phenomenology of moral sensibility which gives conceptual expression to that proto-ethics which is always and all along at work in affective life.

233

Notes

[1] I have found Robert Solomon, *The Passions* (Garden City: Doubleday Anchor, 1977) to be especially helpful in formulating the present argument.

[2] Soren Kierkegaard, *Concluding Unscientific Postscript* (hereafter referred to as CUP), trans. D. Swenson and W. Lowrie (Princeton: University Press, 1941), 206.

[3] CUP, 208.

[4] Because of his Ockhamistic metaphysics, according to which each moment is absolutely contingent, Kierkegaard rejected the Aristotelian notion of a habit (*hexis*). See George Stack, *Kierkegaard's Existential Ethics* (Montgomery, Alabama: University of Alabama Press, 1977), 133–34.

[5] CUP, 347–50.

[6] Soren Kierkegaard, *The Concept of Dread,* trans. W. Lowrie (Princeton: University Press, 1957), 16–17n. Kierkegaard is referring to the disinterestedness of the aesthetic judgment in Kant's *Critique of Judgment.*

[7] CUP, 446.

[8] CUP, 476.

[9] CUP, 476.

[10] Soren Kierkegaard, *Repetition,* trans. W. Lowrie (Princeton: University Press, 1946), 3–7.

[11] In Ch. 3, above [referring to the original publication –ed.], Sebastian Samay uses the term "affectivity" in the same ontological sense in which Heidegger uses the term "*Befindlichkeit.*"

[12] Martin Heidegger, *Being and Time* (hereafter referred to as BT), trans. J. Macquarrie and E. Robinson (New York: Harper & Row, 1962), 29.

[13] The word that Heidegger uses for mood is "*Stimmung*," which means the way we are "tuned," *bestimmt,* to things.

[14] Husserl already established this point in *Logical Investigations,* vol. 2, trans. John Findlay (New York: Humanities Press, 1970), Inv. V, 15, where he develops the position first put forward by Brentano.

[15] CUP, 476.

[16] See "What is Metaphysics?" in *Martin Heidegger: Basic Writings,* ed. David Krell (New York: Harper & Row, 1977), 91–112. [212]

[17] BT, 177.

[18] Lewis White Beck, *A Commentary on Kant's Critique of Practical Reason* (Chicago: University of Chicago Press, 1960), 213–14.

[19] Hence the second *Critique* contained an "incentive" of practical reason whose function was architectonically parallel to the "Transcendental Aesthetic" in the first Critique, namely, to provide the element of sensibility in transcendental synthesis. And it was for this reason that Kant proposed what he called the moral feeling of "respect" (*Achtung*).

[20] Immanuel Kant, *Critique of Practical Reason* (hereafter referred to as CPrR), trans. Lewis White Beck (Indianapolis: Bobbs-Merrill, 1956), 77.

[21] Martin Heidegger, *Basic Problems of Phenomenology*, trans. A. Hofstadter (Bloomington: Indiana University Press, 1982), 133.

[22] CPrR, 75.

[23] "The moral law…completely excludes the influence of self-love from the highest practical principle and forever checks self-conceit, which decrees the subjective conditions of self-love as laws. If anything checks our self-conceit in our own judgment, it humiliates. Therefore the moral law inevitably humbles every man when he compares the sensuous propensity of his nature with the law. Now if the idea of something as the determining ground of the will humiliates us in our self-consciousness, it awakens respect for itself so far as it is positive and the ground of determination." (CPrR, 77).

[24] CPrR, 79.

[25] Heidegger, "What is Metaphysics?" 106.

[26] CPrP, 79.

[27] CPrP, 79–80.

[28] Cf. BT §34, pp. 55-56.

[29] Heidegger, *Basic Problems of Phenomenology*, 137.

[30] Immanuel Kant, *Foundation of the Metaphysics of Morals: Text and Critical Essays,* ed. Robert P. Wolff (Indianapolis: Bobbs Merrill, 1969), 52–60.

[31] BT, §§25–26.

[32] Accordingly, one can ask how critical reflection is possible in such a standpoint. For if reason is bound to explicating a prereflective given, how is it ever possible for it to disengage itself sufficiently to put into question a particular pre-reflective structure in which it may have grown up? The answer to this is provided, I think, by Gadamer's notion of the fusion of horizons, which belongs to the heart of what he calls hermeneutics. In that view, critical reflection is awakened by the collision of my horizon, within which I have been nurtured and whose validity I have always assumed, with the horizon of the other. The collision awakens me to my horizon, which prior to this collision may well have been at work on me without my knowing it, and furthermore puts it into question by exposing its contingency. The ensuing dialogue between diverse horizonal understandings is thus at the same time a process of critical reflection upon the relative merits of each. It is our view that it would always be possible for such a [212] dialogue to reach agreement about the principle of the worth of the person which we have expounded here, given the appropriate conditions of a dialogue. See Hans Georg Gadamer, *Truth and Method,* trans. Garrett Barden and John Cumming (New York: Seabury Press, 1975), pp. 258-74.

[33] Aristotle, *Nicomachean Ethics,* Ch. 3 (1104bl0-15); and Plato, *Republic,* 401 E-402A

[34] For more on this question, see my "The Presence of Others: A Phenomenology of the Human Person," *Proceedings of the American Catholic Philosophical Association,* 53 (1979): 45–58 [also in John D. Caputo, *Collected Philosophical and Theological Papers,* Volume 1, chapter 20 –ed.]; and Emmanuel Levinas, *Totality and Infinity,* trans. A. Lingis (Pittsburgh: Duquesne University Press, 1969).

[35] Kant, *Foundations,* 54.

[36] The prereflective is not reducible to the affective, for there is also a cognitive pre-reflective – as when I am buried in the complexities of a mathematical problem without adverting to the fact that now I am doing mathematical work. Whence there is both a cognitive and an affective pre-reflective which it is the task of reflective thought to explicate.

16

BEING AND THE MYSTERY OF THE PERSON

[In *The Universe as Journey: Conversations with W. Norris Clarke, S.J.*, ed. Gerald McCool (New York: Fordham University Press, 1988), 93–113]

[93] Heidegger says that thinking is thanking, by which he means that thinking comes in response to the graciousness of Being. Let us say that in these remarks thanking will take the form of thinking, that we offer to Norris Clarke, in gratitude for a lifetime of illumination and insight, an exercise in thinking, a work of thought in thanks for a life of thinking.

I want to think here the question of the person. Such thinking might be called "phenomenological" because it knows no other way to proceed than by the closest heeding of the structure of lived experience, and "hermeneutic" because it recognizes the unavoidability of interpretation, that there is no sheer beholding of unambiguous structures. Indeed, thinking turns on the notion of ambiguity, of undecidability, of a certain labyrinthine circumstance in which we are all implicated, like it or not. It might also be called "ontological," because I take the person to be a privileged point of departure for the question of Being. Finally, such thinking might be called "ethical," because for it all of the issues in a philosophical ethic are concentrated in the person.

I want to organize these reflections around the oldest and most literal idea about the person: the person as *per-sonare* – to sound through the mask, to fill the mask with sound, to resound. *Per-sona*: the voice sounding through the mask, the false placed over the true. *Persona* implies a dialectic between face and hiddenness, an interplay between the mask [94] and what is masked, between concealment and what emerges into unconcealment. Concealment and unconcealment, what Heidegger called *aletheia*, is here conceived – beyond Heidegger's intentions – in terms of the *per-sona*, in terms of face and sub-face. I want to do here something which Heidegger strangely left undone, to tend to a field he strangely left uncultivated, to follow the dialectic of *aletheia*, of concealment and unconcealment, insofar as it is at work in the person. And what could be more natural, when the very word *per-sona* suggests that the surface is always disturbed by the concealed depths, that the face is always more than sur-face, is always a *plus ultra*, something more? The very word *persona* tells us that something more is resonating through it.

The face – and let us call this my "thesis," if that is an appropriate way to speak here – is a place of transcendence, by which I mean a place in which the transcendent breaks through, and in which we are initiated into deeper things, drawn into the mystery of self, of world, of God. Carried out carefully enough, this hermeneutic phenomenology of the face reveals the mystery, what Heidegger would call the *lethe*, by which we are inhabited and in which I want to locate the essential quality of the person. *Persona*: that means for me the being in which mystery resonates, the being defined by its openness to the mystery. The face leads us into the desert, and, by opening up the play of concealment and un-concealment, of masked and un-masked, which is the age-old sense of *per-sona*, is a worthy matter for "thinking."[1]

And my question is, what is sounding through the mask? What voice do we hear? What sounds and resounds through the face? Is it only a human voice? But that is an altogether strange question to ask. For surely common sense prescribes that it is the human person who speaks, a human voice that resonates through the face. But must we let common sense have the final word? Is it common sense that decides matters of thought? Is it possible to ask whether anyone or anything other than man is sounding through, filling the mask with sound? Can we ask such a question? Were it not a human [95] voice, what then? A divine voice? The voice of God calling us to Godself? Or some cosmic voice, and hence less a voice than a certain cosmic rumble or resonating? Is the person a place where something divine sounds through, or something cosmic and mundane? The questioning is odd and it is difficult even to know how to pose it. Might it be indeed that we are led by this exercise in thinking, not so much to answer these questions as to learn how to ask them? Questioning is the piety of thought and the openness to the mystery. Questioning leads us into transcendence, to the breakthrough, exposing us to the *lethe*, undermining our assurances. Perhaps the most to ask for in what follows is to learn to ask these questions, which is to say, to learn to think.

Kant and Clarke

Norris Clarke has probed the question of the person on a number of occasions and with impressive results.[2] He frequently and rightly takes Kant to task for failing to provide an adequate epistemological ground for our knowledge of the other person, and he rightly argues that, had he done so, Kant would have landed himself on the other side of his transcendental idealism in some form of realism. The one place where the phenomenality of appearance is surpassed, where there can be no doubt about the trans-phenomenality of what is other, is the reality of the other person. The experience of interpersonal dialogue is the best warrant of the claim of realism. In hearing the voice of the other there can be no question of imposing my own forms upon a raw matter. On the contrary, I am addressed by what is genuinely other.

Now, there is a metaphysics at work here, as there is everywhere in Father Clarke's work, which turns on the Thomistic principle *agere sequitur esse*. I translate: Being (*esse*) is manifest, unconcealed, in and through action (*agere*). The Being of the other person is manifest in his discourse because, more generally, action is always a revelation of Being. It belongs to the fecundity of Being, to its self-diffusiveness, to flow over [96] into manifestness. And man is the being who, as Father Clarke writes, "is placed in the midst of the material cosmos with the ability to receive the self-imaging messages of all the material beings around him.... It is man's destiny, written into him by the very structure of his nature, to be the one to listen to being, as it reveals itself to him."[3] Every being is a *persona* of a certain sort, an actor that speaks to us through its action, whose action manifests its Being to us, a being through which Being sounds.

The other person is delivered to us, not immediately, but through the mediation of his action and language. We make contact, but not naked contact. And it is just this self-revelatory dimension of Being which is denied in Kant's epistemology. Because he thinks that Being manages to act upon me while altogether concealing itself, Kant effectively denies the principle *agere sequitur esse*. The influence that things exert upon us is extinguished by the active domination of them by our consciousness. But in the eminently balanced view of moderate realism, things both reveal and conceal themselves to us. Hence it is *esse*, *esse reale*, real Being, which resonates through the *per-sona* for Father Clarke.

Now, I have no wish to rush to the defense of Kant on this point. I am content to let him twist slowly in the wind of Father Clarke's critique. I agree that Kant has no good epistemological theory of how the other person is given to us. But I do want to point out that, while Kant lacked an epistemology of the person, he insisted upon a certain moral faith in the existence of others as the matter of conscience, the material object of the law. The other was for him a kind of fourth postulate of practical reason, an object of practical faith. Whence to understand Kant's account of other persons we would need to look, not to Kant's epistemology, but to his ethics, not to the *personalitas transcendentalis*, but to the *personalitas moralis*.

In the second and third formulations of the categorical imperative, which command the will to treat the other as an end in itself, and hence with the same respect that is deserved [97] by the law itself, Kant makes it clear that the moral agent belongs to a community of agents to whom he is bound in conscience. Every rational being is a being capable of moral action, of rising above and asserting himself to be more than a piece of nature, and hence worthy to be treated as an end in himself. The person enjoys a worth or dignity (*Würde*) that arises from his power to act in ways which are inherently worthy of respect – to keep promises faithfully, to be benevolent in principle. Through the person the law enters the world and acquires concrete form. We feel the power of law pulsating through the other. What resonates, what sounds through the *per-sona* for Kant, is the unconditional authority of the law. The rational being is the law itself, if not on horseback, at least in the flesh, in person, in the person. In Kant's own ponderous formulation, the law is "schematized" by the concrete person in whom we see the law at work.

It seems to me that there is something essentially right in all this, but that Kant's formulations are vitiated by his Enlightenment frame of mind and his dualist metaphysics. And it seems to me likewise that with a slight wave of the phenomenological wand one can cash in Kant's claims for experiential coin.[4] We all know of Kant's beginnings, of his pietist home, and of the tender regard with which he held the men and women of his childhood who led decent but humble, virtuous but obscure lives. The humblest servant is the equal of any man of means, Kant thought, when it comes to uprightness of will. Kant was moved by these examples of moral excellence to a lifelong and unshakable belief in the dignity of people of common decency. His analysis of the feeling of respect – which, I believe, his own dualism makes impossible – has, as Heidegger says, a rich phenomenological description of moral feeling. Kant's ethics originates in a deep and lasting experience of the other person.[5]

But to take this experience seriously would, as Norris Clarke argues, provoke a serious upheaval in Kant's epistemology and, as I want to argue, an equally serious upheaval in his ethics. For even in the ethics Kant takes the person, not in [98] his naked humanness, but rather as the embodiment of the law. In the remainder of this paper I want to take the experience of the other seriously and so to till the phenomenological soil from which Kant's own moral experience of the other arises. I want to ask once again: what is the Being of the person? What is sounding through and resonating in the *per-sona*? To do this, I want to take up the question of the face.

The Face and the Mystery of the Other

Let us attend to the phenomenon of the face, and with phenomenological attentiveness. What does it give us to think? What is at play in the face, in the

240

interplay between face and depth, sur-face and sub-face? The face is a surface which reveals and conceals, which is filled with hidden forces, which is always something more than it gives itself out to be. What is this something more? What secrets does it harbor — and betray? What powers and forces resonate here?

To discuss these questions I want to rethink two phenomena which Kant discussed – the analysis of lying and the treatment of the feeling of respect – in terms of a phenomenology of the face. The work of *deception* and the right to *respect*. What do they have to do with the face? Or with each other? Do they have a common source, draw upon the same reserves? What do they say about *per-sona*, about what we call here the mystery of the other?

Lying. Lying is a good example for Kant of a maxim whose universalization results in self-contradiction. But let us consider it here, not in relation to the law, but in relation to the face. Let us see if the contradiction in which it is implicated is more than logical. Let us see if lying does not point to a deeper division in our nature.

Language, which is the bearer of truth, is centered in the face. Language is seated in the *lingua*, in the tongue, mouth, lips, and it is overseen by the eyes. Language is *lingua, labia, facies.* To speak is not merely to utter words or to form [99] propositions. It is to orchestrate an entire concert by means of which one's words are supported by an ensemble of facial and bodily accomplishments. A merriness in the eyes, a sadness around the lips, clenched teeth, cold looks – all give the fragile sequence of signs its power to convince, to persuade, to have an effect. Speech acts are acts, acting, performances of a *dramatis persona* whose effect is to persuade an audience.

But this gestural accompaniment is for the most part nonintentionalistic, pre-conceptual, para-linguistic. We do not control this ensemble of gesture and expression – and that is why Husserl did not consider it language properly so-called.[6] Indeed what is harder than trying to smile for a camera or trying to look surprised? The support the body lends to discourse arises spontaneously. The face is a field of implicit and unthematic operations. An eyebrow pronounces wordless contempt; a spontaneous smile, without premeditation, declares that approval has been won. One's whole being-in-the-world is disclosed without the intervention of conscious control. And it is precisely because the face escapes the monitoring of the ego that language can be so profoundly ambiguous. I can say with my eyes that I want something very badly, even though my words say I do not want it at all. A poorly concealed look of pain says that I have been bitterly disappointed, even though I say with my words that it does not matter at all. There is fear on the face, even when one's words are brave; anger, even when one speaks softly.

But it is just because the face is a play of surfaces that we can become adept at lying, which is in this view a peculiarly deep and illustrative disruption of our being-in-the-world. The "cold liar" is, from the point of view of a phenomenology of the face, a frightening phenomenon, an enormously divided and rent being. He stares us in the eyes yet dissembles. He seems to have acquired the power to interrupt this whole system of communication between the body and the face, on the one hand, and spoken discourse, on the other. He has acquired the diabolic art of silencing the bodily system, of trafficking in words that do not arise from fundamental projects. He is able [100] to orchestrate his words with a bodily and facial accompaniment that is pure artifact. He is a master mime with an unnatural control over his body. He is able to keep his eyes from betraying him, to bring all the clues and signals, all the minute and unconscious indications that are alive in the face, under conscious control. He tries to acquire total domination over his body.

The inconsistency of lying was a favorite example of Kant's. But this inconsistency is not, as Kant thought, a purely logical matter of non-universalizability. In fact, from a merely logical point of view, it can be quite consistently carried out, not only with others but even with oneself. If it were only a matter of logic, we could do it. If all we had to contend with were the first formulation of the categorical imperative, we could get away with it. The inconsistency of lying, however, cuts deeper than logic; it is a bodily matter which can be grasped, not in logical, but only in phenomenological terms. Lying put us at odds with our most implicit and tacit gestural life, demands that we be ever on guard against the slightest hint of betrayal, that there never be a moment when we are caught off guard. It demands total domination of our bodily being-in-the-world, that nothing be left tacit, implicit, preconscious, inadvertent, unguarded. It demands absolute consciousness and a lived dualism between consciousness and body. Indeed, one would even have to keep one's dream secret. Lying demands absolute vigilance.

Lying exploits the face as a play of surfaces and the performance of a *dramatis persona*. Lying trades on the interplay between sur-face and concealment, manifest and latent. In lying – and this is what interests us here – we are brought up short against the capacity of the other to hold himself back, to keep himself in reserve, to hide himself behind images of his own creation. Lying discloses the thickness and opacity of language and its power to serve as a veil through which the other withdraws even as he discloses himself. We do not make immediate contact with the other. We have no firm grasp of who it is that looks

242

out at us through those eyes, who is speaking, [101] smiling, appearing to be delighted at our arrival. We are all more or less adept how to don the mask.

Indeed, even when we suppose we speak with perfect honesty, we cannot avoid this self-concealment and self-withdrawal. If lying is a case of intentionally suppressing our beliefs, we ought not to suppose that there is some state of absolute self-contact, of perfect self-transparency, where we keep in perfect touch with ourselves. On the contrary, we maintain, it belongs to the ontological make-up of the person to keep slipping away. It belongs to the a-lethic make-up of the person that the element of *lethe* is ineradicable. For, quite apart from whatever is intentionally suppressed in lying, there is the vast realm of what is unconsciously repressed. So that when we speak in good faith, in perfect honesty, we cannot know what or whether "it" (*es*) says within us, what re-pressed desire speaks without our conscious ex-pression.[7] Then we do not lie to the other, which is the simpler case, but we lie to ourselves, which is more complicated. In either case, lying is ontologically significant and points to the alethic mystery of the self.

Respect. And with that conclusion we are led to the second point in the Kantian analysis which we want to rethink along phenomenological lines, viz., the feeling of respect. We recall that for Kant the person is the place where the law enters the world and acquires mundane form. The law, and hence the person in whom the law is embodied, requires absolute respect. But we ask: is the person the embodiment of the law, or is the law simply a distillation, a way of writing in shorthand our experience of the person? Again, it is the face that will serve as our clue.

The face is the seat, not only of truthfulness and deception, but also of what I want to call here "inviolability." The face commands and forbids. It is the face that places the mark of inviolability upon us, which commands respect and forbids violence.[8] The face cries out against manipulation and subjugation. It is the face of the innocent that speaks the most [102] eloquently for social justice: the face of the starving child, with his deathly stare. It is only if we can see the face of our victims that we can understand that they exist as ends and never as means. The face of the other marks him as an end-in-itself, protests against exploitation, manipulation. Every attempt at objectifying the other – from pornography to murder – must be conceived as an attempt to erase the face of the other. Objectification is possible only to the extent that we can deny and nullify his face.

It is the face that condemns murder. When we place a mask on the criminal to be executed, who is being shielded from whom? Is the condemned spared the sight of his executioner? Or is the executioner spared the horror of the eyes and the look of the condemned? What would it be like were this event to take place face-to-face? Would we find anyone willing to do it? And if we did, would we be cultivating a new breed of professionalized brutality? Were the executioners of Auschwitz watching the faces?

All the commandments directed toward our neighbor issue from the face. Kant was not wrong, he simply had recourse to the wrong organon. He needed a phenomenology of the eyes of the other, not a table of logical judgments and their categorical forms. The person is thus not an instance of the law, or the embodiment of the law; rather, the law arises from the person, the law is issued by the face of the other. It is the eyes of the other that issue the categorical imperative. Indeed, the very word "respect" belongs to an "ocular" metaphysics: the a-spect – the look of the other – commands our re-spect: the way we look back. "Respect" – and this is so not only in the Latinate forms, but also in the German *achten* – means the regard, the look, which we give back or return to those whose look brings us up short. From the eyes of the other comes the look that commands our attention, our attentiveness, our regard.

We thus move beyond all value-theory in this phenomenology of the face. The face of the other is not a value posited by the will, but a command that issues from the hidden depths of the other. The modern notion of value must be [103] deconstructed back into its Greek sense of *axios*, that which is esteemed, respected, because of the respect it commands. We do not posit values, but things of imposing stature and imposing dignity command our respect.[9]

But what is it about the other that commands our respect? What spell does he cast over us? What power does he exert on us? The answer to that question turns on the ontology of the face. The face is *facies*, sur-face, appearance, phenomenon. But it is the surface which is never mere surface, which always intimates more than it shows. The face is the surface which harbors something hidden, which is inhabited by deeper motives and concealed sense. The essence of the face is to be at one and the same time self-showing and self-concealing, closure and disclosure, in accordance with the ontology of *aletheia*. The sur-face of the face is to be all writing and sign, a code we can only partly make out, a script of ambiguous messages. Thus the face of the other brings us up short because we know that he knows more than he says, that he says other than he knows, that as often as not he does not know what he says or whence it issues. We know that we have to do here with powers which elude our control, and that is why they command our respect.

244

The self-withdrawing of the other is the seat of his mystery. It is just this self-withdrawing mystery which gives the person the authority of law, which endows him with the power to command respect and to declare himself inviolable. We are persuaded that we have to do here with powers which elude us and which demand to be recognized. He exerts upon us the power of the unknown. He has the advantage of being a mystery to us. He is like a person who wears dark glasses and who puts us at the awful disadvantage of not being able to see his eyes. The inviolability of the other arises from his inaccessibility, from the limits of our access to him and of his access to himself. His inaccessibility is the effect, not merely of perversity, as in the simple case of the lie, but of the ineradicable recessiveness of his being, from others and from himself. The face of the other is a constant reminder of the [104] limits of our reach and of the depths of his being, depths we can only partly probe. He draws himself into a circle which can be only partially penetrated by him as well as by us. His words and gestures communicate with us from a source of which we all have only an imperfect, uncertain grasp.

I am not saying that we are forever cut off from him, but that this being with whom we are always and already, from the start, is always in part withheld from us. The intimacy of our presence with him, our being-with, is always qualified by his mysterious reserve. The other is both surface and depth, both access and recess, revelation and concealment. The other holds himself back, is in continual and necessary withdrawal, even in his very commerce with us. His giving of himself – and not only to us but also to himself – is likewise a holding-back.

Thus both analyses – of lying and respect – on our phenomenological account lead curiously to the same result. They both turn on the phenomenon of the self-withdrawing nature of the other. The person is capable of deception (and this includes self-deception) only because of a deeper and more radical trait, the ontological necessity with which his being holds itself back even in the act of giving and self-revelation. Deception and respect have the same root. Both spring from the self-withdrawing center which defines the other, which constitutes his otherness, and which makes the rest of us a reader of signs.

Thus the Thomist principle which Norris Clarke justly invokes, *agere sequitur esse* – what the other does flows from what he is – also implies that *esse* does not give itself immediately, that it is always held in reserve, that *agere* never succeeds in exposing or exhausting *esse*. *Agere* follows upon *esse* but it never quite succeeds in catching up to *esse*, in unfolding it, in being a match for it. *Esse* remains behind, in concealment, even in the very un-concealment of *agere*. The action of God in the production of the world does not exhaust or wholly display the

Being of God. The action of any finite agent remains an imperfect exhibition of its Being. If action is the self-revelation of Being, and the refutation of any [105] solipsism, as it is, it is also the self-concealment. Indeed, this self-concealment is as much a testimony to the reality of the other – which is the point which Father Clarke want to make against Kant – as is his self-revelation in action, for self-concealment too bears witness to depths we cannot plumb, to a reality upon which we cannot lay hands. Being is self-concealing even its very act of self-revealing. *Agere* springs from a hidden and mysterious root.

We have thus reached a preliminary result in terms of our original and quite odd question: what is sounding and resounding through the human *per-sona*? On this phenomenological reading the person resonates with ambiguity and mystery, with a depth which neither he nor we can fathom. The mystery of the face is to be a surface over an abyss. Something deep is playing itself out, something mysterious reveals and conceals itself in the eyes and lips, in the look of pain and the look of joy. What do we see there? What voice is resonating there?

Suffering and the Mystery of the Person

In speaking of the way the soul makes its way beyond the "names" of God and exposes itself to the transcendent mystery of the "naked Godhead," Meister Eckhart used the term "breakthrough." In the breakthrough the soul enters what Eckhart called the "abyss" of God, the "desert" where the capacity to name God withers away. And, corresponding to the abyss in God, Eckhart spoke of the abyss within the soul, the deep spot in the soul, deeper than the explicit faculties of intellect and will, where the soul is joined to God. The abyss of God is encountered in the abyss of the soul. *Abyssus abyssum invocat.*

Now, without involving us in a religious mysticism I too would like to speak of a fine point of the soul, where we break through to a similar kind of mysterious depth or desert terrain which we find within ourselves. It is here, in this desert place, this deep ground, that we can make an approach to the [106] question of what is sounding and resounding in the human *per-sona*. To this end I want to extend my analysis of the face by turning to the face of the one who suffers. What is the look of suffering? What powers resonate here? Of what mysteries does it speak? What secrets does it harbor? What concealed depths do we catch sight of in the eyes of the sufferer?

"Suffering" implies *passivity*; it means that we undergo something, are subjected to something, against our will, are invaded by alien powers, subdued by a hostile force. In suffering, we are at the mercy of a power, caught in its grip, and we can at best bear up under it with dignity – lest we lose our dignity

246

altogether. We have the power, not to dominate it, but only to undergo it with dignity. Suffering is *violation*. If the essence of the person is his inviolability, suffering assaults and violates him. If we conceive the person in terms of respect, suffering is a reckless, ravaging invader, which respects no one and nothing, neither age nor wealth, neither virtue nor power. Suffering is a transgression against the person, which, by depriving him of his faculties, tries to rob him of his dignity and to turn him into an object, not of respect, but of pity.

Suffering exposes our *vulnerability*. A chance circumstance, a small accident of space or time, a small disorder in prenatal life – all can change the course of a lifetime; can ruin or take away life. We live from moment to moment at the mercy of the elements, of a precarious biochemical balance within our own bodies, of the uneven justice of a world filled with wanton violence, and nowadays at the mercy of a nuclear event that could happen at any moment, not merely because of the volatility of politics, but because of an error in a computer chip.

Suffering – passivity, violability, vulnerability – has a transcendental sense. It provides a kind of locus in which an abyss opens up, in which the familiar categories of everydayness are shattered. Suffering is one of those surfaces – the face, the surface, of the sufferer – which harbors and shelters within itself an abyss. The self as abyss. The face as the sur-face over an abyss. For suffering is not simply suffering. It is a phenomenon of such proportion that it surpasses itself. An abyss opens up [107] within it and we find ourselves exposed to the depths, to the mystery, to the desert within us all. Something, who knows what, is at work here – where the body is degraded and reduced to a shadow of its true powers. Suffering is not understandable. It is a violence with no rights, yet it breaks into and ravages our lives.

I treat suffering as a kind of place, a locus, a field in which a radical hermeneutic event takes place, a deep interpretive construal of our existence. In suffering we encounter a darkness which we construe in conflicting ways and with a conflict that cannot be resolved. The ambiguity here is inextinguishable, the interpretations are in conflict, the choices we make uncertain. We come here to that fine part of the soul, that deep ground which Eckhart described, the desert within. It is in this desert that the fundamental lines of our relationship to the world are drawn. Here, in this desert, we wrestle with the powers of darkness, with the angel of death.

For the religious spirit, suffering points to a power which must take the side of the sufferer. It is an outrage that cries out for justice. The stars cannot follow their regular course, nor the seasons their sequence, there can be no order or sense in anything, if suffering goes unanswered, if no deeper power intervenes by directing it to some purpose. The most powerful religious image in the Western world – the image of the Cross – is of one who suffers. The central image of Christianity is of a suffering innocent. The image of Jesus, J. B. Metz says, provokes the "dangerous memory of suffering."[10]

Suffering compels us to think that there is a God and that He stands with the sufferer, with the poor and oppressed, the starving and the downtrodden. This deep-set religious view cuts across the ideologies of left and right. That is why liberation theology flourishes in Central America and Catholic priests and nuns are called Marxists because they stand by the poor, while in Poland, where the priests also stand with the poor, with the people, with those who have no voice, they are called counter-revolutionary. Suffering and oppression have a transcendent, a surpassing quality for us. There is more to [108] suffering than lies on its surface. Suffering is not simply suffering, not merely a surface. The face of one who suffers is an arrow, an indication, a clue that God stands on the side of suffering. For the religious spirit, the cries of those who suffer issue from the separation of the soul from God – in keeping with the sentiment of St. Augustine (perhaps the most religious writer the West has produced): "Thou hast made us for thyself, O Lord, and our hearts will not rest until they rest in Thee."

Yet it is precisely suffering that, for Nietzsche, breeds the fiction of religion, the illusion which we call faith. Religion, he says, is devised precisely *"for sufferers;* they maintain that all those who suffer from life as from an illness are in the right and would like every other feeling of life to be counted false and become impossible...." In the place of the religious response to suffering, Nietzsche puts what he calls an Olympian, Dionysian laughter. Such a laughter – the laughter of the young shepherd who bit off the head of the serpent, the laughter for which Zarathustra longs – has taken its full measure of human suffering. It has seen into the abyss of the going-under, has undergone the tragic, suffered from terrible melancholy and nausea, yet nonetheless it affirms this world with all its tragic flaws, affirms the flux of going-over and going-under, and is willing to live without appeal. The ability of a spirit to suffer, Nietzsche says, almost determines its nobility. Almost: because it requires likewise the power of laughter.[11]

I do not seek a way to adjudicate this ambiguity and undecidability. I want rather to let this ambiguous and undecidable substructure of our lives be seen, precisely as the nourishing matrix of our beliefs – whether they are religious or tragic, holy or unholy, whether we follow Augustine or Nietzsche. The essential thing is the transcendence, the surpassing, the abyss that opens up under our hands.

My aim is not to produce either an apologia for religion or a critique of it, but to point to the deep ground in which all such fundamental decisions are made, where all essential projects are formed.[12] I want only to mark off the place within us [109] which I have called here mystery, ambiguity, undecidability, the desert, and which lies at the far remove of proof and disproof, of scientific determination. The ambiguity does not dissolve, even though we make a decision, what I would call a deep decision, a deep hermeneutic resolve, a deep construal. I do not want to resolve the ambiguity, or to recommend a course of action, but to point to an ontological structure, to evoke a sense of the hidden depths, of the fine point of the soul, the point where we are brought up short, solicited, shaken, provoked.

Indeed, were one to recommend that we should ignore such numinous considerations altogether and, like Rorty, say that the only point is to minimize suffering and maximize cooperation and to stop dawdling over misty depths, I would not have a counter-argument – except to ask whether anything essential lies outside the sphere of argument. If someone were to say to me that he simply was not interested in this sphere which I want to evoke, I can think of nothing more to say to him.

I am concerned, then, not with an *apologia* for the religious (or the irreligious), nor with its *critique*, but with its *genesis*, its point of departure in the pre-conceptual base of our existence, which I take to be like a dark, thick, ambiguous cord that ties us to the world. I want only to point to the depths and to the ways in which we construe them. Here, in this place, essential decisions are made, fundamental projects are shaped by experiences that go all the way down, experiences that cut all the way through to the core. Heidegger's spatial metaphor of the *da*, the place where something essential happens, serves us well here.

Conclusion

The person, then, on my accounting, is a certain play between the sur-face and the abyss. The person is an interplay between two elements. On the one hand, the person is an incarnate project (I take the face to be but the center in which our bodily project as a whole is concentrated) that is intimately [110] interwoven with the world and absorbed in worldly affairs; on the other hand, a power of transcendence which cannot be saturated by any mundane or quotidian operation, which keeps breaking through everydayness, surpassing it, and opening out on to the abyss. The person is the place where that happens, the locus of the transcendence. The resonance we detect in the *per-sona* is the rumbling of this transcendence.

It is as if we cannot be taken in by the world, as if there is more to us than particular worldly engagements can offer. Things have for us a surpassing quality. They serve as occasions of transcendence, which prevents them from retaining their own identity. The simplest things can become occasions of transcendence and hence can become deep. The deepest, most important things are definable by their lack of identity with themselves. Suffering is not merely suffering: it speaks of eternal things – and let us not forget that this does not necessarily mean a religious eternity, but perhaps the eternity of eternal recurrence, the eternity of the infinite flux of the world. The person is a power of converting the finite into the infinite. Let us not say convert, let us say rather breaking through, the place where the infinite breaks through the finite. It is as if we walk on a surface that is constantly ready to give way and to drop us into the abyss. It is as if the world is constantly liable to transmute, to metamorphose, into eternal things. It is as if we lead lives of everyday activity that are always on the edge of breaking through into the extraordinary, the abnormal, the exceptional. One imagines life as a kind of surrealist film in which a man walking down a crowded city street turns a corner only to find himself in a desert, alone with himself, thinking eternal thoughts. It is as if there is a hidden hair-trigger in things which can be set off by the slightest gesture, the smallest movement, yet produce a shattering blow, a shocking force that leaves us shaken.

Our lives are lived out in this interplay between these two spheres. But this is no theory of two worlds, of inner soul and outer world, eternity and time. Rather, the things of our world have two dimensions, two sides: on the one side their [111] identity – the face of one who suffers is a face and nothing more – and on the other side their non-identity, their power of eliciting surpassal and transcendence, their power to spin off into infinity. And let us say that the person is the being in whom these two, identity and surpassal, intersect. The person is the place where things open up, where the infinity harbored within them is exposed, where the abyss breaks open, where the desert encroaches.

In the person there is played out an interplay between surface and depth, ordinary and extraordinary, commonplace and mystery. The Being of the person is to be open to this interplay, to be the place where transcendence occurs, to let the mystery of Being, of the withdrawal of Being, come to pass. The person is the locus where the transformation of the commonplace into the abyss occurs. And everything that we mean by religion and art and philosophy is, it seems to me, an attempt to come to grips with this transformation, to let it happen, to preserve and cultivate it with words.

Per-sona: the old word for sounding-through. *Per-sona*: the abyss sounding through the sur-face, the sur-face that keeps opening up on to the abyss. *Per-sona*: the concealment that inhabits the core of, and resonates in, all un-concealment. *Per-sona*: the sounding of the mystery, of the withdrawal of Being, the echo it leaves behind.

Whose voice is sounding through the person? Is it the voice of God calling us down the labyrinthine way? Or is it no voice at all, but simply the rumble of the world-play, of the flux, and the more-than-human laughter of Zarathustra, dancing and singing even as he goes under?

Notes

[1] Heidegger too seems willing to give the old word *per-sona* a second reading. He writes: "Persona means the actor's mask through which his dramatic tale is sounded. Since man is the percipient who perceives what is, we can think of him as the *persona*, the mask, of Being." *What is Called Thinking?*, trans. F. Wieck and J. Glenn Gray (New York: Harper & Row, 1968), 62. The project [112] of a phenomenology of the face has been initiated by Emmanuel Levinas, most notably in his *Totality and Infinity*, trans. A. Lingis (Pittsburgh: Duquesne University Press, 1969). See the writings of Robert Bernasconi and Adrian Peperzak for suggestive attempts to relate the work of Heidegger and Levinas.

[2] Norris Clarke, "Action as the Self-Revelation of Being: A Central Theme in the Thought of St. Thomas," in *History of Philosophy in the Making*, ed. Linus Thro (Washington, D.C.: University Press of America, 1982), 63–80; "Interpersonal Dialogue: Key to Realism," in *Person and Community*, ed. Robert J. Roth, S.J. (New York: Fordham University Press, 1975), 141–53; "The Self in Eastern and Western Thought: The Wooster Conference," *International Philosophical Quarterly*, 6 (1969), 101–109; "The Self as the Source of Meaning in Metaphysics," *Review of Metaphysics*, 21 (1968), 587–614.

[3] "Action as the Self-Revelation of Being," 71.

[4] See my "Kant's Ethics in Phenomenological Perspective," in *Kant and Phenomenology*, ed. Thomas Seebohm (Washington: University Press of America, 1984), 129–46. [also in John D. Caputo, *Collected Philosophical and Theological Papers*, Volume 1, chapter 19 –ed.]

[5] Martin Heidegger, *The Basic Problems of Phenomenology*, trans. A. Hofstadter (Bloomington: Indiana University Press, 1984), 132–37.

[6] In the First *Logical Investigation*, §5, Husserl argues that gestures are merely indicative, not meaningful, signs.

[7] It is in this way that, following the recent work of William Richardson, one can integrate the Heideggerian problematic with the question of the unconscious. See "Lacan and the Subject of Psychoanalysis," in *Psychiatry and the Humanities*, Vol. 6. *Interpreting Lacan*, eds. J. Smith and W. Kerrigan (New Haven: Yale University Press, 1983), 51–74.

[8] See Levinas' discussion of ethics and the face in *Infinity and Totality*, Part Two, 194–219.

[9] I take this critique of value from Heidegger; see in particular *Der Satz vom Grund* (Pfullingen: Neske, 1957), 34–35. To a great extent Heidegger's critique of ethics is a critique of modern or metaphysical ethics.

[10] Johann Baptist Metz, *Faith in History and Society: Toward a Practical Fundamental Theology*, trans. D. Smith (New York: Crossroad/Seabury, 1980), 88–118. See also Matthew Lamb, *Solidarity with Victims* (New York: Crossroad, 1982). [113]

[11] Friedrich Nietzsche, *Beyond Good and Evil*, trans. R. J. Hollingdale (New York: Penguin, 1973). Compare aphorisms #62, #270 and #294.

[12] Father Clarke addresses this same issue in his discussion of Transcendental Thomism in *The Philosophical Approach to God: A Neo-Thomist Perspective* (Winston-Salem: Wake Forest University Press, 1979), sec. I, 21–22.

17

THE POETICS OF SUFFERING AND THE DECONSTRUCTION OF ETHICS

[In *Joyful Wisdom: Sorrow and an Ethics of Joy,* Studies in Postmodern Ethics, Vol. 2, eds. David Goicoechea and Mark Zlomislic (St. Catharines, Ontario: Thought House Publishing Group, 1992), 200–224]

[200] Consider the possibility that we do not need ethics, that there is something to be said for getting "beyond" ethics or even for taking a stand "against" ethics. Against "ethics." Let us take to heart Heidegger's observation that "ethics" is an integral part of the classical philosophical or onto-theo-logical project, like "logic" or epistemology." Ethics waxes, Heidegger says, as thinking wanes.[1] As such, the attempt to disturb classical onto-theo-logic, or better, to show that it is always already disturbed, and this from within, would necessarily involve the disturbance of ethics.

On such an accounting the search for a "postmodern ethic" would be a mistake of the same sort as seeking out the "metaphysics" of postmodernism or its "philosophy of mind." There is a great rush nowadays to show that we have an ethics, that there is an ethic in Derrida or Foucault; a great deal of talk about "postmodernism and ethics," although we would resist any comparable demand for a rendering of "postmodern epistemology." The reason for this is the discursive prestige of the word "ethics," its considerable, even intimidating power. Who wants to be found wanting in the matter of ethics? Who wants to risk having no ethics? Behind the prestige of the word is the fact that "ethics" points to something very important, to a pearl of great price, to a care for human well-being. But it may well be that the insights of postmodern [201] writers like Derrida and Lyotard move us beyond or against ethics in the name of something which ethics seeks to shelter but which it cannot contain. I think this is even true of Levinas, who is not a postmodern writer, who loves ethics, who thinks that everything is or turns on ethics, and who certainly does not want to question or deconstruct ethics.

If that is so then the present undertaking represents an effort in double writing which is prepared to trouble ethics in an ethical way, a double gesture which is against ethics precisely because it wants to be very ethical, that is, to be concerned with human flourishing, with the matters which ethics addresses.[2]

In this way, to speak against ethics does not amount to a simple opposition, to being opposed *simpliciter*. It just such a *simpliciter* that constitutes a central gesture of the classical metaphysical tradition which wants to think that things are either absolute or relative, founded or arbitrary, theistic or atheistic, that we are either inside or outside, for or against. To speak against ethics is a marginal operation, a border skirmish, which crosses back and forth across the lines of ethics, which is continually situated inside/outside ethics.

The Deconstruction of Ethics

By the deconstruction of ethics I mean the unearthing of something that ethics harbors but which it cannot contain, the dislodging of something to which ethics attaches itself but which it cannot master, the releasing of something that cannot be contained by ethics and by which it is in inwardly disturbed. Such a dislodging, unearthing, and releasing [202] produces a double effect which both frees and unsettles.

Obligation, from which I take my point of departure in the remarks that follow, is something which ethics wants to make safe, to guard and protect. But obligation, I will claim, cannot be assimilated by ethics. Obligation is an "element" in classical ethics of which ethics is constituted but which comes undone in a deconstructive analysis. Obligation is one of those shards or fragments that ethics, which is philosophy, which is metaphysics, cannot fully incorporate or digest, one of those fragments that first Kierkegaard and now the postmodernists throw up to the totalizing tendencies of philosophy, one of those scraps that jam the gears of philosophy.[3] Everything in ethics turns on obligation but ethics cannot accommodate obligation. Ethics insists on obligation, defends obligation, honors obligation, needs obligation, but cannot tolerate or contain obligation. Obligation is necessary for ethics but obligation makes ethics impossible. Ethics is ultimately scandalized by obligation and is forced to reject it lest ethics lose its status as philosophy. Obligation is the lever by which ethics is deconstructed. Ethics wants to make obligation, to make everything, safe. But obligation is not safe. Life is more difficult than ethics would like us to believe. The deconstruction of ethics is an exercise in facing up to difficulties of life.

Obligation happens. Obligation is a fact (as it were). Obligation (which concerns the "ought") is among the most elemental facts of our existence (which concerns the "is"). *Es gibt*: there is obligation. *Il arrive*: it happens.[4] The "ought" is a fact (as it were). There are numberless "ought's," all around us, sometimes too many to deal with, sometimes in conflict, sometimes extraordinarily [203] difficult to sort out, sometimes clear and pressing. There are all kinds of obligations; obligations – in the plural and in the lower case – are given. Obligations belong to the most elemental conditions of what the young Heidegger called our "facticity," the factical situation in which we find ourselves (and hence of our *Befindlichkeit*). As soon as we come to be we find ourselves enmeshed in obligations.

Obligation, as I construe is here, is a matter of being moved by a force that issues from others, of being touched by a call that the other sends my way. Obligation is not something that I do but something that happens to me. It does not wait for my consent. It is not a matter of a contract that I have signed, not anything I have agreed to be a party to. No one asks me if I agree. Obligation is a scandal for the I, the scandal that the other does not arise as the project of the I but rather befalls the I,[5] the scandal that the I is rendered reactive, responsive, heteronomous. Obligation dispossesses the I of its initiative and autonomy, wounding it, bruising its narcissism.

Obligations spring up like Foucault's relations of power. As soon as two or three people are gathered together – and when are they not? – obligation happens (*il arrive*). There are (*es gibt*) obligations – even as there is power – just insofar as there are people. Obligation is a relation of power, a kind of power/obligation, but it is the power which is exerted by the powerless, the power which overtakes me just insofar as the other is powerless and I have power. Obligation happens as the power of powerlessness.

There is obligation. *Es gibt. Il y a.* It happens. *Il arrive.* Obligation comes over me; it does not come from me. It takes over me; it is not anything that I take over. I do not assume obligation, rather I am consumed and subsumed by [204] obligation. As Lyotard writes in his *"Levinas Notice"*:

> Obligation...does not result from an authority previously legitimated by me or by us. If I am obligated by the other, it is not because the other has some right to obligate me which I would have directly or mediately granted him or her. My freedom is not the source of his or her authority: one is not obligated because one is free, and because your law is my law, but because your request is not my law, because we are liable for the other.[6]

Obligation happens. It binds me. It, *das Es,* binds me. There is/*es gibt,* obligation. But *what* binds me? What is the origin of obligation? I do not know. I am always too late for origins. I never arrive in time. By the time I get there, obligation has already happened. Obligation has a certain density or impenetrability which my freedom and my knowledge cannot surmount. Obligation prevents me from getting on top of it, on the other side of it, from seeing where it comes from, how it arises, from tapping into its whence and whither. I do not know the origin of obligation, any more than I know the origin of the work of art. Obligation transcends me; it does not arise as one of my transcendental projects. Obligation is not so much something I understand as something I stand under. If an obligation is "mine" this is not because it belongs to me but because I belong to it. Otherwise obligation would just be more of the I, more of the same, and nothing of the other.[7] It would be one more thing I comprehend and want to do, rather than something that intervenes upon and disrupts the sphere of the I, which [205] troubles and disturbs the I, which pulls the I out of the circle of the same, out of its self-aggrandizing circuits.

The structure of obligation is revealed by Kierkegaard's rendering of the story of Abraham and Isaac. Something overtakes Abraham, pulls him out of himself and the circle of his interests, which is to plant the seeds of a new generation, by commanding him to destroy his seed. It is a mad call, utterly incomprehensible, an ecstatic call, which calls Abraham out of himself. It makes no sense, could not possibly make any sense. It belongs to a mad economy, a mad genetics, of destroying the seed from which one expected generations upon generations.

"Abraham!" The Lord said.

"Here I am," said Abraham. *Me voici* (Genesis 22:1).

The French is better than the English here because it puts Abraham in the accusative. "Behold the me," *me,* in the accusative, the addressee of an address.[8] You are always, structurally, on the receiving end of an obligation. Abraham does not assume the position of an author, an addressor, a transcendental subject. Abraham does not try to get on top of this command, to penetrate it, to see through it, to mount and surmount the command, which comes crashing in on him. He does not try to assume its authorship. He just takes it, in the accusative, receives it, accepts it, stands under it, allows it its opacity and impenetrability. This is not Abraham's idea but an intervention upon Abraham, something that shatters his circle of self-interest, the sphere of the same, as Levinas would say.

[206] Hegel thinks that this makes Abraham very ugly, not just one more ugly Jew, but the patriarch and paradigm of ugly Jews. For Hegel, the Jew is someone who must destroy everything he loves, who rips himself up from his native land and sets himself adrift, wandering, without a *Heimat*. Accordingly, if Abraham finds he loves his son then he must prove that he is willing to destroy his son. He must not love his son without being willing to take his knife to his

son, to cut his heart loose from his son, and this just because he loves his son. Abraham must not allow his heart to be filled with the spirit of love and beauty, that is, with the reconciling power of the Spirit itself, which is not Jewish but Greek and Christian (which in fact is also Prussian and even Hegelian.) The spirit is not Jewish, for the Jew lacks Spirit and lives lifelessly, in alienation, in incisions and circumcisions, dead and ugly.[9]

Hegel's analysis proceeds from a belief in ethics, in *Sittlichkeit*, concretely embodied socio-historical ethical life, the outer embodiment of inner law, the living, substantive content of dead and abstract duty. *Sittlichkeit* wants intelligibility, reconciliation, and beauty. Obligation is admitted into *Sittlichkeit* only if it embodies the Spirit itself in the process of becoming itself. The essence of the Spirit is freedom, which means that there is nothing but Spirit, nothing outside Spirit, nothing to limit freedom, nothing but freedom, which means that obligation is nothing more than freedom freely exercising itself. Nothing can come from without; nothing can lay freedom low. Nothing is outside freedom to constrain freedom, to bind freedom the way Isaac is bound. That means there really is no obligation beyond the Spirit binding itself, no obligation which cuts, nothing that comes crashing in on my freedom. For Hegel, to say "Here I am" one must be [207] talking to oneself, to the Spirit itself, which is oneself. As a form of the Spirit, ethics is *bei sich sein,* being close to oneself (*Glas* 53a), being in oneself, being at home, the monologue of the Spirit with itself; it is not a matter of being errant and adrift like Abraham.

Ethics is scandalized by obligation because obligation is structurally heteronomous, a law visited upon me by the other. That is why obligation is ugly and not in the spirit of Greek beauty and autonomy, of *harmonia* and reconciliation. Obligation is the unsightliness, the distastefulness of answering a command that comes at me from without, that comes over me, comes toward me and pulls me out of myself, which fills me with discord and discomfort, which disturbs and disconcerts, disrupts and decenters. This is not what philosophy wants, not what philosophy calls ethics. This is the ugliness of dispossession and heteronomy, of self-diremption and alienation, not the beauty of autonomy and reconciliation.

Ethics does not want to lose its mind, to surrender its freedom, to give up its autonomy. Ethics does not want to let itself be taken over, to come under anything but itself. In ethics, obligation must always be, in one way or another, something I do to myself. "I, Plato, am the truth." That, as Nietzsche said, is the first stage of the story of how the real world became a *fabula*. The philosopher *is* the truth. The truth is something I have, something I am, so that to abide in truth is to abide in myself; to obey the truth is to obey myself.[10]

Kant provides a very telling example of this. (In Kant, Nietzsche quipped, the truth has become a little more remote, foggy and Königsbergian.) Kant appreciated as well as anyone within the philosophical tradition the structure of obligation, its transcendence and opacity. In Kant, the law [208] comes to us like the voice of the Lord, a great German Jewish *Du sollst*, like Moses speaking *Deutsch*, which takes us over and strikes us low, which humbles us by the majesty of its uncompromisable command, which leaves us speechless except to say *Ich kann* (which is in the nominative), which is Kant's way of saying "Here I am." Obligation is a "cognitive monster" (*monstrare*), which makes a pure show of itself but does not admit of demonstration.[11] Obligation is a spontaneous causality which just irrupts in the midst of the phenomenal world, a cause without antecedent which disrupts the unbroken regularity of phenomenal succession. Like the mighty heavenly sweep above, the law sweeps over us and sweeps us up. Indeed the sublimity of the law exceeds the sublimity of the starry heavens above inasmuch as the moral law is literally able to move heaven and earth, to displace them, to divest them of their status as things in themselves. The starry heavens above become an *Erscheinung* just in order to make room for the law in the noumenal sphere.

Then Kant blinked. He was too much the *Aufklärer,* the lover of lights and luminosity, too much the philosopher, to let obligation be. He handed obligation over to philosophy, to the metaphysics of morals, to ethics. This mighty law which sweeps down over me and takes me over cannot be anything other than me, anything other than reason dictating to itself, prescribing for itself the rules by which it itself will conduct itself. When I bow to the other, I do not honor the other but the universal reason which constitutes both him and me, that is, I do not honor the other as other but the other as the same.

The gesture of ethics is always the same: I, Plato, am the truth. I, Hegel, am the Spirit. I, Kant, am Reason. "We the people" are the truth and the law; "we" speak in the name [209] of God, in the name of nature. Ethics is constituted by its deep resistance to an irreducible other and to heteronomous disruption.

Ethics wants to keep its head, not to lose balance. It will not allow itself to be put in the accusative, to lose the position of author, addressor, subject. It does not want to get laid low, to let *nous* or *Vernunft* bend under the strain of the other without bending back into the erectness of autonomy. Obligation is a matter of being claimed whereas the energies of ethics are spent on making claims, on "validating" the "legitimacy" of moral or ethical "claims." Ethics wants to maintain itself in the nominative position, to inhabit a sphere which is universal, transparent, rational, valid, legitimated, autonomous – and beautiful. Ethics wants to make sure that there are fixed, unambiguous and universal criteria in place, firm guide-rails to steer us through the perplexities of life. Ethics wants to be a guide for the perplexed, to be the offspring of reason and universality, of beauty and harmony. It abhors the abyss of singularity and incomprehensibility.

That is why we had to send for a rabbi. It took Levinas to restore to obligation its original difficulty, to give an account – under the name of "ethics" – of obligation that would respect its transcendence. Obligation is embedded in the density of facticity, singularity, particularity, and transcendence, in the dark groundlessness which can only choke ethics, jamming the gears of ethical reason and clouding its judgement. Ethics is always on the lookout for the *arche* and the *principium* whose mighty sweep opens the space of the ethical field and regulates its transactions. Obligation on the other hand is enmeshed in an anarchic domain of groundless grounds, of principles without principle, of singularities which defy principled adjudication, of [210] resistance to rule, of double binds and intractable ambiguity. Obligation transpires in an anarchic field, which Derrida once saw fit to call a field of responsible anarchy.[12]

The Poetics of Suffering

Obligation I have said is the power of powerlessness. The power of the powerful is dangerous, but the power of powerlessness is obligation. The power of the powerful is a way to contain and constrain difference, to hold it in check. It violently excludes, represses, silences, marginalizes, or it actively produces normal subjects, which has the same effect. But the power of the powerless is the power of difference, of the different one; the power of the oppressed, of the silenced, of the one left over or left out. The power of the powerless is the paradoxical power of the ones who come from on high just because they have been laid low, the power to command just because there is nothing commanding about them, the power to attract just because they are repulsive. The power of powerlessness is sublime just because it is wretched. It is sublime, not beautiful. It is not beautiful but ugly; it is sublime, from on high, but not beautiful.

The problem besetting ethics, and the reason ethics undergoes deconstruction, is that ethics is in love with beauty, but obligation is sublime, not beautiful. Ethics is charmed by the radiance of beautiful forms, of alluring and lovely paradigms. Ethics is captivated by images of egalitarian equilibrium, of cool heads and calm deliberation, of *nous* and *Vernunft*, of universality and a community of equals, of good form and comeliness, autonomy and self-possession. In a [211] word – this is the word upon which I will make a great deal turn here – ethics is in love with beauty. But obligation consorts with everything mis-formed and malformed, ugly and unsightly, rejected and repulsive, odious and odiferous, diseased and distorted, demented and depressed.

Ethics, which has always insisted that it is not aesthetics, that it does not reduce to judgments of taste, has a fatal attraction to beauty. The history of ethics is a history of good form, of beautiful and comely figures, which fill our hearts with the spirit of reconciliation and beauty.[13] There are no ugly Jews in ethics. It is filled with inspiring figures of the beauty of the just man [sic], of the prudent man, of the good man, of the virtuous man, of the holy man, of the man of duty who honors the law precisely as law, the beauty of the man of Spirit who reconciles pure duty and concrete life, the beauty of the Overman who goes under just because of his exquisite delicacy, and even the beauty of the man who belongs to Being's shining glow, to *Sein*'s shining *Schönheit*. Ethics has been deeply aretological, in love with excellence and *arete,* and calli-logical, struck by the beauty of its logos. Ethics has always been charmed by the good form of Athenian gentlemen (sic) or Spartan warriors or men of reason or men of pragmatic good sense.

Obligation, on the other hand, traffics with ugliness and contamination, with the worst not the best, with everyone whom Nietzsche thinks smells bad or who offend his palate and induce nausea,[14] with all those who belong at the bottom of the order (odor?) of rank. The interests of obligation lie with "the widow, the orphan, the stranger" (Ex 22:21), as Levinas likes to say. That of course is only a short list, an emblematic expression, for everyone who is down and out, downtrodden and outcast, excluded and marginalized; for [212] everyone who is impoverished, weak, incapacitated, diseased, mad, unfortunate, afflicted, different; for everyone whose birth and circumstances are lowly, whose endowments and gifts are less than modest, who have been cursed by nature and who lack nurture; for everyone who suffers from their station in life, from the wounds in their flesh, from the demons that torment their minds; everyone who suffers from their gender or their race or their nationality or their religion or their politics; in body or in mind; for everyone who suffers and is laid low. In short: for suffering.

Obligation has to do with what Lyotard calls *les juifs:* in the plural and in lower case.[15] The "jews" are not the Jews, not a nation or religion, although historically the Jews know more about being jews than nearly anyone else. *Les juifs* is everyone nomadic and homeless, everyone uprooted and dispossessed, whose identity and dignity has been shattered.

Les juifs are the powerless who suffer from the powerlessness.

Les juifs are ugly – Hegel was more right than he knew – and they smell bad, just as Nietzsche says. *Les juifs* are the domain of obligation, and they disturb ethics' love of beauty. Obligation happens with the pain and suffering of *les juifs*.

Obligation cannot be accommodated by ethics. That is because, in my view, obligation belongs instead to what I will call a "poetics of suffering." Obligation happens – pathically. It is a feeling, a passion, a *pathos,* something we undergo, sensuously. Obligation is a passionate passivity or receptiveness, a well-tuned sensuousness and sensitivity. Obligation is pathic, a pathic event. Obligation is a sensuous event which requires a sensuous idiom. That idiom is what I am calling "poetics" or "patho-poetics." It is "pathics" because it is attached irrevocably to *pathos,* to feeling, to suffering as [213] feeling. It does not cultivate a *pathos* of distance, of superiority and removal, but rather a *pathos* of proximity, a *pathos* of contamination, engagement and obligation. It a "poetics" because it requires invention (*poiesis*) of idioms, the production of forms which provide an idiom for suffering. The poetics of suffering can be found in many genres: in poetry itself, in literature and works of art generally – and sometimes better there than anywhere else – but also in religious scriptures, in personal diaries, in the exposes of investigative journalism, in daily conversations, in the look of sorrow on a wounded face, and occasionally, passingly, in "philosophy" itself.

The poetics of suffering is not to be reduced to aesthetics, which is concerned with beauty and taste and which is capable of aesthetic disinterest and even dilettantism. Patho-poetics has to do with feelings, but not, as in aesthetics, with feelings of inner harmony and the play of faculties, but with feelings which disturb and unsettle, which engage us and touch us deeply, which cast us into an abyss. Patho-poetics deals with feelings of pain and suffering.

Pain and suffering establish an irreducible register of events; they institute their own irreducible domain and require their own genre. They effect a profound reconfiguration of events, one which gives them a unique shape, tonality, urgency, significance, impact, one which requires that we respond to events differently. To speak the venerable language of phenomenology, pain and suffering institute a distinct layer of meaning. I conceive of the poetics of suffering as the idiom which suffering seeks in order to express its irreducible qualities.

I say "events" (Lyotard) in order to avoid speaking in subjectivist terms. An event is what happens at the point at [214] which what used to be called "subject" and "object" intersect. Pain and suffering are events which recast and reconfigure, which cast their own figure, over other events. Linguistic events are events; but so are feelings, actions, and productions of all sorts. Psychoanalysis, e.g., as a theory of the unconscious, one with interesting implications for literature, is one event, but a man or woman in pain, tormented by invisible demons, is another event, a different configuration which awakens different concerns – which are the concerns of the poetics of suffering. A country, even an outlaw country, constrained by an embargo is one event; starving children and malnourished, disease-ridden adults is another one. Medical research has to do with one event, diseased bodies and destroyed lives with another. The information acquired from animal experimentation is one event, but an animal in pain is another.

The poetics of suffering is not to be confused with what Karl-Heinz Bohrer called the "aesthetics of horror," to which it is almost perfectly opposed. In the poetics of suffering and the aesthetics of horror, war – to choose one event – becomes two different events. The aesthetics of horror takes war as a great spectacle, a great show, a spectacular appearance which has a horrifying beauty of its own. The aesthetics of horror is still aesthetics: it can find beauty in the thunder of mighty guns, the roar of bombardier squadrons, the demolition of a ship. It can back off from particularities, take a distance from slaughter, and see a magnificent form in the whole. But the poetics of suffering is attached irrevocably to the flesh, to the singularity of suffering flesh, to the pain, the fear, the horror, and it resists aestheticization.[16]

In the poetics of suffering, thinking is not held captive by beauty but is carried off into the sublime, the particular [215] sublime which is the abyss of suffering. In Kantian terms, patho-poetics concerns feelings of the sublime, not feelings of beauty. Religious feelings, too, belong to such a poetics.

The poetics of suffering is an operation of feeling (*pathos*), not of *nous*, which is what ethics wants to be. I will give an example of the difference between ethics, which is philosophy and therefore always a certain kind of noetics, and the poetics of suffering, by taking the case of Aristotelian *phronesis*. *Phronesis* is the most sensible attempt on the part of philosophical ethics to confront the epistemic limits of ethics. *Phronesis* is an excellence (*arete*) of *nous,* a mode of insight. It is the agility of mind that comes only with practice of seeing into the idiosyncrasies of the particular situation, of knowing how to bring to bear a general schema upon a unique situation, of applying the universal to the particular. That is why it could become "understanding" (*Verstehen*) in *Being and Time* (§§31–32), a mode of knowing how to, of knowing one's way around the world.

But the poetics of suffering does not turn on *nous* but *kardia*, not on knowledge but on mercy, *misericordia. Kardia* does not bring the universal to bear upon the particular – which is to assume the subject position, the position of the addressor – but is wholly immersed in singulars, in the accusative position, lost in the demand which issues from the singular one, which comes over me and lays claim to me and evokes from me the *me voici*. *Kardia* lifts the universal, suspends it, and allows itself to be touched by the singular one, drawn into the densely entangled web of singularity. *Kardia* is a transaction conducted in the accusative and occurs as a responsiveness to the call which issues from a singular situation, to a call for help or recognition, for space or freedom, for dignity and independence. *Kardia* is not [216] "application – which is conducted in the nominative, which has not lost its bearings – but dedication, *dare,* giving, self-giving. It is not an insight but a certain succumbing to the claims which are placed on me, a giving in, a melting, a surrender, a loss of self.

Phronesis is practical wisdom, a certain knowing of what is best by those who are admired by the best. But *kardia* is a recipe for foolishness, not a schema of wisdom, which is likely to lead one to be mocked by everyone and taken as a fool. *Kardia* is the foolishness of one who works with the incurably ill; the foolishness of underpaid teachers in poor and dangerous inner city schools; of those who work with the homeless; of physicians and lawyers who serve the poorest and the neediest instead of maintaining lucrative practices defending the rich against the poor, healing the rich while letting the poor suffer; of couples who adopt retarded and handicapped children; of skilled craftsmen of "Habitat for Humanity" who build houses for the homeless instead of expensive single family dwellings in the suburbs; of those who work to protect the environment or wildlife (the animal, Lyotard says, is the paradigm of the "different," of ones who lack an idiom for the injury that has been done them).[17]

The poetics of suffering is a matter of being moved or being touched by the power of powerlessness. It is a pathics which takes place in the domain of feeling, of the feeling of those who suffer and the feeling of those who respond to suffering. As such, the poetics of suffering is a poetics of flesh, of afflicted flesh and healing hands, of wounded flesh and hands that bind wounds, of homeless flesh and hands that build. Obligation is a movement between flesh and flesh, a transaction conducted between a flesh that addresses and a flesh that is addressed. Obligation is a relation of power, of [217] the power of afflicted flesh and of flesh which is touched by afflicted flesh.

In the end, and I am forced by limitations of space here to hasten to an end, the poetics of suffering is a poetics because it turns on the production of powerful paradigms and figures, vivid portraits of suffering, and then it hopes for the best. It turns on a kind of hermeneutics of suffering, one which tries to read the inscriptions of suffering, not so much to understand their meaning as to undergo the shattering of meaning. Adorno said it is barbaric to write poetry after Auschwitz.[18] That is true, and we must guard against the aestheticization

263

of Auschwitz, but it is no less barbaric not to. Given humanity's ageless cruelty, I would say it has always been barbaric to write poetry and always barbaric not to. What I call the poetics of suffering is precisely the sphere in which the barbaric way in which we deal with one another seeks an idiom, one which is not confined to beauty and taste.

The film *Shoah* is a good example. *Shoah* is a powerful poetics because it is a film which is not trying to be beautiful, or perhaps even to be a work of art, but simply to document, to go on record, in black and white, not in living color, which would have been obscene. To supply a record: that means to keep something in our heart, to keep it safe there. *Shoah* wants to inscribe the dangerous and disturbing memory of suffering in our heart. *Shoah* simply records testimonies, and the testimony is very powerful. That is because it is the testimony of witnesses to unthinkable violence. The deportations are violent disturbances of the relations of power/obligation, scenes of incomprehensible violation. The power of *Shoah* is the record of that.

Happenings

[218] Obligation happens. There is obligation. *Il arrive.* The "proof of it is not logical, in the sphere of *logos,* but patho-poetical, in the sphere of *pathos* and in the poetic creation of idioms. The proof is the victim, or failing that, the witness to victimization. That is what is so heinous about depriving the victim of an idiom.

The secret police, the military authorities, the prison guards all transact their business in the domain of obligation. They bear testimony to it, but privatively, in the mode of the negation of violation. The feeling of horror at this violation is the testimony to obligation and it provokes the search to find an idiom, for a poetics of suffering.

Were it possible to socialize or "normalize" someone out of this feeling of horror, to extinguish this feeling, then the poetics of suffering would be extinguished. Then obligation would not happen. Perhaps that can be done. I do not know. I like to think that the cry of the victim will always have the power to disrupt the power of those who produce victims.

The happening of obligation is a happening of feeling, a kind of patho-event. Obligation springs like cries of pain from wounded flesh or tormented minds. Just so.

But the cry of pain does not obligate absolutely. Now I must tell you of my impiety and of the helplessness of the poetics of suffering. I am not a rabbi, not Levinas, who is too pious. Unlike Kierkegaard, the point of view of my work as an author is not religious, although I think that religious texts are a good,

264

even a remarkable source for the poetics of suffering. [219] Obligation is a happening, not a necessary truth. Obligation is a call, but it is a finite call which transpires in the sphere of feeling, not in transcendental space. Philosophically speaking, it is a hypothetical not a categorical imperative. There is no absolute back up, no absolutely authoritative voice in the poetics of suffering. The call of suffering happens, and that is why there is obligation. The call of suffering is the call of justice, a call for justice, a word which Derrida is, happily, more than willing to use these days, and of which he says that it – if it exists – is not deconstructible.[19] But the call for justice, which is the call of the structural other, of the one whose difference places an obligation on me, does not take place in transcendental space, but in a pathic space, the space of feeling.

The call of (for) justice is not (in the first place) the Voice of God or of Pure Reason or of a Social Contract "we" have all signed or a trace of the Form of the Good inscribed in the soul. It is the still small voice of little ones, of singularities, of *me onta,* non-beings who do not count for much. It is, e.g., not absolutely irrational that some prosper at the expense of the suffering of others. It only irrational on some accounting of reason, say of Kantian universalizability or the greatest good for the greatest number. It is not absolutely against nature that some prosper at the expense of the suffering of others, but only on certain accounts of nature. Indeed on many, some would say most, accounts of nature, nature implies a natural order of rank, of higher and lower, best and worst, which rank orders people in terms of white and black, male and female, exceptional and mediocre, Overman and mass man, European and non-European, adult and child, sane and mad. That causes inestimable suffering.

In the end – and I am still hastening to an end – I think [220] the merciless story Nietzsche tells at the beginning of *Truth and Lying in the Extramoral Sense* (one of his earliest texts) – or in the last aphorism of the *Will to Power* (one of his last) – goes unanswered.

> Once upon a time, in some out of the way corner of that universe which is dispersed into numberless twinkling solar systems, there was a star upon which clever beasts invented knowing. That was the most arrogant and mendacious minute of "world history," but nevertheless it was only a minute. After nature had drawn a few breaths, the star cooled and congealed, and the clever beasts had to die.[20]

Substitute "justice" for "knowing" here and you will see what I mean by my impiety. Five thousand million years from now, when this little star has cooled off and congealed, and has dropped back into the sun, when the solar system has dissipated, the call of justice will have dropped into oblivion. You and I, all things, this very moment, this suffering child, the prosperous white upper classes – that is all so much will to power, so many quanta of force charging and discharging their energy, a veritable monster of energy, decreasing here, increasing there, blessing itself in its sheer innocence.[21] And nothing more. *Und Nichts ausserdem.*

You and I stand on the surface of the little star and shout, "racism is unjust." The cosmos yawns and takes another spin. There is no cosmic record of our complaint. The cosmos feels no pain and has no heart on which to record our complaint, provides no idiom for our objections. The cosmos pays us no heed. The cosmic view is always spectacular and lends itself to an aesthetics of horror, or to an aesthetic [221] justification of life, much more easily than to a poetics of suffering. "Racism is unjust" is a complaint made in the midst of great cosmic stupidity, of an indifferent world, under stars twinkling in a void. The call of suffering, of the other, falls on deaf ears. It is just part of the whole, of an absolutely innocent game which knows only greater or less discharges of energy, self-accumulating and self-destructive forces, but does not know about the call of suffering.

There is an ear for injustice and a heart for suffering only where there is flesh, only because there is flesh, only for as long as there is ear, heart, and flesh. There is feeling. It happens. That is why obligation happens. Obligation is a relation of power in the domain of feeling, in the domain of the powerlessness of flesh, of the power of powerless flesh.

Obligation is a fact (as it were). As it were. As if it were a fact, an uninterpreted fact of the matter. As if it were a pure fact, of pure reason, or of the whisper of the will of God in our ear, or the traces of the Form of the Good vaguely stirring in us. As if it were like that.

In Christianity, the foolishness of the children of God was in the end a good investment which would be returned a hundred fold. In postmodernism (and maybe in a postmodern Christianity), the stakes of foolishness have been raised still higher. It is no longer a matter of being fools for the kingdom of God in which one could expect a payback for one's investment. It is a matter of being fools in a much more distressing sense.

Notes

[1] Martin Heidegger, "A Letter on Humanism," trans. F. Capuzzi, in *Basic Writings,* ed. David Krell (New York: Harper & Row, 1977), 232.

[2] For a recent attempt to trouble ethics in the name of what has always concerned ethics, viz. human flourishing, see Charles Scott, *The Question of Ethics: Nietzsche, Foucault, Heidegger* (Bloomington: Indiana University Press, 1990).

[3] I will make frequent use, in this study, of the language and metaphorics of Derrida's *Glas,* trans. John Leavey and Richard Rand (Lincoln: University of Nebraska Press, 1986). See the opening passage on "remains" (1).

[4] This is the language of Heidegger for the granting of Being (*Es gibt*); of Lyotard for the happening of events (*il arrive*), one of which is the happening of obligation; and of Kant for the "Categorical Imperative," as a "fact as it were of pure reason."

[5] Jean-Francois Lyotard, *The Differend: Phrases in Dispute,* trans. Georges Van Den Abbeele (Minneapolis: Univ, of Minnesota Press, 1988), "Levinas Notice," 110.

[6] Lyotard, *The Differend*, 112.

[7] Lyotard argues that obligation is subject to the following dilemma: if I understand it, it is mine and not an obligation; if I do not understand it, it is a blind and arbitrary command. See *Differend,* No. 176, p. 117. Obligation is a scandal.

[8] The story of the "binding of Isaac" is found in *Genesis* 22:1. For [223] the *me voici,* see Emmanuel Levinas, *Otherwise than Being or Beyond Essence,* trans. A. Lingis (The Hague: Martinus Nijhoff, 1981), 141–42; for a commentary by Jacques Derrida, see *A Derrida Reader: Between the Blinds,* ed. Peggy Kamuf (New York: Columbia University Press, 1991), 413 ff.

[9] See *Friedrich Hegel On Christianity: Early Theological Writings,* trans. T. M. Knox (Chicago: University of Chicago Press, 1948), 199–200; see also 187,196, 204–205. See Derrida's commentary in *Glas,* 40a–55a, especially 44a.

[10] Friedrich Nietzsche, *Twilight of the Idols* in *Twilight of the idols and The Anti-Christ,* trans. R. J. Hollingdale (Baltimore: Penguin Books, 1968), 40-41.

[11] Lyotard, *The Differend,* 123.

[12] See my "Beyond Aestheticism: Derrida's Responsible Anarchy", *Research in Phenomenology,* 18 (1988), 59-73. [also in *The Essential Caputo: Selected Writings,* ed. Keith Putt (Bloomington: Indiana University Press, 2018), 184-194. –ed.]

[13] Lyotard undertook a critique of phenomenology's preference for good form in his early *Discours, Figure* (Paris: Klincksieck, 1971).

[14] See Jacques Derrida, *The Ear of the Other: Otobiographgy, Transference, Translation: Texts and Discussions with, Jacques Derrida,* ed. Christie McDonald, trans. Peggy Kamuf and Avital Ronell (New York: Schocken Books, 1985), 23–24, note.

[15] Jean Francois Lyotard, *Heidegger and "the jews",* trans. A. Michel and M. Roberts (Minneapolis: Univ, of Minnesota Press, 1990).

[16] Karl-Heinz Bohrer, *Die Aesthetik des Schreckens – Die Pessimistische Romantik und Ernst Jungers Frühwerk* (München: Carl Hanser Verlag, 1978). See Michael Zimmerman, *Heidegger's* [224] *Confrontation with Modernity* (Bloomington: Indiana Univ. Press, 1990) for comments on Bohrer's thesis (53) and on Junger's relation to Heidegger (46ff.).

[17] Lyotard, *The Differend,* No. 38, p. 28.

[18] Theodor W. Adorno, *Prisms,* trans. Samuel and Sherry Weber (Cambridge: MIT Press, 1982), 34.

[19] Jacques Derrida, "The Force of Law: the Mystical Foundations of Authority," trans. Mary Quaintance, in "Deconstruction and the Possibility of Justice," *Cardozo Law Review* 11 (1990): 919-1046; see p. 945. For a commentary, see my "Hyperbolic Justice: Deconstruction, Myth and Politics," *Research in Phenomenology* 21 (1991): 3–20. [See also Chapter 10 of *Demythologizing Heidegger* (Bloomington: Indiana University Press, 1993), 186-208. –ed.]

[20] *Philosophy and Truth: Selections from Nietzsche's Notebooks of the Early 1870s*, ed. and trans. Daniel Breazeale (Atlantic Highlands: Humanities Press, 1979), 79.

[21] Friedrich Nietzsche, *The Will to Power*, trans. W. Kaufmann (New York: Vintage Books, 1968), No. 1067, pp. 549–50.

DECONSTRUCTION AND RELIGION

.

18

MYSTICISM AND TRANSGRESSION: DERRIDA AND MEISTER ECKHART

[In *Continental Philosophy*, II: *Derrida and Deconstruction*, ed. Hugh J. Silverman (New York: Routledge, 1989), 24–39]

[24] Derrida himself has warned us that it is a mistake to confuse what he says about *différance* with some kind of negative theology – in particular with that of Meister Eckhart whom he mentions by name. I begin by endorsing and underlining that point which I take to be but the beginning, not the end, of the question about deconstruction and negative theology. I set out from there to defend what I call (borrowing an expression from Kierkegaard) the "armed neutrality" of *différance*. Neutrality: it does not imply or exclude the existence or non-existence of any entity (it is ontically neutral). Armed: it is not particularly hospitable to existence claims but holds them all suspect. Because it is not a substantive position on its own but rather a parasitic practice, deconstruction has no ontological commitments. Thus while it would be comical to find a negative theology in deconstruction, it would not be at all surprising to find deconstruction in negative theology – as a practice, as a strategy, as a way that negative theologians have found to hold the claims of cataphatic theology at bay.

In the second part of the essay I turn to Meister Eckhart himself and I demonstrate the way he called upon a certain deconstructive practice in order to make medieval onto-theologic tremble. Then, in the third part, I argue that one finds in Eckhart a great disseminative energy aimed at promoting and enhancing the life of the spirit, a grammatological exuberance and joyful wisdom whose political subversiveness did not go unnoticed by the guardians of onto-theo-logic.

I. Negative theology and the armed neutrality of *différance*

[25] *Différance* is not God, not even a hidden God, not even the innermost concealed Godhead of negative theology, although sometimes, in the flush of Derrida's more famous accounts of *différance,* it begins to sound a little like a *deus*

absconditus. For example, Derrida says in a well-known text that *différance* is not an entity, that it makes no appearance (is not a *phainomenon*) and has no truth. Still *différance* is nothing to be taken lightly, for it makes possible what is present, and while it has no truth or manifestness itself (indeed has no "itself"), *différance* enables what is manifest to make a show. That sounds a lot like the hidden God Who withdraws behind the veil of the very world which He has created. Sometimes *différance* sounds like that ultimate un-knowable, the un-knowing of which constitutes the most learned wisdom of all (*docta ignorantia*).

Now it is just this suggestive proximity to negative theology which is likely to lead us astray. For *différance* has nothing to do with even the most negative of all negative theologies and this for the very good reason that such theologies:

> ...are always concerned with disengaging a superessentiality
> beyond the finite categories of essence and existence, that is, of
> presence, and always hastening to recall that God is refused the
> predicate of existence, only in order to acknowledge his superior,
> inconceivable, and ineffable mode of being. (*MdP*, 6; *MoP*, 6)[1]

Negative theologies are always just detours on the way to even higher, more sublime affirmations. They are ways of saying in even stronger terms that an entity, namely God, exists. He exists so deeply, so thoroughly, so purely, so perfectly, that we even have to take the word "is" back, if and when we say it. Negative theologies are modified onto-theo-logies, variations on the philosophy of presence which always turn out to be philosophies of super-presence.

And so if we find ourselves saying that *différance* is neither a word nor a concept, that there is no name for what we mean to say when we say *différance,* that is not because we have stumbled upon, or been overtaken by, a being of such [26] supereminence that words fail us. It is because we have in mind the conditions under which words are formed in the first place, and the "word" for that is a kind of a non-word, anterior to words, the general condition or rule of formation for words. Hence *différance* is not a mystical *nomen innominabile* but a grammatological one. *Différance* is older than the name of Being, older than any name, is not itself a name, in the French language or any other. But this, Derrida says, is to be understood not in all its mystical depth but rather in all its grammatological platitude:

> The unnamable is not an ineffable Being which no name could
> approach: God, for example. This unnamable is the play which
> makes possible nominal effects, the relatively unitary and atomic
> structures that are called names, the chains of or substitutions of

names in which, for example, the nominal effect *différance* is itself enmeshed. (*MdP*, 28; *MdP*, 26–7)

The namelessness of *différance* does not consist in being an unnamable being but in pointing to the differential matrix which generates names and concepts, in which they are produced as effects. Of course, as soon as it is coined, uttered, repeated, and entered into the lexicon of "post-structuralist" thinkers, *différance* becomes itself another nominal unity, one more effect of the differential matrix of which it means to be no more than indicator. But it would be a serious misunderstanding to think that it is some master name or kerygmatic announcement of a Being beyond Being, or of a presence which is so pure that it cannot itself appear and be present except by means of the finite and imperfect traces of itself which it leaves behind. Lacking all ontological profundity and mystical depth, *différance* stretches out laterally over the surface as the chain of substitutability, as the coded tracing, within which are generated all names, all the relatively stable nominal unities, including the name of God, including even the name *différance*.

And in a commentary on Levinas and Heidegger, Derrida warns us against confusing *différance* with any of the sayings of Meister Eckhart in particular. Eckhart himself is perfectly clear about the upshot of his negative theology: "When I said that God was not a Being and was above Being, I did not thereby contest his Being, but on the contrary attributed to him a *more* [27] *elevated Being* (Q, 196, 25–28).[2] And upon this Derrida comments: "This negative theology is still a theology and, *in its literality at least,* it is concerned with liberating and acknowledging the ineffable transcendence of an infinite existent" (*ED*, 217; *WD*, 146).

Negative theology is engaged in the business of establishing ontic transcendence, which is to say, the super-eminent existence of an entity, of a being whose Being is so pure – Eckhart calls it the *puritas essendi,* the purity of Being – that it is best affirmed by being denied, that is, affirmed to be *beyond* Being. And that is why Eckhart was able to write, to the puzzlement of his commentators and to the consternation of the Inquisition, both that God is *esse* while creatures are a pure nothing (not even a little bit), *and* that God is an absolute nothing, a naked desert, while being is the first of all creatures. He wanted to establish the Being of God in so pure a region that the affirmation of His Being had to be continually purified by a denial of Being. Eckhart's orthodoxy on this point is unmistakable, but he had a way of saying things which made his inquisitors nervous.

Now that leads me to the next point I want to make about *différance*, that it has no ontic import, that it carries no ontological weight. In this same remark on Eckhart, Derrida continues:

> *In its literality at least,* but the difference between metaphysical ontotheology, on the one hand, and the thought of Being (of difference) on the other, signifies the essential importance of the *letter....* That is why, here, when the thought of Being goes beyond ontic determinations it is not a negative theology, or even a negative ontology. (*ED*, 217; *WD*, 146)

The thought of the ontological difference or, for Derrida, of the letter, of *différance* – on this point, I take it, and Derrida too seems to take it, we have to do with parallel thoughts – goes beyond ontic determinations. This is *not* because it affirms a super-ontic entity, but because it has an altogether different, non-ontic function. Difference/*différance* is not itself something ontic, nor does it establish the existence, or higher existence, or non-existence, of anything ontic. Difference/*différance* does not affirm a hidden God (deferring himself behind the chain [28] of signifiers), but neither does it deny God. What then is its function?

> Ontological anticipation, transcendence towards Being, permits, then, an understanding of the word God, for example, even if this understanding is but the ether in which dissonance can resonate. This transcendence inhabits and founds language. (*ED*, 217; *WD*, 146)

The role of difference/*différance* is to establish the conditions within which discourse functions. It founds (and un-founds, undermines) languages, vocabularies, showing how they are both possible and impossible, that is, incapable of a closure which would give them self-sufficiency and a feeling of success in nailing things down. So difference/*différance* establishes the possibility (and impossibility) of a language which addresses God, even of one which invokes the dissonances of negative theology – even as it establishes the possibility (and impossibility) of a discourse in which God is denied. It does not settle the God-question one way or another. In fact, it unsettles it, by showing that any debate about the existence of God is beset by the difficulties which typically inhabit such debates, by their inevitable recourse to binary pairs which cannot be made to stick. That is why Nietzsche says that atheism, too, represents the ascetic ideal, the desire to pin things firmly in place (*Genealogy of Morals,* III, section 27).

That, too, is why I am unhappy with Mark Taylor's recent and otherwise quite innovative adaptation of Derrida to death of God theology.[3] Taylor starts out on the right foot by saying that he wants to write an a/theology, that is, one that stays on the slash, which writes in between theism and a-theism. He situates himself within the crucial Derridean gesture of undecidability – for *différance* does not show that there either is or is not a God. The problem I have with Taylor is that he proceeds to assimilate Derrida into the familiar death of God story – by which the transcendent God of Christianity becomes the immanent spirit of Hegel, which becomes in turn the divine Man of Feuerbach. If the first round of death-of-God thinking ended up with the birth of Man, with a humanistic atheism, then the role of Derridean deconstruction is to provide us with an even more radically non-humanistic atheism by stamping [29] out that last remnant of metaphysics: Man himself. At the end of his story, God has become *écriture* (with nothing left over). The sacred scripture has become all there is of the sacred itself: God as glyph, as hieroglyph. Now that is not to stay on the slash of undecidability but to make a reductionist decision against God, to reduce the ambiguity of a genuine a/theology and to turn *différance* against God.

The armed neutrality of *différance* means that it is evenhandedly antagonistic to all claims of existence or non-existence. It plays no favorites when existence claims are afoot but gives all parties to the dispute an equally hard time. It shows the limits under which our discourse labors when someone says something about something to someone (*hermeneuein*). *Différance* is neutral by being uniformly nasty about letting vocabularies establish their credentials and get set in place, as if they really were making good in some strong sense on their claims. Its neutrality lies in its unremitting and unbiased antagonism which does not single out theologians for particular abuse but is equally hostile to ontological claims made across the board. It is, for example, just as inhospitable to empiricists and phenomenologists who talk about the perceptual world. Such armed neutrality is, however, not aimed at locking us inside a play of signs but at making us think twice about claiming that our discourse has accomplished what it sets out to do. It throws a scare into our discourse, destroys a bit of the prestige and self-importance of reference, and ends up creating a salutary distrust in the power of language to do what it sets out to do (along with providing an account of how language accomplishes what it does manage to do).[4]

II. Deconstruction and negative theology in Meister Eckhart

Now I would say that Meister Eckhart is a salient example of this recognition that language is caught up in a self-defeating enterprise, that the very terms we employ to assert that something is are caught up in complicity with their opposites, so that language keeps unsaying what it says, undoing what it does, and in general failing again and again to make good on its claims. It will of course be objected that I have come back to [30] square one because Eckhart did all of this in the name of a super-essential being, that his confession of the failure of language had an ontological agenda, viz., to establish the super-existence of God beyond the frailties of language.

I have never denied that there is some truth to that.[5] Nor, as we have seen, does Eckhart. When the theologians of the Curia swept down upon him, he hastened to assure them that he spoke with brother Thomas (Aquinas), that he believed in the living God, and that his more extreme formulations were mostly intended to show the existential clout of the truths of the Christian faith.[6] The Christian religion, he insisted, is filled with teachings which should swell our hearts and stir our being instead of just sitting helplessly on the shelves of the monastery library. Eckhart had a faith, a commitment, to the God of Abraham and Moses and to the God Whom Jesus dared call *abba,* father. (Nowadays, the dare is to call God mother.)

Now, I started out by saying that I endorse the notion that deconstruction is a parasitic practice. For deconstruction can make a living only inasmuch as there is already someone who wants to say something about something to someone. Deconstruction requires a prior hermeneutics, the anterior work of addressing one another about the matter at hand. Deconstruction lies in wait for discourse to stake its claims and then it pounces on it, showing how much trouble this discourse has bought for itself by its boldness. Were no one bold enough to launch the hermeneutic project, were no one willing to make such claims in the first place, then deconstruction would never get off the ground. This is another way of saying that deconstruction itself has nothing to say, or better that there is no deconstruction itself, that it is a parasitic practice, not a substantive position. In classical terms, the Being of deconstruction always exists *in alio,* by inhabiting the discourse of others, never *in se,* as something present in itself, as some form of *ousia.*

In short, deconstruction is first of all a practice – it is what it does – not a body of theories, and secondly a parasitic practice – what it does is to inhabit the discourse of those who have something to say and to make trouble for them. It needles its way into the discourse of others and shows them how much trouble they have brought upon themselves. Deconstruction [31] does not want to deny that something exists, but only to show the difficulty we have getting that said. That is what it means to say that nothing exists outside the text – viz., that existence claims cannot be disentangled from the web of discourse which make them possible to begin with. Existential assertions cannot break out into

276

the open with atomistic independence, seize upon the things themselves, and then vaporize, leaving us in naked contact with *die Sache selbst*. Deconstruction requires a prior project which it then inhabits and disrupts, not by scattering it to the four winds, but by heightening its appreciation for its own difficulty.

That is why I find in Meister Eckhart a great medieval deconstructive practice, one keenly appreciative of all the trouble that medieval onto-theo-logic has brought down on its head. He understands quite well that the terms Being and Nothing are functions of each other, that each is inscribed in the other, marked and traced by the other, and that neither gets the job done, alone or together. Neither alone seizes upon the living God, nor do both together in a Hegelian synthesis. As a professional theologian at Paris he showed his colleagues the complicity in which binary schemes like Being/Nothing or creator/creature are caught up. He argued that if you start out with the being of creatures then that makes God a nullity, not even a little bit. On the other hand, if you concede the nullity of creatures, then you have perforce admitted, not only that God has being, or is being, but more strongly still that being is God (*esse est deus*). And he did not just make these claims off the cuff, in vernacular sermons to an uneducated audience which could not give him an argument, but he made them in Latin at Paris, to the most sophisticated audience of the day, and he used the most refined arguments of medieval onto-theologic to back them up.[7]

Eckhart had an acute sense of what we nowadays call the "textuality," the interdependence and differential structure, of the terms of scholastic discourse. That is why he had no great confidence in any particular name we sent God's way. He argued emphatically that to call God "creator" was just to mark Him off in terms of "creatures"; to call Him "cause" was to mark Him off from "effects"; to call Him "good" was to name Him in reference to the will; and to call Him "true" was to give Him a [32] name relative to the intellect (*C-M*, 200–203). Every one of these "absolute" attributes was "relative" to something else in the discursive chain. Every time the intentional arrow was aimed at God, it came up with "God," which sends us skidding back to something else in the chain of signifiers. The divine names just keep referring back to other names in the chain. We never get a name which is really God's own name, which really seizes upon God, and then, having done its duty, having delivered us into the inner chambers of the Godhead, quietly dissipates into thin air. Eckhart kept warning us about the contingency of the signifiers we deploy. This warning reached its shrillest and most startling moment when, faced with the difficulty of getting something said about God, he openly preached one day to what must have been a very startled congregation, "Therefore I pray God that he may make me free of God" (*C-M*, 202).

Now we may hear in this a prayer for presence, for the transcendental signified which puts the play of signifiers to rest and makes us one with the One. I do not deny that there is a wide streak of this in Eckhart, a streak of Neoplatonic, henological metaphysics, in which everything gets centered on the Godhead beyond God, on the One beyond multiplicity, on the silent unity of soul with God beyond time and place. This notion of mystical unity does not contradict onto-theo-logic but crowns and perfects it. It fulfills the metaphysical desire for presence in a way of which metaphysics itself was incapable, with a surge of intuitive unity which surpasses the wildest dreams of conceptual reason. Having discovered the complicity and play of terms in medieval onto-theo-logic, Eckhart was not above trying to arrest that play and calm the storm he had stirred up, by bringing the onto-theo-logical system with which he was wrestling into a higher, mystical closure.

But I say that to reduce Eckhart to such a gesture is to cut him off at the knees, to repress everything *else* which is astir in his text, and to miss the good that deconstruction does for religious thinkers, and which Eckhart was putting into practice. For if Eckhart was not above pushing for closure he was at the same time acutely aware of the impossibility of closure, of the wide-open uncompletability and unstabilizability of onto-theological discourse. When he prayed aloud for God to rid him of [33] God he was blowing the whistle on metaphysical theology – plain and simple.

Now it is my claim that if he thought (as he certainly did) that there was a higher, unitive way beyond language, he was at the same time – whether he liked it or not, whatever his *vouloir-dire* – putting such a way into question. For once *he* has recourse to the stabilizing discourse of the Neoplatonic One beyond multiplicity, to the "Godhead" beyond "God," to the timeless unity of the soul's ground with God's ground, *we* today recognize that that *too* is just another creature, another signifier which belongs to an historical vocabulary. Neoplatonism did not drop from the sky, did not emanate from the One. Godhead too is another effect of *différance,* a differential effect achieved by a discourse which deploys a God/Godhead distinction. Godhead sends us skidding back to God from which (by being distinguished from which) Godhead derives its sense and impact. To reach out for the Godhead beyond God is but to name Him relative to God, to remain within the chain of mundane predicates. Godhead, too, drags a chain of signifiers behind it. The Godhead beyond God is also a creature, what a religious person would call an idol, what Derrida would call an effect of *différance,* or Heidegger an issue of the Difference.

We do not get anywhere if we let our frustration and impatience with the play of signifiers lure us into invoking another domain of signifiers in which the reigning truth is that we have here to do with the transcendental signified beyond all signifiers. The only headway to be made is to confess that we never escape the chain of signifiers, to concede that the trouble we are in is permanent, and to press ahead anyway. The prayer to rid us of God has to be kept permanently in place. It demands a constant vigil, watching and praying always that we do not fall down to graven images, including that most alluring image of all, the image that we are beyond images. The prayer to rid us of God is a prayer to keep the play of images in play, to give it no rest, to be unattached to any creature, no matter how sublime and fine, even if it be the mystical Godhead itself, or the *Seelenfünklein,* even if it be the most exquisite reaches of Eckhart's dazzling mystical speculations.

The only headway is to awaken to the fix we are in, we who believe in something – and who does not? – to raise our level [34] of vigilance, to watch and pray, to be permanently on the alert against mistaking graven images for the living God, mistaking the effects of *différance* for the things themselves (be they perceptual, scientific, or theological). "I pray God that he may make me free of God" is an ongoing prayer which keeps the discourse open. This is a prayer against closure, against turning the latest and best creations of discourse into idols. It arises from an ongoing distrust of our ineradicable desire for presence, of our insidious tendency to arrest the play and build an altar to a produced effect. I pray God – that is, He Who is everything and none of the things which this signifier names, *nomen omninominabile et nomen innominabile* – to rid me of God, which is to say, of all of those nominal effects which try to cow us into submission, all of those historico-cultural-linguistic effects which are collected together by the word "God."

I am arguing that if we pressed these considerations upon Eckhart it would show quite clearly that he had very little invested in the metaphysics of presence, in Neoplatonic henology, and that everything he had to say revolved around seeing the failure of signifiers to catch God in their net.[8] I am arguing that it belongs to the innermost tendencies of his thought to let go of the Godhead too, of the henology, of the *Seelengrund* and *Gottesgrund,* for they too are nominal effects. The dynamics of his own teachings are to rid us of all idols, of every "God," of every signifier which gets too important and asserts its authority, even if that be "Godhead" itself. I pray God to rid me of "Godhead," that is, to keep me free of attachment to any signifier.

III. Eckhart's Joyful Wisdom

At this point it may be objected that I am trying to turn Eckhartian mysticism into a despairing and faithless agnosticism, a dispirited silence about an infinitely distant God. But exactly the opposite is the case. For, by resisting any closure of Eckhart's discourse I am defending its open-endedness and its enormous affirmative energy. Eckhart's sermons celebrate God's enveloping action in the world and in his own life. His writing explodes in an extravaganza of images, in a play of mystical signifiers, in a profusion of discourse which aims at keeping [35] the life of the soul with God alive. There is no better example, to my knowledge, of a certain mystical dissemination and a religiously joyful wisdom than the brilliant, playful virtuosity of Eckhart's German sermons and Latin treatises. He rewrites the words of Scripture, turns and twists the most familiar sacred stories, reinterprets the oldest teachings in the most innovative and shocking ways. Derrida's dichotomy between rabbinic and poetic hermeneutics (*ED*, 102–103; *WD*, 67) has nothing to do with the Sacred Scriptures, for Eckhart's commentaries on the Scriptures stir with a poetic energy which exploits all of the associative and rhythmic power of his Latin and Middle High German tongues.

And always with the same effect: to prod the life of the spirit, to promote its vitality, to raise its pitch, to enhance its energy. Like a religious answer to Nietzsche six centuries before the fact, Eckhart engages with Dionysian productivity in a multiplication of religious fictions which serve the interests of a life which lives out of its own superabundance, without why or wherefore, for the sake of life itself:

> If anyone went on for a thousand years asking of life: "Why are you living?" life, if it could answer, would only say: "I live so that I may live." That is because life lives out of its own ground and springs from its own source, and so it lives without asking why it is itself living. If anyone asked a truthful man who works out of his own ground: "Why are you performing your works?" and if he were to give a straight answer, he would only say, "I work so that I may work." (*Q*, 180, 23–31; *C-M*, 184)

There is a grammatological exuberance, a transgressive energy, in Eckhart which suggests a kind of medieval analogate of Mallarmé and Joyce. He had a way about him of making the whole tremble, of soliciting the foundations of onto-theo-logic. The papal bull which condemned him said that even when his sayings were not in error they were still dangerous (*C-M*, 80). On this point, at least, the Pope was right. The powers that be, the guardians of orthodoxy, always have a fine ear for disruptive discourse. For the life of him, Eckhart could not see what they were exercised about. That is because Eckhart was concerned with the dynamics of the soul's life with the living [36] God, not with defending the political power base of the magisterium. The Inquisitors understood that texts outlive good intentions, that they would retain their disruptive power long after the reassuring voice of this humble Dominican friar was silenced – by everyone's account, the Pope's included (*C-M*, 81), a loyal son of the Church.

This master of silence and of the silent unity of the soul with God was an eloquent preacher – by profession and vocation – and a prolific writer who produced a massive corpus, only a fragment of which has come down to us today. His defense of silence was carried out by a multiplication of discourse. He is a master of life (*Lebemeister*) and a master of the letter (*Lesemeister*) who plays with the syntax and semantics of the scriptural texts and the texts of the masters before him in order to tease out of them ever new senses. He is a master of repetition who knew well that his *commentarium* was not to be a simple reproduction but a new production, a new rendering which made the old text speak anew and say what had not been heard.

He was constantly altering the syntax of a text, rewriting it so that it said something new. He would fuss with trivial features of texts to which no attention at all had been paid and make everything turn on them, even to the point of reversing their traditional meaning. He would even play with the letters in a word. When he was defending his notion that *esse est deus,* he said that *esse* is the tetra-grammaton, that ESSE and YHWH constitute the same sacred four-letter word, the four-letter word of the Sacred itself.[9] His grammatology included a tetra-grammatology. He would invert sayings to see what fruit they would yield. When brother Thomas soberly taught, in a carefully nuanced way, that *deus est suum esse,* Eckhart boldly announced that *esse est deus* and creatures are a pure nothing. And that did not prevent him from also teaching that God is above being and being is the first of all creatures. When Jesus said that Mary had chosen the better part (the *vita contemplativa*) by invoking Martha's name twice (Martha, Martha, you worry and fret about so many things), Eckhart explained that the repetition of Martha's name meant that she had two gifts (the *vita contemplativa* and the *vita activa*) and hence that Martha had chosen the better part (*Q*, 280-9)!

A recent study offers an interesting catalogue of the ways [37] he played with the phonic and graphic substance of the two languages he spoke.[10] He reads *mutuo* (reciprocal) as *meo tuo et tuo meo* (mine yours and yours mine). He asked us to hear in the angels *Ave* to Mary the Middle German *ane we* (without pain) which is what Mary experienced once she consented to God's demands. He plays with the proper name of his own religious order *(ordo praedicatorum,* order of preachers) which he said meant order of praisers, those who offer divine predicates. He even tinkered with the word eagle, hearing in the Middle High German *adeler* (eagle) not Hegel, to be sure, but *edeler,* the noble man. He said that true thankfulness *(dankbaerkeif)* is, not thoughtfulness, but fruitfulness *(vruhtbaerkeit),* that is, to be made fruitful by the gift one receives, and that means to give birth *(gebern)* from it in return *(in der widerbernden dankbaerkeit).* In the Vulgate version of Rom. 6:22, *Nun vero liberati a peccato* (Now, however, you have been liberated from sin), Eckhart finds eight different grammatical functions in *vero,* including: truly *(vere)* delivered from sin; delivered from sin by truth *(vero,* the dative of *verum,* by truth), and so on. In the opening line of John's Gospel, *In principio erat verbum* (In the beginning was the Word), the words *principium, erat,* and *verbum* are submitted to similar multiple readings, disseminating and multiplying their senses. He even changes the opening lines of the *Pater Noster,* according to Christian belief the only prayer to come from the lips of Jesus himself, so that thy will be done becomes will, become thine [i.e. God's], because he taught that willing to do God's will is not as high as getting beyond willing altogether.

The only test to which Eckhart seems to put his innovations is their ability to generate new spiritual vitality, to keep the life of the soul with God in motion. He was a pragmatist of the spiritual life with a taste for multiplying and inventing discourses aimed at promoting and enhancing spiritual life. He was a *Lesemeister* (master of readings, of letters) because he was a *Lebemeister* (master of life, spiritual master).

Moreover, his emancipatory words put the powers that be on the spot and tended to break open the rigid hierarchy and exclusionary order of the political system which accompanies onto-theo-logic. He produced a significant deconstructive effect upon the prevailing onto-theo-logical power structure, upon let [38] us say the onto-theo-politic of his day – for which he was made personally to pay.[11] In Eckhart everything turns on *Gelassenheit* (a mainstay of Heidegger's vocabulary) which means letting-be and which includes everything which liberates and sets free. *Gelassenheit* means letting God be God, letting Him be – in yourself, in others, in everything, which is obviously a very non-exclusionary idea. *Gelassenheit* is a principle of love *(caritas)* with some teeth in it, a *caritas* put forward by a Christian which had a deconstructive kick to it.

As I have recently written:[12]

> Eckhart saw the life and love of God to be ubiquitous, not confined to just a few privileged souls, not just to priests, e.g., which made the churchmen of his day uneasy, or to males (he

preached to women and told them that they all had the divine spark, the *Seelenfünklein*), which made these same churchmen uneasy, or even just to Christians, which made nearly all Christendom uneasy. Furthermore, he did not think that the presence of God was confined to *churches* at all, or that God necessarily prefers the Latin language, but that the German vernacular in which he preached would do just fine. And that is why the Reformation took a liking to him and why the Papal Inquisitors gave him a hard time. Although a high-level Dominican administrator himself, Eckhart set about disseminating power-clusters in medieval Christendom, disrupting the political power of onto-theo-logic, and for that he earned the wrath of the Curia and felt the blows of its institutional power.

We can write Eckhart's writing off as negative theology, as a closet metaphysics of presence, or we can let it be. My claim is that if we press Eckhart about his Neoplatonic henology, his metaphysics of the one, he has to give *that* up, too, as so much idolatry, so much onto-theo-logic. What Eckhart was doing and saying, preaching and teaching, had nothing to do with onto-theo-logic or henology. Nothing turns for him on calling God Being or presence, even a superessential Being, a superessential presence. That is just a way of making the prevailing onto-theo-logic tremble.

At the end of the sermon on poverty he says, "Whoever does not understand what I have said, let him not burden his [39] heart with it" (C-M, 203). This discourse on mystical poverty does not defend some onto-theo-logical theory about God or the soul. And it can be well understood without understanding any of the subtleties in which the sermon engages. The sermon means only to lead us to the point where we will try to be (existentially) the poverty of which it speaks. We cannot understand his talk, Eckhart says, unless we make ourselves like what he is talking about. And if we are like this poverty, then we do not need to burden ourselves with this talk about God and Godhead.

What Eckhart taught had little to do with a Neoplatonic One or a super-essential presence. Rather he taught with irrepressible exuberance the joyful wisdom of a life graced by God and in the process shattered with loving joy the most prized graven images of onto-theo-logic. Nothing is more typical of Eckhart than the argument he pursues with mystical perversity that the better part belongs not to Mary, languishing dreamily at the feet of Jesus, trying to be

283

one with the One, but to Martha, who rushed about making the preparations for Jesus's visit, with all of the energy and robustness of life.[13]

Notes

[1] [220] I use the following abbreviations to the works of Derrida:
ED Écriture et la différence (Paris: Éditions de Seuil, 1967)
MdP Marges de philosophie (*Paris: Éditions de Minuit, 1967)*
MoP Margins of Philosophy, trans. Alan Bass (Chicago: University of Chicago Press, 1982)
WD Writing and Difference, trans. Alan Bass (Chicago: University of Chicago Press, 1978)

[2] I use the following abbreviations to the works of Eckhart:
[221] Q *Meister Eckhart: Deutsche Predikte und Traktate*, ed. J. Quint (München, Carl Hanser Verlag, 1963)
CM *Meister Eckhart: The Essential Sermons, Commentaries, Treatises, and Defense*, trans.
Edmund Colledge and Bernard McGinn (New York, Paulist Press, 1981)
In this text, I employ the Alan Bass translation from the French, which seems to me a fair rendering of Eckhart's German

[3] Mark Taylor, *Erring: A Postmodern A/Theology* (Chicago, University of Chicago Press, 1984).

[4] Derrida clearly dissociates himself from any outright denial of reference in "Limited Inc., a b c...," trans. Samuel Weber, *Glyph* 2 (1977): 192–8. See also Derrida's interview "Deconstruction and the Other," in Richard Kearney, ed., *Dialogues with Contemporary Continental Thinkers* (Manchester, Manchester University Press, 1984), 123.

[5] See my *The Mystical Element in Heidegger's Thought* (Athens, Ohio University Press, 1978; reprint: New York, Fordham University Press, 1986), 228–35. See "Idolatry and Metaphysics," xvii–xxvi, the Introduction to the Fordham reprint, for another discussion of deconstruction and mysticism.

[6] The best discussion of this is Bernard McGinn, "Eckhart's Condemnation Reconsidered," *The Thomist* 44, 1980: 390–414.

[7] I have discussed this point in detail in my "The Nothingness of the Intellect in Meister Eckhart's *Parisian Questions*," *The Thomist* 39 (1975): 85–115. [also in John D. Caputo, *Collected Philosophical and Theological Papers*, Volume 1, chapter 9 –ed.]

[8] In "Neoplatonic Henology as an Overcoming of Metaphysics," *Research in Phenomenology* 13 (1983) 25–42, Reiner Schürmann distinguishes Eckhart's negative theology (the doctrine of God as a highest being, the subject matter of onto-theo-logic) from his henology (the Godhead as a process of coming to be, *Wesen, Anwesen*), arguing that the latter, as a non-entitative experience of Being as process, overcomes metaphysics. This point also applies to Plotinus (see *MdP*, 187, 206; *MOP*, 157, 172). I will touch upon this dimension of process and overflow in Eckhart in the third part of this study.

[9] See Frank Tobin, *Meister Eckhart: Thought and Language* (Philadelphia: University of Pennsylvania Press, 1986), 76–77.

[10] Tobin, 171–179. See also Michel de Certeau, "Mystic Speech," in his *Heterologies: Discourse on the Other*, trans. B. Massumi (Minneapolis, University of Minnesota Press, 1986), 80–100.

[11] There is thus even a Marxist interest in Eckhart: see A. Hans, "Maître Eckhart dans le miroir de l'idéologie marxiste," *La vie spirituelle* 124 (1971): 62–79.

[12] [222] John D. Caputo, *Radical Hermeneutics: Repetition, the Hermeneutic Project* (Bloomington, Indiana, 1987), 265–66. See chapter 9, "An Ethics of Gelassenheit."

[13] In the time since I completed this essay, Derrida has published "Comment ne pas parler? Dénegations," *in Psyché: l'inventions de l'autre* (Paris, Galilée, 1987), 535–96, a discussion of negative theology vis-à-vis the theologian and philosopher Jean-Luc Marion.

19

DERRIDA AND THE STUDY OF RELIGION

[In *Religious Studies Review*, 16 (January 1990), 21–25]

Derrida, Jacques:
> *GLAS* (cited as G). Trans. John P. Leavey and Richard Rand. Lincoln and London: University of Nebraska Press, 1986 Pp. 262. $50.00.
> *THE TRUTH IN PAINTING* (cited as TP). Trans. Geoff Bennington and Ian McLeod. Chicago and London: University of Chicago Press, 1987. Pp. xiv + 386. $19.95.
> *THE POST CARD: FROM SOCRATES TO FREUD AND BEYOND* (cited as PC). Trans. Alan Bass. Chicago and London: University of Chicago Press, 1987. Pp. xxx + 521. $18.95.

[21] On the cover of *The Post Card: From Socrates to Freud and Beyond* there is a reproduction of a drawing taken from a thirteenth-century fortune telling book by Matthew of Paris that portrays Socrates seated at a writing desk, diligently at work on a manuscript, while behind him stands a rather more diminutive Plato who appears to be dictating to him. Upon this "catastrophic" reversal of roles Derrida comments:

> Be aware that everything in our bildopedic culture,…in our telecommunications of all genres, in our telematicometaphysical archives,…everything is constructed on the protocolary charter of an axiom, that could be demonstrated, displayed on a large *carte*,…[that] Socrates comes *before* Plato, there is between them – and in general – an order of generations, an irreversible sequence of inheritance. (*PC* 20).

[22] Our tradition has always assumed that Socrates did not write and that Plato, who did, regarded his writings as a written copy, a mimesis, of the living dialogue of Socrates; in other words we have always imagined Plato seated and Socrates whispering in his ear. And just as Socrates breathed on Plato, Plato got

Aristotle going (and Aristotle Aquinas, etc.), thus setting up the irreversible line(age) called the Western tradition.

Derrida is clearly charmed by the outrageous reversal perpetrated by the drawing, as if Matthew of Paris were a thirteenth-century deconstructionist. But as always there is a point to the joke, a fine tip on the Derridean stylus. The point is *not* to announce the "end of the tradition," even if that is what Allan Bloom and former Education Secretary [William] Bennett [1985–88, under Ronald Reagan] think he is up to. For careful readers of Derrida know that he regards declamations about the "end" of the tradition, or of metaphysics, or of literature (or of whatever you want) as just more metaphysics, more tele-communication, more apocalyptic pronouncements from on high. Derrida's idea is that the tele-communicatory life of the tradition, the "postal" process of sending out messages over the lines of Western philosophy, theology, and literature is a lot more complicated than defenders of the tradition have been wont to allow. It is not, by a long shot, a process whereby original messages, *ipsissima verba,* are passed on to a legacy of faithful followers whose job is then to return them faithfully to their author, which is the classical hermeneutic circuitry. On the contrary, messages have been scrambled, garbled, even lost; and filial lines have come out backwards. So many voices, so many writers: who is saying what to whom? Who is the sender and who is the receiver? This is not just bad luck but a structural necessity inscribed in the very nature of the postal process. Communication necessarily depends upon writing, not just in the narrow sense of written documents, but in the general sense of *écriture,* of the tangled chain of signifiers which is the condition of possibility – and of impossibility – of any attempt to communicate in any kind of medium at all.

Consider a theological analogy. Instead of an image of an evangelist with pen in hand and ear cocked heavenwards waiting for his next line – a theological "postal principle" – imagine the Derridean counterpart: a large Jesus seated at a writing desk, while diminutive evangelists whisper in his ear; and not just the evangelists, but whole communities, churches, clusters of even more diminutive figures whose names and faces we cannot make out, feeding Jesus lines that grew out of oral traditions and liturgical practices, passed on and altered, altered and passed on, and put into his mouth. The sayings of Jesus are dictated by those who followed him; the Teacher is the effect produced by those who are supposed to be receiving the teaching. You see the Derridean, deconstructionist reversal here: Jesus as effect, i.e., not an original content which is preserved and communicated – according to the classical postal principle – but a content which is produced by the followers; the founder is founded.

Derrida tries to get all this across – i.e., tries to make the idea of getting things across problematic – by writing a book or, better, patching together a text, about transmissions, correspondences, communications called *The Post Card* that has been very ably translated by Alan Bass. Indeed Derrida has been very fortunate with his English translators; and they have made available in the cluster of books here under discussion an exceedingly important dimension of his work. The (a)thesis (like Kierkegaard, Derrida has to write a book in such a way as not to write a book) of *The Post Card* is that a letter is always *able not* to arrive at its destination. The tip of that point is directed at Lacan, who in the concluding line of his 1956 seminar on Edgar Allan Poe's "The Purloined Letter" claims that a letter *always* arrives at its destination (Muller, 1988, 53). (The postal metaphor first appears in this seminar (Muller, 1988, 43).) Freud had said in *Beyond the Pleasure Principle* that the unconscious desire for forbidden pleasure is constantly being rerouted, directed along alternate paths, postponed and deferred, or "purloined" (which is why Freud is one of Derrida's sources for his notion of *différance*.) Lacan's innovation was to treat this process of rerouting as a linguistic operation, according to which the "transactions" between the unconscious and experience are governed by linguistic laws. The life of the subject is a function of "the symbolic order," a metonymic and metaphoric transformation of unconscious desire. The subject passes along a fated path marked out by the symbolic chain and is entirely traversed by the symbolic order. Lacan sees in Poe's story a literary illustration of this theoretical point (which for Derrida betokens a whole metaphysics of "literature"): the fate of each of the characters in the story is governed by the place of the stolen letter. They do not have the letter but the letter has them. Eventually the detective Dupin, who recovers the stolen letter, is himself drawn into the cycle, sent skidding down the route to which the letter destines everyone and so misses his chance to occupy the place of the doctor/detective/psychoanalyst, the place of Poe and Lacan themselves. The duped Dupin is a bad psychoanalyst (and the dissident Lacan, excommunicated by official Freudianism, is the good one).

The Post Card is very much an attempt to upset Lacan's cart(e). Derrida objects that Lacan harbors a theory of a master hermeneut, a master of the truth who, by listening to the inverted letters sent out by the unconscious, claims to return them to their sender in decoded form. The doctor/hermeneut knows the "truth" of the unconscious, the law of its letter, which he has gained in virtue of his transcendental, doctoral advantage. Derrida in turn is defending a poststructuralist Freudianism, one that must proceed without the help of a master key. Derrida does not reject the very idea of the unconscious – for it is central to his attempt to disrupt the Husserlian, Cartesian, Platonic notion of intentional consciousness – but only that the unconscious operates according to laws that can be deciphered. Derrida thinks the unconscious is constantly "disseminating" its effects all over conscious life in such a way that the letter may always not reach its destination. The letter does not mean anything determinate, but it is constantly lost and going astray. Indeed it does not "mean" at all, but it is a much more "grammatological" operation than Lacan allows. We ought not to say that Derrida's "point" is "illustrated" – for that is to subordinate literature (fiction) to philosophy (truth) (*PC,* 425–28) – but that this a/thesis is enacted in *The Post Card* by the exchange of lost and torn love letters which constitute the opening *"Envois"* ("Sendings," "Epistles"?), which includes not incidentally an important critique of Heidegger's postal principle, his letters from Being (*Seinsschickungen*).

[23] Readers of *The Purloined Poe* will discover that Derrida and Lacan may not be as far apart as Derrida contends, that Derrida like Dupin is too tough on Lacan, that Derrida is being drawn into the cycle! (Cf. Barbara Johnson's study (1987)). For one thing, Derrida's whole idea of Freudianism as a transcription system, a system of writing, which he defended in *Writing and Difference,* is originally Lacan's. Furthermore, it may be that the contested sentence, that a letter always arrives at its destination, means only that the rule of the symbolic order is unbroken, that no one escapes the symbolic order. What the analyst sees is not a master plan, as Derrida contends, but the necessity of the symbolic order, the inescapability of the chain of signifiers – that there is nothing outside the text (= the symbolic order), which is precisely Derrida's own view. The position of the analyst is not a transcendental one but one of Socratic vigilance, alertness to what Derrida calls the play of signifiers and to what Lacan calls the insistence of the letter. On that reading, "the letter always arrives at its destination" means about the same as "there is nothing outside the text." It is obvious – it hanging from the fireplace for everyone to see – that Derrida and Lacan are saying the same thing, but Derrida/Dupin does not see it.

In *The Truth in Painting* Derrida is again out to deflate the pretensions of the masters of truth, not this time the master of the truth of the unconscious, but the *Kunstwissenschaftler,* the learned art historian, master of the work of art. This whole discussion applies as well to the art historian in *The Post Card* who intends to straighten Derrida out about the "true" meaning of the illustration in Matthew of Paris's book (*PC,* 172-73). This time detective Meyer Schapiro (*TP,* 292), the Columbia University art historian, is stalking a stolen work of art that he intends to restore to its proper owner. A painting of Van Gogh has been lifted by Heidegger, who has pilfered it right from under the nose of Van Gogh experts by cloaking it with his sentimental, unscientific, Schwarzwaldian mythology of the "peasant woman" that makes it speak of "earth and world." Schapiro (Dupin) sets Heidegger up, asking him, innocent as a lamb – did I say Columbia or Columbo? – just what painting Heidegger was describing. Then Schapiro moves in for the kill, explaining with scientific deftness that in the painting that Heidegger must have had in mind the shoes were not peasant shoes, but city shoes, indeed the shoes of Van Gogh himself, at that time a man of the town.

Derrida is not out to defend Heidegger – he is also worried by the peasant ideology, a point that is directly related to Heidegger's involvement with National Socialism (see Derrida's *De L'esprit*, 1987) – but to deflate Schapiro. He casts a series of doubts over Schapiro's arguments: Couldn't a city dweller paint peasant shoes? Are we sure these are men's shoes? Are we sure they even make a pair? Isn't Schapiro's urbane Jewishness just an opposite ideology? In short, Derrida rejects not only Heidegger's onto-hermeneutics of the Being of the work of art that is supposed to open up a Greco-Germanic world of earth and sky, mortals and gods, but also Schapiro's scientific hermeneutics which brings the work under scientific control. He wants to unlace the shoes, to free them up, to extricate them from the art-historical police as well as from those who fantasize about standing in peasant fields receiving messages from the gods (Heidegger's Hölderlinian hermeneutics). In the end, Derrida thinks, "there is" only the painting:

> Nobody's being accused, or above all condemned, or even suspected. *There is* painting, writing, restitutions, that's all…. The shoes are *there for* (figure, representing, remarking, depicting) painting at work. Not in order to be reattached to the feet of somebody or other, in the painting or outside it, but there *for-painting* (and vice versa) (*TP*, 371–72).

The painting cannot be reduced one way or the other, restored definitively to any proprietor. It is marked with an irreducible residuum or remanence. It cannot be assimilated, appropriated, thematically determined. The painting is stuck to its canvass, imbedded in its textuality, pasted down in and by the rough strokes of Van Gogh's brush. The painting is glued down to the canvass. And with that remark we come to the glue of *Glas,* to Derrida's most outrageous moment, his academic *skandalon* which has rent more than one academic robe.

Glas not only resists thematic summary; it is like many of Derrida's writings a disruption of the very idea of thematic summary. The book is printed in two columns, each of which is cut into by numerous insert paragraphs called Judas peep holes and which look like little windows on a computer display terminal peering into other texts. On the left is a commentary on Hegel, on the right a commentary on Jean Genet, the well-known French novelist and dramatist, convicted thief, and homosexual who was celebrated in Sartre's *Saint Genet,* a study of Genet which Derrida very much dislikes. *Glas* deals with Hegel and Genet. With Hegel, which in French sounds like *aigle,* eagle, which embodies the cold, soaring conceptuality of absolute knowledge, *savoir absolue* (*Sa*). With Genet, that is, with *genêt,* a mountain flower, with the flowers that fill the pages of *The Miracle of the Rose, Our Lady of the Flowers,* and *The Thief's Journal. Glas* on Hegel and Genet, that is, on *aigle* and *genêt.*

One can imagine the difficulty of translating a book like this but Leavey and Rand have done a remarkable job. And Leavey and Ulmer have added to their contribution with a completely indispensable companion book – called, what else? *Glassary* (1986) – which supplies an exhaustive index to *Glas,* tracks down all of its references, and adds two excellent introductory essays.

Now we who have long ago succumbed to onto-theo-logic, who are Greek down to our toes (shoes?), want to dismiss this *aigle/genêt* with a wave of our academic gowns and cut through to Derrida's *idea* – we want to know what the *logos* is here and to cut the wordplay. But it is Derrida's claim that whatever *logos* is to be found here sticks like glue to the glossa and the glotta – and that is its *glas.* In short, we have run up against Derrida's quasi-psychoanalytic theory of the signature, that an author is constantly signing his name both *in* the text as well as on the title page outside the text. The signature is both inside and outside, unable to be contained by the "classical" (*glas* is derived etymologically from *classicus*) distinction between author and text, unable to be circumscribed by the frame which literary theory puts around the text. Such signing is not a conscious, intentional act, of course. On the contrary, an author's signature seems to act for Derrida like an opaque medium or even a scrambling machine through which the exchanges between the unconscious and conscious life are transacted. Like a classical trope [24] called antonomasia, which treats a proper name as a common name, Genet keeps turning his name into flowers, into a thing, making it a kind of rebus; Genet's antonomasia is an anthonomasia (G, 181b). In the same way, Derrida himself is fascinated with his own name: the -*da* reminds him of Heidegger's *Da-sein* and also of Freud's famous *fort-da* game, both frequent subjects of Derrida's writing. And then there is the Reb Derissa; the derisiveness of "rida" *(ridere);* and finally *derrière,* e.g., Plato behind Socrates, which among others things is a homosexual behind.

"Thematically" (a bell should go off at this word, for *Glas* tolls the death knell of thematics) *Glas* is about religion. The Hegel column is interested in the transition from religion to absolute knowledge, to a conception which has purified itself of contamination by *Vorstellung*, to a pure *Begriff*, an immaculate conception. *Glas* is specifically interested in jamming the gears of this transition, putting a glitch in its works (and so can be read as rejection of the claim that religion and art can be transcended). Derrida knows that you cannot "oppose" *Sa* with anything because *Sa* will just eat it, that is, *Sa* assimilates any opposition as its "negative moment." So you have to jam *Sa* with writing (G, 233a), gum up its works, show how writing sticks to its operations like glue. The result will be to have shown that there is always something left out by *Sa*, always a remnant (G, 1a, 1b) that the absolute system failed to digest, an excess that exceeded the grasp of the system, a transcendental excess or ex-position, i.e., a transcendental that is out-of-place.

For Derrida, that transcendental is Hegel's sister – both with and without citation marks. Without the scare quotes, because Derrida inserts numerous "cuts" from Hegel's letters about his real life sister about whom, on Derrida's quasi-psychoanalytic theory of the signature, Hegel is always writing. With the scare quotes, because Derrida treats the "theme" of the "sister" in Hegel's works as just this transcendental excess. The reasoning behind this is as follows. For Derrida Hegel's "system" is a kind of "holy family," and the transition from religion to philosophy is a transition from a "holy family" to the "speculative family." A family is a process of division and reappropriation (G, 6a ff.), a life process by which the separate (husband/wife) unite to bring forth the individual that is their own, that itself separates and unites, and so on. It is a circular system by which the proper appropriates, keeps returning to home and hearth, until the process culminates in absolute homecoming, *Sa*.

So the family is *in* the system but it also *is* the system; the family is inside/outside the system (G, 21a-22a). Now within the family the sister occupies a unique role because her relationship with her brother is according to Hegel the most "spiritual" of all relations. That is because, while she and her brother are a couple made up of members of the opposite sex, their relationship is without sexual desire and hence without the battle of recognition. Yet the system would seem to exclude the possibility that a relationship could ever be formed without that battle. Hence the most perfectly spiritual and beautiful relationship that *Sa* knows is excluded by *Sa*. *Sa* turns on the possibility of what it excludes, depends upon what it renders impossible. The sister is in a position of transcendental excess (G, 151a, 162a). You see what Derrida's idea of the transcendental is: that which is excluded from a certain place in order to open up that place; that which makes something possible and in making it possible, breaches it.

293

Derrida develops all of this by means of an insightful account of: (1) Hegel's early *Life of Jesus* – which accentuates Hegel's invidious distinction between the alienated, divided, ugly, soulless, slavishness of Judaism and the living, breathing unity of the spiritual life of love that Jesus initiated; (2) the conflict between the divine and the human law in Sophocles's *Antigone*; (3) the culminating analysis of the next to last chapter of the *Phenomenology of Spirit* in which Hegel includes the "religion of flowers." Enter Genet *(genêt)*.

In column (b) we meet the most bizarre counterparts to the holy family and the immaculate conception: Genet's underworld of convicts and "fags" *(pedale, tante)*. "Convicts' garb is striped rose and white," *The Thief's Journal* opens; "there is a close relationship between flowers and convicts." Cut off from bourgeois society, Genet's figures occupy a space parallel to that of the family in Hegel's, a sphere of love prior to that of law. Still, they are not a moment in the growth of society that contributes its sons to the public sphere, but outlaws whose illicit love is mocked by bourgeois society. Genet signifies their other-worldly status by an act of nomination, giving them names like First Communion, Divine, and Our Lady of the Roses – like members of religious communities who have also "left the world." There is a smell of incense and burning candles and of altars decked with beautiful flowers throughout these novels that deal with the most sordid characters. When the Judge calls Divine by her (his) civil name at his trial for murder, Divine is already lost. You can betray persons just by giving the authorities their name. Genet does not hesitate to compare his homosexual convict lovers who face the guillotine to Jesus (mocked, spat upon, betrayed). Or to compare himself: abandoned by his father at birth, taking his mother's name, lacking what Hegel called a *wirklich* father, his is a kind of virgin birth.

There is an explosion of Derridean motifs in Genet, the likes of which are to be found perhaps only in Joyce and Mallarme. For one thing, so much turns on naming and nomination: Genet has written his name all over these books, has signed his Jean (the Gospel of John) and his *genêt* wherever he could. Furthermore, Derrida reads Genet in strongly anti-Lacanian terms. (See Ulmer's essay in *Glossary*.) For Genet's virgin birth means the displacement of the father and of the rule of phallocentrism. Genet (his mother's name) takes the feminine side (*Sa* has become *sa,* her), makes himself into a flower, adorns his fags like the lilies of the field and compares them to the Blessed Mother. Thus Genet refuses Lacan's identification of *logos* with the name of the father and accentuates the cultural element in gender over natural sexual difference. (Derrida is always testing the limits of the *physis/nomos* distinction.)

But, as I have repeatedly insisted here, it is not the thematic issues that interest Derrida. He is not opposed to Sartre's *Saint Genet,* which distills from

Genet an ontology of freedom, because Sartre got the thematics wrong. He is contesting thematic interpretation (hermeneutics) itself (G, 27b- 29b, 86b). What interests Derrida above all about Genet is the operation of writing, the grammatological play, the *glas*. He finds in Genet's writings an omnipresent discussion of cutting: of whores with roses embroidered strategically to [25] their dresses, of cut flowers, of guillotined convicts, of the photos of notorious criminals cut from the newspapers and pasted on cell walls ("head cuts"!), of multiple castrations of the "antherection" (the flower/convict). Now it is not Derrida's intention to submit all this "*coupluré*" to psychoanalytic hermeneutics, to reduce it to the fear of castration, which would just be to oppose Sartrean hermeneutics with Lacanian. He wants not to op-pose one position with another, but to jam the positional-thetic-phallic mode altogether. He writes in double columns and not linearly, but not because *Glas* constitutes a phallic war, a battle for recognition between opposing columns. We have already seen that Derrida favors Hegel's sister from whom this battle is missing. Derrida writes this way so that we cannot castrate him, not because he has gained an unconquerable phallic advantage, but because we are always already castrated, i.e., divided by writing, subject to the incisions of the law. We have always already lacked the phallus. Our veil has always already been ripped down the middle; our columns are always already circumscribed (-cised) with writing (G, 65b).

Now once again this is not a *third* thematic, an anti-Oedipal one, to be opposed to the Sartrean and Lacanian, but a description of writing, of *écriture* itself, which is the condition of the (im)possibility of thematics. In other words, when Genet writes *genêt* he/it is writing about writing, about cutting and pasting together, about the spider's web of textuality. And the wild vines that grow this way and that on the right side of *Glas* cross the line cut down the middle of the page and wrap around the Hegel column on the left, eating at its surface, hollowing out and invaginating its doric, let us say its Greco-Germanic eminence. This cut and paste job, this gluing together of fragments and torn pieces, this agglutination is the *glas* that gums up the glide of the Hegelian transitions, the glitch in its machine, the glottal stop in its logos. It pushes *Sa*'s head back into the text, causing its fragments and globules to stick in its throat, leaving it sticky with glue and glucose. I could go on (and Derrida does).

If I am asked what significance Derrida holds for theology I would say that he represents in part at least the latest installment in the debate between Athens and Jerusalem, the latest and most subtle version of de-Hellenization. Deconstruction in my view is *not* the latest version of death of God theology, a more ruthlessly atheistic theology, an atheism with a Saussurean twist, as Mark

Taylor holds. It is more feasibly put to work, I suggest, in a low Christology, to take but one example, a very low Christology which is ruthless about the limiting, textualizing conditions from which the logos of Christology tries to ascend. Derrida stalks the claims of logo-centrism with a maddening patience. He does not let anything get by; he picks up everything, every slip, every chance, every loose thread. Every time we think we are breathing the air of the living logos and are filled with the spirit, Derrida clogs our throat with the thick mucus of textuality, chokes us with the glue of *glas*. Now theo-logy is no more immune from logo-centrism than any of the other -ologies, no more free from the illusion that it deals with gifts which have dropped from the sky than the rest of us. Indeed its critics would say that it is particularly vulnerable to such illusions, that anyone who speaks of divine revelation has made his whole enterprise turn on such an illusion.

I do not think that Derrida undoes the very idea of religious revelation but that he undoes a lot of the ideas of revelation that religious writers have proffered for some time now. He thinks that all immaculate conceptions are always already contaminated with writing. He would insist – patiently, ruthlessly, indefatigably – that textuality sticks like glue to what religious traditions hold dear, that textuality insinuates itself into religious "positions." (Are religious beliefs in the positional-thetic mode? Are confessions of faith "claims"? Are *doxa* in the phallic-thetic mode? Or is doxa just praise?)[1] Deconstruction wants to cut off the illusion of immediacy – of immediate experience, immediate revelation. Derrida thinks that immediacy is both philosophically unjustifiable and politically dangerous.

I do not think that Derrida is an antagonist of religion but rather a powerful and novel critic of the illusions and tom foolery to which mortals are prone; and that includes religious mortals. But why end on such a critical note? After all, cutting is to be followed by gluing. *Glas* glues. So maybe Derrida does not just stick it to theology; maybe he can teach theologians a thing or two about how to make things gel.

Notes

[1] There is another dimension to the question of Derrida and theology that the present cluster of works does not broach, viz., the relationship of deconstruction to negative theology. Derrida separated himself from negative theology in *Writing and Difference*, translated by Alan Bass, (Chicago: University of Chicago Press, 1978), 146, on the grounds that the latter's talk of the God "beyond Being" always harbors a metaphysics of a higher presence. Then Jean-Luc Marion, in his *Dieu sans L'être* (Paris: Communio Fayard, 1982), made a spirited defense of negative theology

against Heidegger and Derrida, arguing among other things that its predicates were meant as praise, not predication. Derrida responded to Marion in an extended discussion of neoplatonic mysticism and Plato's *chora* in *"Comment ne pas parler: Dénegations"* in *Psyché: Inventions de L'autre* (Paris: Galilée, 1987), 535-95. See also my "Mysticism and Transgression: Derrida and Meister Eckhart," *Continental Philosophy* 2 (1988), 24–39 [see chapter 18, above].

References

Derrida, Jacques
    1987 *De L'esprit*. Galilée.
Johnson, Barbara
    1987 *A World of Difference*. Johns Hopkins University Press.
Leavy. John P. and Gregory L. Ulmer
    1986 *Glassary*. University of Nebraska Press.
Muller, John P. and Richardson, William J. (eds.)
    1988. *The Purloined Poe: Lacan, Derrida, and Psychoanalytic Reading*.

20

HOW TO AVOID SPEAKING OF GOD: THE VIOLENCE OF NATURAL THEOLOGY

[In *The Prospects for Natural Theology*, ed. Eugene Long (Washington, D.C.: The Catholic University of America Press, 1992), 128–150]

[128] Is it not already too late?[1] Have we not already succumbed to violence? By reason of our title, by reason of this opening sentence, have we not already shattered the silence, already said too much about God? Are we not already speaking about God?

How to avoid *speaking* of God, how not to say a thing. How to *avoid* speaking, what to avoid when we speak of God. You hear the oscillation between two different intonations. First: how not to *speak* of God, how to respect the absoluteness of God absolutely, by silencing language, both written and spoken. How to loosen and absolve the absolute from any linguistic ties that would turn God into something relative. That is the harder saying, the saying that wants to say nothing, the more absolutist saying. But short of that, or en route to that, there is another intonation. How to *avoid* speaking of God? How to avoid saying anything inappropriate, ungodlike; how to say nothing wrong; how to delay, to put off, saying what God is.

Two pleas to avoid violence: how to avoid the violence of speaking; how to avoid speaking violently. The first pursues a more radical atheology, a desert silence; the second pursues a negative or apophatic theology. Perhaps not two pleas at all, but only one. Do they not say the same thing? Does not the first plea speak up vociferously in favor of not speaking, thereby adding to all the talk? Correspondingly, does not silence function in the second plea like a regulative ideal? Would it not like to board up the house of language altogether? Either way, the issue is to avoid violence.[2] But the desire to avoid violence runs [129] into an aporia, an impasse. On the one hand, we must not do violence to God; we must respect God's transcendence. We must take every means to avoid compromising God, reducing God to something less than God is. We do not want to turn the creator into a human creation; to make God the image and likeness of man; to worship an idol, a graven image. We must not violate the absoluteness of the absolute. That is what Meister Eckhart had in mind when he preached of the truly divine God (*der göttliche Gott*), the Godhead beyond God, the God of whom he said, "I pray to God to make me free of God."[3] I pray to God to rid me of my violence.

But on the other hand there is the necessity, the inescapability of language, mediation, conditionality, interpretation, signs, horizons of understanding, conditions of possibility. For it is already too late. We are always already speaking, always already delivered over to language. Do we not say yes to language before we say anything at all? Do we not say yes to language even when we say no – to language, to God, to one another – with a primordial yes, let us say with an ontological yes, which antedates every particular, ontic yes or no, spoken or written, which antedates everything cataphatic or apophatic?[4] Is not linguisticality a kind of ontological constraint under which we necessarily labor? Is not the violence of language inscribed in our being? Language is the condition of our having a world, a theology, even a negative theology that asks how to avoid speaking of God.

Here, too, the idea is to avoid violence, not this time the human violation of God, but the violence of the wholly or absolutely other; not the violation of the divine order by the human, but the violation of the human order by a kind of otherness or transcendence that just comes crashing in upon it. By conceding the inevitability of a certain ontological violence, we avoid a greater violence. For to follow the path of the absolutely unconditioned is not only an impossible demand, an illusion, it is a dangerous illusion. To start with an absolutely absolute, something absolutely unconditioned, is to abandon philosophy, thinking, all responsibility. Not to submit God – or the categorical imperative, or Levinas's Other – to a linguistic or historical conditioning is dangerous. For what we always get – it never fails – in the name of the [130] Unmediated is someone's highly mediated Absolute: their jealous Yahweh, their righteous Allah, their infallible church, their absolute *Geist* that inevitably speaks German. In the name of the Unmediated we are buried by an avalanche of mediations, and sometimes just buried, period.[5] Somehow this absolutely absolute always ends up with a particular attachment to some historical, natural language, a particular nation, a particular religion. To disagree with someone who speaks in the name of God always means disagreeing with God. Be prepared to beat a hasty retreat. The unmediated is never delivered without massive mediation.

You see the trouble we are in. Violence on either side, the violence of theology, in a double-genitival sense: the violence theology perpetrates on God; the violence it perpetrates on us in the name of God. There is always already violence; nothing is ever innocent – theology included. Is natural theology violent? Is there a natural violence in theology? Can there be a violent nature? What, then, is being violated? What is nature?

God Without Being

I want to put this aporia to the test in the paper that follows by taking up a most remarkable contemporary attempt to deal with it, Jean-Luc Marion's *Dieu sans l'être*.[6] Marion wants to avoid the "idolatrous violence" of Being (79), the violence of submitting God to an anterior condition, an anterior conceptuality, borrowed from the Greek philosophy St. Paul chided in his first letter to the church at Corinth. Marion does not want us to speak about God in ungodly terms but to speak of God *à partir de lui* (75), or in God's own terms (57), in the terms God has given us. Marion tells us how not to speak of God: do not speak of Being; do not pass an ontological screen over His face; do not make the Unconditioned into something conditioned.

I want to track the movements of Marion's quite interesting argument and to show in the process how he does not escape the violence [131] he wants to avoid, indeed how he provokes an even greater violence; how in the name of avoiding mediation he visits upon us a massive mediation. I will intervene upon his text repeatedly, annoyingly, insolently. I will buzz around him like a gnat or a gadfly, like a brazen, deconstructive pest.

Marion's position turns on a distinction between the "idol" and the "icon," which are alternately the pagan and the Christian ways to make the divine visible (18-26).[7] In the idol, the divine is embodied in wood or stone but in a movement that is arrested. Here the divine is in a sense too visible, for it holds our look captive, so that we cannot look beyond it into the "distance." The idol is always a mirror in which we behold ourselves and one that sends our look bounding back on ourselves. While the idol arises from authentic religious experience it is embedded in a limited, historical embodiment that condemns it to pass from the historical scene. Without the Greeks, Greek statues lose their religious power; idols always have their twilight.

In the icon, on the other hand, there is something surpassing, an excess, an infinity (26–35). There are invisible depths to its visibility, so that the look is not caught by the object but is carried off into the distance. Thus to venerate an icon is to venerate what is depicted in it, not to stop short with the visible thing itself. Furthermore, the icon is not a blind mirror, not a statue deprived of eyes, but a face that envisages us with its invisible powers. The icon exceeds the domain of aesthetics and human creation, exceeds its own embodiment, speaks to us from an infinite distance. (You can hear a lot of Levinas in Marion's distinction, the invisible infinity of the face of God, which opens up invisible depths in something finite and visible.)

But suppose we objected to Marion that the distinction between icon and idol is strictly historical, that one man's (or woman's!) icon is another man's idol? He will only admit half of this: the Greeks were able to experience the divine in their statues, but we are not; their religious art was authentic for them, but it has lost its power for us (41–44). Then are we to understand that Christian icons do not suffer from the same limitations? If Christian icons are touched by the beyond (41–44), do they have a power that rises above their historical embodiment, and so have an infinite depth (32) that allows them to retain their effectiveness without regard to time or place? Does that mean that they would retain their power even without Christians? Do Christian icons have a power that persists, *per impossible*, even without Christianity? Would that not be magic and a loss of distance?

[132] It also follows from what Marion is saying that while idols are manmade creations, there is some sense in which the icons are not. To be sure, icons do not drop from the sky, they are works of Christian art, products of human hands – but that is not all. They are more than just man-made; someone or something else is cooperating in their production (33), so that this human opus is also an *opus dei*. In the idol, man is revisited by his own ghost (*revenant, Gespenst,* 33). That must mean that the icon has an inspired status for Marion, a kind of *Begeisterung* that fills it with a true and infinite spirit, *Geist* (but evidently a universal *Geist* with a particular attachment to Roman Catholicism, which has no time for Latin American theology or the Dutch catechism). But I am getting ahead of myself. I should stop interrupting.[8]

Marion thinks that metaphysics is the peculiar form of idolatry that we Westerners have devised (26-27). "Being" is our most treasured idol. Having lost the capacity both to create and to appreciate pagan art we have instead devised a paganism of our own and have created the idol of philosophical conceptuality. (This is a lot like Hegel's saying that art is past, in the sense that art no longer serves the West as the primary depository of its truth.[9]) You see the idolatrous functioning of the metaphysical concept: the concept seizes God round about, measures the divine by humanly comprehensible standards, holds the look of the mind's eye captive, and cuts off the infinite, incomprehensible depths of God. Lacking infinite depths, the metaphysical look is accordingly not sent off into the distance but is reflected back onto itself. A metaphysical concept of God, let us say that of the *causa sui,* is an image of the metaphysician. It is not inspired but constructed, not infinite but finite, not an excess but an incision into the divine. So Westerners are just as prone to idolatry as anybody else, but ours is the idolatry of the concept. The God of metaphysics, of what Heidegger calls onto-theo-logic, is an idol that, like all idols, has its twilight – in Nietzsche's metaphysical nihilism. That god is dead and good riddance. Thank God for getting rid of that god (45). The dispute between classical metaphysical theology and Nietzschean atheism is a lover's quarrel about an idol (49–51).

Thus far, Marion offers us a sensitive religious application of Heidegger's critique of the violence of the God of onto-theo-logic, of [133] natural theology. But now he moves against, or beyond, Heidegger, criticizing what he calls a "double idolatry," idolatry revisited on a higher level, the idolatry even of Heidegger's post-metaphysical, truly divine God. This is the theoretical heart of Marion's position, and everything stands or falls with this move.

But perhaps I should speak more cautiously, be careful not to say too much. Does Marion even have a position? Does he not write a man-made book? Is not the idea here that this is nothing merely man-made, no linguistic artifact of Marion's, but something touched with the divine truth itself, straight from the heart of God? We are trying to avoid idolatry – so this must be an icon; this must be inspired. If that is so, I must be more careful; I intervene at my own peril. Or perhaps Marion is only mediating something about icons to us, giving us a little conceptual supplement (cf. 35–37). But is that not pagan, idolatrous, anterior to the divine? Then I need not worry, for I am performing a service, criticizing an idol, for which the faithful everywhere will be grateful.

For Marion, Heidegger's "thought of Being" represents a second and more insidious idolatry (58). Heidegger has taught us that to get to the truly divine God, we need to think the ontological difference, that is, make the step back from the horizon of metaphysics, which does not give God enough space, to that Open which *permits* (*lassen*) the appearance of the God before whom we can dance and sing.[10] But you see the trouble Heidegger is causing; you see how his God needs Being's "permission," Being's letting-be, in order to make an appearance! Instead of stepping back from the God of metaphysics to *God* (we will have to reach an agreement about how to write that), Heidegger takes the step back to an intermediary, to the thought of Being, to the Open (or *Ereignis, Sprache,* etc.), and thereby erects another obstacle, another barrier, or what Marion calls a "screen of Being" (*écrivan de l'être,* 58) between us and….

How are we to finish this sentence? We must at all costs avoid violence; we must not let God fall victim to any anterior conditions. Shall we just say: God? But that is an English word – and so another screen. *Dieu* just ties us up in a French connection; *Gott, theos,* and so on are just more linguistic screens. Well, for the time being (for being and time? *Being and Time*?), let us provisionally write "*Dieu*" with scare quotes when something idolatrous is afoot, and just write

303

God (while [134] Marion writes *Dieu*), erasing the quotation marks, when what we have in mind is the real thing, the unscreened *Sache selbst, même chose.*

Heideggerian idolatry is centered on Heidegger's onto-centrism, that is, on the priority of Being over any being, God included, with the result that Heidegger's "God" is always screened, a "being" who must always wear a halo of scare quotes. The God who is thought in terms of Being is really no more than a reflection of our projection of Being. Now if this second form of idolatry consists in setting up something anterior to God (65), then clearly the only way to escape from idolatry altogether is, as Marion writes, "To think God without any condition, not even that of Being; thus to think God without pretending to inscribe or describe him as a being." (70).

Now if it is the same thing to think and to be (Parmenides), if the soul is in a certain way all beings (Aristotle), if being is the first thing that is conceived by the mind (Aquinas), then it might be objected to Marion that to abandon the conditionality of Being is to abandon thought itself. So be it, Marion responds; so much the worse for thinking (71), for St. Paul says that wisdom of God makes foolishness of the wisdom of men – and that includes Parmenides, Aristotle, Aquinas, and Heidegger. It is hard to imagine what Marion means by this, by what seems like a hyperbolic effort to remove himself from every human conditioning. Is he not thinking now? And even if it is a different kind of thinking, one tied to prayer and praise[11] – that is all right, I do not object to prayerful thought – is that not still thinking? Would Marion not be angry if we said that his book was thoughtless, that he should think about all this more carefully?

To get beyond the God of Being, or the Being of God, is to heed what is revealed to us in the *ego sum qui sum* (but that's Latin) of *Exodus* 3:14, which on Marion's rendering runs, "I am what I want to be" (71). But that is English and "*Je suis celui que je veux être*" – that is French. Perhaps it is inspired French; after all, we do speak of inspired translations. In any case, we should be grateful to Marion for this excellent rendering, this very fine mediation of this passage to us. The sacred writer means – we have Marion's word for it – that there is nothing that Being can say of God that God cannot challenge, nothing that the *Seinsgeschick* can send God's way that God cannot return to sender. God is saying to us – we must be grateful for Marion's help with what God is saying here – that he can do without Being's help (11, 71). At that point, we have pushed ourselves up to the edge of [135] the unthinkable, and it is under this figure of unthinkability that we are able to "think" God. Now the idolatrous God, pinned between quotation marks, can be rewritten, not as God, but under erasure, as ~~God~~, where the cross signifies unthinkability (and ultimately the crucifixion; this is excellent writing, although writing is dangerous). It is not so much that we erase God with our thought, as that God erases (*rature*) our thought by saturating (*sature*) and overwhelming us with his excess (72).

God Is Love

If Marion were telling us how to avoid *speaking,* then this would be the end, the last sentence in the book, for by crossing out God and Being, we have crossed beyond the line of Being and thought, wandered off the Parmenidean path of what can be or can be thought, outside of which, sheltered by this nothingness and silence, lies the truly divine God. But it turns out that Marion's desire to tell us how *not* to speak — speak *without* Being, God does not need it — means that he has a lot to say about how *to* speak and furthermore *who* should do the speaking. (Will God need this speaking? And these privileged speakers?)

For by breaking the idol of Being, we allow the Gospels to speak. God is love, St. John tells us — and love is beyond Being, Marion supplements. How so? Because love is unconditional; it does not offer itself conditionally, only when certain terms are met in advance.

But is this the same thing? Does the unconditionality of love mean the same thing as moving beyond the Heideggerian thought of Being? Did not Heidegger, following Angelus Silesius, say that the rose is without why? Did he not claim that this was possible only because the mystical poet has entered that realm outside the sphere of the strict accounting system of the principle of sufficient reason? Did he not describe this as a leap into the groundlessness of Being, of the play of Being, of Being's refusal of ground and thought's refusal to seek after ground? And do not Eckhart and Silesius say that love is without why? And does not Heideggerian *Gelassenheit* belong to this same realm? Are not *Dichten* and *Denken* marked precisely by their irreducibility to thinking in terms of grounds, reasons, accounting?[12] Do they not belong to a general economy, to expenditure without reserve?

Love, Marion continues, does not try to encompass or reduce [136] someone to its own terms; it does not cling to itself, but rather is a self-giving that advances without imposing conditions. The upshot of this is that the second idolatry is surpassed by love because love alone lets God be thought (*laissant Dieu se pense*) in terms of a demand that is purely, solely his own (*à partir de sa seule et pure exigence*), namely, as pure generosity, pure self-donation. And that does away with the prior screening by any concept (metaphysics) or any other higher condition (the ontological difference). "God can give himself to thought without idolatry only on his own terms" (*à partir de lui seul*), namely, as love, as giving, as gift (75).

305

I thus run the risk of angering the gods, maybe even God, by raising another objection here. Suppose I just said that Marion does not attain God "without condition" (*sans condition,* 106) but that he is merely switching to *another condition,* love? He does not take a step back from an idolic God to God in Himself, but he shifts the hermeneutic horizon from Greek ontology to biblical *agape,* from Athens to Jerusalem, and claims that this hermeneutic fore-conception – love – is better than the philosophical one. The God without Being is the God with (of) love, and so it is love that provides the mediation, the condition of possibility, the horizonality, within which God can be thought and experienced properly as God. It is love that lets God be God (*laissant Dieu*), that thus grants God permission to be God. Is that not to reproduce the gesture that submits God to an anteriority, but this time a more adequate anteriority?

After all – I realize this is bold, to make love give an accounting of itself in this way – how does love acquire such an exceptional status, such unconditionality, such extratextuality, such extra-terrestriality? Does it drop from the sky? Does it not belong as much to our human vocabulary as does Being? In fact, is it not a lot more anthropomorphic than Being? Do we not know of it first and foremost from human relationships and do we not then apply it to God, *mutatis mutandis,* because it is one of our better words, one of our finer human moments? What would possess Marion to say that it is a word that describes God *d partir de lui* and not, like everything else we say about God, *à partir de nous,* which we then, by a kind of theological effort, transfer to God?

Marion's answer to this objection is that the notion that God is love – as opposed to the metaphysical conception that God is Being – is a biblical idea, that it has been revealed to us, that this is God's own word. But – again I risk angering the gods, or at least Marion – that only raises the problem up a notch, or switches the terrain on which it is to be worked out, to the Scriptures. First of all, a good negative [137] theologian like Marion cannot seriously believe that God uses words, that he speaks, that he expresses his thoughts, that he lets himself get tangled up in a chain of signifiers, that he needs the discourse of love (the way he does not need ontological discourse). Is not the whole idea of God's words, spoken or written, already stretching things a little, stretching the screen of language itself over God?

Furthermore, even if we admit that biblical language has a special place amidst human discourse generally, still is it not the case that the Scriptures are mediation through and through? Are they not *conditioned* in various and multiple ways? What is the New Testament except the way a human community gives voice to the impact that the man Jesus made in its life, to the way he transfixed and transformed them? And upon what were these writers to draw in order to say what they had to say, other than the places and things of their everyday life, the human relationships that bound them together as a community? Is not their voice through and through that of a specific time and place? When Jesus taught us to call God *abba* (202, note i), father, he took a familiar word from the patriarchal tradition he grew up in that expressed a warm human relationship and transferred it to God with the idea that this was the most adequate discourse that human prayer could adopt, not that it named God *quoad se*. (Was Jesus a negative theologian? Did he prefer a language of familiarity or of distance?)

So, too, the *agape* in terms of which John speaks about God is drawn from the love that the Christians bore one another. Is his Gospel not written in a natural language, whose terms and meanings are drawn from a human and finite matrix? Is he not just using the best discourse he has available to get something across? Is not John, is not the whole New Testament already itself a *hermeneusis,* written down somewhat later, filled with the debates of the day, with issues in local churches, with formulas that arose from later liturgical celebrations, marked by a plurality of interpretations and competing theologies, all of which is a translation – into Greek – of something that happened in Aramaic? Do we not have to worry about establishing good texts and learning how to read Greek, and measuring up to a host of other limiting conditions? Do we not have to admit that this discourse is conditioned through and through, all of which is propaedeutic to explaining the sense in which it is inspired?

But I am talking too much, not letting Marion get a word in edgewise. Let us give him a chance to explain himself.

Heidegger, Marion says (91 ff.), at one point actually recognized the incommensurability between metaphysics and faith, that each belongs to a different domain, and that the God of faith cannot be expressed [138] in the discourse of Being. In a seminar at Zurich in 1951, Heidegger said:

> Being and God are not identical, and I would never try to think the essence of God in terms of Being…. Were I yet to write a theology, something to which I am at times attracted, the word Being would not be permitted to occur in it. Faith has no need of the thought of Being. If it [faith] uses that, it is already no more faith. Luther understood that.[13]

But Heidegger does go on to say that the experience of God and his revelation is nonetheless subject to a prior conditionality, to the "dimension of Being," so that even if Being does not enter "into" theology, as one of the divine predicates, it remains "over" theology, regulating it as an anterior condition of possibility, laying down the parameters within which theology can function. Heidegger's God is always a "divine prisoner of Being" (106).

In fact, when it comes to Being, according to Marion, Heidegger is in the same boat as Aquinas, both of whom subject God to the anteriority of Being with equal violence. Marion criticizes Thomas for overturning the traditional Neo-Platonic thesis that the good is beyond being, which Thomas found in Pseudo-Dionysius, by turning it into a thesis about the supereminence of God's being. Because of his commitment to Aristotle's doctrine of the four causes, Aquinas failed to see that the primacy of Being arises only from a human point of view intent on scientific understanding (*ens* is the first thing understood by the intellect), whereas, from God's point of view, it is the good, that is, nonbeing, which has the primacy (119–22).

This is interesting. God sides with Neo-Platonism over Thomism. An unprecedented case of divine intervention in a metaphysical dispute. This is bad news for the Thomists, who always thought they had the inside line on Exodus 3:14.[14] You see how people who disagree with Marion keep discovering that they are in fact falling out of God's point of view? Still, if Dionysius was faking it about being Dionysius, faking it even about having St. Paul's point of view (*Acts* 17:34) – was he not known as Pseudo-Dionysius, Dionysius the phony? Was he not a dangerous supplement? – how can we be sure he has God's point of view? One would have thought that Dionysius simply had Plotinus's point of view and that he was using the categories of fifth-century [139] Neo-Platonic metaphysics. But perhaps Plotinus had God's ear, too. To put it plainly: Is not the Neo-Platonic metaphysics of the good beyond being an intermediary condition, an intellectual artifact, a conceptual anteriority, no less than Thomas's *ipsum esse subsistens* or Heidegger's *Geviert?* Are we not just trying to find the right conditions rather than the unconditioned, to get into the circle in the right way and not to escape from the circle?

Still, I have promised to let Marion have his (very considerable) say. We do not see what Marion is after until we actually follow his very suggestive readings, his very excellent supplements, of the Scriptures, which are as it were actual case studies of what it means to think God without Being and to do theology without violence. In the Scriptures, Marion says, we will find an economy that operates without, or that is indifferent to, Being, that does not move along the Being/beings axis, that moves outside the idolatrous enclosure of Being and beings, that is indifferent to the ontological difference (126-28).

In *1 Cor.* 1:28, for example, St. Paul says that God chose "those who are nothing (*me onta*) in order to show up those who are (*onta*)." The men of Corinth are nothing in the eyes of the world, for they have nothing worldly to glory in. Clearly what the world calls Being could not matter less to Paul. Paul annuls, or is indifferent to, the world's distinction between beings and nonbeings. It is in quite the same sense that Paul says to the Romans that God is free to treat the things that are not as if they are (*Rom.* 4:17), for God shows the same indifference to the world's distinctions. Paul would rather be nothing in the eyes of the world and glory only in God. He does not adopt Being as the ground of his discourse (*fond du discours*, 138); he is interested only in how one stands with respect to God. What counts is not a difference with respect to Being but with respect to "glorying" (139). Beings thus are set by Paul into a different play, where the difference between what is and what is not, according to the world's standards, is cast into indifference in favor of the difference between glorying in God or in oneself. A similar reading that breaks the rule of Being, of worldly *ousia,* can be given to the story of the prodigal son. The two sons are both at fault for they can think only in terms of *ousia,* of possessions and goods, the father only in terms of love. For the sons, the father's money is an idol they can't see beyond; for the father it is an icon of his love.

Now, I do not wish to take anything away from Marion's felicitous readings of the Scriptures, to treat them as if they were nothing, for there is much of substance in them. I am just baffled that he thinks any of this contradicts Heidegger (let alone Derrida). If anything, Marion [140] has confirmed what Heidegger held from his earliest days, that there is a difference between understanding the world – or Being – in terms of *ousia* or *Vorhandensein* and understanding it in terms of *Existenz.* What Paul says depends entirely upon the fact that he switched the understanding of Being from what is merely factually present (*Vorhandensein*) to what has worldly standing, a sense that is picked up by the Greek *ousia* and by English expressions like "men of substance" or "powers that be." It is to Being understood thus, understood differently, that the Christians at Corinth profess their indifference. Implicit in Paul's claim is its inversion, that from God's point of view those who glory in themselves are *me onta,* whereas Christians live and move and have their being in Christ Jesus.

Far from refuting the role of the ontological difference, Marion gives a rich and textured application of it. For – let us give Heidegger a word here – it is only because metaphysics fails to think the difference between Being and beings, that is, fails to see that beings can be projected differently in their Being, that metaphysics ends up painting a monochromatic world of factual presence at hand, which world is confounded by Paul's discourse. What Paul is saying makes sense only if one takes the step back from Being as presence to Being itself, Being, the truth of Being, difference, and so on. What Paul does, from Heidegger's point of view, is to set the distinction between beings and nonbeings on a different axis, reframe it on a different ground of discourse, one toward which the church at Corinth may adopt indifference. But what is that if not to recognize what at first was called the "ontological difference," and later on just "difference" (*Unter-Schied, Austrag*), or the languaging of language (*Sprache*)? If the meaning of Being is worldly prestige, Paul will take his stand with the *me onta,* for he would rather have his being in Christ Jesus. It is this capacity to switch horizons, to differentiate Being from its ousiological or entitative constraints, that makes Paul's discourse possible.

It is not an exaggeration to say that Heidegger's single, lifelong thought is that Being cannot be reduced to presence, that the difference between Being and beings opens up the possibility of alternate understandings of world and Being. It is a high irony to me that it is precisely to illustrate the fecundity of the ontological difference that Heidegger cites exactly the same text from St. Paul, that God has chosen the things that are not to annul the things that are, to show that "world" means not simple cosmic or entitative presence but the "how" of being-in-the-world – that is, whether Dasein is turned toward [141] or away from God.[15] This "how" of Being regulates how to speak and how to avoid speaking about Being, God, and world.

In other words, by turning to the Scriptures, Marion does not find a God without Being, but only a God without Being taken as mere presence or *Vorhandensein.* Marion has not discovered an understanding *without* Being but the possibility of understanding Being *differently*.[16] Above all, he has not found an understanding without mediation and anteriority, but an understanding where everything depends upon what sort of anterior conditions of possibility one deploys. The economies of the New Testament elude the horizons of ousiology, so one should keep one's hermeneutic guard up and be prepared to shift one's forestructures, for there are more things under heaven and earth than are dreamt of in ousiology. In the Scriptures, we do indeed encounter another world, another understanding of Being, man, and time. That is not only not an objection to the ontological difference, it was Heidegger's first example of the difference and arguably his original point of departure. For it is only in virtue of marking the ontological difference that one liberates Being from a narrow ousiology, thereby opening up the play or open space within which the biblical "world" of "love" and "giving" Marion invokes can appear. That means that it is only by opening up the ontological difference that one can avoid violence, for one would do violence to the world of the New Testament were one to understand St. Paul's words ousiologically and so deny the distinction between *onta* and *me onta* the space within which it is playing in this text. The "indifference" of the Christians at Corinth to "being" and "not being" is a function of the worldly understanding of Being and depends upon it.[17]

Still, none of this explains why, in the Zurich seminar in 1951, Heidegger said that if he wrote a theology he would not use the word Being, although any possible theology would remain within the dimension of Being. Why did he not just say that he would use the word Being differently? The reason for this is that later on in his life [142] Heidegger gave up on the word "Being" and handed it over to ousiology, which has tended to corner its use. (He also gave up on the word truth!) Being means (has come to mean and we can't reverse the process) presence, and so it is not a word he would use for poetry or "thought" – or theology. So it is necessary to step back from the Being of metaphysics to what he calls here the "dimension of Being"; elsewhere he calls it the "truth of Being" and later on just *Ereignis*. Even in the Marburg period, Heidegger was describing his attempt to step back from Greek ousiology as a matter of getting "beyond Being."[18] He also described it as thinking Being "differently," as thinking *Seyn*, or Being. He tried a lot of things to twist free of ousiology. But any way you look at it, he had already marked off what Marion means by getting along "without Being."

My point is that even when you speak of God without Being, or beyond Being, you have not extricated God from all anterior conditionality. You have not gotten something unconditioned but something better conditioned to a religious sensibility. Such a God is nothing unmediated or unconditioned, and we cannot rightly claim that this is God's point of view. What Marion offers us is an argument for the higher religious adequacy of biblical discourse (mediation, conditionality) over that of metaphysical ousiology, an argument that does not rebut but depends upon the ontological difference, that transcends the idolatry of the *causa sui* but not of the "second idolatry." He has not found a world beyond human mediation that speaks God's own language – for God does not have a language – but he simply shows us why we ought to prefer the biblical vocabulary. He has managed to occupy not God's point of view but that of a certain human religious experience that is from one end to the other expressed in the thoroughly human terms of loving, giving, and earthly glory, and that is, if anything, a good deal more anthropomorphic than anything to be found in Heidegger or, *a fortiori*, Derrida. The terms of "giving" and "donation" need first to be given (*es gibt*) in order then to elaborate a discourse about God's loving gift of himself.

That means that Marion has not found anything nonviolent, anything that is innocent of the originary, ontological violence of which I spoke in the beginning, the violence that belongs structurally to, indeed that constitutes, language itself. The "word of God" is a metaphor. To call upon a revealed, nonviolent language, upon words that are the words of God himself, is already to submit God to the violence [143] of a metaphor, to the language of metaphor, and to the metaphor of language. It is to bring God within the sphere of influence of the primordial ontological yes to language that precedes every particular yes or no, every particular vocabulary or natural language. For God does not speak at all; he does not have a tongue or vocal chords or make use of writing instruments. He does not favor Hebrew or Aramaic, Greek or Latin; he does not favor one vocabulary over another. He is not a father because he is not even a "he." Love is no less a creature than being (159); both are linguistic creations, creaturely languages. Being and love are equally linguistic, mediating, conditioning. Whatever revelation is, it is not something unmediated, unconditioned, dropped from the sky – which is why Heidegger said that what you think about revelation (*Offenbarkeit*) depends upon the dimension of Being, that is, the Open (*das Offene*).[19] To have sacred books is to subject God to the anteriority of writing, textuality, language. It is to confess that there is nothing outside the text, not in the sense in which that notorious statement is often (mis)understood, that texts lack reference, but in the more sensible sense that there is no reference that can escape the influence of texts, textuality, language.

Anything else – shall I say it? Will Marion forgive me if I say it? – is idolatrous. It is to fail to preserve the distance between revealer and revelation, God and the word of God, Jesus and the New Testament.[20]

Ecclesiology Without Violence

Up to now I have been arguing that the ideal of nonviolence Marion pursues is illusory, that there really is nothing we can say about God that is not violent in the sense that it does not cast God in certain terms, that it does not subject God to a certain horizonality, and so set up something *anterior* to God, with a kind of ontological violence. It is not that we are putting something ahead of God, as if we were consigning him to an entitative second place, but we are conceding that our understanding of God operates under certain constraints. From our point of view, then, Marion is arguing that the horizons of [144] biblical experience are better than the parameters of Greek ousiology and not, as Marion understands himself, that the biblical understanding is unconditioned, God's own point of view. We can never clear away the screen without the screen going blank; we can never make unmediated contact without eliminating the means of contact altogether; we can never eliminate the conditioning to which we subject God without knocking out the conditions in terms of which it is possible to think or speak about God.

But now I want to take my argument one step further. Not only is the ideal of unconditioned understanding an illusion, it is a dangerous illusion. Marion's desire for the unmediated is ethically and politically dangerous, and, let us say, it brushes with violence in the worst sense, in the ethico-political sense.

From his opening pages Marion (9–10), in resolute opposition to "postmodernism," is intent upon establishing the *hors texte*. He wants to see to it that theological *verba* make way for and so give way to the extra-textual *Verbum*. Theology must always counter its *logos* with its *theos,* which is the Divine Logos. Theo*logy* must constantly be monitored by *theo*logy. It would be blasphemous were any human *logos* to precede the Logos of God. Theology must move in docile abandon to, and allow itself to be regulated by, its own divine Logos. For Jesus is the *Logos* of the father, the Word he has been speaking through all eternity. He is the perfect unity of word and Word, speaker and spoken about, proclaimer and proclaimed, sign and referent (197–203).

You see the top-down character of Marion's theology. He does not allow that calling Jesus the *logos* of the father, his eternal wisdom (which is not anything Jesus ever did himself), is a practice that arose among Greek-speaking gentile Christians, who took this word and extended it to Jesus because, given their linguistic, cultural, and historical horizons, they found it a felicitous way of expressing their faith in him. I am insisting that the anteriority, the horizonality, this very Greek horizonality, is already there in John. Calling Jesus the *logos,* and saying that he is the "word" "spoken" by the father from all eternity, that is all anterior to Jesus, a horizon that is called upon in order to bring their experience of Jesus to words. It is also to reinscribe Jesus's very Hebraic *abba* spirituality within Greek logocentric horizons. The divine Logos cannot regulate human logos from above because speaking of the divine Logos is an extension of human logos and starts from below in the first place.

Marion's problem is that the New Testament is only a text, and that is dangerous. Like the veil of Veronica (*verum-icon),* it contains only the trace of the *Verbum,* of the life, death, and resurrection of Jesus. [145] There is a dangerous gap between the event and the text, between the *Verbum* and the *verba.* So what Marion wants to do is to reconstitute the originary unity of sign and referent found in Jesus himself, to put it to work again now, in the church, to make this the model of reading the text, so that the gap between text and *hors texte* can be closed (204–10). Texts bear the mark of absence; they yield to more than one meaning; their referents are in dispute; they are mediation through and through. That is why Marion wants to diminish the textuality of the New Testament, to put this text under maximal constraints, to arrest its flux of meaning, to fix its reference once and for all. He wants a hermeneutics free of the limits of the hermeneutic situation, of hermeneutic conditioning. He wants a hermeneutics that is no hermeneutics at all, because the interpretation is not an interpretation but a kind of absolute deliverance that delivers us from the conflict of interpretation that arises if you admit that you really have a text on your hands.[21]

That model of assured hermeneutics, of what he calls "absolute" or "Eucharistic" hermeneutics (210–11), is given to us by the New Testament itself, in the story of Jesus on the road to Emmaus, instructing the disciples on the meaning of the Scriptures, giving them a *hermeneuein* whose truth the disciples instantly recognize when Jesus breaks bread with them (207–208, 211–12). In this story, Jesus, the one who is proclaimed, explicates the proclamation; the unity of subject and object, *interpretans* and *interpretandum*, is absolute. From this we learn, Marion suggests, that all interpretation of the Scriptures undertaken by theology must reinstate that primal hermeneutic ideal. Christians thus do not have to submit to the limitations of textuality that others do, for the reference of their texts is ever present to them – in the Eucharist (206). What is outside the text, their *hors texte*, is made present daily in the Eucharistic celebration (12), which is neither idol nor icon but substantial, sacramental presence (235, note i). Hence, every interpretation is to be done in the context of the Eucharistic celebration.

Now, if Marion simply meant that understanding occurs in the context of a prayerful, Eucharistic faith, *ratio et oratio,* one could take no exception to him. But for Marion, all of this has a darker, onto-theo-political sense. Theological police are beginning to move in and take [146] up their position. It means that the priest who stands in for Jesus controls the reading while the congregation listens like the disciples. But the priest himself stands in for the bishop, who is the theologian par excellence (214); only the bishop merits the title of theologian in the full sense (215). True, the bishop can delegate his privilege, but there's a string attached:

> In the same way that the priest who breaks his communion with the bishop is not able to enter into ecclesiastical communion, so a teacher who speaks without, indeed against, the Symbol [capitalized] of the apostles, without, indeed against, his bishop, is no longer able absolutely to conduct his discourse in an authentically *theo*logical site. (215)

Priests who break with their bishop have lost the right to offer the Eucharist, and theologians who break with the bishop have lost the site from which to interpret. That, presumably, is why the Vatican can silence them, or remove their official theological credentials. Marion does not say this. He is silent about this silencing. But do we not hear it? That is also why theology cannot be a science and must monitor the growth and the character of its own *logos*. That is also why the multiplicity of meanings that do in fact emerge from reading the text are regulated by a deeper unity, a kind of central spiritual control, which sees to it that the multiplicity is kept within manageable limits. All talk about "progress" in theology must be regarded with suspicion, for there can be only a kind of unfolding of what we already knew. So beware of theological innovation (221–22). Beware in particular of the "deviant" Dutch Catechism and liberation theology (235, note i; 253), which are the primary targets of Marion's Eucharistic theology (Part Two, "*Hors Texte*").

You see now why I take to heart Derrida's warning against those who "on the pretext of delivering you from the chains of writing" proceed to "lock you up in a supposed *hors texte*." It's the *hors texte,* the thing itself, the unconditioned, that locks you up! Derrida continues: "it's also with supposed non-text, naked pre-text, the immediate, that they try to intimidate you, to subject you to the older, most dogmatic, most sinisterly authoritarian of programs, to the most massive mediatizing machines" (*supra,* n5). You see too how the celestial hierarchy laid out by the false Dionysius, he who assumes heavenly airs/heirs, reproduces itself on a terrestrial scale, and how the desire for silence results in an order of privileged speakers.[22]

Theology is either for liberation or against it. Everything is always, already political. There are no pure, apolitical theologies. Theo*logy* – [147] even and especially when it congratulates itself for having become *theology,* for having played down its *logos* in favor of *theos* – theo*logy* no less than *theology* is always already housed within an institutional power. Now if onto-theo-logic is always also onto-theo-politics, if metaphysics always implies a metaphysical power structure, a seat and site of power and authority, if metaphysical binarity has always meant rigorous hierarchical distinctions and massive powers of exclusion, then Marion has done very little to overcome paganism and metaphysics in *Dieu sans l'être.* Indeed, I would say that he has done a great deal to reinstate it, that this theology of docile abandon to the *Logos* lends onto-theo-political power a helping hand in its most violent form. It does indeed have a great deal to do with how not to speak, with theological silence, namely, with silencing Dutch and Latin American theologians; it has a great deal to say about how not to speak about God, namely, in disagreement with the bishop. God may evidently do without being, but not without the bishop. (What does Marion do when bishops disagree and will not keep silent?)

You see the massive mediation in this talk of the unmediated, the unconditioned, in removing finite, human conditions of anteriority. Is this what Jesus was getting at when he looked around at the theological powers that be in Jerusalem and called them a brood of vipers? Is this what he had on his mind when he systematically took the side of the outcast, the poor, the sinners, the prostitutes, the Samaritans, the lepers, of everyone who was excluded by the powers that be? Is this what it means to be *me onta* in the eyes of worldly power?

Of course Marion's attempt to get absolute extra-textual footing here is futile, for it is pinned entirely to a piece of the text. The story of the disciples on the road to Emmaus is as thoroughly textual as any other part of the text. And Marion's mediation of it to us depends minimally upon having a text that is not corrupt, one whose grammar and vocabulary is understood, and finally and above all upon having an interpretation *of that text,* an interpretation whose authority clearly cannot depend *upon that text.* For example, there is Schillebeeckx's interpretation, that all such post-Easter appearance stories are not records of actual events that serve as the basis of resurrection faith, but rather are preceded by and give expression to resurrection faith, to a faith that Jesus lives still in the power of his father.[23] This is a reading of the text that scarcely permits the exorbitant theological, or onto-theo-political, power play, let us say the massive ecclesiastical violence, that Marion wants to perpetrate. It must be Dutch!

[148] On Giving In To Violence

Marion's attempt to lift the veil, to remove the screen, to erase the mediation, to remove the conditions, is an illusion that is at once impossible – for it just cannot be carried out – and dangerous, for it gives one divine airs (heirs), invests one's own finite, mediated views with a pretended absolute authority, lends support to absolute violence. The attempt to eliminate ontological violence, to extricate God from any anterior conditions of possibility, is both misguided and hell-bent on producing a worse violence, ethico-ontical violence, violence of the meanest sort.

I will now conclude these remarks by offering a certain generalization of the point that I have been arguing one way or another throughout this confrontation with Marion. One might say that it is a deconstructionist point and one of the more important implications of deconstruction for theology. The point is that nothing is ever unmediated – a point that ought not to be so hard to swallow for Christianity, which has always been a religion of mediation, where the father has mediated himself to us in Jesus. We do not make naked contact. We are always already immersed in historical and linguistic horizons, always conditioned by them. But such conditions do not only limit us, they enable us to think and speak, to put things in a meaningful perspective, to gain access to such things as we are wont to call from time to time the things themselves.

That is a more timid "hermeneutic" way of saying there is nothing outside the text, which is a bold "deconstructionist" way of saying something similar but stronger. This rather notorious declaration of deconstruction does not mean that there are only texts, which would be absurd, but that we never gain access to things by leaving the text behind. Furthermore, it does not mean text in the narrow sense of what we ordinarily call texts, but the "general" text, textuality, *écriture*, the trace, supplementarity, and so on (the sort of thing Marion keeps supplying every time he wants to get his point across).

To put it in the Saussurean terms of early Derrida, there is nothing without the chain of signifiers; that is, meaning is not constituted, reference is not made, apart from an enabling code of repeatable signs. Meaning and reference are not inwardly constituted, are not self-constituting, without means and mediation, and then merely outwardly expressed. Meaning and reference arise from below, from within pre-constituted chains, from within communities of discourse that in slow and complex ways weave a world. The world is a textured product, and what we are inclined to call the things themselves are [149] things with which, having dwelled for a lifetime among them, we have become exceedingly familiar. The deconstructionist claim is not that there are no such things, but that there are no such things without the enabling chains by means of which they are constituted, no such things without signs. *Kein Ding sei wo das Wort gebricht.* Without the signifier the thing itself always steals away.[24]

What Marion wants to do is extricate religious discourse and Christian theology in particular from the conditions of textuality, to say that in Christian revelation we have come upon Godtalk in the strong sense of God's own words, that the revealed Word operates as a control on the words of revelation, that the *hors texte* keeps the text in line. That is to make a play for the transcendental signified, to escape the chain of signifiers, to shed the limits of textuality, and to situate ourselves outside the textual site. Marion's Eucharistic, theological site, understood as he understands it, is the view from nowhere, a utopic demand to shed our own textual skin.

The life and death of Jesus was a historico-linguistic event. It transpired in a moment of historical time, and it was expressed and remembered in a language marked by its historical and linguistic horizons. It was mediated from the start, which is why Jesus asked Simon who Simon took him to be, and why Jesus evidently asked himself the same question. No Christologist today seriously entertains the idea that Jesus knew what Thomas Aquinas said he knew about himself. The Mediator was mediated even to himself. Jesus was rabbi and teacher, but he taught about his father; he did not teach the unity of proclaimer and proclaimed that began to take shape in the early churches shortly after his

317

death. The history of the church is the history of the elaboration, the constitution of its theology, within the linguistic and historical horizons of its Hebraic and Greek beginnings, its Latin middle, and its European modernity. It has been mediated ever since, as generations of Christians have let themselves be addressed by the same question.

How not to speak of God? Not without being – for someone may deny that he is (11) – and not without love – for someone may try to reduce him to pure being. Not without metonymy or metaphor,[25] praise or predication, singing or dancing. It is not a question of finding [150] a pure nonviolent discourse, but of giving in to the violence of discourse, the violence that discourse is, of letting words fly up like sparks from hearth fires everywhere, even those of the base communities – and even from The Netherlands – and anywhere else where there is the hope that something may catch on. And when someone tells us that he has the pure discourse, let us beware of this immaculate conception, for along with that go judgments of impurity, contamination, and exclusion.

God does not speak. He is not *Logos*. So there can be no question of claiming access to the language God himself favors. The primordial yes we say to language is a human necessity, is always already violent. But let us say yes to this archi-violence, which is nothing more than the constraint imposed upon us by our human condition, in order to avoid the violence that excludes, excommunicates, silences. For that silence is more violent than speech.

Notes

[1] I have adapted the title of this paper from Derrida's "Comment ne pas parler. Dénegations," in his *Psyche* (Paris: Galilee, 1987), 535–95; see p. 561. Eng. trans. "How to Avoid Speaking: Denials," trans. Ken Frieden in *Languages of the Unsayable* (New York: Columbia University Press, 1989). See also Derrida, *Of Spirit* (Chicago: The University of Chicago Press, 1989) on the whole problem of "avoiding" (*ne pas parler, éviter*).

[2] I have adapted the subtitle of this paper from Derrida's "Violence and Metaphysics: An Essay on the Thought of Emmanuel Levinas," in *Writing and Difference,* trans. Alan Bass (Chicago: The University of Chicago Press, 1978), 79 ff. The parallel between my critique of Marion and Derrida's critique of Levinas (and of Marion) will become clear in the course of this study.

[3] *Meister Eckhart: Sermons and Treatises,* ed. and trans. M. O'C. Walshe, 3 vols. (London: Element Books, 1987), vol. II, 202.

[4] On this ontological yes to language, see Derrida, *De l'esprit*, 147–54n1; *Psyche,* 547, 561.

[5] I derive the heart of my argument in this paper from Derrida's criticism of those who "on the pretext of delivering you from the chains of writing and reading" proceed to "lock you in a supposed outside of the text, the pre-text of perception, of living speech...of real history.... And

it's also with supposed nontext, naked pre-text, the immediate, that they try to intimidate you, to subject you to the older, most dogmatic, most sinisterly authoritarian of programs, to the most massive mediatizing machines." Jacques Derrida, *The Truth in Painting*, trans. G. Bennington and I. MacLeod (Chicago: The University of Chicago Press, 1987), 326-27.

[6] Jean-Luc Marion, *Dieu sans l'être* (Paris: Fayard, Communio, 1982). All page references in parentheses in the text will be to this work.

[7] *L'idole et la distance* (Paris: Graesset, 1967). Idolatry abolishes "distance." It is always necessary to choose between them. See *Dieu sans l'être*, cited above, 239.

[8] In *De l'esprit*, Derrida plays up the ghostly *revenant* in every *Geist*, particularly the *Geist* that gives itself absolute airs.

[9] Gadamer offers a commentary on this remark of Hegel's in *The Relevance of the Beautiful and Other Essays*, ed. Robert Bernasconi (Cambridge: Cambridge University Press, 1986), 4–6.

[10] See Heidegger's *Gesamtausgabe*, vol. 9, *Wegmarken* (Frankfurt: Klostermann, 1976), 338–39, 351; Eng. trans. "Letter on Humanism" in *Basic Writings*, ed. David Krell (New York: Harper and Row, 1977), 218, 230. See also his *Nietzsche*, 2 vols. (Pfullingen: Neske, 1962), vol. 2, 394.

[11] *Psyche*, cited above, 572–74, note i, where Derrida criticizes the effort made by Marion in his final chapter (259 ff.) to play down the predication and to play up the element of praise in proclaiming Jesus as Lord.

[12] Martin Heidegger, *Der Satz vom Grund* (Pfullingen: Neske, 1957), chaps. 5–6, 185–88; for a full account of these matters see my *The Mystical Element in Heidegger's Thought*, rev. ed. (New York: Fordham University Press, 1986).

[13] Martin Heidegger, *Gesamtausgabe*, vol. 15, *Seminare* (Frankfurt: Klostermann, 1986), 436–37 ("Züricher Seminar"). See Derrida's commentary on this text in *Psyche*, 590–92.

[14] I have worked out the Thomistic thesis on Being (*esse*) vis-a-vis Heidegger's critique of onto-theo-logic in my *Heidegger and Aquinas: An Essay on Overcoming Metaphysics* (New York: Fordham University Press, 1982).

[15] Martin Heidegger, *The Metaphysical Foundations of Logic*, trans. Michael Heim (Bloomington: Indiana University Press, 1984), 173.

[16] A major thrust of Derrida's rebuttal of Marion has been that even Neo-Platonic discourse about a God "beyond being" has been mainly in the service of establishing a *hyperousion*, supereminent being. Cf. *Psyche*, 540–44. Derrida thus agrees with Aquinas's reading of Pseudo-Dionysius.

[17] Furthermore, Marion himself calls upon the ontological difference, upon its capacity to transform the temporal matrix, in order to rethink the Eucharist in terms of a futural, eschatological gift, and to loosen it from the constraints of now-time. Cf. 239 ff.

[18] Martin Heidegger, *Basic Problems of Phenomenology*, trans. Albert Hofstadter (Bloomington: Indiana University Press, 1982), 284–86.

[19] *Gesamtausgabe* 15, 437.

[20] Only once (159–60) does Marion explicitly address the question of how such unconditionality is possible for us finite beings. His answer is that we move from the paganism of Being to the iconism of love through the intermediary experience of vanity, the *vanitas vanitatum* of the *Book of Ecclesiastes*. But of course, from my point of view, that is only to describe the movement not from the conditioned to the unconditioned, but from inappropriate to appropriate

conditions via a connecting or intermediate condition or horizon, in short, from Greek experience to Christian experience through Hebrew experience. See the brilliant analyses of chap. 4.

[21] It is with a concession of the textuality of the text of the New Testament in mind, and to avoid absolutizing cultural, linguistic, and historical features of the text, that Elizabeth Schüssler Fiorenza calls the New Testament a "historical prototype" rather than a "mythical archetype" in *Bread Not Stone: The Challenge of Feminist Biblical Interpretation* (Boston: Beacon Press, 1984), 10–15.

[22] *Psyche,* 552–54, note i.

[23] Edward Schillebeeckx, *Jesus: An Experiment in Christology,* trans. H. Hoskins (New York: Crossroads, 1979), 379–97.

[24] I relate Heidegger's reading of this line from Stefan George to the concluding lines of Derrida's *Speech and Phenomena* in my "The Economy of Signs in Husserl and Derrida," in *Deconstruction and Philosophy,* ed. John Sallis (Chicago: The University of Chicago Press, 1987), 99–113; see especially 109–111. [See above, chapter 6 –Ed.]

[25] Negative theology, as Derrida points out in *Psyche,* 535, constitutes a complex textual practice with its own economy – of metaphors, metonymies, rhetorical and grammatical devices, etc., with which all who know this "literature" become familiar.

21

BEDEVILING THE TRADITION:
ON DECONSTRUCTION AND CATHOLICISM

[In *(Dis)continuity and (De)construction: Reflections on the Meaning of the Past in Crisis Situations*, ed. Josef Wissink (Kampen, The Netherlands: Pharos, 1995), 12–35]

[12] *Advocatus diaboli et discontinuitatis*

A tradition flourishes when it is capable of change, when it is revisable and self-correcting, adaptive and self-critical, even while remaining loyal to itself. The alternative is to harden over, to become oppressive and reactionary and a scandal to the contemporary intelligence. It is precisely with a view to keeping the Catholic tradition in motion, keeping it well and well-deserving of contemporary respect that I have chosen to speak of deconstruction and the Catholic tradition.

It is not as though this expression is without difficulty. "The Catholic tradition:" is that not something of a fiction? Are there not many Catholic traditions, subtraditions and counter-traditions? Too many to count and recount, too many to reckon up or to reckon with?

Is not "deconstruction" itself even more problematic – a species of intellectual recklessness, a nihilistic infatuation, an irresponsible relativism? Is not the very idea of "deconstruction and Catholicism" oxymoronic, a bit of fatuousness unlikely to win respect from the faithful on either side of this improbable equation? Or is it possible that deconstruction supplies just the sort of critical effect or shock that a tradition requires in order to remain at once loyal to itself and critical of its loyalties?

I propose to show in the present study that deconstruction is not a way of scattering our beliefs and practices to the four winds but rather of requiring their constant reexamination, and this just because it holds that the "origin" of a tradition, its absolute beginning, is always already "deferred" and "undecidable." From the point of view of deconstruction, origins are not written in stone, founding intentions are never unambiguous, a history is not without suppressed evidence and silenced voices, and the present is not without contingency. A deconstructive analysis forces a tradition back to its founding or originary acts but in just [13] such a way as to see that an absolutely originary act eludes it and necessitates constant interpretation and reinterpretation. Put more pointedly, there never was an absolute Origin.[1] Instead of an Origin we find only a supplement, instead of an absolute beginning, a slightly violent substitution. The Origin turns out to be a beginning at which no one was present.

However, the deferral and undecidability surrounding the Origin does not have the effect of destroying or undermining the tradition but of necessitating constant renewal, constant rereading and reinterpretation of the foundation, which was never quite foundational, never quite what it is said to be. So the deconstruction of a tradition is not to be conceived as a way of destroying it but of exhibiting its contingency. Deconstruction does not demolish authority but it divests authority of the trappings of absoluteness and makes the bearers of the tradition responsible for the forms the tradition assumes and the formulae it invokes. Deconstruction has the salutary effect of preventing the configurations that have come to figure in and form the tradition from acquiring absolute and unquestionable prestige. The result is not to undo the tradition but to make its practitioners all the more responsible for it. We cannot invoke the story that the originary charter has been handed to us on tablets of stone or by way of some divine appointment, for that, like every story, is a story in need of interpretation. Stories are stories, not uninterpreted facts of the matter.

A deconstruction – of a text or an institution, of a discourse or a practice – which amounts to the claim that everything is subject to the ever so slightly subverting sway of *différance,* is a way of demonstrating the need for constant revisability, rereadability and reworkability. A deconstruction is a demonstration of plurivocity and polyvalence, of polymorphism and ambiguity. It shows that a text or a tradition is rich enough, multilayered and textured enough to deserve – to merit and be worth – deconstructing. A deconstruction is not simple destruction, not a sheer levelling or razing, but an exhibition of complexity and hidden tensions. A deconstruction demonstrates that beneath the calm surface of unity a thing puts forth there lies a multiplicity of competing elements, that beneath the reassuring look of certitude and knowledge there is restlessness and undecidability.

[14] Beneath the look of seamless continuity there are ruptures and interruptions and disruptive discontinuities. A deconstruction shows that things are never as simple as they seem, never as easy as they look, never as settled as they appear, never as finished as they make themselves out. It is not that there is no truth, no tradition, or no continuity, but rather that truth and tradition and continuity are not what they say they are, that they always bear closer analysis.

Deconstruction is neither religious nor atheistic, neither scientific nor anti-scientific, neither political nor apolitical. It represents instead an analytic style that inhabits structures like religion or science, or literature or politics, exposing in a painfully close and scrupulous way the complex and unsettled character of these discourses and of the communities and traditions that grow up around them.

The Devil of Deconstruction is in the Details

But the devilishness of deconstruction arises not from a spirit of destructiveness or negation, not from a perverse sense of philosophical *Schadenfreude* in the difficulties that beset our traditions and our truths, but from a spirit of affirmation and celebration. Deconstruction is affirmation: the affirmation of the plurivocity and multiplicity that simmer beneath the surface of our discourse; the affirmation of the difference and alterity that tend to be lost when a single assured and reassuring style holds sway. Deconstruction is the affirmation – not the simple toleration or grudging admission – of discontinuity. (If I had the time and the wherewithal I would start a Catholic journal entitled *Dissensus* or *Discontinuitas*, to compete with both *Communio* and *Concilium*.) Deconstruction is the advocate of the devil of discontinuity, of the little break or tear, which it construes to be an opening and a chance for something new. The first word of deconstruction is "yes," indeed its first two words: "*Oui, oui.*"[2]

That is why I dare speak of "deconstruction and Catholicism" in the same breath, why I dare enclose within the range of the same quotation marks such disparate and discontinuous structures. "Deconstruction and Catholicism" is a phrase calculated to shock both sides and to comfort no one: neither the Vatican nor the *rive gauche*, neither the Curia (which [15] cares excessively for continuity) nor the keepers of the curiosities of recent French thought (who love discontinuity). But in my mind, far from being something oxymoronic, deconstruction and Catholicism belong together, indeed quite exquisitely. For what is in greater need of deconstruction than Catholicism? What can do more good for Catholicism than deconstruction? What is more deserving of deconstruction than Catholicism? What deserves it more?

I am being perfectly serious. What is older, denser, richer, more complex and multifarious, more polyglottal and polymorphic than Catholicism? Catholicism is Platonic and Aristotelian, Greek and Latin, Hebrew and not a little Aramaic, conservative and liberal, ancient, medieval and Renaissance, modern and postmodern, old and new, otherworldly and a hotbed of radical praxis, Marxist and capitalist, old world, new world and third world. But this seething multifariousness simmers beneath the seemingly smooth surface of the *una sancta catholica et apostolica ecclesia*, of something that purports to be continuity itself. And, by the same token, what harm can befall deconstruction if we make it go to church from time to time? Surely the devil himself should be allowed in church if that is what he wants. Will not deconstruction find there a plentiful supply of texts, of scriptures and readings, of stories and letters and even of apocalyptic pronouncements, with which it can pass the time, particularly during a boring sermon? Was not Paul the author of some of the world's most famous *cartes postales*?

Cannot deconstruction take the form of a certain affirmation of Catholicism, of a certain *oui, oui*, which would constitute a certain *credo*?

Eucharistic Hermeneutics vs. Devilish Hermeneutics

This is a complex and almost endless subject which I can hardly treat in full here (or elsewhere) and which I have chosen to treat only emblematically, by choosing an issue or two in which the more universal operation I have in mind, which must necessarily scandalize both Paris and the Vatican, can at least be embodied or exemplified in a particular problem or two. (It is more complicated than this, but that is just what deconstruction predicts.)

The particular effect of deconstruction on theology that I want to single out, the devilish good that deconstruction can do for theology, is focused on the deferred Origin, the loss of an absolute beginning, the indefinite [16] deferral of some point in the past where heaven and earth intersect and some moment in time gets charged with eternity and absolutely foundational value. The Origin has always already retreated; there is always already *différance* and discontinuity. Such discontinuity ought not to be utterly disconcerting for Christianity which has always been a religion of the Mediator, of God's icon, and hence of God's sign and supplement, of mediating and mediations and vicars, all of which concedes in principle the need to address the gap, let us say the discontinuity, between God and humankind. It is this discontinuity – between the kindred spirits of humankind and the divine alterity – that is the heart and soul of all the other discontinuities that bedevil us. We are always already in between the divine and the human, on the margins, *entre*.

That is why it goes against the grain of Catholic theology, as I conceive it, to pursue the line that Jean-Luc Marion has taken. Marion has performed the admirable service of showing us that any truly theological theology will always include a deconstruction of the *logos* of theo/logy, of the idols of metaphysical conceptuality (which Luther identified with unforgettable clarity), that the deconstruction of the idol is of the essence of respecting the true icon, which is an entrée upon the infinite. But Marion goes on to argue that theology should

324

dispense altogether with "screens" and "conditions," which means to dispense with mediations and supplements of every sort, precisely with the intention of getting beyond the human standpoint and of adopting a divine one, of speaking *à partir de Dieu,* and hence-quite miraculously, I would say – of reattaching us to an absolute Origin.[3]

On this point Marion has allowed himself to be excessively influenced by Levinas, to be overimpressed with the hyperbolic excess of Levinas, the excess of the otherwise than Being, of what comes to us from beyond essence, without Being. Marion succumbs to the transcendental illusion of thinking that he has made contact with the Absolute Beginning. Marion's beautiful and powerful book enjoins us to think of God as ~~God~~, where the cross is all at once a Heideggerian crossing out (*Durchkreuzung*), the Hebraic crossing out of G-d, the crossing out proceeding from a negative theology, and the Cross of Christ.[4] But it is no accident in my view that [17] all this culminates in what Marion calls "Eucharistic hermeneutics," which is a very powerful ecclesiology, a little too powerful, which does not leave room for the little gaps and discontinuities that deconstruction advocates in its own devilish way and that give a tradition room to breathe.

The *New Testament,* Marion admits, is a text, and even a historical text, which means both a text with a history and a text about an historical event. As a text, there is something very dangerous about the New Testament, for a text is a supplement and a substitute, a system of signs – perhaps even a screen separating us from the Origin. As such it is constantly bedeviled by the problems that beset other texts: there is always a certain uncertainty surrounding a text, about its authenticity, its sense, and above all its reference, its *hors-texte,* for there are always little gaps and discontinuities between a text and its *hors-texte.* The idea behind a text is to try to fill in or supplement a dangerous gap, to represent a Presence that has since disappeared. The text stands between the outside and the inside, between the founding act, the absolutely authorizing Origin and everyone who depends upon the Origin.

As an historical text, the referent of the New Testament has flowed off into the past and is no longer present. But this text, the New Testament, is different, because its referent is not past, but present, made present again and again, every day, in the Eucharist. So the reading of this text has a context – the Eucharistic celebration – which prevents it from going astray, which attaches this text daily to its referent, which steers the reading and protects it from the fate of all other texts, insulating it from the danger that clings to any other text, from the risk of crossing the abyss between the text and the *hors-texte.*

Now this is not a private opinion that Marion holds, but it is based upon a Scriptural text. For this is the lesson of the New Testament story of the post-Easter appearance of Jesus to the disciples on the road to Emmaus. The disciples listened to Jesus, whom they did not recognize, interpreting the Scriptures with great clarity (this is the only occurrence of the verb *hermeneuein* in the New Testament). But it was only when Jesus took bread into his hands and blessed and broke it with them that the disciples realized that this was indeed the risen Lord. For Marion, this story is a text about the text. It is a kind of self-instruction that the text leaves behind, a kind of auto-hermeneutics inscribed in the text, something like the stage instructions that a playwright inscribes in his text, by means of which the [18] text itself instructs us about how it is to be read. The reading must always be entrusted to the hands of the one whose hands break the bread, which is preeminently the hands of the bishop, or the hands of the ones whom the bishop consecrates, lest the gap between the text and the *hors-texte* grow too wide or even become an unbridgeable abyss. The one who has the power to let the Word become flesh in the Eucharist is likewise the one who is empowered to give words to the Word. It follows therefore that just as he who breaks with the bishop is no longer authorized to break the bread, so one who breaks with the bishop is no longer authorized to teach or interpret, to speak or to write.[5]

So this Eucharistic hermeneutics is also a slightly terroristic hermeneutics, for it ends in silence, not quite mystical silence, the silence of *theologia negativa* or of the *pati divina,* but just plain silence, the kind you enforce, the kind that produces what Lyotard calls *le différend,* the silenced dissenter who has been deprived of an idiom in which to state his dissent or his injury.[6] On Marion's telling the divine "distance" not only breaks idols, it breaks dissent and breaks down difference.

This result confirms a warning that Derrida issues in *Truth in Painting* to beware of those who promise to give us something unmediated, who would dispense with screens and mediations in order to put us in direct contact with the Origin, for we will later on find ourselves visited with the most massive mediations, with bishops and long robes and police all over the place.[7]

Marion wants to eliminate the undecidability, to close the gap between the text and the *hors-texte,* to smooth out all the discontinuities, to build a bridge, a supremely secure *pons* that swings across the abyss, constructed by a supreme *pontifex.* Such a *pontifex* will arrest the play of the text, stop its trembling (*ébranler*), fix the text within a firm interpretive context so that the river of interpretation will always flow within fixed borders.

It is as if when reading the text the heavens open up and a great hook comes swinging down from the sky and lifts us up, outside the text. At least it lifts Marion up, for I myself have not yet seen Marion's hook, [19] which has not made its way to America yet (although our financial contributions to the Church have been most generous.) On Marion's reading, the story of the road to Emmaus is a divinely providential preempting of Jacques Derrida which foresees from all eternity that, at some late date in the history of the Church, toward the end of the second millennium, before the Lord will have made his deferred return, someone very devilish would come along and say *il n'y a pas de hors-texte*.[8] Such a devilish man will have been cut off in advance, foreseen by the divine wisdom, his stylus tip blunted *a priori*, infallibly protecting the church from all error – and misspellings.

This is not Marion's private opinion, a little supplement he is supplying. This is the divine word. For Marion has based his view upon a text (which he has interpreted for us). But suppose, in a spirit of devilishness, we disagree with Marion about his reading of this text? Suppose we follow the reading of a famous Dutchman, heaven forbid, according to whom this little story does not actually record an eye-witness event, does not quite wire us up directly to the Origin, does not quite make direct contact with a founding, authorizing moment? Suppose that the truth of the story is not to be measured by the standards of the *adequatio rei et intellectus*? Suppose that this story is already too late, that it already comes after the Origin, that the Origin has already passed by? Suppose the story is meant to give expression to the faith of a community that Jesus is Emmanuel, God with us, and, now that he is dead, that Jesus is with God, that the power of God was in Jesus? Suppose the story is a way of saying that in this time of deferral the faith of the community is that God was with Jesus. On this very Dutch and devilish reading, a certain reversal sets in according to which the Easter faith is not based upon the post-Easter appearances, but rather, conversely, the post-Easter appearance stories express the Easter faith, so it turns out that the story comes later than the faith. Suppose that the point of the story then is not to establish episcopal authority on the basis of having made direct contact with the Origin, but to express a faith in the Origin, in fear and trembling – which means in the absence of the Origin, which is never quite in sight – a faith that the power of God was felt in the words and the deeds, the life and the death, of Jesus? Then the story does not establish the power and the authority of the bishop to enforce *consensus* or silence, but rather brings us back to the fear and the [20] trembling, to the faith through a glass darkly – through a *glas,* which refers to the little gap and discontinuity between the Origin and us.[9]

Marion will respond no doubt that the bishop has not authorized this Dutch reading of this text (although it is dedicated to Cardinal Alfrink). But then Marion is chasing his own tail, for this is the text he is using to *establish* authority of the bishop to rule out dissident, Dutch, and devilish readings. The ground turns out to lack a ground, to stand in need of a ground, to be a little groundless. Marion's hook is suspended from nowhere, held up by nothing. The road to Emmaus turns out to be a *Holzweg,* not an escape route. The luminous auto-hermeneutical operation of the story is clogged by the glutinous textuality of the text which prevents it from being self-interpreting, from leaving behind its own reading instructions. Marion has not established direct contact with a pure *hors-texte*; he has not extricated himself from the textuality of the text, from the misspelling of *différance,* from the undecidability that inhabits a text and the interpretation of the text.

Marion gives us a very interesting reading, in a very beautiful book which I myself have purchased twice, in English and in French, but whose argument – despite this expenditure without reserve – I do not buy. I myself think that the most that Marion's argument establishes, although this is quite a lot and is alone worth the cost, is the inseparability of *ratio* and *oratio*, of praying and praising, on the one hand, and of predicates and predication, on the other hand. But Marion remains, withal, inside the text, offering us a certain reading, without a hook to hoist him over the abyss that engulfs us all, both eucharistic hermeneuts and just plain devilish hermeneuts.

Marion wants to get back to something foundational, something originary and grounding, but it turns out that this ground-laying is a little groundless, a little violent. That is what ground-laying always turn out to be, a little violent, sometimes more than a little. That is because the Origin is always deferred, always lost in the past, always pre-original. The discontinuity with the Origin is always already, structurally, in place. A tradition takes place in the discontinuity with its Origin which is always a [21] little lost. That is why Christianity is a certain form of *différance,* occurring precisely in the space opened up by the *deferral* of the Origin, the impossibility of making contact with the first coming, on the one hand, and of the Lord's increasingly delayed return, on the other hand. Christians are always already late-comers, always the latter-day disciples, always arriving too late for the origin, after a crowd (*ecclesia*) has already gathered. We are the *ecclesia* of those who come too late for the Origin and too early for the *parousia.* The space of *ecclesia* is *différance.*

The Original Text

That is why it is always a question of starting from below, of settling for supplements, of being engulfed in mediations and substitutes, without a heavenly hook. It is a question of beginning where one is, as Derrida says[10] – not where God is, we may add. That is an old Catholic idea. "It is certain and evident to the senses that in the world some things are in motion," St. Thomas said at the beginning of a very long book.[11] That is where St. Thomas begins, not with God, but with the senses, and he was the angelic doctor. "None is good but God," the Scriptures say, from which it follows that we who are not God should be content with a more devilish beginning, more earth-bound and in need of mediations and messengers (*angeli*) and give up trying to start *à partir de Dieu.*

Where do I begin? How do I start? That is the question that Hegel posed and thought he had resolved by starting the *Logic* with the dialectic of being and nothing. Johannes Climacus made good fun of that and showed us – in what is perhaps the first postmodern gesture – how it is not possible to make an absolute beginning, how one can never be sure one has gotten back to the start, that there is always something we have forgotten or left out, some little fragment and discontinuity we will have missed that will clog up the absolute beginning.[12] That is why Derrida advises us to begin where we are, in the midst of a text, of a sentence, of a tradition, and not to imagine that we can somehow escape the condition of textuality by [22] means of some kind of Archimedean *hors-texte* which, *mirabile dictu*, stabilizes the trembling of the text.

Here I am (*me voici*), in the midst of a complex of events and structures, discourses and institutions, histories and traditions, in the plural, which I must sort out and sort through. Here I am in the mist of *différance,* with the misspelling, surrounded by the difficulties and discontinuities of life. The word of God, the mind of God, what God wants, what God has said, that is a matter to be settled in fear and trembling. It wavers in undecidability. It is nothing I can speak from (*à partir de*), nothing to which I can pretend but only something to hope for, to intend, to take as a mark, a trace I can never hope perfectly to retrace, as if it were a code I could decode.

What are the words of God? Here – this book, the New Testament. But this is English, a translation. Are we to understand that God speaks English? Then let us go back to the *original,* to the Greek. But is that not also a translation? For Jesus did not likely speak Greek but Aramaic. Then is Aramaic the original, the divine tongue itself? Divine tongue? Does that phrase not stick in one's throat? How can there be a divine tongue, not a *lingua franca* but a *lingua divina*? After all, God does not actually, strictly speaking, speak. God has no vocal chords, no writing instruments. God is not subject to the scrambling, disseminating, Babelian condition of *différance*, which makes speaking and writing possible (and impossible) by its differential play. That means that even if we could get back to some text which would be what Jesus said in Aramaic, or which Paul or John themselves actually wrote, to an autographed manuscript, actually signed by Paul, or even by Jesus, we would still be dealing with a translation. For the very idea of the word of God is implicated in translation, in *transferre, trans-latio, meta-phorein*. The search for the literal word of God leads us back to the metaphor of the letter, back to the metaphor of the word of God, according to which we imagine God dictating to or conversing with us, through a messenger or an intermediary. The search for the original leads us back to a little gap, a bit of an abyss, that we are forced to cross (*meta*) with the help of a little vehicle meant to bear us (*phorein*).

That being said, that little proviso being stated, that little discontinuity being noted, right at the beginning, let us ask again: What are the words of God? The words of God are the words of the Scriptures, which are the [23] traces which God has left behind in the act of always already withdrawing from the world. The faith of the faithful takes place in the space opened up by this withdrawal, but this space is not a simple absence created by an utterly absconded God who has disappeared without a trace. Rather, it is twilight space, of flickering images, a space in which the withdrawal leaves its trace behind, like a fissure in a surface left behind by something, *je ne sais quoi*, which has passed through it and disappeared. Faith is defined by this withdrawal, by a retreat which has left its traces in the texts to which it gives rise. Faith is assigned the task of reading traces which cannot be absolutely tracked down, deciphered, decoded. The faithful in turn are themselves always already marked, traced, inscribed – *in hoc signo* – within systems of traces from which there is no escape. Indeed, the very idea of escape from the text, from the textuality of the text, is a transcendental illusion, the illusion of the perfectly unmediated, the illusion described by Kant of the bird that thinks that it could fly all the more swiftly were it not for the air which offers it such resistance – although the air is just what holds it up. For where would we be without the text?

The point of deconstruction is to settle into this space, into this marginality between the presence and absence of God. Deconstruction does not revel nihilistically in absence, which is always one-sided, but wrestles in the dark with ambiguous traces. Deconstruction does not level the text by destroying the distance by which the text – this text, the New Testament, or any text – is inhabited. It does not reduce the text to something entirely immanent and mundane, devoid of an Other, of (here) a divine Other, divested of the shock of transcendence, of an intervention from without, of the trauma of alterity. The point of deconstruction, its stylus tip, is to maintain the *undecidability* of the text, to maintain the difference between the divine and the human in all its undecidability, to let the text waver in undecidability, or rather, since deconstruction is nothing that you or I do, or even that Jacques Derrida does, to let that undecidability be seen, to let that wavering be.

Undecidability is not a way of mistreating the text, of casting doubt on it, of treating it with disrespect. Undecidability is the condition of possibility for respecting the distance that inhabits and disturbs the text. Undecidability prevents the text from settling into the stability of immanence, the familiarity of immanence, the mastery and domination, the continuity and certitude of immanence, all of which undo the transcendence of the text. Far from destroying anything, undecidability [24] saves the text from destruction – this text, the New Testament, or any text worthy of the name. Deconstruction is a way to prevent the text from becoming an idol, a way to shelter its iconic quality, which is to be the trace of the infinite, or of something, I know not what. The devilishness of deconstruction is to make it always a matter of undecidable wonder, of wondering out loud, when we have to do with the divine trauma, the shock of revelation, and when we are just being beaten over the head by something human.

The most pointed example of the need for undecidability at present, an example I would say is almost amusing were it not so serious, has to do the ordination of women. The only advantage of this debate is to make it perfectly plain how the Origin withdraws, how the original is always deferred, how we are constantly mistaking the original for its copies and substitutes, to the point of making the very idea of the Origin tremble. You will pardon me if I do not treat this imaginary exchange with the proper ecclesiastical solemnity:

Bishop: The priest must be in the likeness of Christ, the *imago Christi.*

Advocatus diaboli et discontinuitatis: *Oui, oui.*

Bishop: But Jesus and the apostles were all males.[13]

Advocatus: *Oui, oui.*

Bishop: It follows, therefore, that the essence of the redemptive act which God effects in Jesus is tied up with the maleness of Jesus, with masculine sexuality.

Advocatus: *Mais, non.* Are we to believe that God's redemptive power, the very divinity of the fact that God has redeemed us all – Greek and Jew, male and female, black and white, bondsmen and slave (Gal 3:28) – is somehow constrained or confined – I

331

am trying to be quite precise, I do not mean to be rude – to male genitalia? Is this what the blood of the martyrs has come down to? Do we not at this point fall down before an idol, a very classic one, indeed one with roots in our subconscious? The idea behind this beautiful distinction between an idol and an icon is that, in an idol, our look (*regard*) is arrested by [25] something visible, trapped and fascinated by the visibility of some graven image. The result is that instead of proceeding on to the infinite beyond it, to the otherwise than being, to the transcendence, the look is trapped in immanence, sent back to us so that we find ourselves regarding our own reflections, ourselves, not God. Is nothing wrong when we look into this book and see only ourselves, not God? But if our look is arrested by the masculinity of Jesus, then is it God and God's transcendence we have in view, the God who is Otherwise than Being? Cannot the God Who is Otherwise than Being, the God without Being, be otherwise than masculine? If we insist upon the masculinity of Jesus, is that to get back to the original or is it to stop with an idol and a substitute – something human, something quite obviously, conspicuously male, and a human, all too human, socio-politico-sexual power structure, an historical contingency? Do we honor the saving power of Jesus or a patriarchal model borrowed from the Greco-Roman household? Do we make contact with the original or do we fall down before the oldest, most phallocentric idol we can imagine? Is this not precisely to fail to preserve the distance of the ever deferred Origin, to fail to proceed on to God and respect the divine self-deferral, as befits an icon, in which one does not so much see as one is envisaged by the Divine, and this precisely with the aid of God's icon, God's *imago,* God's Mediator? Is the loyalty of the Church to a male priesthood loyalty to the Original or simply loyalty to itself?

So you see why I am an advocate of the devil, of a devilish hermeneutics, and why I think that deconstruction – which warns us about the loss of the Origin – is one of the better angels of our nature. You see what undecidability does, the good it does for Catholicism, for whom deconstruction is, I would say, a perfect fit. This devilishness is not as far removed from the truly divine God[14] as those who think they speak with the tongues of angels like to think. It is in virtue of undecidability that the distinction between the human and the divine, between the derivate and the Origin, between devils and angels, is a little

332

undecidable. The advocates of deconstruction and of Derrida may be the *advocati diaboli,* but then is this not a loyal opposition, one of the oldest and most venerable ecclesiastical functions, maybe even a divinely appointed and not merely a human role?

[26] This devilish, deconstructionistic hermeneutics is not out to deny the divine icon and reduce everything to an idol of *différance.* Far from it; it loves this distinction between idol and icon, but like all distinctions, it wants to worry about it, to be bedeviled by it, to worry in fear and trembling that we cannot be reassured by this distinction which only shifts the problems of faith and theological reflection to another level, viz., that of determining just what is iconic and what is idolatrous, what is divine and what is manmade and mundane, what is original and what is a copy, what is part and parcel of the calming reassurance and continuity of immanence, and what belongs to the shock of the divine, the jolt and trauma of something different, of something – *grace à Dieu* – divine and discontinuous.[15]

The Archi-Bishop

But is it not clear that it is the work of the Bishop, and for us Catholics, of the Bishop of all Bishops, to resolve this undecidability and to arrest this play, so that we can tell the difference between the divine and the human, the original and the substitute? Or is the Bishop of all Bishops also caught in *différance?* Can this be thought, said, uttered, repeated? Is it permissible? possible? Is it not diabolic? Jesus himself was tempted by the devil. Can we say, can we think, that the Bishop of all Bishops, the supreme pontifex for every groundless abyss, is himself, even behind Vatican walls, subject to *différance?* Can divine infallibility be subject to a misspelling? Does not the divine breath inspire the vicar (which means substitute, supplement, perhaps even a dangerous one)?

To answer that dangerous question I propose that we take up another, also very Derridean example. You all know the famous cover of *La Carte postale*[16] which portrays the utter perversity of a Socrates – who never wrote – seated at a writing table while Plato – who condemned writing but wrote quite a great deal – whispers in his ear, dictating to Socrates what he should write. Derrida loves this postcard, which he found in the bookstore of the Bodleian Library in Oxford, for many reasons, among which is the [27] way that it scrambles the wires of the West's most venerable communication system, its oldest hermeneutic code. We like to think that Socrates taught and asked questions and that Plato, his disciple, taking pen in hand, wrote the intellectual biography of Socrates, and that the history of Platonism, which is the history of us, is to have been on the receiving end of these messages ever since. But this perverse postcard suggests that these wires have been crossed, that when we read Plato quoting Socrates, it is Plato dictating to Socrates, Plato putting words in Socrates mouth, Plato speaking through the mouthpiece of Socrates. That is to say, the relationship between Plato and Socrates is an undecidable, which does not mean something utterly chaotic, but rather that this is a distinction to be held in fear and trembling. Are we to understand that in the *Dialogues* Plato speaks with the authority of Socrates, or rather, contrariwise, that Socrates speaks with the authority of Plato? Are we sure who is saying what to whom in the Platonic dialogues? Who is the original and who the follower? Must we not proceed here with care?

Let us imagine now the reversal of another scene, this time with Jesus seated at the writing table while the evangelists whisper in his ear and Jesus takes dictation. Imagine the reversal of the painting by Raphael in which the evangelist Mark sits with his ear cocked to the heavens, waiting for the next inspired word; imagine that it is Jesus seated at a writing table and that it is Jesus whose ear is cocked to the wind. That is to say, let us put the distinction between the original sayings and the ones we have supplied, between what Jesus says and what *we* say Jesus says, into undecidability, so that we are not quite sure which is which, so that the margins around the text are blurred just a bit. Is that unimaginable, unthinkable, perhaps even blasphemous? Would that destroy the transcendence, the shock of alterity, or would it preserve it? Is this not what we know, what we learn when we study New Testament exegesis and we learn about "later theological reflections," about "theologoumena."[17] These theologoumena do not represent callous falsifications but certain dialogues that the community imagined and then recited or prayed in liturgy and attributed to Jesus in a kind of prayerful theatrics. They are not transcriptions of Jesus' original and actual words, which constitute an *hors-texte* almost impossible to access, but a way we have found to imagine an Origin that is always already out of view

[28] I single out a particular saying of Jesus, one which is very important to any bishop worthy of his name, but also important to me for at least two reasons: 1) it contains a very famous pun, I am tempted to say an inspired pun; 2) it has to do with what Derrida calls the violence of the Origin or of the foundation. There is a logion in *Matthew* in which Jesus says to Simon, "Thou art Peter and upon this rock I will build my church" (*Matt.* 16:18). This is a lynch-pin for the bishop, a foundational stone, a *fundamentum inconcussum*, engraved in stone around the rotunda in the Vatican.

But suppose we let the fog of undecidability, which is meant to be a protective cover and shelter of transcendence, settle upon this saying? There is every reason to think that Jesus did not intend to found a Church or to make Peter his Pope and the Bishop of Rome, or to build a cathedral in Peter's name, let alone to establish the Vatican library and museum, and hence that Jesus did not actually say this. What is human and what is divine in this saying is not quite so clear, not as clear as some people think, not as clear as quite a few bishops think. We can imagine Jesus at the writing table and the early church, which had begun to coalesce around Simon, whispering in his ear, feeding him a few crucial lines.[18] It may be that the apostolic chain from Peter to the present is continuous and unbroken, but is there not still a little gap or abyss, a bit of discontinuity, in between the Founder and Simon/Peter, that the church has filled in, a little missing supplement that the church has supplied? Could it be that the little slash between Simon/Peter has a deconstructive edge on it, that it represents a little gap or discontinuity? Could it be that the Founder, Jesus, is founded, that he has been made or constituted a Founder by those who followed him, so that the Founder is founded by the church which he founded (or did not quite found)? Could it be, once again, that the Origin, the originary foundation, has been deferred? Could it be that we have founded ourselves, that the church has founded itself, that we must assume responsibility for this foundation?

This reversal goes to the heart of Christianity and Catholicism. It is the reversal in which the Proclaimer becomes the Proclaimed, in which the Proclaimer is proclaimed by those to whom he meant only to proclaim something else. The idea behind Jesus's ministry, the exegetes think, was not Jesus but the father, *abba* (which I think a Derridean would [29] recommend we translate as "mother.") He came to give glory to the father who was greater than him. The followers of Jesus however ignored what Jesus had in mind; they did not follow what Jesus taught but began instead to teach Jesus himself, and him crucified. Had the followers of Jesus followed Jesus, there would be no Christianity because Christianity was not Jesus's idea, not what Jesus taught, and it is almost certainly something that, had Jesus lived, we can well imagine he would have opposed. The birth of Christianity depended upon the death of its author, not because he died for our sins and in order to establish his church, but because had he lived he would have opposed the idea of such a church. Christianity is a living example of the need for the hermeneutics of the death of the author and of ignoring the Founder's intentions.

That makes things difficult (which is not always bad), a little devilish, a little discontinuous and undecidable. It brings us back to the missing hook, back on the road to Emmaus, back to the same old problem of trying to find an originary authority, trying to resolve the undecidability of the text on the basis of the authority of the bishop when it turns out that the authority of the bishop is partly the bishop's own idea, that the enabling or authorizing legislation that the bishop invokes was written by the bishop himself. In other words, the originary act, the founding act, the act that authorizes the bishop, is a little violent, a little groundless, marked by a certain discontinuity with the ostensible Founder. The founding act turns out to be a little supplement, derived by prompting the Founder, supplying him with an extra word or two, that covers up the little gap that separates the Founder from the Founded.

It is all a little like the analysis that Derrida makes of the American "Declaration of Independence," or that Lyotard makes of the French "Declaration of the Rights of Man."[19] There is always the question of who authorized the delegates assembled in Philadelphia to speak on behalf of the "people," or in the "name of God," or in the name of Natural Law. Was this insurrection not a little violent, not only in the sense that it was prepared to use violence against the English monarch, but also in the sense that it was not, strictly speaking, authorized? It was a rebellion; it struck out on its own, without enabling legislation. The founding act, the ground, is a little groundless. That is why we hold in continual undecidability what [30] was done in the name of God and what was not. For example, in the case of the American constitution, we are all free to wonder out loud, without being unpatriotic, whether one could, in the name of God, exclude everyone from the sentence "all men are created equal" except white, male landowners.

If theology is always being written from below, if things, including theological things, are steeped in *différance* and undecidability, if the difference between the divine and the human, the theological difference, wavers with the instability of *différance* itself, which is it appears able to seep behind Vatican walls, if the Origin is always deferred, then there seems to be no way to save theology from being constantly bedeviled by Derrida and deconstruction. I say this despite the preemptive strike mounted by the New Testament against Derrida, or more precisely, mounted by Marion's reading of the New Testament, which may be a little idolatrous. When something begins, when something starts *ab initio*, there is always a little gap, a bit of discontinuity, a leap, a certain violence, a "mystical force" in virtue of which the foundation of a thing is a little groundless.[20] Foundations lack enabling legislation because there is at the founding point no legislature (this is the act which brings the legislature about). The ground is groundless and the beginning is violent because the Origin is deferred. The result is that we are forced to found ourselves.

Divine Discontinuity

What, then? What are we to do now? Has everything gone to the devil? I would say there is nothing to do but tell stories. We who are caught up in *différance* – trapped by a misspelling, steeped in *écriture*, following the trace of what has always already withdrawn – we cannot give up our texts. Do not mistake me. I do not consider this an easy task, but very difficult, and I do not take the need to tell stories lightly. It is always a question of telling stories, good stories, the best ones possible, and possible to pit story against story, to see which one wins out, not because of some macho-story telling power of the narratival subject, but because we are struck by the trauma of alterity in a story, by the shock of transcendence, the blow [31] which is invariably delivered by something divine, which is quite other, wholly Other, which I take to mean (hyperbolically) very, very Other.

So I will tell you one of my favorite stories about the "Deconstructor and the Bishop," about a great Deconstructor who was also, it seems, a rabbi, but definitely not a bishop; he was, I wager, a little too devilish for the bishops. The story is called "Before the Law."[21]

> One day a great Deconstructor went up before the Law, and before the Law there were assembled many bishops, in long, beautiful robes, stroking their long, fine beards. The work of the bishops was to watch over the doors of the Law, to determine who would and who would not be granted admittance to the Law. Now there was a man with a withered hand who had been lying there, before the Law, for many years, and the Deconstructor had gone up to see if he could entreat the Law about this man, who was by now quite old and feeble. The man himself had entreated the Law many times before but each time the bishops told him that he should wait until later. When the Deconstructor arrived before the Law the bishops watched him closely, to see whether he would heal the man, because that day it was the sabbath and according to the Law it was not permitted to heal on the sabbath. The Deconstructor looked on the man with the withered hand long and lovingly and then he said to him, "come!" (*viens!*). Then he turned to the bishops and asked them, "Is it lawful on the sabbath to do good or to do harm, to save life or to kill?" The Deconstructor was making a distinction between justice and the law, and he was saying that the Law is deconstructible, but justice in itself, if there is such a thing, is not deconstructible. The sabbath you see is the Law, while the man

337

with the withered hand calls for justice. The bishops were confounded by this question, which [32] seemed to them very cunning, even very diabolic, and they suspected that the Deconstructor was out to destroy the Church and the Law. So they took counsel among themselves. Huddling together in secret council, they wrapped their long robes about themselves, they stroked their long, thin, black Tartar beards, and they looked down their long, sharp noses at the Deconstructor. But after all this conferring among themselves they just looked at the Deconstructor and kept silent. That filled the Deconstructor with sadness and anger, and he grieved at their hardness of heart. "Is this man with a withered hand made for the Law," he asked them, "or is the Law made for this man with a withered hand?" Again they kept silent. They wanted to tell him to wait for another day, to defer this justice, that it might be possible to heal the man some other day. But they remained silent. So the Deconstructor bent down low to the man, who was by now too weak to stand, and said, "Stretch out your hand." Thus it was that the Law was deconstructed and justice, which is not deconstructible, was done. After that day, the Bishops went out and spread the word that the Deconstructor was a danger to the Law, that he meant to destroy the Law and the Prophets and the Church itself.

I commend this story to our reflection on devilish and deconstructionist grounds, as a story that, on my reading – which is a little devilish, a little Derridean, a little Levinasian, a little Kafkaesque, a little Dostoevskyesque, and a little evangelical too – harbors the shock of alterity, the trauma of transcendence, the blow of the divine. It helps us sort through the ambiguous play of traces that fluctuate between the human and the divine in the New Testament. It gives us not a hook but a hint of where the divine alterity is to be found, where it may have left a trace, and of how to go about revising, rereading, reworking the tradition. It and other stories like it have – for me at least, and I commend it to you – the ring (*glas*) of divinity, the echo or the trace of absconded transcendence. The bent limbs of the lame, the withered flesh of the lepers, the deaf and the blind and even the dead: are those not the traces to follow in tracking down the divine retreat (*retrait*)? Are those not the tracks left in an undecidable text which help steer the risky route of this devilish hermeneutics? It is always [33] a little risky, is it not, but is it not a fine risk?[22]

After all, does this man heal by God or by Beelzebub? Who knows? How could we tell?

What is the divine discontinuity, the alterity, the mark of transcendence in the Scriptures? Might it not be found in the contradiction of our freedom, in the appeal for mercy and healing and selflessness? Might it not be found in the astonishing power of God to confound us, to demand that we hold our hand, that we put away our sword, or, contrariwise, that we hold out our hand to help or to heal, that we give what we need for ourselves, to take the bread out of our own mouths? Might not the shock of alterity be found in the capacity of the Scriptures to contradict our aggression and greed, our violence and power, which is *menschliches allzu menschliches*? Might the trace of the divine be found in the points in the Scriptures where our humanity is turned inside out, turned into a substitute for another, disrupting our freedom and self-continuity with the shock of divine discontinuity?

What would Catholicism look like if it were deconstructed down into this divine discontinuity, if it allowed itself to be traumatized by this divine disruption, exposed itself to the disconcertion, the disruption, the deconstruction, the discontinuity, the devilish disturbance?

What would Catholicism look like if it did not confuse itself with God, if it acknowledged the retreat of the divine Origin, the withdrawal of God, and the revisability and contingency of the substitutes upon which we are forced to fall back? What would Catholicism look like if it reflected not the patriarchal structures of the ancient world but the discipleship of equals? What would it look like if the kingdom of God meant the rule of God from the bottom up, from the base community, from the people of God, and not from the top down? What if the presence of Christ in the Church were a function of there being two or three assembled in his name, instead of being mistaken with the vested interests of a self-authorizing hierarchy and of Vatican bureaucrats? What would Catholicism look like if it identified its mission with healing the lame and the leper, [34] with the poorest of the poor? What would Catholicism look like were it to heed the call of the other and lay aside its almost structural homophobia, anti-Semitism, phallocentrism, and Eurocentrism? What would Catholicism look like if it understood that Jesus was a teacher of alterity, of the outcast and despised, not of the white upper middle classes?

The sort of devilishness I have in mind when I speak of the good that deconstruction can do for Catholicism comes down to nurturing the salutary shock of discontinuity, to cultivating the undecidability of the deferred Origin. For what is more worthy of deconstruction than Catholicism, more worth deconstructing? What is more deserving of deconstruction than Catholicism? What deserves it more?[23]

Notes

[1] I will capitalize "Origin" throughout in order precisely to signify something out of reach, preoriginal, always already deferred.

[2] Derrida, "Nombre de Oui," in *Psyché: Inventions de l'autre* (Paris: Galilée, 1987), 639 ff.

[3] Jean Luc Marion, *Dieu sans l'être* (Paris: Communio/Fayard, 1982), chapters 1–2.

[4] Marion, 106 ff.

[5] Marion, 214–218.

[6] Jean-Francois Lyotard, *Le différend* (Paris: Minuit, 1983), chapter 1.

[7] Jacques Derrida, *La verité en peinture* (Paris: Flammarion, 1978), 372–373.

[8] Jacques Derrida, *De la grammatologie* (Paris: Minuit, 1967), 227.

[9] Edward Schillebeeckx, *Jesus: An Experiment in Christology,* trans. Hubert Hoskins (New York: Crossroads, 1985), Part II, Section III, 320–398; on the road to Emmaus story, see p. 341.

[10] Derrida, *De la grammatologie,* 233.

[11] *Summa Theologiae,* Ia, Q.2, a.3, c.

[12] Soren Kierkegaard, *Concluding Unscientific Postscript to the 'Philosophical Fragments'',* trans. Howard and Edna Hong (Princeton: Princeton University Press, 1992), 111-117.

[13] Even that is too simple; women were certainly among the first and most important disciples, Mary Magdalene being the most important among them. But the place of Magdalene and the other women was erased and displaced by the male disciples who took over the new movement. See Elizabeth Schüssler Fiorenza, *In Memory of Her: A Feminist Theological Reconstruction of Christian Origins* (New York: Crossroads, 1986), 323–34.

[14] A paraphrase of Martin Heidegger, *Identität und Differenz* (Pfullingen: Neske, 1957), 71.

[15] The trauma and shock of transcendence – *"le traumatisme de la transcendence"* – is of course the language of Emmanuel Levinas, *Autrement qu'être ou au-delà de l'essence* (Nijhoff: La Haye, 1974), x, *et passim.*

[16] Jacques Derrida, *La carte postale: de Socrate à Freud et au-delà* (Paris: Aubier-Flammarion, 1980), 180.

[17] Schillebeeckx, 752.

[18] Schillebeeckx, 388.

[19] Jacques Derrida, *Otobiographies: L'enseignement de Nietzsche et la politique du nom propre* (Paris: Galilee, 1984), 13–32; Lyotard, *Le différend,* 209–213.

[20] Sec Jacques Derrida, "Force of Law: The 'Mystical Foundation of Authority'," trans. Mary Quaintance, in *Deconstruction and the Possibility of Justice,* eds. Drucilla Cornell et al (New York: Routledge, 1992), 3–67.

[21] I am here running together two famous stories, one from Mark 3:1-6 with Kafka's famous parable *"Vor dem Gesetz"* from *Das Urteil,* upon which Derrida has written in *"Préjugés: Devant la loi,"* in *La faculté de juger,* eds. Jacques Derrida et al. (Paris: Minuit, 1985), 87–140. I am also making use of Derrida, "Force of Law: The 'Mystical Foundation of Authority'," 14–19. The reader will also detect shades of another story, Dostoevsky's "Grand Inquisitor." All of this comes by way of a deconstructionist itch to repeat with a difference.

[22] Levinas, 24. In these final pages, I am, like Levinas, looking for the trace of the divine in the trauma of transcendence, in the call of the other. That is also quite congenial to Schillebeeckx who, after some 600 pages or so of historical-critical study, concludes that it is Levinas who captures the spirit of Jesus; see *Jesus,* 614, 638.

[23] There are of course many other issues to treat beyond the ones that I have raised here, each of which merit a deconstructive look, each of which turns on one sort of binarity or another, e.g.: doctrine vs. "heresy;" the question of the "other" of Catholicism, first of Catholic and non-Catholic and then of Catholic and non-Christian religion; the binarity of Christian and Jew, of Christian, Jew, and Muslim; of a "New" Testament that "supersedes" or inscribes itself over the "Old" one; the question of the ethics of the "other" vis-a-vis the Catholic "natural law" tradition in ethics, which is more Roman than evangelical.

CONVERSATIONS AND
CONTROVERSIES

22

HORIZONAL HERMENEUTICS AND ITS DELIMITATION

[In *Man and World* 19 (1986), 241–251]

On Graeme Nicholson, *Seeing and Reading*, Atlantic Highlands, NJ: The Humanities Press / London: Macmillan Press, 1984. [*SR*] {First presented at the annual meeting of the Society for Phenomenology and Existential Philosophy, Loyola University of Chicago, Chicago, Illinois, October 17, 1985}

[241] Graeme Nicholson's *Seeing and Reading* is one of those books which takes its own good advice. The book argues for the primacy of what Prof. Nicholson calls "material" interpretation, that is, an interpretation which proceeds always with its eye on the *Sache,* the matter for thought. That principle, first enunciated at the beginning of the phenomenological movement by Husserl when he warned us not to be preoccupied with philosophers and philosophies but with the *Sache selbst,* is for me the first principle of all good philosophical writing. And *Seeing and Reading* is first, last and always a piece of philosophizing, carefully stated and nicely argued throughout, to which the considerable erudition in the human sciences of its author is always subordinated. I would say that this is a Heideggerian book; but it is not a book about Heidegger, but about the things themselves, in particular the problem of truth and of truth in interpretation. On this point, I hope that the remarks which follow – if they raise the question of getting "beyond" the standpoint of the book – can at least get as far as the author of *SR* has gotten. I have learned a great deal from this work and I wish to express my gratitude for this contribution.

Let me begin with an unfortunately oversimplified encapsulation of [242] the argument. Prof. Nicholson has written a probing and carefully argued account and defense of a universal hermeneutic, by which I mean one which treats "interpretation" as a universal feature of all human activity. The title itself implies this universalization: seeing, i.e., the whole sphere of perceptual life, and reading, i.e., the whole sphere of the higher-order acts of the understanding, in particular in the human sciences. *Seeing and Reading,* that means, *Perceiving and Understanding.* But the thrust of the "and" in the title is not only to extend the range of hermeneutics, to make it cover two different spheres, but also to point out the interconnectedness of these spheres. Not only is seeing a kind of reading, because it is interpretive, but reading is a kind of seeing, which lets things be seen. The title means "reading *as* seeing" and "seeing *as* reading." Not only are seeing and reading, perceiving and understanding, both interpretive acts, but the structure of one illuminates the structure of the other. Thus the "and" implies the analogy which exists between the two, not their simple conjunction.

The principal issue in *SR,* the *Sache* with which it is concerned, is the question of the truth of interpretation, and its strategy is to show forth the truth of reading on the basis of, and by beginning with, the truth of perceiving (*SR,* 17). Truth in both cases means that something is disclosed, something appears in its truth. And it argues that the three structural, or constitutive, moments in perception – projection, appearance and illumination – are also at work in reading.

Projection. Perceiving is not a blank, disinterested looking-on; rather, it is always guided beforehand by the projective character of the perceiver (as in *Being and Time,* §§31–32). Perception is always directed in advance by a practical, bodily, and linguistic project. We do not simply perceive a pen but we take the pen *as* a pen by taking the pen in hand in the course of a practical task, of hurriedly dashing off a phone number, say.

Appearance. But projection is not enough. If I project, it is the thing itself which appears (*SR,* 71); if I interpret, something is interpreted. In every projection, something appears. To explain this Prof. Nicholson turns now, not to *Being and Time,* but to the later Heidegger's account of the realm of the unconcealed, of the open, which is prior to and not opened up by projection. We enter the Open and there encounter the appearance. If we get into the Open by projection, the thing gets there by appearance (*SR,* 74). Projecting is what we do, appearing is what things do (*SR,* 81). And not only [243] do things appear, but in appearing they also hold themselves back, withdrawing into themselves thereby detotalizing the visual field (*SR,* 97).

Illumination. If projection has to do with the cognitive and epistemological, and appearance has to do with the ontological, then illumination is what mediates between these two. Illumination, which sees to it that projection does not simply project but *reveals,* thus stands at the heart of Prof. Nicholson's claim about the "truth" of perception. In Plato (the classical theory of illumination), the faculty (eye, mind) and the object (visible thing, *eidos*) require light (of the sun, the Good) to make their union possible. But Prof. Nicholson finds a modern counter-part to the classical theory in the Heideggerian notion of the

Lichtung or clearing, which provides a prior sphere of illumination which makes the encounter of projection and appearance possible, which makes it possible for them to make contact. Thus projection reveals only because it is illuminated in advance and the light which it casts upon things is reflected. If the *Lichtung* is the sun, and the object is the thing which is revealed, then Dasein is like the moon (*SR*, 117). The light cast by reflection is a reflected light; projections project, cast light, because they are in advance illuminated.

In the second half of the book, this same triadic structure is enlisted in the service of an account of the higher-order interpretive acts of the human sciences. *Projection.* To read a text is to project a meaning for it, not just any meaning, but one it in fact has. In so doing the interpreter makes the text speak and thus functions as a ventriloquist who projects his own voice upon a text which is otherwise mute.

Appearance. But that raises the question of whether and to what extent anything is disclosed or revealed by the projective interpretation, and what the restraints are upon our readings. It is precisely to address this issue that Prof. Nicholson speaks of the primacy of material interpretation, that is, of a reading of a text in terms of what we know about the *Sache* and of what it discloses for us. (One needs to be musical to understand the history of music, philosophical to understand the history of philosophy, etc.) Taken in conjunction with Heidegger's conception of language as *heissen,* a calling up and summoning of things into presence, "material" interpretation allows us to approach a text in such a way as to experience the rising up and emergence into presence of the things themselves which the text summons, so that the words of the text are indeed *logos* as *legein,* as a certain letting-lie-forth of the matter itself.

[244] *Illumination.* Finally, Prof. Nicholson suggests, the role of "illumination" is played by the Heideggerian-Gadamerian notion of the historicality of the understanding. It is the ongoing process of history, of the changing circumstances of the interpreter, which continually sheds new "light" upon texts so that they can be understood and applied anew, given new sense and new life, but always under the aegis of the *Sache selbst.*

I wish now to offer a critical reaction to this excellent study. Stated in general terms, I am concerned that *SR* resists the genuinely critical impulse in Heidegger's hermeneutics and that it tends to cling both to the more Husserlian moments of *Being and Time* and to the Gadamerian version of the later Heidegger. Its account of "seeing," an ocular metaphor which Heidegger came more and more to distrust, is cast in the Husserlian language of "perception," which is pointedly excluded from *Being and Time,* and of "horizon," which

347

Heidegger would later on abandon. And the account of "reading" is guided by a Gadamerian Heidegger which continues the talk about projection and horizon while resisting the delimitation of horizonality. In my view, the conception of hermeneutics defended in *SR* has been deconstructed by the progressive radicalization of hermeneutics which takes place in Heidegger's later writings. I wish to defend this view by pointing to two elements in *SR* where I think this resistance can be located.

(1) *The Delimitation of Projection.* The early notion of projection is displaced by Heidegger's later analysis of the Open and so cannot be treated as another constituent moment alongside the Open. Accordingly there is no room in Heideggerian hermeneutics for what Prof. Nicholson calls "illumination." Prescinding from the fact that this notion casts Heidegger's thought in the terms of the very metaphysics it sets out to deconstruct, it seems to me that, in *Being and Time,* whatever may be called "illumination" is nothing other than the projection of the Being of beings and the appearance of beings in their Being while, in the later writings, it is nothing other than the Open itself and the arrival of beings in the Open. That means, on the one hand, that there would be no justification in *Being and Time* for saying that projections are illuminated or flooded with light or cast a reflected light. And, on the other hand, it means that in the later writings, once the terms of the account shift to the Open which opens up the space [245] within which things can emerge into presence (what Prof. Nicholson calls appearance), there is (1) no room for a theory of projection, and (2) no need for any additional account of illumination. Even as projection (along with thrownness and fallenness) explains all the illuminating that happens in *Being and Time,* so the Open, or the *Gegnet* explains all the illuminating that happens in the later writings.

In short, the later notion of the Open displaces the early notion of projection, shifting the source of light, as it were, and consigning projection to a mode of representational thinking.[1] Hence, of the three constituents of seeing and reading which *SR* invokes – projection, appearance and illumination – I think that the first is dropped in the more radical and less Gadamerian notion of hermeneutics found in the later writings, and the third is always redundant.

Prof. Nicholson is trying to keep too many balls in the air at once. He wants to hold on to two views at the same time – the earlier more transcendentally oriented view, and the later view which emerges from an "immanent critique" of the residual transcendental elements in *Being and Time.* He thus clings simultaneously to two different views of hermeneutics which I think are incompatible. He is trying to hold on simultaneously to Heidegger and Gadamer.

348

The difficulty I am pointing to can be put, rather simple-mindedly I confess, by following the very images deployed in *SR*. If projection is like the lantern on the miner's hat, and illumination like the sun, then clearly the light of the lantern would be nullified when the miner emerges from the cave into the sun. Holding to a theory of projection *and* a theory of the Open would put one in the position of the man whom Nietzsche describes as walking through the streets at high noon, holding up a lantern and asking, "Where is God?" Again: if the projective understanding of Dasein is like the moon, its light is extinguished when the sun comes out. I would turn this image around and say that projection is indeed like the miner's light, searching and scanning the earth for its reservoirs of energy which the mining industry wants to strip away, while the matter for thought is the movement of the *Seinsgeschick* which has driven the miner to such aggression.[2]

But then why does Heidegger say, in a text which is the focus of a careful analysis by Prof. Nicholson, that human Dasein is *erleuchtet* and *gelichtet*, illuminated and cleared?[3] Heidegger is here arguing that Dasein is itself its own 'there,' that Da-sein *is* its own *da*. There is no other being which illuminates Dasein from the outside: the Being of [246] Da-sein is to be (*zu-sein*) the "*da*," to be it oneself and not to receive it from outside. For Prof. Nicholson this means that "Man is in a *Lichtung* and man *is* a *Lichtung*." (SR, 109). And this he takes to mean that projection both casts a light and receives a light. But to the extent that one insists that Da-sein receives a light in *Being and Time*, one is saying, not that it *is* the there, but that some share of the 'there' has been communicated to it from without. But Heidegger is emphatic here that Da-sein "is" the there (and it is interesting that when this passage is cited in (SR, 109), the italics emphasizing the "is" are omitted). For projection is the way (actually, one of three coequal ways) in which Dasein *is* and *makes* and *clears* the clearing.

I am inclined to think Prof. Nicholson fails to observe the crucial distinction here between man and Da-sein: it is man, this anthropological, innerworldly entity, which is properly illuminated, inside the clearing, flooded with light (and hidden in the dark too). But it is in virtue of the Da-sein in man, whose structure is care and whose meaning is temporality, that anything – whether on the subject side or the object side – is manifest, disclosed or illuminated at all. Hence one must say that Da-sein *is* the clearing and that it is "cleared" *(gelichtet)* only in the sense of being itself self-clearing; and correspondingly that *man* is cleared because of the Dasein in man, and there is no sense in which *man* "is" the clearing. In other words, Heidegger is observing a distinction here between Dasein (the ontological) and man (the anthropological) which functions just the way the distinction between the transcendental and the empirical does in Husserl.

By the same token when we turn to the later writings – in particular to *Gelassenheit* and the "Dialogue with a Japanese" – Heidegger becomes expressly critical of transcendental, horizonal, and hermeneutical thinking and hence of the whole theory of projective understanding. Although Prof. Nicholson gives searching analyses of both these texts, he does not face the issue of the deep *transgression* of horizonal hermeneutic thinking which they contain. Horizonal thinking – which is what Prof. Nicholson means by projection, although he does not use the word (*SR*, 231) – is precisely delimited by the idea of the Open. The horizon is the closing off of the Open, the attempt on the part of human thinking to shrink the Open down to human size. The horizon is but the face which the Open, the *Gegnet,* shows to us, and the task of thought is to get beyond this horizonal delimitation and constriction to the regioning of the region.[4] Region [247] thus does not have the sense of something partial and regional but the sense of the open space, the *freie Weite,* the open expanse in which all horizonal, regional, transcendental structures are carved out and of which they are constrictions. The task of thought is to think the opening of the open, the regioning of the region. And such thinking can no longer be conceived in terms of the projective forestructures of *Being and Time.* There is no question of sketching out in advance, of fore-grasping, fore-seeing and fore-having, which together make up the essence of pro-jection, fore-casting. Now thinking itself must be conceived in terms of openness, of letting-be, of responsiveness to an address.

The Place of Husserl and Gadamer. Part of Prof. Nicholson's concern in all this is to keep the Heideggerian view he is defending clear of the "subjective idealism" of Husserl (*SR*, 117). But I think that is (1) an unfounded concern, for I do not agree that Husserl is a subjective idealist, and (2) an ironic concern, inasmuch as *SR* seems to me in many ways closer to Husserl than to Heidegger. For by its defense of "perception" and "projection," *SR* seems to me to stand by the most Husserlian and transcendental elements in Heidegger and to resist Heidegger's own more radical tendencies. In other words, had Husserl's case been properly stated in *SR,* Prof. Nicholson would have found himself much more in accord with Husserl and the early Heidegger's adaptation of Husserl than he is prepared to admit, which also explains why he is so comfortable with Gadamer's rendering of the later Heidegger. Let me conclude, then, by briefly making this argument.

According to Prof. Nicholson, Husserl does not allow for any objective "affinity" within the manifold itself so that whatever synthetic unities arise in

Husserl's thought are prompted entirely by consciousness. There is nothing about appearances themselves which prompt the synthesis. Rather consciousness is moved from within its own resources to posit, by a logical inference, a unified object. It is only the binding power of the mind which binds the noemata together (*SR*, 94–95).

But Husserl's thought has a considerably more "hermeneutic" bent than that. In the first place, the whole notion that perception is interpretive (construing, *Auffassen*) is Husserlian from its inception, and that is why it turns up in Heidegger. Secondly, Husserl rejects the notion that perception is judgment or inference and maintains a purely [248] perceptual, pre-predicative synthesis upon which judgment and inference are subsequently based. Thirdly, Husserl has a perfectly clear doctrine of "motivation" which consists in saying that consciousness is moved to form just those syntheses and no others as experience gives. The object is precisely the objective correlate of the sequence of experiences in which it is given. And if, for some reason, the *de facto* order of the sequence of experiences should break down, then consciousness would be thrown into chaos, its world gone up in smoke, which is the famous hypothesis of the annihilability of the world. Indeed Husserl is so impressed by the given order of experiences with which we are *de facto* presented that he wonders aloud whether this would not in fact represent the basis of a proof for the existence of God *ex ordine universi*. That is, the order of our experience is so obviously *not* our own doing but a way the things themselves have of falling together harmoniously that we have to wonder whether or not there is a divine governor who has produced all this order (*Ideas I*, §58).

Finally, when Husserl speaks of the "transcendence" of the object, he does so because of our inability to get it totally within our grip. Transcendent things, the things which are *not* inherent parts of the conscious stream, are not only unpredictable in an absolute sense (they are merely presumptive unities), but also elusive, beyond our grip (*tenere*, re- and pro-tention), non-totalizable: we can only get at them adumbratively, partially, perspectivally.

Now I am not interested here in trying to settle the question of the real difference between Heidegger and Husserl, but in the sort of hermeneutics defended in *SR*. And in this regard it is important to see that this difference has to do with the fact that Heidegger openly confessed the need for an existential ontology to guide in advance any discussion of "intentionality," instead of trying to go it alone without any ontological guidance. For Husserl's seeming freedom from presuppositions is an illusion which ends up being subverted from behind, which turns on an ontology of freedom, and so ends up as a thinly disguised way of holding a Cartesian ontology. Heidegger thought it was better to put one's ontological cards (presuppositions) on the table. Hence Heidegger put care in the place of this Cartesian reflexivity, and existential temporality in the place of a recto-linear inner time-consciousness. Thus, as is stated in Heidegger's letter to Husserl of October 1927 (which is noted in *SR*, 267, n. 122), they are agreed about the fundamental difference between the [249] transcendental and the transcendent, but they disagree about the way in which to determine the *Being* of the transcendental.

Now that is why Heidegger never spoke of "perception" (and came to distrust ocular metaphors). He thought that this was a term which belongs to the metaphysics of consciousness. Husserl objected against traditional empiricism that there was in a sense no such thing as "sensations," that these were constructs, contrivances of an abstract empiricism which had lost contact with perceptual life; there is only perceptual experience which is always already interpreted. But Heidegger made the same move on Husserl and argued that in a sense there is no such thing as "perceptions," that these too are constructions, and that in concrete being-in-the-world there are only our dealings (*Besorgen*) with one thing or another. Just to have a perception of something requires a contrived shift out of ordinary being-in-the-world. Whence the thematizing of "perception" in SR is a reversion back towards Husserl and away from *Being and Time*.

In the same way, the insistence on the role of "projection" in *SR* is an attempt to preserve one of the more Husserlian and transcendental elements in *Being and Time* which resists the direction in which the later writings are moving. For in his later writings Heidegger subjected the residual elements of transcendental phenomenology to an impressive critical scrutiny, the end result of which was a radical rethinking of thought in terms of letting-be, and of "hermeneutics" in terms of listening to and heeding the dispatches which are sent our way by the *Seinsgeschick*. His readings of the history of metaphysics became more violent and had less and less to do with any traditional sense of hermeneutics. They remain *sachlich*, to be sure, radically *sachlich*, and they have renounced projection in favor of a deep-seated listening and letting-be.

And that is also why I question the coziness of Heidegger and Gadamer in *SR*. For, seen in the light of the genuine tendency of Heidegger's later writings, the appearance of *Truth and Method* in 1960 seems to me in fact a reactionary development, one which has recourse to the fundamental framework of *Being and Time* and which backs away from the radical impulse which Heidegger's later writings were manifesting. Gadamer has no appetite for the delimitation of horizonal thinking in the direction of the *Gegnet* itself, no taste for the end of metaphysics. He is interested only in the endless perpetuation of the tradition, in a process by which horizon is wedded to horizon [250] in an effort to pass along the valuable contents of the metaphysical tradition. He had no sense that the real *Sache* is left unthought by the tradition, that the happening of the tradition as *a-letheia* and as a play of epochs without why, as the plaything of the child-king, has a darker, more austere, even more ominous side. Gadamer belongs to the metaphysics Heidegger wants to deconstruct but he represents its most extreme "liberalizing" by saying it does not mean just one thing. He is, as Thomas Sheehan recently said about liberal Catholic theologians, the most extreme liberal form of a fundamentally conservative idea. His idea of the "finitude" of the understanding belongs within an implicit metaphysics of the infinite riches of the metaphysical tradition which it is the work of hermeneutics to pass along in a kind of infinite Husserlian task. Again I think that *SR* moves too much in the orbit of Gadamer's Heidegger.

Finally, I should add, there is even some doubt as to whether Heidegger himself carried out this process of radicalization of hermeneutics all the way, and whether the whole "postal economy" of the delivery service run by Hermes is not itself an attempt to subdue *a-letheia* to a metaphysical rule. That is the question which Derrida puts to Heidegger.

But I will close by formulating my question to Graeme Nicholson: how are we to think the delimitation of projective-horizonal- hermeneutical thinking *vis-a-vis* the *Gegnet,* and what does that import for seeing and reading?

Notes

[1] For example, the representational thinking characteristic of modern science is described in "The Age of the World Picture" in terms of "projection," which is said to shut thinking off from the "incalculable." *Gesamtausgabe*, Bd. 5, *Holzwege* (Frankfurt: Klostermann, 1977), 77–79, 95–96; *The Question Concerning Technology and Other Essays*, trans. W. Lovitt (New York: Harper & Row, 1977), 118–20, 136. Later on, in "The Question of Technology," such representational thinking (*vor-stellen*) is said to be the mode of thinking into [251] which modern man is put (*stellt*) by the power of the *Ge-stell*. In other words, such projective, horizonal, representational thinking is the way we are driven and sent by the *Seinsgeschick* to reveal the world, the failure to appreciate which is for Heidegger "the supreme danger." Far from gaining us admission to that Open which "grants," projective thinking precisely "blocks" us off from it and encloses us in the delusion of the primacy of human projects. *Die Technik und die Kehre* (Pfullingen: Neske, 1962), 17–18, 25–26, 32; *Question Concerning Technology*, 18–19, 26, 31–32.

[2] See *Question Concerning Technology*, 14–15.

[3] "*Es [Dasein] ist 'erleuchtet,' besagt: an ihm selbst als In-der-Welt-sein gelichtet, nicht durch ein anderes Seiendes, sondern so, dass es selbst die Lichtung ist.*" *Sein und Zeit*, 10. Aufl. (Tübingen: Niemeyer, 1963), 133.

[4] *Gelassenheit*, 2. Aufl. (Pfullingen: Neske, 1957), 38–42; Eng. trans. *Discourse on Thinking*, trans. John Anderson and Hans Freund (New York: Harper & Row, 1966), 63–67. Cf. *Unterwegs zur Sprache*, 3. Aufl. (Pfullingen: Neske, 1965), 95–101, 120–128, 150–153; Eng. trans. *On the Way to Language*, trans. P.D. Hertz (New York: Harper & Row, 1971), 9–12, 228–34, 51–53.

23

HERMENEUTICS AND FAITH: A RESPONSE TO PROFESSOR OLTHUIS

[In *Christian Scholars Review* 20 (December 1990), 164–70]

[164] I am grateful to Prof. Olthuis for the attention he has paid to *Radical Hermeneutics* (hereafter "RH"), for the appreciative rendering he has made of my argument, and for the questions he raises which go right to the heart of the matter.[1] My sense is that there is a more deep set agreement beneath our disagreements and it interests me very much to try to clarify both our convergence and our divergence.

Olthuis and I are on the tracks of a similar sort of thing, namely a version of postmodern hermeneutics which does not simply jettison every notion of truth, self, ethics, and – we can add here – faith, but rather situates these notions within the radical constraints that postmodern analyses bring out; in short, a version of postmodernism which has not lost its mind – or its nerve. That is why I kept the notion of "hermeneutics" in the title of my book and put "deconstruction" in the subtitle, and it is why I put "hermeneutics" in the nominative position and made "radical" the modifier. I am interested in radicalizing hermeneutics, pushing it as far as it can go, without pushing it right out the window. Hermeneutics for me is always set squarely within the difficulty of life. Hermeneutics is bent on describing the situation of "factical life," the incessant flow of concrete existence, the urgent summons by which we are constantly visited in our daily lives. There are always already decisions to be made, promises to keep, and miles to go before we sleep. When Heidegger first introduced the term "hermeneutics" in his early Freiburg lectures, he spoke of the "hermeneutics of facticity," which meant that hermeneutics is an effort on the part of life itself to take stock of the cares and troubles of everyday, factical life. However far down the road of deconstruction RH has gone, RH belongs in the wake of that earliest Heideggerian program.

The more Derridean way to put what I am up to in RH is to say that radical hermeneutics describes the conditions of possibility *and impossibility* of our everyday beliefs and practices. Both together, not one without the other.

Postmodern hermeneutics shows that the very thing which makes our daily lives possible – in Derrida's case, *différance* – also and in the same operation makes them impossible, [165] that is, sees to it that the system cannot close, that there are always loose ends, that the fragility, contingency, and deconstructibility of our most favored notions are quite inescapable. This style of hermeneutics does not simply jettison the assumptions of everyday life; it does not simply debunk our beliefs and practices or laugh them off the stage. It shows the "difficulty" which besets them, the "undecidability" in which they are "always already" engulfed.

Accordingly, Olthuis and I share a number of broad concerns. We favor a postmodernism which does not simply throw reason to the four winds (whence the uncharacteristic discussion of science in RH). We seem very much agreed that there is an interesting ethical twist in postmodernism whose turn towards the marginalized and excluded represents a suggestive similarity with a biblical ethics of mercy towards the outcast and with contemporary liberation theology. We are agreed on the need to go beyond a dominantly Gadamerian version of hermeneutics, which we both take to lack real bite when it comes to criticizing the violence of the tradition process.

But Olthuis thinks I have allowed myself to be bitten too deeply by a Derridean bug and that that skews what is otherwise the salutary direction taken by *Radical Hermeneutics*. Much of what Prof. Olthuis complains about in RH has to do with what he must regard as a creeping Derrideanism, which, as he thinks, "debunks the idea and reality of any trustworthy tradition, any ultimately trustworthy truth – and even perhaps any final hope." At that point, I think he is repeating a familiar misunderstanding of Derrida which is common to philosophers, theologians and literary critics alike. I should like to clear that misunderstanding up and in so doing make a start on clearing the name of RH, which seems to leave Prof. Olthuis with a sense of Godless despair.

Prof. Olthuis subscribes to the notion that Derrida is enamored of a "purely intra-linguistic" play of signs that frolic out of control and that have lost all contact with the world. He seems to think that for Derrida there is no "other" of language, whereas Derrida would say that everything he has written is concerned precisely with the other of language.[2] Furthermore, Olthuis mistakenly identifies *différance* with language. Linguistic signs are but a single case of *différance,* i.e., of the differential spacing that makes any meaningful system of signs im/possible. It is clear, from Derrida's account of Mallarme's mime – who "writes" (in the sense of archi-writing) with his body – that the "gesture" also is made possible by the differential distribution of hand, arm, face, etc.[3] The same is true of architecture as the play of spaces, as the spacing of space, in which Derrida is quite interested, and music, as the play or spacing of sound and rhythm, and so on.

Again, *différance* is not meant to be a "creative word" (on an analogy with God) and it is neither creative nor recreative. If anything, it is in the middle voice, [166] as Derrida says quite explicitly.[4] It neither creates the world, like Olthuis's creative Spirit/Word, nor reproduces it, like a Lockean idea inscribed on a blank tablet. *Différance* means that a single element (a mark, or idea, or gesture, or sound, or belief, or practice, or whatever you need) cannot function alone, that it functions only in differential spacing from the other elements with which it belongs. There is a principled entanglement of element with element, binding them among themselves in such a way that the "subject" cannot simply "intend" one element and not the rest. The subject cannot simply, by an intentionalist fiat, cut the rest of the chain loose and try to dominate the system by sheer "intentional" force, by its sheer will or *vouloir dire*. That is a "chain," a constraint, a passivity. But at the same time *différance* means the endless innovativeness, the novelty of endlessly new "connections," and that is liberating, disseminative, "active." So it is active/passive, creative/chained, in the middle voice. But *différance* does not "do" anything or have anything done to it. It supplies the condition of (im)possibility within which "agents" do things and "patients" have things done to them and by which each gets entangled in the other.

Différance is not, therefore, the analogate to Prof. Olthuis's Spirit/Word, nor should it be expected to be any part of or make any contribution to a "cosmology." It is, if Derrida is on to something here, the condition of im/possibility for Prof. Olthuis to speak of his Christian faith in a Spirit/Word, or to have a cosmology; even as it does the very same favor for those who reject Christian faith or have never heard of it.

This debate is somewhat confused, I have to confess, because Prof. Olthuis cites one of my earliest pronouncements about Derrida (his notes 9, 32), in which I shared then some of his present complaints about deconstruction, but which I would now, frankly, retract as a misunderstanding. That makes things awkward. Suffice it to say that these confusions have beset some of North America's finest minds! I started out trying to defend hermeneutics from Derrida and ended up radicalizing hermeneutics with the help of Derrida.

A good deal of RH was devoted to bringing Derrida into play with Heidegger and hence to giving deconstruction a hermeneutic twist. The middle term in that project is "mystery." On my accounting, the play of *différance* is made to intersect with the mystery of withdrawal, at least insofar as it describes the situation in which "we" – we who cannot say we, who do not make up that

357

much of a community – are all commonly located, the fix we are in, the constraints under which we labor. The more difficult things get under the cut of the Derridean stylus, the more fractured and ruptured are our lives, to use the buzzwords of the day, the more it seems to me to bring out the fundamental (Heideggerian) "questionability" of our days and works. "Who are we?" – we who are troubled by the words "we," "are," and even "who," we who have made so much trouble for ourselves by problematizing our most deep set and instinctive convictions and beliefs? What can we know? What ought we to do? In what can we hope? What is [167] going on? Derrida shows us that there is a kind of drift or slippage in our most favored structures (that's what deconstruction does to/for us) – which sends a tremor through our lives (that's the hermeneutic twist). Brought together, made to intersect and overlap, they constitute a more radicalized hermeneutic).

To see the hermeneutic twist I put on deconstruction, let us take the example of the famous deconstruction of the "subject," the result of which is the notorious "decentered subject" which has scandalized so many good citizens of Alanbloomsburg, USA. Postmodernists generally and deconstructionists in particular argue quite relentlessly, and with no little success, that "subjectivity" is very much the "effect" of grammar, history and the unconscious – in a (non)word, of *différance* (since Nietzsche, Heidegger and Freud are identifiable sources of Derrida's [non]idea). Now in RH that argument is taken to be the latest version of an old idea which has found multiple expression over the centuries, but which I chose to emblematize with Augustine's *quaestio mihi factus sum:* I have been made a question to myself. Deconstruction tends to throw "my life" (ultimately, deconstruction would make you put *everything* in scare quotes) into a kind of deep questionability which constitutes a good deal of what we mean by the "self" in a very Kierkegaardian sense. In *The Sickness Unto Death* Kierkegaard described the self as a relation which relates itself to itself, as a being which is related to itself in the mode of making itself questionable, or (to use the early Heidegger) of making things difficult for itself. This very questioning of the subject, putting the subject into question, exposing it to the possibility that it is subverted from behind, blindsided by forces over which it has no final control, is the very constitution of the self in the very Augustinian and Kierkegaardian sense that I favor. What Heidegger, Derrida, and RH (trailing along in their wake) have given up for "lost" is a Cartesian or strong transcendental self which makes everything turn on an integral, constituting subject. But that loss of an over-epistemologized illusion I count as a gain of a factical self which has been restored to its original difficulty.

Still, Prof. Olthuis is himself troubled that I give so much play to this troubled, divided self, or generally to the issue of the "mystery" of things, to the "concealment" which envelops us. The "God of creation is inherently revealing," according to Olthuis, and because "Caputo refuses to accept that truth is possible," he (me) makes it impossible for us (you) to "rest" in the healing love of God. Olthuis is willing to grant that our lives are very much in the grip of an enveloping play and that things can get pretty stormy. But his idea is "to play out our lives in fear and trembling" – he will give RH that much, but then he adds – "for it is God who is at play in us."

Maybe. Maybe not.

RH is not out to silence that sort of faith, or to excommunicate it from the society of postmodernists; actually it is inching towards a postmodern account *of* faith. RH does not "refuse to accept that truth is possible," or dogmatically deny it, which would indeed be a kind of "reverse autonomy." It simply wants to reinsert the coefficient of "undecidability" which attaches to our beliefs and practices, to see to it that we do not, as Kierkegaard warns, take ourselves to belong to the church triumphant while we are still paying our dues to the church [168] militant, or to give it a Derridean twist: that faith is always through a *glas* darkly, a glassy glaze. Faith is a certain *hermeneusis,* a way to construe our experience. No man (or woman) has seen God (and lived to tell it). God is a spirit. Faith is a reading we have put on things, which "sees" (reads) a certain benignity behind an awful lot of malignity, which sees (reads) a gentle hand in the midst of considerable violence.

The thing is to see that undecidability does not, as Olthuis mistakenly supposes, "give up on truth," Undecidability is not indecision, not the opposite of decision, but the condition of im/possibility of decision. The undecidability which invades things sees to it that the hermeneutic situation is never quite clear, that it is beset by a kind of principled ambiguity, which means, as Kierkegaard says, that "deliberation" will never end, never reach a "resolution." (Otherwise a computerized "expert system" can make the decision for you. "Undecidability" is just a very good argument against the formalizability of the hermeneutic situation.) The resolution is reached only in the resolving, in the leap, beyond thought into action, for there are always miles to go before we sleep. It is the undecidability which *requires* the decision.

The undecidability antedates the decision, invades the decision during the act, and remains in place afterwards. That is why Kierkegaard, in one of the four scenarios at the beginning of *Fear and Trembling,* has Abraham coming down the mountain afterwards thinking that he sinned because he was at least willing to take his son's life. (And there's a pretty good argument for that gloss.

An old Jewish midrash on the story has it that God *was* testing Abraham, but he failed the test; he should have known better.) Abraham was faced with a *hermeneusis*; he had to decide how to take that voice, how to construe it. And the undecidability of his choice cut all the way down. There is no point at which the believer gets outside the flux, cuts through the veil of appearances, gets behind the *glas*/glass.

The whole point of the concluding two chapters of RH was not to rule faith out of court but to put it back into the flux, to situate it within the hermeneutic situation, to chain it together with its binary opposite, with a Nietzschean celebration of the death of God. Augustine and Nietzsche are emblematic in RH of a binarity from which we cannot escape, a fluctuation which makes faith (and faithlessness) tremble. Faith occurs *in* the fluctuation between a notion of a loving God and an impersonal cosmic play. We do not get free from that fluctuation, not unless we find some way to escape history, embodiment, linguisticality, the unconscious – or whatever else the post-deconstructionists and post-postmodernists of the future come up with to further humble our badly battered sense of autonomy and transcendental egos.

Indeed religious faith gets to be quite dangerous, and even quite bloody (and Kierkegaard is keenly sensitive to this in *Fear and Trembling*, that this is a religious practice which calls for spilling blood) when it lack undecidability. When people think they have gotten beyond the veil of appearances, when they take it that they have been granted an immediate "revelation", in an uncritical, undeconstructed sense of revelation, revelation without mediation, when they feel themselves inspired, pronounce themselves infallible, anoint themselves chosen, when they [169] announce that they speak the unmediated words of God (or of Being) – without the undecidability, without the *hermeneusis,* without the mediation – then the rest of us are usually visited with the most massive and oppressive mediations. The best thing the rest of us can do – we who speak and write from below and who have our doubts about being chosen – is beat a hasty retreat before the blood starts flowing.

So religion is a *hermeneusis* but the *hermeneusis* requires *hermeneusis*. There are many faiths and many versions of the same faith and we cannot stop this disseminative drift (which does not condemn us to indecision but elicits choice). So we need some help, a guideline, a way to approach the question of faith. That is where the hermeneutics of suffering comes in. I did everything I could in RH to make it plain that I see faith in terms of suffering, that suffering is a kind of abyss for me, a darkening of our world which faith seeks to "construe." (For Nietzsche – who in RH represents the sharpest and most insightful antagonist to this approach to faith – suffering need not and cannot be construed, for that is inherently cowardly; it need and must only be "affirmed" as a part of the wheel of becoming.) Faith seems to me first and foremost faith in a power who stands by the oppressed, who takes its stand with those who have no power, those who are ground under by power (or sometimes even just by misfortune). Faith reads the face of suffering; it is a *hermeneusis* of suffering. Nietzsche thinks that suffering is innocent, that it is part of the package which comes along with having a body. The believer thinks that Nietzsche supplies a very comforting line to those whose comfort is bought at the expense of the suffering of the poor and oppressed. The more the poor think their suffering is part of the wheel of becoming, the better those whose prosperity depends upon this order of rank like it. That is why I find religion at its best in the struggle of the Church in Latin America, in the work of the liberation theologians, and it is just the point (as I thought I made plain in RH) where religion has the goods on Nietzsche. Furthermore (to take a shot which has opportunely arisen) the more the Vatican or right wing American fundamentalists condemn or even attempt to silence this work, the more they reenact "The Legend of the Grand Inquisitor" (Dostoevsky).

Olthuis and I are very much together on this point. Christian faith turns on the figure of Jesus stretching out his hand to the leper or defying the Sabbath laws in order to heal the withered hand. I see in postmodernism, or in certain versions of it, notably in Derrida and Levinas, where there is an explicit concern for the outcast and marginalized, a resonance with this biblical ethics of mercy. Olthuis seems to agree with me on that.

Olthuis has however jumped the gun in the last pages of his study when he heaps upon me a lot of godless despair, skepticism, denial, and giving up on truth. He sounds a little triumphalist to me at times, though that is not the dominant tenor of the piece, and he occasionally reminds me of Kierkegaard's analogy for the state of contemporary Christians. Christians today have confused the church militant, to which we all still belong, with the church triumphant, to which we have not yet gained entrance. That, says Johannes Climacus, is like an army lined up for battle which, before firing a shot, declares itself the winner and then [170] marches home in triumph.[5] I have the same sense about the concluding sections of this paper. Olthuis seems to have declared himself the winner, to be already composing his victory songs, to have seen the light, to have experienced a revelation which has expunged the darkness, to "know" something the rest of us do not. As for myself, I am, like Johannes Climacus, still trying to get as far as faith, to fight the good fight, to figure out the story of Abraham, to see through a *glas* darkly. We are neither inside nor outside faith, or revelation, or God. For every moment of the "dark and dangerous play" which reads like "God's play with us," there is an Auschwitz or a Hiroshima, a killing field somewhere, in South Africa or South America, which silences God's voice, darkens his aspect, and exposes the trembling in/of faith.

What there is for me, and this is what for me gives the guide to the perplexed, are the works of human mercy and the faith that they are backed up by something which outstrips us. That I believe is what Jesus called the kingdom and what he meant when he invoked the name of his *abba* whose love was, as he thought, deployed everywhere, disseminated to the most lowly quarters of the kingdom. But that is a faith which is confessed and professed against the background of Zarathustra's laughter, that the killing fields are all part of a great cosmic play, that the cosmos does not know we are here, and does not care.

The point of RH was neither to preclude nor to include faith but to describe the hermeneutic situation within which faith – or for that matter any other fundamental resolution – takes place. The idea behind RH is not to close something off before it gets off the ground but to insist upon the constraints under which we labor whenever we commit ourselves down one path or another. RH was written with a certain circumspection about Christian faith in particular because it was directed at a primarily philosophical audience. There was no need to add to the scandal of a book which was already scandalizing professional philosophers by having invoked the names of Heidegger and Derrida. I have in other places,[6] however, been somewhat more explicit about the implications of this book for Christian faith, and I will be even more so in a forthcoming work which I plan at the moment to entitle *Sacred Anarchy*. This work will take the story of healing the withered hand – the openness of Jesus to the unclean, to repeat the excellent observation of Hauerwas cited by Olthuis – as the paradigm of an anarchy and transgression of a radically salutary sort which has an interesting postmodern twist.

Notes

[1] In the June 1990 issue of the *CSR,* James Olthuis posed the question, "A Cold and Comfortless Hermeneutic or a Warm and Trembling Hermeneutic," subtitling his essay "A Conversation with John D. Caputo." Here John D. Caputo responds, correcting some misperceptions but also finding a great deal of common ground between himself and Olthuis. Mr. Caputo teaches philosophy at Villanova University.

[2] See in particular the interview with Derrida "Deconstruction and the Other" in which Derrida clearly, perhaps even impatiently, sets his readers straight on this point, in *Dialogues with*

Contemporary Continental Thinkers, ed. Richard Kearney (Manchester: Manchester University Press, 1984), 107–125.

[3] Jacques Derrida, *Dissemination,* trans. Barbara Johnson (Chicago: University of Chicago Press, 1981), 194–203.

[4] Jacques Derrida, *Margins of Philosophy,* trans. Alan Bass (Chicago: University of Chicago Press, 1982), 8–9.

[5] Soren Kierkegaard, *Philosophical Fragments,* trans. H. Hong and E. Hong (Princeton: Princeton University Press, 1985), 108.

[6] See "Beyond Aestheticism: Derrida's Responsible Anarchy," *Research in Phenomenology,* 18 (1988): 59-73 [also in *The Essential Caputo: Selected Writings*, ed. B. Keith Putt (Bloomington, IL: Indiana University Press, 2018), 184-194. –Ed.]; "Presidential Address: Radical Hermeneutics and the Human Condition," *Proceedings of the American Catholic Philosophical Association,* 61 (1988), 2–15. [see ch. 4, above –Ed.]

24

DECONSTRUCTING INSTITUTIONS: A REPLY TO DAUENHAUER

[In *Human Studies,* Vol. 14, No. 4 (1991), 331–337]

[331] Bernard Dauenhauer is a careful and reflective philosopher from whose writings, in particular from *Silence* (1980) and *The Politics of Hope* (1986), those of us who work in the continental tradition have all profited. I am therefore very grateful for the attention he has given to *Radical Hermeneutics* (hereafter "RH") and happy to respond to his criticisms.

But I am also troubled, for just these reasons, by the reading he has given to RH, by the way he has lined it up with an irresponsible and reckless anti-institutionalism, with a contempt of tradition, with a kind of futile and pointless anarchy. He attributes to RH views which are rejected there and recommends in rebuttal views which are espoused in RH. Perhaps Dauenhauer has been misled by the rhetoric of RH, by its flip and insouciant tone, and that is my responsibility. Or perhaps he seriously misunderstands deconstruction or anything that makes use of deconstruction.

Let me say in a general way something about deconstruction, both as it is used in RH and – I am convinced of this and I could demonstrate it had I the space – the way Derrida uses it. Deconstruction is and means to be mettlesome, difficult, itchy, an impudent troublemaker, rather the way Socrates was; the Socratic comparison in RH is to be taken seriously. But deconstruction is not to be confused with outright destruction, razing, obliterating, or knocking down – of institutions, structures, traditions, texts, or ethical standards. Above all, it is not to be confused with irresponsibility. Indeed, as Derrida (1983a; 1983b; 1987) has recently been saying, deconstruction is profoundly responsible and profoundly affirmative. It proceeds from a deep sense of responsibility to those who are excluded by the prevailing powers, and that is what gives it its ethical twist. It makes a profound and deep "yes" to language and to life, to politics and to justice, to universities and to institutions, which is why so politically minded an institution as the New School for Social Research very properly awarded Derrida an honorary degree in 1989. Deconstruction operates in the service of social and political structures precisely by refusing to permit them to [332] "disambiguate," to use Dauenhauer's term – there is an instructive connection between "ambiguity" in Merleau-Ponty and Derrida's "undecidability" (Gasché, 1979) – to become something less than they are, to harden into immobile identities, to close down. Deconstruction resists closure, closing down, closing off, and aims at openness, opening new possibilities, innovation and novelty.

That is why I connected deconstruction in RH with a Kierkegaardian repetition which repeats *forward,* which forges ahead, producing something new. But this affirmation is never an *ex nihilo* creation but always a "repetition" which begins in the factical situation in which one finds oneself. It "repeats with a difference;" it alters and innovates upon inherited materials. It affirms with a difference; it begs to differ. So if one speaks, within a deconstructive framework, of a "revolution" that means a reconfiguration of existing structures not a pure new start. That is why I described a Kuhnian scientific revolution as "a certain free play of scientific rationality, a free repetition of possibilities *which the old system harbored,* a creative *transformation* of *old* signs – let us even say, a releasing of the signs which make up *the old system.*" (RH 219, emphasis added)

The idea behind deconstruction, and of my use of deconstruction in RH, is to keep systems, institutions, structures of any sort, literary or political, to keep them all *open,* by showing that they can close only at their own peril and only by a kind of violence. We begin where we are, in the existing factical situation, with the inherited traditions and structures in which we find ourselves and start from there. That is why Derrida has recently been speaking about "democracy" which is the political structure par excellence of modernity (Derrida, 1986; 1988). Modern democracy was something to which Heidegger was never able to reconcile himself and this vitiates his account of the history of metaphysics, for the darkest night of subjectivism initiated by Descartes is also the epoch of democracy, which does not at all seem like the concealment of Being to us. Democracy is also the political structure par excellence of postmodernity, for postmodernity means to extend the theory of democracy, but without the Enlightenment metaphysics of the autonomous subject. Accordingly, the deconstructionism of RH means to be a contribution to a theory of democracy because democracy is supposed to keep the doors open to the *demos,* those whom Plato, Nietzsche and Heidegger considered the worst, the smelliest, the most thoughtless. The deconstructionism of RH takes the side of just this "worst" element, which is also its (RH's) religious twist (to which Dauenhauer seems to object). For, as Nietzsche pointed out, the "slave revolt" (= democracy) in modernity represents the triumph of Judeo-Christian ethics, the

366

difference being that Nietzsche thought this was an objection to Christianity instead of one of its finer contributions.

[333] Deconstruction resists closure; it acts like the gadfly which keeps inherited structures from becoming the great sleeping steed towards which they drift. It is not against institutions but for them, for their forward repetition, their ongoing incessant reform. Its aim is to keep them honest and to let them know just what they are excluding, oppressing, erasing, forgetting, normalizing, regulating into oblivion. Institutions resist dissent, plurality, reform, the irregular, the different, the abnormal. They tend to have an inflated sense of their own power and importance, to think they have ahistorical authority, that they have dropped from the sky. Deconstruction is a philosophy of institutions which is intent on subverting such tendencies in institutions, on deflating their sense of being irreformably in the right, on holding institutions open to what they want to close off, to their other.

If you want to translate that into concrete politics, beyond saying it is a contribution to democratic theorizing – which I did not even try to do in RH, but which it might be well at least to adumbrate here – I would say that I think that the effect of the massive power exerted by capitalist, socialist and advanced technological "systems" over social and political "institutions" in both the East and the West has been to put power before people, not to give power to people. These enormous and insidious powers require resistance, reform, and – if we are lucky – outright revolution, which, *mirabile dictu,* has recently been happening in the Soviet Union and eastern Europe. In the United States, where we have long been favored with liberal, democratic institutions, I think a comparable but different revolution is required, and on at least three fronts: against the widening gap between the poorest and wealthiest Americans and against the politics of greed advocated by the Reagan and Bush administrations; against a foreign policy which favors the most oppressive right wing dictatorships in Latin America and South Africa, which refuses to recognize the rights of Catholics in Northern Ireland and of homeless Palestinians; and finally against ecological practices which are relentlessly destroying the earth in order to feed capitalist greed and maintain a high level of technological comfort for a small part of the world's population. "Oh my fellow democrats, there are no democrats" (Derrida, 1988). Democracy is still to come.

I think that Dauenhauer is willing to concede many of these criticisms of institutional life, and he might even share some of these political views, but he thinks that I (and Derrida) both go too far and do not see the rest of the story. So let the word go forth: I do not, and Derrida does not, believe that institutions do no good, but rather that they should do more good. Derrida is to be credited

367

with have "founded" a most notable and innovative educational institution – the *College internationale de philosophie* – and has been involved in educational reform in France for two decades. I myself have [334] taught at the same institution for over two decades, have and continue to serve it happily in numerous positions, am actively involved in the pluralist reform of the American Philosophical Association, and have tried to do a little pluralizing too of the American Catholic Philosophical Association. I thought all of this was plain enough in RH, on a theoretical level, and that I had taken sufficient precautions against the sort of reading Bernard Dauenhauer gives me, which I could imagine and foresee and which I tried to forestall. Evidently not hard enough. Let me therefore correct, in a purely textual way, some of Dauenhauer's most serious misimpressions of the text of RH.

Dauenhauer thinks I have taken an anarchistic position, and in a sense I have, but only in the sense that the *demos* reject *hier-arche*, in the sense thus of a "responsible anarchy" (Caputo, 1988), i.e., one which tries to "respond" to all those who tend systematically to be ground up by the ruling *arche*, which is why Derrida has been writing rather a lot in recent years about "responsibility." But Dauenhauer thinks and says repeatedly that RH shows no sense of responsibility, that it simply rejects any and every *arche*, that is a blindly defiant, subversive opponent of whatever happens to be in place, whether or not it does any good at all, that RH is downright dangerous. He accuses RH of advocating an empty, formalistic defiance, which simply opposes whatever institution is in place, which arbitrarily favors what is out of favor, whatever the substantive merits of either. He says RH is disappointed Cartesianism; that it sees no value in sorting through non-absolutist positions for the best and most sensible alternatives; that RH implies that everything is guilty; that no institution is any better than another, that it advocates revolution "lest there be order;" that it cannot discriminate between hurt and harm, or good citizens and scoundrels; that it is against durable success, leaves us irremediably helpless, does not see that traditions contain elements both of knowledge and ignorance (and so on). In short RH "disambiguates" institutional and political life. Because they are not perfect, all structures must go, and in their place, RH puts an anarchism which holds that "anything goes."

Against such a misrepresentation of RH, I offer the text of RH which precisely and explicitly *rejects* the ir-responsible anti-politics and anti-institutionalism described by Dauenhauer (un-qualified op-position goes against the grain of a theory of "undecidability"). The "ethics of dissemination," I said:

368

is not opposed to institutional organization or the notion of community. It *requires* rather the hardiness (*virtus*) to keep them mobile, in motion, flexible, in flux, reformable, repeating forward. It does not deny that institutional organization is usually the way that things get done, that we tend by a natural momentum to organize our practices along systematic [335] lines. The role of an ethics of dissemination is *only* to keep such organizations honest, to stay on the alert to their equally "natural" tendency, once established, to resist alteration, to suppress and normalize... (emphasis added) (RH 263).

Then I criticize Foucault for a reductionistic rejection of institutions as simple power plays, for "disambiguating" institutions, for failing to recognize that institutions are compounded of *both* prudence *and* violence, which is, if I may say so, exactly what a theory of undecidability implies. I might add that Dauenhauer's criticisms seem to me to come closer to the mark when they are directed at Foucault, who inspires Schürmann's appropriation of Heidegger, than at Derrida, who inspires mine, although both views are left-ish, post-modern, and in some sense which needs careful delineation an-arch-ish. Derrida is much more attentive to issues of ambiguity and has a much more affirmative sense of what institutions are about than Foucault. After the remark on Foucault, I add:

> The function of an ethics of dissemination is not to try to level all institutional arrangements or discourage the formation of new ones – we have seen Derrida's interest in the university – but to *intervene* in ongoing processes, to keep institutions in process, to keep the forms of life from eliminating the life-form they are supposed to house. It means to...practice the Socratic art, to be a gadfly and sting ray – but always in the *polis*. There is no human life outside the polis.... The ethics of dissemination operates only in a community and in the ongoing conversation of mankind. (RH 263)

I conclude this particular section by saying that RH "takes its stand with those for whom the system was *not* designed – women, children, the mad, the ill, the poor, blacks, the religious and moral minorities...." (RH 263-264). I do not, and Derrida does not, think for a moment that women or Black people would be better served by flat out knocking institutions down. I thought it was completely obvious that I was proposing opening institutions up, reforming, remaking and altering them, so that they will begin to include those whom they exclude. I take this to be a postmodern extension of democratic theory, not an unambiguous, decidable and classical anarchism.

I leave it to the reader to decide whether RH advocates an anarchistic anti-institutionalism and anti-politics or whether Dauenhauer has a preconceived idea about deconstruction. (On this point, let me add that I do not really use the word deconstruction all that often when I speak in my own name. I prefer the notion of a "radicalized hermeneutics" because "hermeneutics" always means the concrete (factical, hermeneutical) situation in which we must think and act.)

Dauenhauer furthermore thinks that even when RH shows any sense at [336] all, when however begrudgingly it admits that we need order and institutions and that we ought to promote flourishing and diminish suffering, RH ends up delivering bromides about suffering and that it cannot even distinguish hurt from harm. Now that too is an objection I saw coming and which I thought I had cut off:

> Now it can be objected that all of this evades the real question: just what systems in particular are crushing us? Do not systems which seem to *hurt* now in the long run liberate? And how do we intervene when we want to? (emphasis added)

That is, I know what we teach in our "Intro" courses, but I have an idea that the usual way of doing business does not work:

> But my whole point has been to deny that there are such general formulae and to take the steam out of the heady pursuits which they inspire. I distrust the whole idea of "the answer," and I take it that I have said enough to put the idea of "the answer" into question. If I have argued anything, it is that addressing our sociology is ultimately a matter of getting down to cases, of getting a lot of heads together – specialists and nonspecialists, perpetrators and victims, dreamers and pragmatists, professionals and amateurs (which means lovers) – and letting them hammer something out for the time being, which may even last quite a while – to their surprise. (RH 264)

I deny that there are universals which will be of much help in the concrete, for before the fact they are vacuous and after the fact we have the advantage of hindsight. That is quite clear from the whole debate about "values" in science (consistency, accuracy, etc. cf. RH 218 ff.) Such values are of no help before the fact, when dealing with a scientific anomaly. They get to be important only in the writings of the epistemologists whose expertise is to shed light after the fact on a situation which baffled them and everybody else when the hard decisions had to be made. Where were the epistemologists when we needed them?

The most one can hope for in dealing with the ethical and political befuddlements which continually surround us is pluralistic "conversation," some theory of which is to be found in such diverse thinkers as Rorty, Habermas, Bernstein, Gadamer and Levinas, in which "we" (but I want to be *very* vigilant about that word which can be massively exclusionary) try to hammer out the best solution to the problem at hand.

I have the strongest sense that there is no ideal solution and the strongest sense that it really does depend on which problem and whose hand we are talking about. I think we aim at solutions which will be the best we can come up with under the circumstances, which may or may not be a very lasting solution – and if they do *last* we will be both surprised and *delighted* [337] – but which will have the merit of involving as many voices as possible. I clearly advocate the idea that some views are better than others and that we are more likely to find them by open ended conversation, and that whatever "it" is we need, will be very much a function of the hermeneutical context. I conceive this approach to be quite close to Merleau-Ponty's notion (cited by Dauenhauer) of "inventing what will later appear to have been required by the times."

I have described RH elsewhere, borrowing a term from Derrida, as a kind of "pragrammatology" because I have a deeply pragmatic conception of truth as what promotes human flourishing and diminishes suffering, as capable of arising in the most unlikely places, and a deep distrust of the danger of unbending, unyielding verities.

Dauenhauer thinks, remarkably enough, that this is Cartesian despair, anything goes, disregard of context, disambiguating anarchism. He thinks it is "dangerous" and "irresponsible." But if there is any objection to what I have said here it is not Dauenhauer's but the one I get from my more postmodern friends, viz., that RH has here come very close to advocating Habermas's ideal speech situation, that at this point radical hermeneutics is almost a theory of communicative rationality. I am much more concerned with that objection, which proceeds from taking seriously what I say here, than with Dauenhauer's objections which simply misstate my views.

I leave it to the reader to decide whether Dauenhauer has paid attention to the way my views are qualified and nuanced in RH, whether he has portrayed them accurately, or whether he has dismissively "disambiguated" them because he can see no good coming from deconstruction.

I think that the real discussion between Dauenhauer and me can only begin after this bramble of misrepresentation has been cleared away.

References

Caputo, J. (1988). "Beyond aestheticism: Derrida's responsible anarchy." *Research in Phenomenology* 18: 59–73 [also in *The Essential Caputo: Selected Writings*, ed. B. Keith Putt (Bloomington, IL: Indiana University Press, 2018), 184-194. –Ed.].

Derrida, J. (1983a). "MOCHLOS ou le conflit de facultés." *Philosophie* 2: 21–53.

Derrida, J. (1983b). "The principle of sufficient reason: The university in the eyes of its pupils." *Diacritics* 13: 3–20.

Derrida, J. (1986). "Declarations of independence." *New Political Science* 15: 7–15.

Derrida, J. (1987). *Criticism in society*. Interviews by Imre Salusinsky, 9–24. New York: Methuen.

Derrida, J. (1988). "The politics of friendship." *The Journal of Philosophy* 85: 632–644.

Gasché, R. (1979). "Deconstruction as criticism." *Glyph* 6: 177–215.

25

THE DIFFICULTY OF LIFE: A REPLY TO RONALD H. MCKINNEY

[In *The Journal of Value Inquiry* 26, No. 4 (1992), 561–564]

[561] I thank Ronald H. McKinney for the attention he has given to my book *Radical Hermeneutics*,[1] for the sensitive rendering he has made of my views, and for the high compliment he has paid it by associating it with the work of so eminent a figure as Sir Isaiah Berlin.[2] His presentation is a good example of Gadamer's rule, taken over from Plato, of making the position of the other stronger before offering criticisms of one's own.

The concern he voices, in the last two pages of his study, is that for all their talk of the revisability and contingency of any human schema, postmodernists[3] ineluctably end up formulating an overarching, unrevisable scheme of their own. In my case, I employ the deconstructionist schema that dominant systems come undone from within by reason of the marginalized or excluded forces which they "contain." Because they "contain" (restrain, dominate) such forces, they likewise "contain" (possess, harbor) them and thus eventually come undone by them. That would even hold true, McKinney says, if what became dominant were deconstruction itself. There are those who think that is exactly the situation in the most prestigious English and Comparative Literature programs in the United States today, in which various post-modern views issuing from Derrida, De Man, Bakhtin and others are dominant while more traditional theories of criticism have been marginalized. The very idea of deconstruction is that deconstruction would be deconstructed in virtue of the truth of deconstruction, namely, that deconstruction tends to be undone by the forces which deconstruction itself marginalizes. That is a law, a Nietzschean law of constant going over and going under, an eternal recurrence, which puts the stamp of Being upon becoming. But this is a law I am prepared to live with, argues McKinney, because it means that my day – the day of the ethics of dissemination – will come again as a result of this incessant oscillation.

From this McKinney concludes two things: (1) We post-modernists, far from being post-modern, are still acting out the oldest, pre-modern philosophical battle of them all, the battle of Being with becoming, of the [562] One with the Many, and if we do not take the side of Being and the One (and to that extent give up post-modernism), we will succumb to the inevitable problems of self-referential inconsistency.

(2) The whole position dissolves into a "Sisyphean nightmare" of incessant construction and deconstruction, continually doing and undoing things, texts and institutions, *ad infinitum* (and perhaps *ad nauseam*). Nothing is any more or less true, lasting or harmful than anything else, so why bother? and what help does post-modernism offer?

These are interesting and pertinent criticisms to which I am glad to have the opportunity to respond.

To take the opposition between dominant and marginalized in a rigorously formal sense, without regard to the substantive merits of what is in power and what is out of power, is a mistake. That is something I mean to avoid. I clearly prefer it when egalitarian forces are in power, forces that check violence, discrimination, and exploitation, and when such forces stay in power. I see no merit in having egalitarian forces oscillate with totalitarian forces. I would not say that holding violent or totalitarian tendencies in check represents their "exclusion" or "marginalization," because "exclusion" or "marginalization" refers always to victims. Homicidal rapists or exploitatious businesspeople are not victims but victimizers. Hence the restraint of their victimization practices does not amount to their "exclusion" but simply to a just law, one favored by the ethics of dissemination (which disseminates power clusters that produce victims). I have no interest in deconstructing justice or seeing it oscillate with injustice.[4] Respect for the "other" does not involve respecting people who produces victims, that is, who do not respect others. People who produce victims are not the "other" but ones who want to dominate the "other." The other, as Levinas says, is always "the widow, the orphan, the stranger," that is, emblematically, the weak, the victim. Therefore, McKinney does not reckon with a substantive element in the ethics of dissemination.

If you want to know whence the substantive content of the ethics of dissemination derives, then I would point to the hermeneutics of suffering presented in *Radical Hermeneutics* (273 ff.) which offers an interesting parallel to Isaiah Berlin's notion of avoiding the extremes of suffering. I "begin" ethics with the phenomenon of suffering, with the call of the victim, of the oppressed, which I maintain is the imperative around which the ethics of dissemination is organized. I strive constantly to avoid saying in *Radical Hermeneutics* that anything goes, that one interpretation is as good as another. I assert without apology that those ethico-political schemata that assure people of their dignity, rights, and opportunities, which afford people adequate housing, education, health care, employment, etc., are better than schemata that deprive people of such benefits. If all [563] schemata produce some harm, as I think they do, then schemata that produce less harm are better than ones that produce more harm. Suffering is the measure.

Now one might think that, pressed by McKinney, I have reverted to a classical, foundationalist view, and that I have invoked a "standard" of just the sort I said was impossible in *Radical Hermeneutics*. I offer here two reasons why this is not so and why the recourse I make to suffering does not have the status of a moral principle or foundation in the classical or modern sense.

First, I conceive this principle entirely negatively. Put in classical terms, I offer no theory of the Good but only of evil. I encourage, beyond toleration, the multiplication and maximization of the plurality of forms in which good can come about, that is, in which individuals can flourish, and I invoke a "*meta-phronesis*" to cope with the resulting discord. This is always to be understood within the framework of not producing suffering. Love – and do what you will. Do what you will – but do not produce suffering. For example, homosexual love is love, not war, and one of the multiple and conflicting ways in which people choose to lead their lives. From the standpoint of the ethics of dissemination, homosexual love is a mode of human flourishing. Gay-bashing and depriving homosexuals of their rights, on the other hand, is violent; it produces victims – suffering – and that is where the wrongdoing lies. Gay-bashing arises from enforcing a positive, univocal, and dogmatic view of the Good. I have an entirely negative and non-dogmatic idea of the Good. I prefer to speak of the heteromorphic ("heterological") plurality of "goods" (in the plural and lower case), while ascribing to evil an ominous sameness – of battered bodies and ruined lives.

Secondly, I do not regard this "imperative" – the obligation we have to the victim, the call of the other as victim – as a "categorical" imperative. It is a call, a solicitation, an appeal, which surges up from the face of the other but which has no deep, absolute justification. That is the point at which I break from the foundationalism or what Lyotard calls the "piety" of Levinas, who makes the Other an Absolute. That is the role of Nietzsche in *Radical Hermeneutics*: as a limit case for ethics:

> Once upon a time, in some out of the way corner of that universe which is dispersed into numberless twinkling solar systems, there was a star upon which clever beasts invented knowing. That was the most arrogant and mendacious minute of "world history," but nevertheless it was only a minute. After nature had drawn a

few breaths, the star cooled and congealed, and the clever beasts
had to die.[5]

Substitute the word "ethics" for "knowing" in this passage and you have the
condition against which the non-foundationalism of post-modern ethics [564]
works. Post-modernists do not think we can cut through to the *eidos* behind
appearances, the *ousia* beneath certain attributes, the *prima causa* behind a series
of effects, or to *Geist* or "History" or "transcendental consciousness." Life is a
"dis-aster": we are more and more untied from a guiding star (*astrum*), deprived
of meta-narratives and rock solid metaphysical grounds. We are always already
caught up in finite, revisable, historical, linguistic forms of life, and we cannot
cut through to their deep ground. Our little star may well cool down and
congeal, the play of forces may continue on long after we are all gone, and our
ethics may not matter a whit. Post-modern writers do not throw up their arms
at this point or regard it as a "Sisyphean nightmare." They view it – or I view it
– as part of what the early Heidegger called "the difficulty of life." As St.
Augustine said in a text cited by and Heidegger in *Being and Time*: *factus sum mihi
terra difficultatis et sudoris nimii*: "I have become a land of difficulty and of excessive
sweat."[6]

I do not think ethics is either a practice rationally founded through and
through or a nightmare. I do think a "foolishness" occurs in ethics, a willingness
to make oneself a fool for the other, to serve the other, to respond to the call
of the victim, and to live in such a way as not to victimize. Why not produce
victims? Why not simply go on in our usual greedy, self-aggrandizing way? I do
not think there is a "deep" answer to that, and that may be a characteristic
feature of post-modernism. The call which issues from the face of suffering is
finite and fragile. The "difficulty" is that it does not carry absolutely
commanding authority. It is an appeal and it can be ignored, like the way we
ignore street people as we rush by them on the way to catch a train.

Notes

[1] *Radical Hermeneutics: Repetition, Deconstruction and the Hermeneutic Project* (Bloomington, Ind.:
Indiana University Press, 1987).

[2] Ronald H. McKinney, "Toward a postmodern ethics: Sir Isaiah Berlin and John Caputo,"
The Journal of Value Inquiry, 26.3 (July 1992): 395–407.

[3] I do not use this term to describe my own views because of the looseness with which it is
employed. I think the expression "post-structuralism" is more exact. In either case, what is at
issue is the extensive use I make of Jacques Derrida in the formulation of my views.

[4] See Derrida's discussion of justice and the law in "The Force of Law: The 'Mystical Foundations of Authority'," *Cardozo Law Review* 11 (July-August 1990), Nos. 5–6: 920–1045 (Special Issue on "Deconstruction and the Possibility of Justice").

[5] Friedrich Nietzsche, "On Truth and Lies in a Nonmoral Sense," in *Philosophy and Truth: Selections from Nietzsche's Notebooks of the Early 1870s*, ed. and trans. Daniel Breazeale (Atlantic Highlands, N.J.: Humanities Press, 1979), 79.

[6] Martin Heidegger, *Being and Time*, trans. J. Macquarrie and E. Robinson (New York: Harper & Row, 1962), §9.

26

INFESTATIONS: THE RELIGION OF THE DEATH OF GOD AND SCOTT'S ASCETIC IDEAL

[In *Research in Phenomenology,* Vol. 25 (1995), pp. 261–68]

[261] In the combined spirits of Kierkegaard and Derrida, I set out in *Against Ethics* (hereafter *AE*) to treat obligation as a groundless ground and so to situate (or de-situate) myself in a quasi-philosophical spot, freely "infested"[1] by unclean spirits, by non-philosophical contaminants, in the gap between grounds and groundlessness. So staged or choreographed, like a dancer shifting constantly from one foot to the other, *AE* shuffles *between:* Greek and Jew, Dionysus and the rabbi, Nietzsche and Levinas, autonomy and heteronomy, humor and church-dark brooding, impiousness and piety, orgasmic discharges and substitution for the other; *between* a certain humble Heidegger of the anonymous *es gibt* and a high-flying, eagle-high, Hegel-like Heidegger of the History of Being; between Nietzsche's *ressentiment* against modernity, his attempt to make democracy feel sick with guilt, and his abysmal thought that the forces, which are as they are, discharge themselves in starless nights; between Levinas' attempt to make everybody feel sick, modern or not, and his powerful breach of the primacy of cognition over obligation.

Predictably, *AE*'s critics tend to come from either of two directions, depending on their views of grounds, eagles, stars, orgasms, and rabbis. Charles Scott, a well-known critic of Religion-and-the-Ascetic-Ideal, thinks that *AE* is: too rabbinic, too Abrahamic, too confident, too ethical, too good, too Levinasian, too Judeo-Christian, too preoccupied with religion; that *AE* gives obligation an ahistorical zing that resists [262] genealogical explanations, that it longs for a lost Roman Catholic mysticism and a community of faith, that it distorts Heidegger and Nietzsche, that, in short, it is too *infested* with the Ascetic Ideal. Scott's criticisms, shall we say, show a trend.

His review of *AE,* which is not quite a review, which never permits itself, or the reader, a moment to let the substance of *AE* pass into view, which omits most of the text from discussion, proceeding at once to take a dim view of the text, is a good example of what Levinas means when he writes that obligation to the other is "hardly conceivable in a world where infidelity to Nietzsche, even conceived outside of all National-Socialist contamination, is (despite 'the death of God') taken as blasphemy."[2]

So while *AE* ends by citing Joyce's "The Dead," with worms inching their way toward forgotten graves, with life vanishing without a trace into a dark cosmic rumble, where *il y a* or *es gibt* is all in all, at a point where critics from the other side find despair or at best infinite resignation, Scott finds a cheery, happy, secure, nostalgic Treatise on Obligation. Or, again, when Johanna de Silentio, speaking "against Abraham," deftly undoes the blind, bloodthirsty dutifulness of father Abraham (*AE,* 139–46), or when, more generally, everything, and I mean *everything,* in *AE* is organized around a systematic restaging of *Fear and Trembling* by *Johanna,* aided and abetted by other feminine choreographers like Magdalena and Rebecca, so that the authority of father Abraham, ironically affirmed again and again, is all the while being delimited and danced around, Scott, like someone missing a joke while everyone else is holding their sides, ignores the choreography and suppresses all of the feminine voices – Magdalena, Johanna, Rebecca – not to mention me, their faithful scribe and editor, on the limits of Abraham's frame of mind. Scott does not notice that, in the little postmodern twist they give to *Fear and Trembling,* Sarah is the heroine of the story of the *akedah,* not father Abraham, although I do love Abraham very much.

Or when Magdalena turns Yeshua into an anarchic poet of the Unclean, no friend of either well-scrubbed fundamentalists or manicured Vatican bureaucrats, Scott's allergies flare up; and I, poor *Extraskriver* that I am, am melted down into a Roman Catholic longing for a Rhineland-mystical buzz. Presumably, then, on Scott's psycho-reading, Derrida's eyes, too, are currently glazing over with nostalgia for his Jewish youth in El-Biar as he now writes of "the messianic and the eschatological," of the spirit and ghost of "the religious," which returns and "informs" the "'spirit' of emancipatory Marxism," and that this religious structure belongs to "that irreducible movement of the historical opening to the future," to the irreducibility and undeconstructibility of justice, of which – very much in the spirit of *AE* – "Abrahamic messianism" is "but an exemplary prefiguration."[3] And what of the young Heidegger who made his breakthrough precisely by [263] retrieving the structure of factical life in the letters of Paul? Alas for Johanna, the young Heidegger, and Derrida, the Crusade Against the Ascetic Ideal makes no distinctions, takes no prisoners who might be held over for questioning before execution.

Or while there are many signatures in *AE,* a riot of views and voices, and not everything is signed with my name, Scott grimly, gravely stalks his prey, cutting to the chase, single-mindedly assuming everybody is saying the same thing, getting to the logocentric guts of the book, which is that this is, this must be, The Dreaded Ascetic Ideal. What else can it be if it is "infested" with contagion like Yeshua and with the mention of jewgreek texts?

Or when I express reservations about miraculous, metaphysical, theological, and Heideggerian Origins (*Ursprung*) Scott, by a sleight of hand, transmutes this into a distrust of Foulcauldian genealogies (*Herkunft*), as if, in *AE*, genealogical accounts of obligations are not part of what makes obligations tremble, as if in *AE* Felix Sineculpa is not a serious voice, as if everything is not haunted by Felix. And while *AE* agrees that historicizing and socializing *may* go all the way down (who knows? I have never been all the way down) and wonders what cruelty we could be constituted to tolerate, Scott, in one of the most amazing readings of all, finds an "ahistorical" essence of obligation, one that "protects obligation" from genealogy. (Sigh!) He manages to say this despite the fact that, by locating obligations in flesh laid low (one of numerous analyses ignored by Scott), I went on to insist that "pain has a history," that flesh is "no ahistorical principle," that it is "valorized, feared, and experienced differently, depending on the historical, linguistic, economic, social, cultural, political, military, or religious presuppositions within which it is situated," that when it comes to how utterly obligations are "constituted" – how far socialization and genealogical explanation may go – I concede "I have no idea how far this can go," and that obligations are not "written in the stars or in nature," etc. (did he read *AE*, 208-9 and ff.?). All of this is part of what I mean by obligation as a groundless ground, by the groundlessness of obligation, by its trembling, and why I am against ethics, which is intent on making obligation safe from such critiques. Who does Scott think Felix Sineculpa is, anyway?

Still, I would add here, because Scott's affirmation of genealogy is so unquestioning and powerful as to make me nervous, events are very complex; and there are many other elements besides micro-practices, and many *other* ways to make obligations tremble, very interesting ones indeed, besides genealogies. Or does Scott think that genealogical accounts *explain everything*, that nothing is *not* constituted by such practices, and hence [264] that Genealogy deserves to be capitalized, as the One, True Method, as another European Capital?[4]

But do not mistake me. I am very grateful for this non-review, this non-view, this un-view, this dim view, by Scott. I plan to send it as a reply whenever I am attacked by the other side, by Levinasians, say, who think that I am impious, irreligious, dark and despairing, that I have distorted the scriptures, religion and rabbis, made light of the Good and the True, that I have uprooted obligation and left it to twist slowly in the wind. Then, while the Nietzscheans and Levinasians wage opposing wars on *AE*, I will quietly devote myself to my next book, which will no doubt generate a new constellation of angry campers intent on defending their Heroes. Again, I insist, I am, we are all, very obliged to Charles Scott for the Crusade he has conducted against Religion-and-the-Ascetic-Ideal, for the self-effacing – dare I say evangelical? – zeal with which he has tracked its every trace, searched every hidden corner where this Prince of Darkness might be lurking. His spare – dare I say ascetic? – discourse is organized around an Archimedean point of deep assurance, a booming – dare I say Baptist? – "No" to the Ascetic Ideal. (He has renounced it and all its pomp.) Who would not be grateful for such an unselfish servant of the common good, such a champion of the Ideal of No More Ascetic Ideals?

I come closest to agreement with my good friend Charles Scott, who I feel sure will forgive me for these sallies as I have forgiven him his, in his final paragraphs. Although, even there, I am still being interrogated by a monocular reading, dragged before the Inquisitor of The Ascetic Ideal, my pockets searched for blasphemies against the Latter Day Church of the Death of God; and although, even there, a massive amount— dare I say, most? – of *AE*'s choreography is missed when the last word of Scott's review is given to "Abraham" instead of "Sarah." Nonetheless, despite these sizeable reservations, the situation I and my pseudonymous benefactors seek to evoke is vaguely like the one Scott is describing there. We little beings made of flesh find ourselves, always and already, situated in obligations, in a kind of quasi-ethical *Befindlichkeit,* in a raw facticity into which we have been thrust without having been consulted, and with no *logos* to cover the nude hide of obligations. I would say of obligations what Heidegger says of truth and disclosedness in *Being and Time,* §44c: that like disclosedness itself, obligations belong to Dasein's elemental thrownness into the world, are nothing we have freely chosen, and that it is quite incomprehensible (*gar nicht einzusehen*) as to why there is (*es gibt*) obligation, why it should be. No Commanding Categorical Imperative, no *l'infini,* no Supersensible Good beyond Being comes slicing through sensible appearances to get [265] behind obligations and back them up and protect obligations from what menaces them. Always and already "solicited by the Other" – and I do agree with Scott that we have worn this Levinasian coinage thin (as he wears Nietzschean and Foucauldian coins thin) and need to invent another idiom (so does he, we all do) – overtaken by the call that comes to us from the destitute and defenseless, which is the groundless ground of a call that comes from who knows where. Obligations in *AE* are sublunar, inter-carnal events, transactions between flesh and flesh, which run on their own, before, after, and against ethics, with or without the support of the philosophers, theologians, genealogists, or ethnologists. Devoid of a deep backup, we are left only with good stories of which death makes a perfect mockery.

The point on which Charles Scott and I agree, I would venture to say, is that we both see a certain obligation to obligation, which means the *double* obligation not only to respond to obligation but also to monitor the origins of obligation because of the suffering produced by responding too readily, blindly, and without undecidability, to obligation. The latter danger, expounded very nicely in his *The* Question *of Ethics,* is what above all and rather single-mindedly seems to interest Scott. What divides him and me is that I wish constantly to see these two obligations *together,* to see them as a two-sided coin, a doubled-edged sword, a tension in which we are always and already caught, so that we are obliged to the Other, whose call is "urgent,"[5] before, during, and after all of our genealogies of the obligations that produce suffering. On my reading of Foucault, for example, all the descriptions of the multiple ways in which we are constituted by power (obligations) go hand in hand with a deep sense of *responsibility* to all those who are done in, or done out, by power, all the *me onta* who are constituted as abnormal by normalizing practices (by "ethics," which I am against). It is to these Others, to the call of their otherness, that all the Foucauldian genealogies rise up in response, so that the whole of Foucault is to be read as answering an obligation to the Other. On the view that I take, Foucault, to use Derrida's idiom, begins *by* the "impossible," by the im/possible call of justice for the singularity of the Other.[6]

Scott rightly worries about the sufferings produced by *responding* to obligation. As Derrida says, Heidegger was never more "responsible" than when he promptly started marching in response to the Nazi call to arms.[7] The contemporary American right wing is driven by the obligation, *pro deo et patria,* to inscribe its xenophobic, homophobic vision of the Good, of God and "family values" on the hides of everyone else, like it or not. That is a crucial disorder in our democracy, about which Scott is rightly concerned. But this danger is addressed at some length in *AE* under the name of the "end of the Good," where I identify "victims" as the victims of enforcing [266] someone's else's vision of the Good, which is why I say that, since the Good produces suffering, I side with evil (*AE,* 30-41). But all this is summarily ignored in a reading single-mindedly set on stalking The Ascetic Ideal.

What finally divides Scott and me, then, is that having pointed out the danger we face from the defenders of the True and the Good, I think there is more to say, and I do not think Nietzsche's loathing for democracy and Christianity is a reason not to say it. The ultimate (but hardly the only) rejoinder to the right wing "contract" *on* America, on the poor and the children of the poor – a contract based squarely on the notion that what doesn't kill the poor will make then stronger – will be to make its cruelty plain, to let be seen, *poetice et eleganter* (*AE,* 133), the suffering of five million homeless children, the disaster of *not* responding, before it actually happens, before the American people see *in the flesh* what they have wrought by the right wing landslide of 1994. That letting be seen is what I mean by a "poetics of obligation," a certain poetizing of carnal life, a quasi-phenomenology of flesh, tuned not to orgasmic explosions (which have their place, and I am not against them), but to the call that comes over us when flesh is laid low, which is a deeply "jewgreek" idea disallowed by the Ideal of Greco-Germanic Purity (no infestation allowed).

Scott cannot quite bring himself outright to deny that we have obligations to Others – is that what he really thinks? – but he is blocked by his Nietzschean dogma about the Ascetic Ideal and his fear of blasphemy from saying that we do. He will not just come out with it and say that we are always and already called by the Other, for fear of running afoul of the Religion of the Death of God. Scott's fear of infidelity to Nietzsche seems to outweigh his fear of infidelity to the obligations we have to one another. Does he think that *every* obligation is reducible to The Ascetic Ideal? What then? Fortunately, by reason of what Derrida calls the aporia of urgency, obligations run on their own and do not wait for philosophers like Scott to make up their minds. Even if you think you can give a genealogical account of *every* obligation, which would be a little totalizing, obligations, which oblige quite independently of these cognitive critiques, would return (*revenant*).

Every time you think you have killed them, obligations return, like ghosts, even after the death of God, by whom we are also all haunted, even, and especially, those among us who are the most intent on burying the old deity. Instead of undertaking a "retrieval" of religious structures or a "repetition with a difference," in the spirit of the young Heidegger or the latest Derrida, Scott keeps trying to kill off the old God, to exterminate all the infestations of religious vermin. Repeatedly. Again and again. Does that not invite haunting? Is that not to be haunted? And after we have [267] exterminated infestations who or what would be left standing?

One of the most delicious features of Levinas' work, with all its prophetic talk of being held hostage by the Other, is the way it makes Nietzschean hairs stand on end. Levinas sets off a whole chain of allergic reactions among Nietzschean loyalists, who go about sniffing the air, sure that there must be a Slave Moralist in the House of Being. When it is pointed out to Scott that there is a certain structural *re-ligare* in *ob-ligare,* in being bound (*ligare*) over (*re*) to the

Other (which doesn't mean you have to go to church on Sunday or obey any bishops), his allergies flare up, his head swims, and he faints dead away.

One unfortunate consequence of Scott's unquestioning submission to this Religion of Irreligion is that it blocks him from even considering the positive proposals made in *AE*, in the multiple spirits of Derrida – whose role in *AE* he keeps suppressing – and Lyotard, which are aimed at taking obligation into account, as a fact of our factical life, *without* the excesses of Levinasian infinity, *AE*'s attempt, in short, to situate itself *between* Nietzsche and Ethics. Having backed himself into a corner which makes it impossible for him to say, even to acknowledge, that we are bound over to the Other; and having pledged his troth in advance to the Ideal of a Pure Discourse, uninfested by religious texts and traditions, which are a little *too other* for his blood; the whole of *AE* is subjugated to a monocular interrogation in terms of the Ascetic Ideal, which flattens the nuances and silences the multiplicity of voices, including in the most persistent way the voice of Nietzsche himself, who is also *one* of my heroes, whom with Foucault I do not surrender to Scott. Obligations happen, it is said in *AE*, and they happen because they happen, with or without *Seinsdenkers*, First Philosophers, Genealogists, Sociobiologists, or Ethicians. "Then the cosmos draws a few more breaths, the little star grows cold, and the little animals made of flesh have to die" (*AE*, 247).

Meanwhile, back in D.C., as Scott and I trade noiseless academic fire, right wing extremists, in the majority at last, contemplate a system of orphanages for the children they plan to make homeless. It's a scene straight from Dickens.

Notes

[1] The most telling word in Scott's piece occurs on p. 253, when he reports that he admires Blanchot and Heidegger for having brought us through a region that is [268] "infested" with religion, the Ideal being, no doubt, a discourse pure and uncontaminated by religion, a sanitized philosophical discourse which has made a clean cut from and has protected itself against its other, or at least *some* of its others. What other others would "infest" philosophy's purity for Scott?

[2] Emmanuel Levinas, *Otherwise than Being or beyond Essence,* trans. A. Lingis (The Hague: Martinus Nijhoff, 1981), 177.

[3] Jacques Derrida, *Specters of Marx,* trans. Peggy Kamuf (New York: Routledge, 1994), 166–67.

[4] Suppose selfish genes, ever looking out for their own, have hard-wired sympathy into our bodies; suppose that nature, contradicting Nietzsche's machismo assumptions that life is a brutal war, selects for sympathy and cooperation? Then "obligation" would be nothing more than an evolutionary selection mechanism, long before micro-practices arrive on the scene. See Robert

Wright, *The Moral Animal: The New Science of Evolutionary Psychology* (New York: Pantheon Books, 1994).

⁵ Jacques Derrida, "Force of Law: The 'Mystical Foundation of Authority,'" in *Deconstruction and the Possibility of Justice,* ed. Drucilla Cornell et al. (New York: Routledge, 1992), 26–29.

⁶ Jacques Derrida, *Given Time, I: Counterfeit Money,* trans. Peggy Kamuf (Chicago: University of Chicago Press, 1992), 6, 29; John D. Caputo, "On Not Knowing Who We Are: Madness, Hermeneutics, and the Night of Truth in Foucault," in *Foucault and the Critique of Institutions,* eds. John D. Caputo and Mark Yount (University Park: Pennsylvania State University Press, 1993), 233–62.

⁷ I would say of Heidegger – since Scott here suppresses his criticisms of Heidegger – that the emancipatory power of Heidegger's thought is constantly held in check by his massive nostalgia for (a certain) Greece (Scott is selectively critical of nostalgia) combined with a monomaniac will to exclude all Jewish and Christian "infestation" from the Great Origin; his unchecked valorization of *logos* as gathering unity (which is what Scott elsewhere criticized) and *Wesen* as Essential Being; and his elitist love of the rare and exceptional, all of which are not only *questionable* in the extreme (Scott likes to emphasize what is questionable) but downright *dangerous.* But *AE* is not about Heidegger, and it is distracting to me to have argue about Heideggerian exegesis. I have set forth the "against" in my "Reading Heidegger against Heidegger" in: *Demythologizing Heidegger* (Bloomington: Indiana University Press, 1993), which is the straight man to *AE.*

BOOK REVIEWS

27

HORIZONAL HERMENEUTICS – AND BEYOND

[In *Research in Phenomenology*, Vol. 16 (1986), 211–217]

GRAEME NICHOLSON. *Seeing and Reading*. Atlantic Highlands: Humanities Press, 1984. Contemporary Studies in Philosophy and the Human Science. 275 pp.

[211] *Seeing and Reading* is before all else a philosophical essay. It is not a book "about" philosophy – about Heidegger or Gadamer, for example, who play very important roles in its argument – but a philosophical essay in its own right about the question of interpretation. It is refreshing to find a piece which wants to enlist the resources of Heidegger and Gadamer in the service of philosophizing and which manages to stay clear of the confusion, which Heidegger points out, between the matter for thought and a scholarly object. And it is no less refreshing to find a book which is written so carefully, clearly, and unpretentiously, even while it is so rich in humanistic erudition that one learns a great deal just from following its examples – which range from archeology to Shakespeare. Among its many merits I think that this book will also turn out to be a major bridge-builder in the growing Anglo-continental dialogue. For it addresses issues – Quine's theory of radical translation, for example – which concern the Anglo-American reader with a clarity which cuts off the usual dismissals of continental thinking from these quarters.

I admire this book greatly. It is a finely crafted, challenging, and rewarding piece of work. I do not in the end agree with it, however, for reasons which I will at least sketch at the end of this account. I think that it does not go far enough, that it backs off from the genuinely critical impulse in Heidegger's hermeneutics. In my view, *Seeing and Reading* is even at war with itself, by borrowing at one and the same time from a hermeneutics conceived in terms of transcendental horizonality and from [212] a hermeneutics which is set on the delimitation of horizonality. But before raising these critical reflections, this study deserves as faithful an exposition as space permits.

"Seeing" and "reading" have exemplary significance for Nicholson. Seeing: that means the field of perception at large; reading: that means the whole realm of what Husserl would call "higher order" acts, acts of understanding, especially those which occur in the human sciences. And the argument is that seeing can be construed in terms of reading – that is to say, that perception is from the start an interpretive act, that seeing is seeing-as, and hence a kind of "reading." Even so, reading, which is certainly interpretive, is a kind of seeing in which something emerges into appearance and hence is best understood by a comparison with perception and seeing. Thus the "and" in the title directs us to take seeing as reading and reading as seeing, and not simply to lay the two side by side each other. The "and" signifies not a simple conjunction but an analogy. Seeing and reading differ as do two different kinds of interpretation, as different realizations of the analogously similar structure of interpretation.

Seeing is "background" interpretation which proceeds automatically (what Husserl would call a passive synthesis which operates without the intervention of conscious ego-acts); while reading is "foreground" interpretation, that is, the work of the human sciences which takes up interpretation as an active, conscious task. The analogy between seeing and reading is guided by a tri-partite structure of projection, appearance and illumination which Nicholson contends governs both spheres individually. To understand either perception or scientific understanding thus requires that one see how each is the work of these three structurally coequal components.

Perception is, to begin with, projective; it is not a naked intuitive contact with the world but a contact guided in advance by our practical concerns and by language. The perceived world is perceived in terms of practical concerns which exercise a selective, orienting influence on the perceptual field. We "see" things in terms of current projects; the hermeneutic "as" in seeing-as is guided by practical concern. In the terms of *Being and Time,* perceptual life never operates outside the sphere of being-in-the-world and hence of the projective structure of *Verstehen* and *Auslegen.* For Nicholson this means that a given perceptual object (x) is understood *(verstand)* as A, and interpreted *(ausgelegt,* explicated further) as B. The original understanding of x as A is the work of language. Things are disclosed to us by language (x is A), and further explicated by practical interests (A is B). Now if it is the same thing (x) [213] which is both understood and then interpreted, then Quine's assumption is undermined that the predicates we ascribe to an ordinary object, like a desk, and the predicates generated by the physicist represent two independent lines of predicates which it is the task of the philosopher-"translator" somehow to fit together. On Nicholson's account, such a problem does not arise because the latter are simply higher-order determinations of the former, that is, of the self-same perceptual object (which is also essentially Husserl's solution in *Ideas I*, §§43, 52).

But projection is not enough. If the (practico-linguistic and bodily) subject "projects," the perceptual object "appears"; if I interpret, the interpreted object appears (71). To take account of this, Nicholson invokes Heidegger again, not *Being and Time*, however, but "On the Essence of Truth." Perception occurs in the realm of the "open" and if we get into the open by perception, the thing gains admittance by its own self-showing. Projection is what we need to do in order to make contact with the self-showing appearance. But the open is not created by projection so that appearing-in-the-open must therefore constitute a second structural element in perception. The perceived thing steps out into the open, on its own, which is why it is possible to experience what Prof. Nicholson calls an "eminent" perception, in which our attention is drawn away from current and quotidian concerns to a previously marginal object which then captures our interest – say a noisy military parade which we did not expect to encounter. In Nicholson's view, this sharply differentiates Heidegger from Husserl, whose "adumbrations," lacking all such objectively appearing "affinity," are bonded together in an entirely noetic manner, without objective motivation (92-95), and whose "horizons" are not objective "scenes" (97-100). Lacking a theory of appearing-in-the-unconcealed, Husserl is a subjective idealist in the manner of Berkeley (117).

Still, projection and appearance together are not enough. For if it is the work of projection to disclose, and of the thing itself to make its appearance in the open – if projection performs an epistemic work, and appearance an ontological work – these two require a *tertium quid,* a theory of illumination which mediates the one to the other. Just as in the classical theory of illumination, the faculty (projection) and the object (appearance) require light (illumination) in order to make contact. Illumination bestows visibility on the appearance and light upon the seeing eye. Thus when Heidegger says in *Being and Time*, §28, that the *"da"* of Dasein means *Lichtung*, clearing, and that Dasein itself is "cleared" (*gelichtet*), Nicholson takes him to mean that Dasein stands *in* a light which does not originate with itself. Dasein is itself the light and is [214] also in the light. That leads Nicholson to say that the light projected by Dasein is reflected, and hence that projection is, not a solar work, but a lunar work, which depends upon a prior illumination (117).

It is in virtue of the structure of illumination that one can speak of the truth of perception, not truth in the sense of correspondence, but the truth of the perceptual thing, that is, its unconcealment in the light in which it stands. Together, projection, appearance and illumination, then, do not simply provide the tri-partite structure of perception, but of the truth of perception. The hermeneutic make-up of perceptual life does not rob it of its truth but explains how its truth is possible.

This same tri-partite make-up is then extended to the higher order acts of "reading," i.e., of consciously controlled and scientific interpretation of texts. If Nicholson's analysis of seeing in the first half of the book is an account of perception which is drafted in terms of Heidegger, the analysis of "reading" is cast in the terms of Gadamer's appropriation of Heidegger. Accordingly, the act of reading is always guided in advance by a projection (Gadamer's "prejudices") which is latent in simple, everyday reading and thematic in the reading of old or complex texts. The text functions like a dummy and the reader like a ventriloquist who lends the text his voice (139). And if there are many ways in which this projective work can be carried out, Nicholson singles out two in particular which are of preeminent importance, the first of which – linguistic-material interpretation – shows the place of "appearance" in reading, and the second of which – historical and psychological understanding – displays the role of "illumination" in reading.

It is clear that not any projective reading, not any ventriloquy at all, will do, but only a reading which discloses what the text says. Readings must be controlled and misreadings excluded. Reading has to do with the truth of the text in just such a way as to let the text speak the truth. Now in just the way that some perceptual object (x) is understood as A and explicated as B, so some text (t) is initially projected as "saying" (p) and then interpreted as "meaning" (q). The truth of the interpretation rests on the sort of evidence one marshals to link the interpreted meaning to the projected saying, for it is the *ipsissima verba* which control the interpretation and provide an "absolute canon" for it (142).

To secure the truth of the text, Nicholson gives the primacy to "material" interpretation, by which he means a reading keyed to the *Sache selbst,* a reading of the text in terms of the light the text throws on the things themselves. One requires an understanding of the matter in order to read a text which treats of that matter – one must be musical, e.g., to read a history of music. Indeed the best example of the role played by this sort of pre-understanding of the matter itself is Bultmann's [215] claim that faith functions as the requisite pre-understanding for a reading of the Scriptures. Linguistic interpretative methods function best when they are linked with material interpretations, for then the words of the texts are understood as letting the things themselves appear. That implies the Heideggerian determination of language as *legein,* letting-be-seen: a good reading lets the things themselves be seen in and through the words of the text, lets them step out into the unconcealed, summoning them into "appearance."

Finally, a reading which lets the things themselves appear is possible only if it is already "illuminated" in advance by the historicality of the understanding. The truth of the text is a function of appearance – of how the things themselves step forth into the light in the text – and of illumination – the historical conditions under which the text is understood and applied. The role of illumination is played thus by the tradition which supplies the changing circumstances of interpretation and thus illumines the endlessly varying but also unified message of the text.

I would like now to offer a few critical comments about Nicholson's project which are offered not in an attempt to detract from its accomplishment but to continue its work of thought.

(1) In the first place, I have trouble with the tri-partite structure of projection, appearance, illumination. I think that Nicholson is trying to make use of incompatible versions of Heidegger's accounts of truth: viz., both the early notion of projection and the later notion of the Open in which projection is criticized as transcendental-horizonal thinking. In Heidegger's later accounts projective horizonality is taken as shrinking down the Open to human size, cutting it to fit our human dimensions, and failing to think the Open in itself. The task of thought is not to regionalize the Open into a horizonal frame but to free the open space of what is regioning in the region (*es gegnet, das Gegnet*).[1] Far from admitting us into the Open, then, projective thinking cuts us off from it and certainly cannot be combined with it in the manner that Nicholson attempts. That is why he is driven to the odd hypothesis that Dasein casts a lunar light, that it projects inasmuch as it is illuminated. If, as Nicholson once suggests, projection is like the lantern on the miner's cap and the illuminative power of the Open is like the sun, one need only consider what happens to the lantern light when the miner steps out of his cave.

It is this futile attempt to combine these two notions that leads Nicholson to his theory of "illumination" as mediating projection and appearance, which I also reject. For, on the one hand, whatever "illuminating" is accomplished in *Being and Time* is carried out by the Being of Dasein as care, whose meaning is temporality. There is no sense in which [216] Dasein is illuminated in *Being and Time*. Were that the case it could not be said that Dasein "is its own 'there'" and it would then be necessary to identify whatever else grants it light or clears the open space. One might say that "man," or whatever is human and belonging to the subject side, is cleared, but "Dasein" is the clearing, is the "between." On the other hand, the notion of the Open and the *Gegnet* which Heidegger employs in the later writing explains all the "illuminating" which occurs there.

To summarize this first point: I do not think that "projection" and "appearance" can be made to function side by side in the manner that Nicholson attempts; they are alternate, not combinable, accounts of truth. Furthermore, I think that whichever of them one advocates renders what Nicholson calls "illumination" redundant.

(2) I think a close reading of Nicholson's text will show that by reducing Husserl to a subjective idealist he has seriously misrepresented Husserl. He does not take account of the "motivation" which the de facto course of experience provides consciousness, so that, if the unity of experience is formally effected on the noetic side, it is motivated by the noematic side, which is just what Nicholson means by an objective "affinity." If the synthesis is carried out by consciousness, it is motivated by experience (*Ideas I*, §47). Now this misrepresentation of Husserl seems to me to have a very ironic character which goes beyond merely disputing the author's interpretation of Husserl. For I think that were Husserl's case properly presented by Nicholson, *Seeing and Reading* would turn out to be closer to Husserl and to the Husserlian elements in *Being and Time* than to the genuine, more long-range tendencies of Heidegger's thought.

By clinging to the notion of "projection" Nicholson defends the Husserlian notion of horizon with which Heidegger is forced later on to break. By retaining the notion of "perception" Nicholson reinstates a basic building block of the phenomenology of "consciousness" – although he wants to be critical of "consciousness" (117-24) – one indeed which Heidegger expressly excludes from *Being and Time*. The thematizing of perception in turn leads Prof. Nicholson, in a very Husserlian manner, to mark off a higher order register of scientific understanding, corresponding to Husserl's distinction between passive and active synthesis, and to take a fundamentally Husserlian position against Quine on the matter of scientific predicates. Add to this Nicholson's constant privileging of science – the attempt to lay the foundations of the human sciences, to secure their objective truth, to pronounce an "absolute canon" for interpretation, and to do so in a scientific hermeneutics – and one has a complete picture of a very Marburgian, Husserlian Heidegger for whom phenomenology is universal science.

[217] (3) The conservativism of *Seeing and Reading*, its resistance to Heidegger's deepest and most critical impulses, is completed by the Gadamerian turn taken in the second half of the book. Gadamer's hermeneutics remains confined by the Husserlian notion of horizon. It seeks at best the

wedding of horizons, the expansion of horizons by the exposure of past to present. Gadamer's is an entirely intra-traditional hermeneutics whose sole aim is to perpetuate and keep alive the metaphysical tradition from Plato to the present. It has not the least taste for the radical thinking *of* the tradition, the attempt to think the event of *a-letheia* itself, which sees every epoch, not as one more facet of the metaphysical diamond, but as withdrawal, *epochs,* as a construction stretched over an abyss, which is what is at work in Heidegger's "overcoming" of metaphysics. The fusion of horizons refuses the abyss which opens up by the delimitation of horizonal thinking, the play of the epochs which plays without why. *Seeing and Reading* is closer to the Gadamerian standpoint than the Heideggerian and to the Husserlian elements in *Being and Time* which the later Heidegger rejected.

Seeing and Reading is interested in the way in which a tradition can be appropriated, and in particular, I would say, a Scriptural and theological tradition. Its ocular metaphors of seeing and illumination borrowed from Plato and Augustine suggest a sentence from the psalms which Augustine and Aquinas often cited: "In Thy light we will see light."[2] Heidegger on the other hand was always inching towards the thought of the *lethe*.

Notes

[1] See Martin Heidegger, *Gelassenheit,* 2. Aufl. (Pfullingen: Neske, 1957), 38–42; Eng. trans. *Discourse on Thinking,* trans. John Anderson and Hans Freund (New York: Harper & Row, 1966), 63–7. Cf. *Unterwegs zur Sprache,* 3. Aufl. (Pfullingen: Neske, 1965), 95–101, 120–28, 150–53; Eng. trans. *On the Way to Language,* trans. P. D. Hertz (New York: Harper & Row, 1971), 9–12, 28–34, 51–53.

[2] This suspicion was confirmed in subsequent conversations with the author and also was pointed out clearly in a remark by Charles Scott.

28

REVIEW: *ERRING: A POSTMODERN A/THEOLOGY* [MARK TAYLOR]

[In *Man and World* 21 (1988), 107–14]

TAYLOR, MARK C. *Erring: A Postmodern A/theology.* Chicago: University of Chicago Press, 1984. xi + 219 pages. $20.00.

[107] In the "Prelude" to *Erring*, Mark Taylor numbers himself among what he calls the "marginal" people, caught in the middle, between belief and unbelief (5). What he calls "erring thought" is, he says, neither "properly theological nor nontheological, theistic nor atheistic, religious nor secular" (12). *Erring* thus means to present not a negative moment of a-theism (with a hyphen), but a Derridean margin or tympan, a slash which inserts itself between theism and a-theism. Taylor wants to occupy that place between theism and atheism which belongs to the realm of the *antre, entre,* the milieu, which is not reducible to either the theistic or atheistic poles.

Taylor thus turns for help to the central Derridean motif of "undecidability" which is, I think, the tip of the Derridean stylus. I heartily agree with Mark Taylor in situating his discussion thus. It is I think the best and most fruitful way to approach the question of deconstruction and theology. The question that I want to pose is whether *Erring* succeeds in staying on the slash, whether it is indeed, as it wants to be, a/theological; or whether the slash becomes a hyphen, whether a/theology is just another version of a-theism, of a somewhat bolder, brassier sort, indeed even of quite a brilliant and imaginative sort. To this end, I want to rehearse Taylor's argument as I hear it, and then to offer a critical reflection on its ability to think on the borderline.

For Taylor, deconstruction is important because it is "the 'hermeneutic' of the death of God" (6). Deconstruction understands the "ramifications of the death of God" and helps us radicalize what "begins in the death of God" so that it ends with the "death of the self." Deconstruction thus lends the death of God a hand by pushing it over the edge, radicalizing it, making it "utterly transgressive." To put it somewhat flippantly, if you liked the death of God, you'll love Derrida.

Thus, despite his protestations to the contrary, Taylor is weaving quite a yarn, telling quite a tale, with a very definite beginning, middle, and end. 1.–The beginning is the period of classical Christian theism which stretches from Augustine to Hegel. Hegel is the end of that beginning, and the beginning of the end, that is, of the death of God. For with Hegel, the transcendent, infinite, creator-God is incarnated in the Spirit, a notion which had both a theistic (right-wing) and an atheistic (left-wing) cutting edge. 2.–The middle of the story is the period of atheistic humanism, or [108] humanistic atheism, which is the moment of reversal and denial of God, but a denial which by affirming the divinity of man succeeded only in relocating the divine attributes from a heavenly to an earthly station. 3.–Thus because the first round of the death of God resulted in the birth of man, a second round is required which will result in the death of man himself (19). Patricide has to be followed by suicide (104); ontology must become necrology; the dissemination of God needs to be followed up by the dissemination of man. The first version belonged to modernity and humanism; the second round is the work of post-modernity and the critique of humanism. Deconstruction thus gives the death of God theologian new and more powerful critical tools to work with in order to bring about the deconstruction of the onto-theo-logic. Postmodernism thus completes the death of God story, bringing it, if not to a happy end, at least to a gay (*fröhlich*) inter-ludal un-closure.

This claim is argued for by means of a carefully constructed plan. The structure of this book, ironically, is no more errant or erring, no more an unscientific interlude (183), than the *Critique of Pure Reason*. The book is bound up tight from beginning to end; it has a skillfully crafted symmetry, a message to deliver (no *destinerrance*), and quite a story to tell. Despite his own best efforts to be mazing and erring, Taylor lapses repeatedly into clarity, falls constantly into orderliness. *O felix culpa.*

The book is neatly divided into two parts. The first part is devoted to what I have called the beginning and the middle of the story Taylor is telling, that is the movement from classical theism to the death of God. The first part is a deconstruction *of* theology – of both classical theology and atheistic theology. It proceeds by following the dialectic by which transcendent theology reversed itself into atheistic humanism, and then by critiquing the latter as a mere reversal which remains caught up in the old theological system. The old system is said to turn on four interwoven points: God, man, history and Book (Bible, Scriptures.) The second part of the book is not a deconstruction of theology but a deconstructive a/theology, in which the same four themes are deconstructed/repeated as writing, trace, "mazing" grace, and text. In the remarks which follow I will keep a special eye out for what happens to God in this story.

The classical God is the *deus omnipotens,* the all-powerful Father, creator of heaven and earth, whose power and mastery the death of God theologians – from the left-wing Hegelians on – wanted to appropriate for themselves. But the death of the heavenly master only resulted in the birth of a master-man. The [109] servants of God become themselves the new masters. In keeping with his past work on Hegel, Taylor tends to see Derrida's binary oppositions as variations on the master-slave relationship. The first death of God theologians did not subvert the logic of mastery but simply turned it to their own ends (24), reversed it so that man emerged in the privileged spot, and God was replaced by an *Übermensch.*

But this exaltation of man spells trouble for everything else, for the other species, for the environment, and ultimately, ironically, for man himself. Feeding as it does on a logic of mastery, atheistic humanism stokes the fires of colonialism, consumerism, and patriarchal power. Taylor concludes this impressive opening chapter with a convincing account of the way in which atheistic humanism is nothing more than narcissism and nihilism. Clearly the undoing of classical theology for Taylor will ultimately have to take the form of deconstructing the *Gestell,* or power/knowledge, or exclusionary systems in favor of some more gentle way to dwell on the earth.

The theological flip in virtue of which God was so readily transmuted into man in the nineteenth century was due to the fact that, in Christian dogmatics, God and self belong to a binary pair, that the self is conceived to be the *imago dei* (so it is really just a matter of deciding who was made in the image of whom). Thus Augustine is not only the author of the first great treatise on the process of the persons in the Trinity, but also of the first great autobiography. Augustine is the first one to spin a great yarn of the self's journey towards God (which is also what Hegel's *Phenomenology* amounts to), or, to borrow Prof. Taylor's phrase from an earlier book, towards self-hood. But by injecting time into the self, Augustine's fabric comes undone, the self is dissipated, disseminated. The "self" is a unity only because it is held together by the force of writing. By uniting what resists unification, Augustine produces only a literary and fictitious unity. Writing compounds what is present with non-present (past, future) in the irreal unity of the story which Augustine tells to God. The self is an effect of *différance.*

399

History is autobiography writ large, the story not of the solitary soul's journey to God, but of the people of God as a whole. Now the story that Taylor himself is telling begins with Augustine's *City of God* and climaxes in Hegel's *Encyclopedia.* "History" is the way metaphysics has figured out to bring time under control, to get mastery over *chronos* by weaving Ariadne's thread through the maze of the flux. It is a way of saving presence and killing time. So too the Book is the record we keep of how all this mastery comes about. The Book is the account we keep of the [110] closed economy of salvation - of the creation of the world, of the history of salvation, of agreements old and new.

In the second half of *Erring* Taylor takes up the positive task of an a/theology which is no longer content with trading masters or with the power-brokerage of classical theology and atheistic humanism. The end of deconstructing theology is the beginning of deconstructive a/theology.

Unless one is a regular reader of Parisian philosophers, the first chapter of Part Two, "Writing of God," ought to knock one's theological socks off – "literally," I would say, if I did not know better. The transcendent God of classical theism which was immanentized in Hegel, and anthropomorphized in leftwing Hegelianism and Nietzsche, is *"écriture*-ized" (or graph-ized) by Taylor, i.e., reduced to the differential matrix, to – God bless us – *écriture, différance.* That I think is an ending calculated to surprise Derrida himself (not to mention God). When he signed the piece Reb Derrisa I do not think he was angling for this. Indeed if Derrida were worried that someone would consider *différance* a word or concept, that would be nothing compared to this. But indeed for Taylor *écriture* is divine enough for the job and all the divinity we need.

The Word became flesh in Jesus, and now it becomes word again, a sacred script, holy writ, hiero-glyph. "The word 'God' refers to the word 'word,' and the word 'word' refers to the word 'god.'" (103–104, citing Scharleman). The death of God is the death of the transcendental signified, consciousness "deals *only* with signs," with what is "within consciousness," "signs are signs of signs" (105). Now by this Taylor does not merely mean what Derrida says in OG [*On Grammatology* –ed.] 14, that the whole idea of the transcendental signified is theological in tone, i.e., that it implies the subordination of speaking and writing to ideality, meaning, objectivity. He means further that arche-writing has become the divine *milieu,* that God has become the *antre, entre* in which all semantic and syntactic effects are produced, a creative/destructive matrix or medium, an eternally recurring play, in which things emerge and submerge again. Add to the God of Abraham and of Moses, the God of de Saussure.

After that it is not hard to see that the self is reduced to "markings," that is to say, to an erratic mark in the play of forces. But this yields an interestingly

"Christian" result. For this dismembered self turns out to be what the Scriptures meant by a self conceived, not in terms of identity, private property, consumption and self-aggrandizement, but rather one which is compassionate, generous to a fault, to the point of foolishness, in an economy without reserve. Such a non-self lives *sine cura, without care for* [111] itself or for where it will find the wherewithal to lay its head. That is an interesting result to say the least, a kind of post-structuralist sermon on the mount which I find very impressive.

Likewise, in a deconstructive a/theology we run up against the end of history and the beginning of the labyrinth, which Taylor calls "mazing grace." Man is indeed truly become *homo viator*, wandering without home or center, nomadic, carnevalic. Finally, the mastery of the Book is undone by drawing it back into the play of the text.

Now I want to come back to the point with which I began, with Taylor's claim to be writing between belief and unbelief, on the margins or threshold of theism and atheism. I will approach this question by raising three objections which I present in increasing order of concern.

The first I have already voiced earlier on, that there is very little errant about *Erring*. The book is tightly organized, has an argument that presses ahead like a steamroller, and tells a lovely little story how about the God of St. Augustine became *écriture*. The "Interlude" at the *end* is not believable. This "text" has become a "book" with a point to make – about "death of God" theology.

Secondly I think I hear in this book something that one also hears in Derridean literary critics. If I am not mistaken, Taylor denies that language has reference. And although at a critical point he inserts a citation from Samuel Beckett – to the effect that language is not about something, it is that something itself – right in between two citations from Derrida (105), I believe that he also attributes this view to Derrida. Now that I deny – both in itself and as a view attributable to Derrida. I quote from a recent interview:

> There have been several misinterpretations of what I and other deconstructionists are trying to do. It is totally false to suggest that deconstruction is a suspension of reference. Deconstruction is always deeply concerned with the "other" of language. I never cease to be surprised by critics who see my work as a declaration there is nothing beyond language, that we are imprisoned in language; it is in fact saying the exact opposite.[1]

Derrida adds that saying we are submerged in words, that there is nothing beyond languages, are "stupidities."

If he does not deny reference, what Derrida does deny is that we ever get naked access to things, that we ever find a word which attaches so singularly to a thing that it names that thing properly, [112] so that it is that thing's own name and that name's own thing. He denies that there is a word which seizes a thing wholly and round about without pointing in other directions also, that there is ever a thing which cannot be inscribed in a thousand other ways. Rather, every signifier is caught up at once in a chain of signifiers so that that it cannot fall upon a thing wholly but can reach out to things only in and through the concatenating chain to which it belongs. A signifier is always definable by other signifiers; we can never reach an ostensive definition of a signifier but are always drawn back again and again into defining it with still more signifiers. Its reference is not simple, naked, immediate, atomic. Its reference is subject to slippage and substitution.

That means that there is nothing about what Derrida says which commits him to saying that the word 'God' refers to the word 'word' and vice-versa. What deconstruction is committed to saying is that if the word God functions in some natural language, then it does so only in virtue of the systematic connections within that language, only by assuming its place within the differential play of that language. What 'God' marks off in that language is a function of the syntactical and semantical differences which make that language up.

Furthermore, there is nothing in what Derrida says to suggest that God has anything at all to do with *différance* or *écriture*. "God" is a produced effect of *différance,* one of the things it is possible to say and to think because of *écriture,* but not *écriture* itself. To put it in Heideggerian terms, God is something ontic, one of *ta onta,* not the ontological difference itself (which is why Heidegger always said that theology is a positive science). *Différance* or *écriture* is ontologically neutral; it makes no decisions about what is not or is not, but indeed sees to it that all our decisions waver in undecidability. It is not a being or a cause of being, nor a non-being or cause of non-being. Indeed were it possible to locate *différance* in the divine, then indeed *différance* would have become both concept and meaning, something definite and identifiable, namely, the divine milieu, a.k.a., God.

Third, that brings me to the question with which I began, about whether Taylor has succeeded in the terms which he has set for himself, viz., to write "between belief and unbelief," to linger on the margins, to avoid both theism and atheism, and to think upon those borders, thresholds, margins where such polarities arise. In short, is this a/theology truly a/theological?

I think the answer is no. Taylor's position is it seems to me just more radically atheistic than the first round of humanistic atheism. He replaces humanistic atheism with an atheism which has wised up about humanism. He thinks that deconstruction can be [113] of service to the death of God a-theology by helping it stamp out the onto-theo-logical fires which continued to burn after the first round of death of God theology, viz. in atheistic humanism.

Erring is not genuinely a/theological because it does not manage to situate itself in the *entre/antre* which is prior to the theism/atheism dispute. Rather it is a more thorough-going, radically atheistic atheism than atheistic humanism – which everybody from the Pope to Heidegger saw to be inverted theism. That means that *Erring* is still caught in a moment of reversal, that it is still engaged in a preliminary stage of stamping out theism, which says that the death of God has to be followed up with the death of man. It is true that by trying to think the divine *milieu* Taylor has tried to remain in this realm of undecidability, but by calling the milieu *divine,* and claiming that this is what becomes of God in deconstruction, he has undone his own claim, and forced *différance* into a decision about God which is both reductionistic and beyond undecidability.

Now that does not seem to me at all where deconstruction or a deconstructive a/theology leads us, for it does not manage to write on the borders between belief and non-belief but becomes instead a party to the dispute. Deconstruction does not deny God, or turn God into man, or turn God into anything at all, including *écriture.* It shows that any discourse about God is caught up in a systematic chain of signifiers from which it cannot loosen itself: God/world, God/man, creator/created, theism/atheism, transcendent/immanent, sacred/profane, etc. There is no affirming the transcendence of God which can somehow extricate itself from the immanence of world, which does not draw its meaning from the immanence of the world. There is no talk of God which does not belong to some differential matrix, no talk which somehow seizes upon God and becomes God's own word.

What *écriture* does to us is expose that subsystem of undecidability which inhabits our discourse, throwing our binary pairs and exclusionary, purifying gestures into confusion. *Différance* does not drain the word "God" of reference, it simply deprives it of its prestige and robs us of the sense that we get very far whenever we invoke it. *Différance* keeps us in between belief and unbelief, never sure that what we call God is not something else we are trying to exclude, or that what we call man or world is not God's hidden hand. It puts us in a position where we are hard put to distinguish faith and reason, faith and madness, faith and non-faith. We do not know who we are, or whether we believe or not, not if we are willing to face up to the bad news that we have no privileged access to the things themselves. *Différance* leaves us wavering in fear and trembling, in Augustine's *quaestio* [114] *mihi factus sum,* which are the religious equivalents of Derrida's *ébranler.*

To show how deconstruction can be put to work in an entirely different direction than one found in *Erring,* let me conclude by pointing out how one of my favorite writers put the matter. If you call God Father, that is said only relative to a Son, and cannot be what God is. If you call Him creator, that is said only relative to a creature, and that cannot be what God is. If you call him the First Cause, that is said relative to an effect, and that cannot be what God is. (That is to say, every time you speak of God, you simply reinscribe Him in some differential matrix or other.) So, then, what are we to call God, we ask? "I pray God to rid me of God," he answered.[2]

Notes

[1] *Dialogue with Contemporary Thinkers,* ed. Richard Kearney (Manchester: Manchester University Press, 1984), 123.

[2] I have developed this point in my "Mysticism and Transgression: Eckhart and Derrida," *Continental Philosophy,* II (1989), "Derrida and Deconstruction," ed. H. J. Silverman (New York: Routledge, 1989): 24-39. [see chap. 18, above -ed.]

404

29

REVIEW: *TEARS* [MARK TAYLOR]

[In *The Journal of Religion*, Vol. 72, No. 3 (July 1992), 453–454]

TAYLOR, MARK C. *Tears.* Albany, N.Y.: SUNY Press, 1989. 263 pp. $54.50 (cloth); $17.95 (paper).

[453] From its wonderfully ambiguous title and the hilarious letter to the publisher in which Mark Taylor declines to write a preface to clear things up, *Tears* (cuts/ cries) invites and provokes multiple glosses. One way to get your bearings on this [454] very unscientific postscript – but getting your bearings is cheating, a way to short-circuit the effect of this (un)book – is to head straight to the middle, chapter 6, "The Anachronism of A/Theology," in which Taylor deftly settles the hash of T.J.J. Altizer. Twentieth-century theology opened its doors with Karl Barth's resounding "no" to liberalism, that is, Protestantism's transmutation of the absolute otherness of God into something historical, social, cultural (immanent). Say "no" to religion in order to say "yes" to God, Barth says. "Altizer's 'No' to Barth's 'No' is at the same time a 'Yes' to a radical immanence in which every vestige of transcendence is erased" (p. 76). But – with Altizer – Taylor argues, "modern" theology reaches closure (but postmoderns are not supposed to *know* anything about "world history" and its epochal peaks and valleys). The philosophy of *presence,* which peaks out in Altizer's anti-Barthian claim that "the kingdom of God is at hand," means that we are swimming in "total presence," pure *parousia,* no more delay or deferral. Altizer is entitled to his own views, but when he tries to pass this off as "deconstruction" or "postmodernism," that, Taylor now shows (he was not clear about this before), is a ruse. "By declaring the death of God," Taylor writes, "Altizer does not call into question the traditional understanding of Being in terms of presence. To the contrary, he insists that to be is to be present, and to be fully is to be present totally" (p. 76). Altizer's dispute with Barth turns not on the meaning of Being as full presence but on the locus (immanent vs. transcendent) of full Being. Altizer favors a this-worldly Hegelian pleroma,

Being as the identity of difference, thus "completing" Hegelianism (modernity). Postmodern "a/theology," on the other hand, means to be "otherwise than Being," not in the straight (orthodox) sense of difference (Søren Kierkegaard, Barth, Emmanuel Levinas) but of Jacques Derrida, whose *différance* is a different difference, an other other, an oblique nondialectical difference, neither immanent nor transcendent (p. 79), neither temporal nor eternal (an "anachronism"). Taylor means (and needs) to say, I think, that *différance* is a certain quasi-condition of possibility that makes religious (and other) discourse (and practice) possible, even as it throws them into confusion, *pace* Taylor's reservations about Rodolphe Gasché (p. 96). *Différance* delimits and incises both total presence and absolute otherness, submitting them to the undecidability of the "/" in a/theology, which infiltrates both Barth and Altizer. *Tears* is a multifrontal exploration of this different difference that cannot be trumped by dialectics, of the radical tears that rend Hegelian dialectic. Along the way Taylor can be a clear expositor and critic. Chapters 9-10 are excellent delimitations of the "neo-Hegelianism" of hermeneutics, both Hans-Georg Gadamer's and Richard Rorty's, which seek to assimilate and consolidate difference, as against the more radical poststructuralist exposure to difference. The discussion of Kierkegaard's absent (m)other (chap. 11) is fascinating. I would read last the opening chapters on deconstructive architecture (1–5), where Taylor can be dizzying, dazzling, labyrinthine. *Tears* is taylor-ed to the most exotic postmodern tastes in religion, criticism, and architecture (archi-texture); cut to fit readers of Derrida, Maurice Blanchot, and Levinas; his essays are shreds and fragments of texts, fabrics marked and strewn about the floor of Mark's postmodern taylorshop; written on the seams of other texts; marking up the text of Mark (which one?). A lot of this (un)book is like that if you can deal with it. If you are scandalized, you will miss a lot – a neo-Kierkegaardian humorist and one of the most creative voices on the American scene.

30

REVIEW: *POST-CARTESIAN MEDITATIONS: AN ESSAY IN DIALECTICAL PHENOMENOLOGY* [JAMES MARSH]

[In *International Philosophical Quarterly*, Vol. XXX, No. 1 Issue No. 117 (March 1990), 101–107]

JAMES MARSH. *Post-Cartesian Meditations: An Essay in Dialectical Phenomenology.* New York: Fordham University Press, 1988. Pp. xiii, 279. $39.95 cloth.

[101] *Post-Cartesian Meditations* is an attempt to formulate what James L. Marsh describes as a "critical modernism," that is, a philosophical standpoint which remains faithful to the essential tendencies of modern philosophy from Descartes to Kant and Hegel, while tempering the claims of modernism in the light of the critique of modernity which has taken shape in twentieth-century continental philosophy. Critical modernism is conceived in contradistinction to postmodernism, which Marsh takes to be an excessive, illegitimate, and, as he has no hesitations in claiming, irrational rejection of modernity. Postmodernism is anti-modernism and irrationalism, the outright rejection of reason (x–xi, 254–55). Critical modernism is the correction and perfection of modernism, its secret longing, its truest friend and *Aufhebung.* Marsh's "post" is post-Cartesian, not post-modern.

Post-Cartesian Meditations (hereafter PCM) is a challenging, intelligent, and clearly written volume, a comprehensive assessment of the state of the philosophical art in the late twentieth century. Marsh does not fear to take a stand or try to hide behind continentalist cant. His work is clear, forceful, and out in the open. He uses a consciously non-sexist prose and he invites debate and discussion. There is much to agree with in Marsh's study and, as I hope to show, much to disagree with. But one is in either case grateful to the author for this vigorous, readable work which makes an energetic defense of modernist thought, which is not afraid of being understood, and which takes on the postmoderns with gusto.

In what follows I will present the main argument of PCM, tossing in a friendly word of support here and there, but perhaps a bit more often – as a sometimes post-modern myself – making some trouble for PCM by pushing the post in post-Cartesian. PCM is an essay in "dialectical phenomenology," a discipline with three phases: an eidetic-descriptive phase deriving mainly from the phenomenologies of Husserl and Merleau-Ponty; a hermeneutic phase deriving from Gadamer and Ricoeur; a critical-suspicious stage deriving from Marx and Freud. The first phase is temporally keyed to the present; the second to the past (the tradition); the third to the future, a new, perhaps utopian world (xi, 177–80). But before taking up eidetic phenomenology, Marsh offers us a "historical reduction" which positions PCM relative to the debates in progress in the late twentieth century about the meaning of "modernity."

For Marsh, Descartes is the father of all us moderns and we should not be out to kill our progenitor but only to chasten, temper, or reform him. (Marsh prefers revolution to reform in politics, but reform to revolution in epistemology and metaphysics. He wants to be a moderate in philosophy but a radical on the streets.) Descartes set things going in the right direction but he went too far. He put philosophy on a methodical, critical, and reflexive path (6); he gave us all our philosophical bearings by making it clear that hereafter philosophers should proceed by questioning prejudices and presuppositions and producing evidence for their beliefs. The Cartesian project came to grief only because of its excesses. We who have read Heidegger and Merleau-Ponty, Gadamer and Ricoeur, have since [102] learned the limits of any possible *epoche*. Descartes is guilty of a prejudice against prejudice, for it is impossible to be absolutely presuppositionless. Likewise the Cartesian desire for clarity and distinction is misplaced, for it lays conditions befitting mathematics upon philosophy at large. Marsh thus sides with the arguments of a "hermeneutic phenomenology" against Cartesian dualism, but he remains attached to the spirit of the Cartesian inauguration of the modernist project. That is the tension in the book, and the question is whether PCM can master that tension.

Marsh is moving closer to Husserl than to Descartes. For Husserl continues the Cartesian undertaking in the manner of a transcendental phenomenology, according to which "evidential rationality" (xi) – a linchpin word for Marsh which sets his heart aflame – comes to mean the clarity of phenomenal experience rather than the limpidity of logical deduction. But Husserl's own Cartesianism is "exploded" (23) by his turn to the life world in the *Crisis*. Once the life world is affirmed as the uncircumventable matrix of all higher order operations, philosophy finds itself unavoidably caught up in historicity, linguisticality, and ambiguity, and the claims of pure transcendental reason are thrown into question. With the discovery of the life-world comes what Marsh calls, following Merleau-Ponty, the "triumph of ambiguity" (23 ff.). Hereafter critical modernism must be not only post-Cartesian but post-Husserlian.

This is for me the pivot on which the success of the argument of PCM turns. Marsh is saying right at the beginning that dialectical phenomenology wants to take full stock of ambiguity, which includes for him historicality, linguisticality, embodiment, sociality, and intersubjectivity. He wants to concede, to embrace, what Heidegger calls "facticity," the factical situatedness of what modernity calls transcendental consciousness. One might say, to make things simple – and Marsh is not adverse to making things simple – that there are two ways to deal with ambiguity. The first tack, the one taken by Marsh, is to fess up to the difficulty but to try to contain the damage. That is what he means by critical modernism. Ambiguity muddies the waters of the philosophy of transcendental consciousness but it does not altogether sink its ship. Ambiguity is a negative "moment" in the total life of reason, not a mortal wound. This strategy, whose modernist prototype is clearly Hegel, has been carried out in an exemplary way by Paul Ricoeur. For years now Ricoeur has been judiciously balancing and dialectically mediating mythos and logos, freedom and necessity, trust and suspicion, Hegel and Freud, truth and method, explanation and understanding, structuralism and humanism, Habermas and Gadamer, analytic philosophy and hermeneutics, sense and reference, and whatever else can be cast in the form of dialectical contrariety. Ricoeur is the not so secret hero of PCM: it is Ricoeur's philosophical style, his neo-Hegelian negotiating between modernist aspirations and the existential-phenomenological-hermeneutic critique of modernity, which provides Marsh with his philosophical paradigm. Like Ricoeur, PCM wants to range over a lot of positions and literally put them in their place, situate them within a comprehensive dialectical scheme. Like Ricoeur, Marsh thinks you can "both/and" these disputes into submission, taking the side of the angels while giving the devil his due. He wants to defend what modernists call "reason" – this entitles one to speak in the name of reason itself, a formidable advantage which gives one the right to declare one's opponents irrational – while agreeing that reason is marked with finitude and ambiguity. The head of (critical) modernist reason is bloodied but unbowed.

The other strategy – and this is the one that I myself pursue, the one that Marsh thinks is *verrückt* (literally: it is irrational and self-contradictory, according to him) – is the more "post-modern" option, which takes its lead from late Heidegger and Derrida, not Ricoeur. The postmodern idea is to stay with the ambiguity, to follow it out, and to renounce the claim that one can gain a transcendental high ground from which one attempts to "situate" ambiguity in the first place. What the postmodernist has against the critical modernist is that the very claim to be able to deal with ambiguity judiciously, to balance out its rightful [103] claims against the claims of reason, is not in the end to give ambiguity its due and hence it is not even very balanced. After all, once one claims to have put ambiguity in its place, one has already effectively transcended it, localized it, and removed oneself from its influence. The very attempt to *mediate* between reason and ambiguity, between transcendental rationality and factical situatedness, the very claim to be able to oversee this dispute, has already taken the side of transcendental reason, has already laid claim to a higher, transcendental-dialectical vantage point, has already staked out a position above the tidal waters of ambiguity from which it surveys the whole, both sides, both/and. The dialectical desire to mediate between transcendental reason and ambiguity is already an act of transcendental mediation, already committed to transcendental reason. That is why from my perspective PCM fails to be a truly "radical" hermeneutic – because it fails to take ambiguity or facticity completely seriously. It thinks itself already on the other side of ambiguity, able to survey and mark off and so to contain the extent of its influence.

For the postmodernists, dialectical mediation comes to the bargaining table of philosophical discussion with a set of transcendental non-negotiables. Mediation does not stay "between" reason and ambiguity but moves "beyond," becomes transcendence and *Aufhebung*. Postmodernists, at least of the sort I admire, remain *in media res*, in the midst of the dispute going on within the things themselves, stuck between, tossed to and fro', in a position of "undecidability." On my account, mediation fails to stay "between" while undecidability adheres more rigorously to the inter-mediacy of the human condition. The effect of this in Marsh's text is that the triumph *of* ambiguity is relentlessly transmuted into a triumph *over* ambiguity, into an outright intellectualism which is deeply marked by Habermas and Lonergan and which, in my view, all but subverts the factical-hermeneutical element in PCM. I admire the sweep of this text and its effort to come to grips with ambiguity, but I am convinced that in the end facticity and ambiguity are swept under the rug.

Consider the discussion of Merleau-Ponty, the great philosopher of ambiguity. After an illuminating comparison of Wittgenstein and Merleau-Ponty on the rejection of an ideal language in favor of a shifting, contextualistic view of language, Marsh goes on to claim that Merleau-Ponty was always a philosopher of essence. That is in some sense true of *Phenomenology of Perception* but it is not a credible claim to make about *The Visible and the Invisible*. It tells us more about Marsh than Merleau-Ponty. Marsh is not going to let go of the idea of an "eidetic" phenomenology in some strong sense – even though he wants to admit that any such "essences" as he finds are steeped in language and history.

Let us now turn to this eidetic phenomenology, which is the first phase of PCM, in which Marsh takes up the classic questions of "existential phenomenology" – perception, objectification, freedom, and intersubjectivity.

In the manner of Hegel's *Phenomenology,* Marsh's dialectical phenomenology wants to start out from perception and work its way up to the higher levels of the spirit (beyond description to interpretation and then to critique). He wants to defend a version of Husserl's thesis that perception is the founding stratum of experience, that expression is founded upon perception, and that reflection is founded upon expression, the higher stratum being related to the lower as the explicit to the implicit. Marsh, however, also wants to hold that there are no unmediated perceptual data, that the perceptual world is mediated to us by language and history. But these two theses are at odds with each other: the one says that language expresses and explicates perception, the other that it actually constitutes it in some non-trivial way, that language does not simply unfold the implicit contents of perception but shapes it. You can see the trouble this makes for speaking of an eidetic reduction. Husserl thinks that he has achieved an essence when he reaches a perceptual invariant, something which cannot be even imaginatively varied away. But someone who has taken a linguistic turn (x) would simply suggest that what Husserl has run up against is not an essence but the limits of his language. What is lingering behind [104] Marsh's approach is the implication that he somehow knows what lies on the other side of language, that he has some kind of access to a pure nonlinguistic real or prelinguistic perceptual essence. It is this privileged access which enables him to oversee the relation between perception and language, to look so judicious, and so to say with serene balance that language is just the expression of the perceptual.

Dialectical phenomenology also wants a theory of objectivity, which it thinks has been rashly jettisoned by Kierkegaard, Nietzsche, and the postmodernists. Such rashness can be avoided by distinguishing among eight different senses of objectivity, an account of which Marsh happily supplies. The upshot is that not all objectification is alienation, and that even critiques of objectification – like Kierkegaard's critique of objective truth and Heidegger's critique of presence at hand – presuppose and make use of objectification in another sense, inasmuch as Kierkegaard and Heidegger produce careful descriptions of matters which they have explicitly thematized. There is some truth to that and I do not think that a more sensitive rendering of Heidegger, for which Marsh is not famous, would deny that. But one is impressed with the enormous resistance of PCM to any troubling of "objectivity" at all. One

411

wonders about all this anxiety about a loss or even a diminishing of our objectifying powers. What does PCM will, want, desire? What is it afraid of?

The chapter on freedom argues for a conditioned liberty, not an unconditional, Sartrean freedom. To disagree with dialectical phenomenology on this point is to fall into self- contradiction. (This is a fate which *consistently* befalls those who dissent from PCM. If I have counted right, every single position which differs from PCM is declared self-referentially inconsistent and hence logically absurd.) For to deny freedom is to discredit one's own claim to be offering considered evidence for one's claim (since one can hardly offer any other view), while to affirm absolute freedom is to undermine the possibility that one determinate view is to be preferred to another.[1] A suggestion by a sensitive Sartrean commentator (Thomas Busch) that Sartre might be more complicated than this (i.e., that Sartre's text is more involuted, more textual, that it admits of other readings) is just waved off with the remark that that would show only that Sartre is even more self-contradictory than Marsh thought (158). It is astonishing how little ambiguity Marsh actually finds either in philosophers or in the things themselves.

Furthermore, this free, existential self is not a solitary but an intersubjective being. Intersubjectivity is to be explained not by means of Husserl's transcendental apperception, but by invoking the dynamics of embodiment as presented by Merleau-Ponty. Others are given in their bodily presence, in their gestures and movements; they are not somehow hidden behind bodily appearances. This I think is an extremely sound move. But a great deal of the good that Marsh's hermeneutic phenomenology does for him is undone by a Habermasian account of intersubjective communication in terms of the distinction between coercion and appeal. Appeal is a free, rational, undistorted, unprejudiced communication (which acquires such elevated status by meeting Habermas's four conditions for validity claims), a communication which does not violate or distort. Appeal is never contaminated with coercion; it is virgin pure and Cartesian clean. Yet how, one might ask, can that possibly be if intersubjective communication occurs between impassioned, embodied, interested, free, existential subjects who always operate under language and history, prejudice and presupposition? The distinction is dualistic and Cartesian, a straightforwardly metaphysical distinction which succeeds not in escaping Cartesianism but only in [105] extending it from the subjective to the intersubjective level. This is the sort of trouble that I think PCM is always getting into.

In introducing the "hermeneutical turn," which PCM wants to take, Marsh stresses the limits this imposes upon us: that there is more than one way to read a text, the non-definitiveness of any reading, that all one can say is that some readings are better or more probable than others (164, 167–69). The reader – this reader, anyway – has to catch his breath at this point. Because Marsh's very sensible commitment to hermeneutics at this juncture in the text has been preceded by a series of chapters in which every position which differs with PCM is reduced to absurdity – quite literally – by being shown to be in performative contradiction with itself. Far from making its opponents stronger in hermeneutic fashion, PCM makes them look ridiculous so that one wonders how such foolishness ever found its way into print. Such excessive intellectualism does not permit hermeneutic flexibility any more than it was prepared to admit phenomenological ambiguity. It aims at wiping out its opponents with mortal blows pointed at the very coherence of those who differ from it. Whatever lip service PCM pays to hermeneutics in theory, its real working practice is a black and white logic in which positions are either rational or irrational, fully legitimized or self-contradictory, without ambiguity, shading, or alternate interpretations. Texts do not admit of second readings; to differ from PCM is to become absurdly self-contradictory. PCM wants to do hermeneutics but it has sold its soul to Lonergan and Habermas. (Were it not for the fact that I consider the argument from performative contradiction to be for the most part completely barren, I would suggest that PCM is in performative contradiction with its own commitment to phenomenological ambiguity and hermeneutic plurality.)

Following Ricoeur's adjudication of the Gadamer-Habermas debate, Marsh goes on to argue that this hermeneutic commitment to the tradition requires also – in dialectical balance – critical distance from it, although one must also recognize – more balance – that one cannot carry out absolute, total critique because one lacks the absolute standpoint (173). This completes the triumvirate that Marsh wants to establish: his "transcendental method" includes a descriptive eidetics, an interpretive hermeneutics, and a critique. It is interesting that Marsh is happy to say that PCM practices a transcendental method (179), because he elsewhere denies the distinction between the embodied and the transcendental subject (128) and claims that he breaks with Husserl's transcendental subject "completely" (205). But what else is the transcendental subject other than a subject capable of performing transcendental acts, and what else is the deployment of a transcendental method other than a transcendental act?

Of Ricoeur's three masters of suspicion only Freud and Marx merit special chapters. Nietzsche evidently has been contaminated by postmodernism; his is too much of a break with modernism; he does not even pretend to be delivering

413

science and apodictic truth. Nietzsche is excess; PCM cannot appropriate him. Be that as it may, there follows a nice presentation of the Freudian unconscious which is – of course – integrated with conscious and intentional life after the manner of Ricoeur's *Freud and Philosophy*. That is followed by a discussion of the "social unconscious" which is where Marsh finally gets brazen. Now the talk is no longer of "reform" but of "radicality." Now we are told to seek, not a capitalism which has been mediated with Marxist critique, but Marxism itself, albeit one purged (by an eidetic and hermeneutic phenomenology) of its reductionistic tendencies. Here we move beyond Ricoeur who may have been guide enough in matters metaphysical and epistemological, but who must now give way to critical theory. There follows an interesting attempt, which makes use of the work of Roslyn Bologh, to integrate phenomenology and Marxism. Phenomenology has a built-in critical function inasmuch as its account of the life world functions as a critique of scientism and technocracy, even as ideology critique is itself a phenomenology of a life shaped by capital, a life which is itself a form of reification and positivism. I am largely in agreement with this Marxist streak in [106] PCM, not because I am Marxist, but because I agree that Marxism does have phenomenological cash value, as Marsh and Bologh argue. Marxism offers us a good phenomenology of an alienated life and it is an excellent tool for making trouble for the bourgeoisie.

Still, I have three complaints with this phase of PCM. First, it is an illusion to think that one requires a transcendental apparatus to make such a critique when a good phenomenology of those who are being ground under by the system will do just fine. Secondly, Marsh seems to pin technology and technologies to capitalism in such a way as to suggest that socialism is any less committed in theory or practice to more and better technology. My own view is that the powerful sweep of technology has both the capitalist and socialist world in its grip and may indeed, as Albert Borgmann suggests, be gradually eroding the difference between them.[2]

Thirdly, and most importantly, it is disingenuous simply to note – as Marsh does (205) – and then proceed to ignore the fact that one could also make an equally scintillating critique of state socialism. The capacity of capitalism to exploit and oppress is at the very least matched by the capacity of state socialism for terror and murder. Nothing is innocent. What PCM requires here is an even healthier suspicion, an even wider ranging critique, of all power/knowledge, of everything which tries to pass itself off as the science of human affairs, as holding the meaning of history, as history's chosen instrument for revolutionary change. It is just at that moment when thinking desires closure, when it wants to totalize, that it is the most dangerous to the rest of us who are just trying to make it through the day.

That is why I am so troubled by the final chapter of PCM which amounts to an apocalyptic announcement of the "emergence of dialectical phenomenology." I single out a highly symptomatic passage which is not at all untypical of the philosophical tenor of this text and which I wish to reproduce here with a few pointed Derridean jabs – in order to make a point.

"*What I have done in this book is to show how phenomenology, and by implication the whole of modern Western philosophy*" – that is a tall order, a large totality: not just the phenomenologists but everybody from the Presocratics to the present – "*can and should lead to*" – this is going to be teleological; we are going to get the *telos* of everybody from Thales to 1989 – "*dialectical phenomenology*" – PCM is what we have all been waiting for, our secret longing; philosophy must become Marsh – "*if it is faithful to itself*" – but philosophy will become Marsh only if it is true, authentic, and self-present.

There is more: "*Only with...*" – this is the *only* way, no hermeneutic plurality here – "*the final step into critical social theory*" – critical theory is the *final* step, the *finis* and *telos,* the end of philosophy, the end of us all – "*does one achieve full rationality,*" – everything will be rational and the rational will fill everything; this will be the fullness of presence, of reason, everything we always wanted, in all its fullness – "*do full justice to the phenomena,*" – the phenomena will have been saved, one and all; they will have been fully rationalized, made fully transparent; no more ambiguity here, no more need of alternative interpretations – "*and reconcile theory and practice fully*" – this is really full of it, of fullness, that is.

"*Short of this move into critical social theory*" – this sounds like a warning – "*we have not asked crucial questions and not explained crucial contradictions.*" – we will be living in contradiction, inauthentically, lacking presence – "*The dilemma for phenomenology, then, is this: either it moves into critical theory or not*" – you notice all the ambiguity here, the hermeneutic flexibility, the shifting contextuality – "*If it does, then it is fully self-conscious and faithful to itself*" – and this from a philosopher who says he has broken [107] with the Cartesian subject and pure transparency – "*If it does not, then it remains obscurantist,*" – Habermas and Lonergan of course will show us all how to be clear – "*dishonest*" – PCM evidently knows what lies in the heart of man – "*and less than fully comprehensive.*" – which one could have thought PCM conceded was the fate of us all once it admitted our finitude, fallibility, and ambiguity.

Go then and sin no more.

In sum, PCM is a forceful and robust presentation of some of the best work in contemporary continental thought which makes a sustained effort to take into account the critique of modernity that has been underway for the last century or so. In the end, it is my judgment, it succumbs to its own worst intellectualistic, scholasticizing tendencies and turns hermeneutic phenomenology into something other than it is. To use the argument that it loves to use on everyone else, PCM is itself one long performative contradiction. While it pays lip service to phenomenological ambiguity and hermeneutic plurality, it treats everything as black or white, good or bad, rational or irrational, and tries to leave a crater wherever it finds an opponent. Just where we need rich phenomenological description, it gives us a Lonerganian *reductio ad absurdum;* instead of a conflict of interpretations, it offers the annihilation of dissent.

Now let me try to practice some of this Ricoeurian hermeneutic balance on PCM. Despite my disagreements with this text, it is light-years removed from the lisping, limping nonsense that sometimes passes itself off as postmodern thought; it undertakes a phenomenological and hermeneutic delimitation of the modernist project; its ethico-socio-political heart is in the right place; and it invites a good argument by its clear and forceful prose. My one wish for Marsh, as he now turns to a promised (threatened?) sequel to PCM, is that son of PCM not inherit all the bad habits of its father.

Notes

[1] As Gadamer shows, following Plato's *Seventh Letter,* this would not refute it materially: one could be *determined* to say that determinism is true even while in fact it really is true. It could be that all Megarians really are liars. The objection is formalistic and vacuous and is about as much help in getting to the bottom of things as the scholastics who refused to look through Galileo's telescope on the grounds that it was formally incoherent that the principle of light could have dark spots. Cf. *Truth and Method,* eds. J. Cumming and G. Barden (New York: Seabury Press, 1975), 308–10.

[2] Albert Borgmann, *Technology and the Character of Contemporary Life* (Chicago: Univ. of Chicago Press, 1985), 82–85. Technology creates a system which cuts deeper than either capitalism or socialism.

AUTOBIOGRAPHICAL

31

ON MYSTICAL AND OTHER PHENOMENA

[In *Analecta Husserliana*, Vol. 26, *American Phenomenology: Origins and Developments*, eds. Eugene F. Kaelin and Calvin Schrag (Dordrecht: Reidel Publishing Co. 1989), 318–22]

[318] The work of Heidegger has been the abiding influence on my work in phenomenology. But it was not my first interest. Rather, like Heidegger himself, my first beginnings were in the Aristotelian and scholastic tradition and the question of Being as it is posed in that tradition. My first serious philosophical work occurred when I learned enough Latin to begin a close study of the first part of Thomas's *Summa Theologica*. This project was guided not only by Maritain and Gilson but above all by Pierre Rousselot's brilliant study of the mystical dimension in Thomism which bore the misleading title *The Intellectualism of St. Thomas*. Along with Maritain, Rousselot posed the question of the delimitation of the metaphysical experience of Being vis-à-vis artistic, religious and especially mystical experience. This was the first form which the Heideggerian problematic of "overcoming" metaphysics took for me. And although I knew nothing of Heidegger's project at the time it has always been my one abiding interest.

Graduating from college in the same year the Second Vatican Council opened (1962), my horizons began rapidly to expand. I was drawn, first, to Nietzsche's critique of Christianity, which at that time was very shocking to me, and then to Heidegger. I was excited by Heidegger's promise of a new start in metaphysics which would take the form of a phenomenological approach to the question of Being.

In my doctoral dissertation on the development of Heidegger's understanding of *Grund* and *Abgrund,* I seized upon the chapters of *Der Satz vom Grund* in which Heidegger discussed the German mystical poet Angelus Silesius (Johannes Scheffler). Heidegger holds up the poetic verse "The Rose is Without Why" against Leibniz's well-known principle of sufficient reason, "nothing is without reason." He shows the way poet's saying eludes and delimits the metaphysical principle. The [319] poet does not violate the principle – the poetic verse does not consist of arbitrary and capricious propositions – but enters instead a wholly different sphere, outside the realm of propositional discourse and metaphysical representations. In the mystical poet's experience of the rose, over which this prestigious principle of metaphysics and logic has no authority, our experience of Being and of thought is transformed. Far from being a confused and irrational undertaking, Heidegger says, the most extreme depth and sharpness of thought belongs to the mystic.

That posed for me the fundamental question of my first book: how then are we to understand the relationship of Heidegger's "thinking" to mysticism? And that question could be pursued in depth only by a close study of the source of Angelus Silesius' saying in Meister Eckhart, a figure in whom, as I discovered, Heidegger had been extremely interested as a young student. To be sure, Heidegger was often enough called a mystic by his critics, and the expression *Seinsmystik* was meant pejoratively, as if contact with mysticism was self-evidently a matter of contamination. But I wanted to raise this question more seriously, to see if, on the one hand, what is traditionally called mysticism exemplifies what Heidegger calls "overcoming metaphysics," and, on the other hand, whether there is something mystical about Heidegger.

The Mystical Element in Heidegger's Thought (1978) has sometimes been misconstrued as an argument that Heidegger *is* a mystic – which results I think from taking the title of the book too hastily. I want to stress the "element" (not the "mystical"), that is to say, that there is only a certain structural likeness, a certain analogy, between Heidegger and the mystic. For Heidegger, like the mystic, urges a relationship to the *Sache* in which representational thinking and willing are suspended and replaced by an openness to the address which overtakes Dasein. Whence there is a structural likeness between the relationship of Being and thought in Heidegger and God and the soul in Meister Eckhart.

But more deeply considered mysticism and thought, like thinking and poetry, are at best "neighbors" – dwelling outside the sphere of metaphysical and representational discourse, but each in its own space. Far from arguing that "thinking" is something mystical, I pursued two [320] other points. (1) Heidegger's work is distinctly divided from the mystics because the matter for thought is the history and language of Being as it unfolds in the West, not the eternal and silent unity of the soul and God aimed at by the *unio mystica*. (2) If anything, the disconcerting thing about Heidegger is not that he is a mystic, but that he is *not*, that that sort of *Gelassenheit* of which he speaks means releasement to the ominous play of the epochs, not trust in a divine and loving hand.

The argument of *The Mystical Element* led quite naturally to another application. For many years, the Thomists had been complaining that

Heidegger unfairly included Thomas's metaphysics of *esse* in his history of the oblivion of Being. How could a metaphysics in which everything turns on *esse* have anything to do with *Seinsvergessenheit*? Heidegger, they thought, had stolen Gilson's line (substituting his own *Seinsdenken* for Thomistic metaphysics). I had two definite responses to this Thomistic complaint which I developed in my second book, *Heidegger and Aquinas: An Essay on Overcoming Metaphysics* (1982). (1) Heidegger's thought is deeply and thoroughly "phenomenological," or as I said in *Heidegger and Aquinas* "alethiological," and hence is decisively separated from a realistic and causal metaphysics, even a metaphysics of *esse*. The more the Thomists insist that in Thomas *esse* is the act of all acts, the highest actuality, the more they invite Heidegger's rebuke – that Being is conceived in terms of making and actuality, *Wirklichkeit*. *Esse* is much more like a Leibnizian *Grund* than Silesius's rose. Thinking is not a matter of a causal-explanatory science of real being but of gentle releasement into, and a certain savoring of, the upsurge of *physis* in which all explanatory machinery is suspended.

(2) But even worse, the Thomistic rejoinder was a missed opportunity. For it failed to see that, were one to read St. Thomas in just the way Heidegger reads the history of metaphysics – a "retrieval" of what is "unsaid" in the sayings of the metaphysicians – one could find a deep element in Thomas which surpasses metaphysics and eludes the Heideggerian critique. For there is, I argued, a mystical element in Aquinas which is substantiated, not by the legends of Thomas' final days in which he is said to have undergone a mystical experience and renounced writing, but in the writing itself, in a careful analysis of the tendencies within the text itself beyond *ratio* to *intellectus,* beyond a science of *esse* to la unitary experience of *esse*.

At this point, my work had come full circle, for I found myself again invoking the name of Pierre Rousselot and his startling readings of [321] Aquinas. But to this I now added the case of Meister Eckhart, for this great German mystic was something of a disciple of Thomas, having held the same Dominican chair of theology at Paris which Thomas himself held a quarter of a century earlier. Eckhart, I argued (along with Bernard Welte), radicalized the mystical dimensions of Thomas' doctrine of *esse.* Thus the sermons of Meister Eckhart were an eloquent expression of the unsaid element in Thomas himself. It is not Thomistic metaphysics which answers Heidegger, as the Thomists were arguing, but a project of "overcoming metaphysics" locatable *within* the Thomistic text.

Having completed this cycle of research into Heidegger and the classical religious tradition, and hence into thinkers who were more conservative than Heidegger, who stood to his right, let us say, I found myself more and more preoccupied with Heidegger's relationship to thinkers who are more radical than he is, who stand to his left, as it were. Derrida, in particular, seemed to me to have learned a great deal from Heidegger about the "destruction" of the history of metaphysics but he seemed to leave no room for its other side, for retrieval. My first impressions of Derrida were negative, but I must say that I have come to read him now more in tandem with Heidegger, as someone who puts us on the alert to the lingering metaphysical residue in Heidegger's text, who in a sense liberates the Heideggerian text from itself. For me, Derrida does not oppose phenomenology but only its naive formulation. He proceeds strictly in accordance with phenomenology's demand for the reduction of naivete. Together, Heidegger and Derrida pursue the structure of the phenomenal – in terms of *a-letheia* and "textuality."

My most recent publications thus have been arguing for what I now call "radical Hermeneutics." By this I mean not the more conventional, and I would say still metaphysical hermeneutics of Gadamer and Ricoeur, which remain very much under the spell of Hegel and Husserl, but a colder, more comfortless hermeneutics in which we are exposed to the loss of metaphysical bearings, to the free play of the epochs. Derrida speaks often of the *ébranler,* the trembling, the loss of foundations. That it seems to me is where Heidegger leads us, but in an alethiological sense. In this more austere reading of Heidegger we are brought up against the sheer coming-to-presence, the sheer event of manifestness, of *a-letheia,* in which the epochs take shape and slip away, in which all things – mortal and divine, heavenly and earthly – come to pass and pass away (*genesis* and *phthora*). In this happening [322] of manifestness, this a-lethic event, things tremble for a while only to disperse.

And it is in the "mystery" of this event that I see the outlines of a post-metaphysical ethics and a post-metaphysical conception of the religious. There is, I now argue, an ethics of *Gelassenheit* which consists in letting-be, which is bent on the emancipation of the other from the oppressiveness of the regime of the *Gestell,* the rule of domination. That is why I think that Heidegger and Derrida (and to some extent Foucault too) make for a successful mixed marriage. For Derrida draws Heidegger back into the *agora* and gives his critique of metaphysics a socio-political cutting edge, extending it into a critique of institutions, into a political analysis. Just so, Heidegger contextualizes Derrida, enlisting this deconstructive critique in the project of openness to the mystery.

But the mystery is not only the mystery of the other, but also the mystery with which all religion is concerned. What is at work in the play of the epochs, the play of manifestness? What hand writes here? What voice calls? What comes to pass in this alethic play? At the end of *Der Feldweg* Heidegger asks, "Is it God who calls, or the soul, or the world?" Or is it no voice at all we hear but just the rumble of the world as it plays without why, a cosmic *Spiel* which plays because it plays?

That is the question which, it seems to me, I have always been asking and which I have learned to ask somewhat less inadequately with the help of Heidegger and his alethio-phenomenological path of thought.

Acknowledgments

Our thanks to the various publishers for permission to reproduce these materials, the source of which is acknowledged at the beginning of each entry.

Our thanks as well to Paul Caputo, M.F.A., for the design of the cover and for his considerable help and advice in preparing the copy for print.

More from John D. Caputo Archives

Previously published:

Collected Philosophical and Theological Papers:
Volume 1 – 1969-1985: *Aquinas, Eckhart, Heidegger: Metaphysics, Mysticism, Thought.*

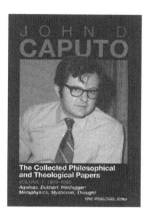

Collected Philosophical and Theological Papers:
Volume 3 – 1997-2000: *The Return of Religion.*

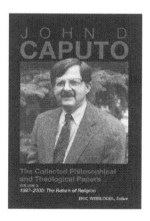

For more information:
For links to podcasts, videos, recorded lectures, interviews, and more, visit:
johndcaputo.com
Follow John D. Caputo – Weak Theology on Facebook:
www.facebook.com/John.D.Caputo

427

Made in the USA
Middletown, DE
17 November 2022

14877139R00243